THE BUSINESS SPEAKER'S ALMANAC

EDITED BY

JACK GRIFFIN ◆ ALICE MARKS

PRENTICE HALL
Englewood Cliffs, New Jersey 07632

Prentice-Hall International (UK) Limited, *London*
Prentice-Hall of Australia Pty. Limited, *Sydney*
Prentice-Hall Canada, Inc., *Toronto*
Prentice-Hall Hispanoamericana, S.A., *Mexico*
Prentice-Hall of India Private Limited, *New Delhi*
Prentice-Hall of Japan, Inc., *Tokyo*
Simon & Schuster Asia Pte. Ltd., *Singapore*
Editora Prentice-Hall do Brasil, Ltda., *Rio de Janeiro*

©1994 by
Prentice Hall

10   9   8   7   6   5   4   3   2   1

Library of Congress Cataloging-in Publication Data

The Business speaker's almanac / edited by Jack Griffin and
Alice Marks.
    p. cm.
   Includes index.
   ISBN 0-13-177544-8
   1. Public speaking. 2. Business presentations. 3. Speeches,
addresses, etc., American. 4. Business communication.
I. Griffin, Jack. II. Marks, Alice.
PN4121.B885   1994   94-13653
815'.089265'09049—dc20   CIP

ISBN 0-13-177544-8

PRENTICE HALL
Career and Personal Development
Englewood Cliffs, NJ 07632
Simon & Schuster, A Paramount Communications Company

Printed in the United States of America

Contents

CHAPTER 1
Management ▪ 1

CHAPTER 5
Competing Today and Tomorrow ▪ 119

CHAPTER 6
The Work Force ▪ 139

CHAPTER **7**
Government and Regulation ▪ 179

CHAPTER 8
Ethics and Values ▪ 237

Index by Audience and Occasion

This special index is designed to assist readers in finding speeches tailored to specific audiences, venues, and speaking occasions.

ANNUAL MEETINGS

AWARD PRESENTATIONS, BANQUETS, AND TESTIMONIAL OCCASIONS

COMMENCEMENTS

CONVENTIONS AND EXPOSITIONS

FORUMS AND SYMPOSIA

GUEST LECTURES

GOVERNMENT COUNCILS AND COMMITTEES

INTERNATIONAL GATHERINGS AND SYMPOSIA

SERVICE AND FRATERNAL ORGANIZATIONS

SPECIAL-INTEREST CLUBS AND ASSOCIATIONS

TOPICAL SEMINARS

Foreword

Each year, hundreds of business leaders deliver thousands of speeches. Addressed to employees, sales forces, managers, business and professional associations, community organizations, religious groups, high school, college, and university students, and government leaders, these speeches reflect the broad spectrum of business today, expressing with an immediacy and intimacy available neither in books nor even in newsletters and magazines the concerns, the issues, the strategies, and the outlook of contemporary commerce. Business speeches are created and presented by the doers of our society. They afford a view from on high as well as from the trenches.

Only a very few speeches in any generation are preserved. The vast majority are written, spoken, reach relatively few listeners, touch a few lives, and then disappear. This is the fate of speeches in almost all areas of endeavor, but it is particularly true of those delivered in the world of business. Our society is equipped to preserve at least a precious handful of political, literary, religious, and academic speeches, but it seems to regard the pronouncements of our commercial movers and shakers—those who generate and control our very wealth—as entirely and instantly disposable.

The Business Speaker's Almanac is offered in the belief that, each year, business leaders in the United States and Canada say a great deal that is not only worth hearing and thinking about, but also preserving and returning to. Furthermore, the editors are convinced that managers, aspiring managers, sales personnel, customer service directors, students, community leaders, and many others recognize the vital importance of staying in touch with the ever-changing currents of the business community in order to acquire and maintain a competitive edge. In addition, when business people are called upon to make speeches themselves, they face a frightening dearth of up-to-date models to help and inspire them. We seek to provide those models.

In this, the inaugural volume of *The Business Speaker's Almanac*, we have endeavored to collect, select, and publish in their entirety fifty-five of the best—the most representative, the most vital—recent business speeches.

For the reader's convenience, we have arranged the speeches into chapters according to general topic. The chapters are

Chapter 1: Management
Chapter 2: Research and Development
Chapter 3: Education and Business
Chapter 4: In the World Market
Chapter 5: Competing Today and Tomorrow
Chapter 6: Work Force
Chapter 7: Government and Regulation
Chapter 8: Ethics and Values
Chapter 9: Media and Communications
Chapter 10: Women in Business
Chapter 11: Minority Viewpoints
Chapter 12: Trends and Predictions

Each chapter is introduced by a brief "how to" discussion, complete with speech-writing tips based on what is best—that is, most effective as business communication—about the speeches in the chapter. As for the speeches themselves, each includes the name and affiliation of the speaker, place and date of delivery, and a concise executive summary. As a useful appendix to the speeches, we have included a miniature anthology of the most effective openings and closings, the best anecdotes and illustrations, the funniest stories, and the most quotable lines.

While the editors believe that an annual collection such as this is most effectively organized by theme—and have structured the book accordingly—it is true that business people are often required to produce speeches suited to specific occasions, including retirement dinners, award presentations, annual shareholder meetings, and the like. A list, alphabetically arranged by type of event, follows the general table of contents at the front of the book to make it easy for readers to locate models for those "occasional" speeches they may be asked to give.

The speeches presented here do not necessarily reflect the opinions, beliefs, or political orientation of the editors, and in no case was a speech included in (or, for that matter, excluded from) this collection on the basis of the opinions it contains. In all cases, we have endeavored to present speeches that deal with subjects of particular concern to the business community. And, again in all cases, we have endeavored to present speeches that exemplify highly effective business communication. We believe that the speeches included in this volume of *The Business Speaker's Almanac* not only communicate a wealth of valuable information and insight, but do so with a degree of skill that makes each of them a revealing pleasure to read.

We trust that our readers will profit from the many business leaders who were generous enough to share their words with us.

CHAPTER 1

Management

As the speeches included here demonstrate, the topic of management demands particular clarity and focus. Although the dictatorial management style is a thing of the past, and a participatory work-group or team approach is generally favored as more effective, the members of the "team" still look to the manager for leadership. At its most basic, then, a speech addressing the issues of management is a speech defining leadership.

The speeches included here demonstrate the importance of recognizing this essential focus. Michael Ramundo makes a detailed, pragmatic presentation; Barry Sullivan takes a philosophical approach to the subject; and Jay Van Andel uses autobiography. All the speakers take the kind of risks that make for a stimulating speech. None hesitates to take a stand. But, without the thematic focus on leadership, there is a real danger that practical instruction will strike the listener as something that could better be expressed in an instruction manual rather than a speech, philosophy will come across as hollow rhetoric, and autobiography will sound like meandering.

A good speech on the topic of management should itself embody some of the qualities of an effective manager. It should be clear and bold, unafraid to point a direction, without, however, bullying. It should be focused, so that it strikes the audience as the product of a coherent *system of thought and action* rather than an expression of airy philosophy on the one hand or a laundry list of DOs and DON'Ts on the other. Finally, like a good manager—an effective leader—the management speech should always define goals and objectives. Especially in this speaking situation, nothing commands an audience's attention more powerfully than a sense of working with the speaker toward a clear set of goals.

Commitment to the Customer:
Inspiring the Customer Service Team

MICHAEL RAMUNDO
Chief Executive Officer
MCR Marketing, Inc.

Delivered to the Association for Service Management International in Chicago and San Francisco; the International Customer Service Association in San Diego; the National Association of Service Management in Boston, Chicago, and Orlando; Sales and Marketing Executives in Hawaii; the AFSMI in Sydney, Australia; and the Society of Consumer Affairs Professionals in Atlanta, Denver, and Seattle, various dates, 1993

SUMMARY: In this highly structured presentation, marketing expert Michael Ramundo emphasizes the crucial importance of effective customer service operations, and he outlines specific management techniques to foster the individual and team excellence needed for maximizing customer satisfaction and lifelong loyalty.

INTRODUCTION

SPEECH TIP: Ramundo's presentation is an excellent example of the "how-to" speech. It clearly defines an overall goal, a set of tasks designed to achieve that goal, and a set of methods for performing those tasks successfully.

Forming lifelong relationships with customers can only be accomplished with committed organizational and front-line employee support. Creating commitment in the front-line team can only be accomplished with continuous management reinforcement.

Reinforcement must support the cultivation of customer-oriented culture and individual attitudes so important for generating the customer orientation. Individual behavior is critical to the process, as the total corporate attitude-of-service is made up of and can only be as good as the combination of all individual attitudes held by employees.

This presentation suggests specific areas of focus for management attention. We learn the most from the best of the service professionals among us who, in our workshops, frequently champion the cause of customer service. They constantly inform us of ways they are improving their ability to serve and suggest ways we might help them improve.

1. CUSTOMERS AND PRODUCT FOCUS

Needs are personal in nature, but they cannot be seen; therefore, they must be inferred. Products are only purchased in order to fulfill individual personal needs. Effective customer servicing means having the ability to understand how the product is being used to serve the customer in his personal circumstance. The customer is satisfied only when he perceives himself as being so. The actual product is not the product sold, but the result, value, or benefit the consumer receives from the product; and benefits are only tangentially related to the product shipped.

The corporation will always need to measure and focus on product shipments and the relationship among shipments, profits, and costs. It must to survive in a free market environment. Yet, it is the responsibility of the customer-servicing arm to create focused attention on how the product is being received and used by the consumer.

Effective customer response teams build permanent customer loyalty and word-of-mouth selling and advertising by focusing on the product from the user's perspective rather than the sales perspective. While the marketing and advertising cost of replacing a lost customer is high today, it will undoubtedly be in the stratosphere by the end of the decade.

Continuously evaluate how service develops value for the customer and how effective product usage is being reinforced. Train your people to service what the customer believes he or she bought, not what you think you sold. Focus organizational effort on:

- What do we do, without adding cost, to expand value customers receive from us?

- What do we do to create a unique customer perception which no competitor can duplicate?

2. COMMUNICATE IN BUSINESS LANGUAGE

SPEECH TIP: Effective communication is often a matter of definition. Ramundo drives his presentation by making one provocative definition after another, then working out the implications of each.

Money is the ultimate yardstick of business, and, to be heard, customer service operations and issues must be translated into dollars—the only language business understands. Even if the ship's captain and all hands are highly interested in service, organizational understanding is significantly enhanced when those responsible for customer servicing communicate results and needs in the fundamental language of business.

Business, like any organized event, needs a scoreboard to measure progress toward the ultimate win. For business, that scoreboard is cash flow, and successful business evaluates cash flow continuously. Measuring things such as number of complaints handled, length of each service call, number of outstanding calls, etc., is helpful as a support measurement. The *important* measure, however, is how service positively or negatively impacts cash flow.

Recognition of customer service comes from communicating good and bad performance in terms of impact on cash. In designing a system, key issues to address are:

- What is the continuing or cumulative negative or positive effect of problem circumstances previously identified?

- Priority: What key issues should be addressed to produce the maximum positive impact on cash flow?

- What are longer term improvement or efficiency targets and how are they to be addressed? What is the expected investment to achieve efficiencies and how will the investment be recovered?

- What are future opportunities for gains? What is the expected investment to achieve these gains and how will the investment be recovered?

3. TRAINING

SPEECH TIP: Ramundo's use of short, imperative sentences to introduce his subjects demonstrates his willingness to lead, as well as advise. By rallying his audience to join him as leaders—here, with specific community-based actions—he lends urgency to his topics and promotes his listeners' shared investment in their discussion.

Get to every trade school, community college, and university. Demand that social skills training be just as important as technical skills training in each curriculum. Your entire customer satisfaction program is based upon the social skills of your people; a front line *incapable* of understanding, using, and dealing with power responsibly cannot be empowered. However, don't assume any institution can perform the training function for you.

The explosion of information-gathering technology is causing a complementary explosion within the power available to the front line. This power, in turn, is accumulating and destroying the vertical organization chart. You do not have the time, luxury, or money to support or follow the supervisory review decision-making process that existed in years past. Service technicians with inadequate technical skills will obviously create tremendous customer dissatisfaction; however, service engineers with only good technical skills cannot necessarily create customer satisfaction. Customer satisfaction requires the use of both technical and social skills. Focus social training efforts on developing five specific characteristics:

- Social Competence: How well can they look for and gain cooperation from others?
- Affiliation: How strongly do they feel they belong to the team and are they able to help others develop a sense of belonging to that team?
- Autonomy: How well can they exercise personal choice and make logical, well-thought-out decisions within a reasonable span of control?
- Preference for Variety: Are they eager to seek fresh and inventive ideas?
- Creativity: Are they capable of having original and viable cost-saving thoughts that can be implemented?

4. CUSTOMER SATISFACTION

Everyone has a customer, and creating customer satisfaction is everyone's responsibility. The customer, either the one purchasing the product, building the product, or approving the promotion, is the one who pays your salary. Rework job descriptions, not only written job descriptions, but the entire concept of the job and the work environment. Job descriptions, written and implied, are usually focused on minimum technical standards describing minimum technical performance. However, even the best technical performance is not sufficient enough to create customer loyalty.

Customer satisfaction and the concept of continuous improvement must be discussed, modified, and emphasized in all jobs in order to produce permanent customer loyalty and corporate innovation. Consider how these points relate to your company and, more importantly, how they are reinforced:

- Everyone is required to find and make positive and constructive changes.
- Everyone is required to make some improvement in our ability to satisfy customers without incurring an increase in cost.
- Everyone, in each customer contact situation, is required to do something that helps the relationship with the customer become a lifelong relationship.
- A personalized presentation is required with every customer contact.

5. LIVING PLANS

Sporting events have little meaning without the centrally located and always visible scoreboard. The scoreboard tracks team progress toward the goal, it tracks past performance, and it recognizes individual stellar accomplishment. It makes all team members aware of their particular performance in relation to the competition's.

> *SPEECH TIP*: Sports analogies can misfire—and even alienate some listeners—when a speaker presumes too much audience interest in or intimacy with the specific rules and jargon of football, baseball, or any other *particular* game. Ramundo avoids this pitfall by using a more generalized sports metaphor.

The corporate scoreboard is the planning and implementation schedule and the system for measuring accomplishment. Whether visible or invisible, this scoreboard controls customer satisfaction. For service technicians to be a part of the team, they must be involved with modification, implementation, coordination and direction of the total plan. Here are some specific suggestions on the overall design and operation of living planning systems:

- Time lines should be long enough so that everyone involved can see the overall direction, goals, and purpose of the department, division, or the entire company. The activities to be done should reflect the overall goals as well as demonstrate how individual performance relates to the total plan.
- Everyone on the team should be given the opportunity to operate, adjust, and influence the evolving plan.
- All key customer-focused activities to be accomplished should be clearly listed. These activities should reflect the overall corporate goals through time.
- The system should be able to demonstrate moments of excellence and indicate areas where improvement needs to occur.

▨ Activities should be adjusted as necessary and people should be assigned to the activities, not vice versa.

6. FIXERS

Be a fixer. Surround yourself with fixers. Reward those who find problems to fix, and then help them fix the problems they find. Surround yourself with those who get satisfaction from the task itself, those who cannot stand to leave a job half finished, and those determined to cause the changes necessary for improvements to occur.

Make decisions. Push on and eliminate problems. Draw attention to people who work on a problem until it is solved. Don't find fault with things as they are; ignore those people who do. Look for things to improve; then improve them! Make heroes out of those who improve things.

Ignore the "Why-don't-they-do-something-about-that?" game, and turn off employees who spend time playing this game. Even massive and overwhelming problems will eventually be solved. They will be solved because they must be solved. Incremental improvement will undoubtedly occur. Make heroes out those who find and fix a portion of the overall problem: Nibbling on the issue long enough will eventually fix it.

Work just below the budget approval threshold. Reward those who don't always ask permission to do things and just do things. Micro-improvements lead to major accomplishments. Focus on what can be slightly modified and what can be improved within the given constraints. Police things, create change, identify problem solvers, and turn them loose. Hold people accountable for creating incremental solutions.

7. MEASURE SATISFACTION—DISCOUNT MEASUREMENT

Invest more on measuring satisfaction. Train all people in the organization to study where the customer currently is, what he thinks of you, and exactly where he wants you. Measure the customer's perception through every customer contact. However, heavily discount the information you receive. Seldom will others willingly and without reservation tell us we have bad breath. Studies suggest that dissatisfied customers are remarkably complacent and tolerant of negative experiences. The customer tells us what he thinks only after we invest a considerable amount of energy in earning his confidence. We must earn the right to his involvement in our self-improvement program.

Proactive customer servicing means that you are reaching out and actively seeking information. It means that, like any research professional, the customer service representative is trained to seek the real truth existing beyond the apparent truth. The authentic, objective, sincere, and enthusiastic attitude of the front-line people is critical to uncovering hidden problem areas. Create and nurture a work culture that breeds enthusiasm, and then:

- Develop formal measurement methods specifically designed to uncover complacent but dissatisfied customers.

- Design a system that actively seeks out perceptions gathered by the front line. Make the system evaluate and convert these perceptions into changes which are beneficial to the organization.

8. ACCOMPLISHMENT

Achievement is a precious thing; focus all your energy on nurturing this rarity. Focus on specific accomplishments rather than general goodness. Look for specific excellence, find and reward heroes demonstrating exceptional behavior. Set up a "What did you accomplish?" program.

Most employee-of-the-month systems focus on general good performance—which is fine. However, general goodness does little to clear new territory or plow virgin fields. Heroes and achievers create higher levels of excellence for tomorrow.

To create loyal, lifelong customers in an overwhelmingly fragmented market, it's necessary for individuals to identify and positively handle specific incidents with speed, commitment, and dedication. Therefore, create management reinforcement systems that reward individual speed, commitment, and dedication.

Measuring specific excellence or particular accomplishment is typically difficult. Therefore, rewards should be as random and unpredictable as accomplishment. As many have said: "A leader in business can be either a devil's advocate or a cheerleader." Cheerleaders produce more results.

What are the characteristics of high achievers? They:

- Take moderate risks.

- Need immediate feedback.

- Find accomplishment interesting in itself.

- Are preoccupied with the task or goal at hand.

Nurture these people.

9. SUPERVISE LESS, GUIDE MORE

Information is power, which is rapidly becoming the only thing of value, and, thanks to the tumbling price of computing power, information is growing in the hands of the front-line people at an exponentially increasing rate. Information produces knowledge; knowledge produces power. The concept of supervisory management is becoming obsolete. The classic management pyramid is being replaced with networks, special projects, and special assignments. Building relationships, rather than managerial structures, is the key to obtaining power.

There are the front-line people, and there are those who guide the front line. Leaders have time to lead, but they don't have the time to supervise.

Leadership is not magic. It is guiding, developing, coaching, and counseling. It is finding and nurturing champions. It is building teams and spreading an enthusiastic attitude of service. Leadership is inspiring others. It is practicing sincerity. We don't know much about sincerity, but we do know that it can't be faked.

Tomorrow's leader recognizes the tremendous power possessed by the front line and does not underestimate front-line performers. He does a lot of guiding and very little supervising. The true leaders are those who can help the front line interpret and use information properly. They are those select few who aren't making all of the decisions, but who are capable of assisting the front line in making effective decisions. Increase front-line accountability and involvement by broadening their responsibility on a project basis. Avoid vertical pyramids. Instead of promotions, find ways to increase responsibility and authority on a per-project basis.

10. FOCUS ON THE POSITIVE

A person can perceive either the positive or the negative—by choice. If one person focuses on the positive, others will follow. The positive side creates more success, more involvement, better followership, and it produces greater customer satisfaction.

Yes, there is a role for the negative as well. After coaching and training, if the individual continues to perform poorly, he should be removed from the position or, better yet, removed from the company. However, focusing attention on the positive puts pressure on the poor performer to adopt a more positive and constructive attitude himself.

Customer service and sales management professionals are the counselors for the corporation. They are the conscience. They are customer champions. Others in the organization can make negative comments. Customer servicing professionals cannot.

Is there such a thing as the impossible customer? Of course there is, but the impossible customer does not become less impossible when we focus our valuable resources on his negative behavior. More importantly, overall customer servicing is not improved by focusing on the negative.

Is focusing on the emotional positive side too fluffy or not macho enough? Abraham Lincoln said in the Gettysburg Address: "We cannot dedicate, we cannot consecrate, we cannot hallow this ground. The brave men, living and dead, who struggled here have consecrated it far and above our poor power to add or detract." The issue is not how macho or emotional we are. The issue is the integrity and conviction we have in what we do and say.

11. RISK TAKING

Reward risk taking when you see it. It is a valuable resource. Help people understand the basis of true power and authority. Four forms of authority are

- Formal: This type of authority is usually delegated from above and derived from position or ownership. Typically this form of power is not available to the customer response position. It is in the hands of the customer.

- Acceptance: This type of authority comes from below. Others grant the power to lead. It is earned based upon the strength of personality and is available to anyone, including front line customer response people.

- Contract: This type of authority resides in a contract or, more specifically, in the problem at hand. The psychological contract includes any problem that the customer wants solved. The customer service representative has considerable power within the limits of the problem solving process.

- Knowledge: This type of authority comes from one's knowledge about a given subject. The individual with the knowledge has considerable power as he/she educates others.

Understand and help others to understand the real sources of power, and reinforce those who take risks.

12. DIVE INTO CHANGE

The status quo is always dead, yet we fight to preserve it. Most organizational change efforts eventually run into some form of employee resistance. The concept of change triggers rational and irrational emotions in people because of the uncertainty involved. Resistance comes from

- Self-Interest: People fear losing something they consider valuable.

- Misunderstanding: Those who do not fully understand the reasons behind the change will resist it.

- Lack of trust: Because of past experience or past perception, some people simply don't trust the organization.

- Different perceptions: There are always trade-offs. What one sees as very positive, someone else will see as negative.

- Fear: Some are afraid they will not be able to develop the new skills change requires.

Don't assume change will be resisted. Dive into change and get others involved through

- Education: Once persuaded, people often will help with the implementation process and communicate their support to others.

- Involvement: Participation causes commitment.

- Support: Understand and help others create change—nothing works better in helping people adjust.

13. PERSONALIZE YOUR WORLD

High levels of customer satisfaction are created by individuals, not companies, policies, or procedures. Champions are everywhere. Stand up and be counted. Look for and discover the other champions around you. Find ways to instill a sense of ownership in others.

Bureaucracy and regulations stifle creativity and a sense of ownership. Bureaucracy creates losers. It assumes the worst, and it protects the masses against the one-in-a-million exception.

Overwhelming momentum in a given direction suggests that nothing can change. Find the little victories. Look for ways to personalize relationships. Don't try always to guess what the boss wants. Look around, look at your customers, look at the competition, and use your own senses. Don't always look for the rules. Use judgment, thought experience, and your colleagues. Then try something. Take a small risk. Develop your own influence sphere, and then help others develops theirs.

Experiment, but have patience. Typically, experimenting does not produce immediate positive results. Usually, results are slow, and they need time to build, which is why it is so important to reinforce the small wins. Small wins build momentum. The momentum will diffuse inside the culture, and change will occur.

14. FIND SOMEONE TO SERVE

Henry David Thoreau said all that needs to be said on this topic: "Be not simply good; be good for something."

> *SPEECH TIP*: A single well-chosen quotation can make a strikingly effective conclusion. Closing his speech almost suddenly, Ramundo spares his audience any repetitive summary of the material he has already presented, thereby respecting—and rewarding—his listeners for their attention throughout.

Closing the Impact Gap through Leadership

BARRY SULLIVAN
Electronic Data Services

Delivered to the Information Processing Interagency Conference, 1992, Austin, Texas, November 19, 1992

SUMMARY: *Electronic Data Services executive Barry Sullivan notes that history has always shown a time lag between technological invention and its productive application in the work place. Today, as electronics and information technologies advance at lightning speeds, businesses may best compete by shortening that time lag, re-engineering their production processes through leadership, better communication, and responsive innovation.*

Good evening, ladies and gentlemen. It's a privilege for me to be here today, and I'm honored that you would ask me to speak.

Before I begin, I'd like to answer the question I know you're too polite to ask: "How long is this going to take?"

Let me answer this way: Lincoln's Gettysburg Address used 266 words, the Ten Commandments used 297 words, and the Bill of Rights used 463. I hear that the latest Federal directive to regulate the price of cabbage in America contains 26,911 words.

My comments will fall somewhere in between.

> *SPEECH TIP*: Using humor, Sullivan introduces a reference point—Lincoln's Gettysburg Address—that he will be calling upon throughout the speech. This technique acknowl-

edges the obvious differences between two concepts or events while at the same time smoothing the way to draw parallels between them.

Today, November 19, is an important day in the history of the United States of America. In 1863, on a brisk, cloudy, windswept Pennsylvania afternoon, Abraham Lincoln dedicated a new national cemetery "as a final resting place for those who gave their lives that [the] nation might live." Today is the 129th anniversary of the Gettysburg Address.

Now, I believe that there aren't too many people who would disagree that the Civil War was one of the most pivotal events in American history, perhaps *the* most pivotal event. Nor are there too many folks who would take issue with the statement that Lincoln was one of the greatest *leaders* this nation has ever known. So, I think it's worth noting that, in the middle of that turbulent time, Abraham Lincoln not only dedicated a cemetery, but, he also asked for a renewal and rededication to the basic, fundamental principles upon which the nation was founded.

"It is for us to be dedicated to the *unfinished work*," he said.

"It is for us to be here dedicated to the *great task* remaining before us," he said, "that we here *highly resolve* that these dead shall not have died in vain, that this nation shall have *a new birth of freedom.*"

Here was a perfect example of leadership at its best—an inspiring leader providing purpose, and hope, and renewal—during a time of great change, of great crisis, of great expectations.

Well, it's 129 years later. But we, too, are in a time of great change. All you have to do to realize this is look at any world map and see how out of date it is! In the last year alone, *National Geographic* changed its map six times, trying to keep up with the times. Any *new* map is, at best, a mere *snapshot* of current events.

Many people would also say that today is a time of great economic crisis. Some of the leading economists state very forcefully that we are in the middle of a worldwide economic recession. But, there are others, like Lester Thurow, Dean of the MIT Sloan School of Business, who say that we're not in a recession. Rather, we're in a five-to-ten-year restructuring.

Well, I don't know, perhaps it's a little bit of both. But, I do know that what's called for today is strong leadership. And I also know that both private enterprise and government organizations are undergoing major restructuring. They're downsizing, flattening organizations, and re-engineering processes. They are being asked to do *more*—with *less*.

And, so, I'd like to spend the next few minutes discussing this "re-engineering process" and the role that leadership plays.

Now, I find that it's somewhat difficult to explain process re-engineering, so let me relate a story to make my point. A hundred years ago, nearly every factory in the country was powered by steam engines. A long drive shaft was hooked up to the engine, and machines were serially connected to it. Back then, factories looked like bowling alleys.

> *SPEECH TIP:* Creating a vivid scene to illustrate an abstract idea, Sullivan further engages his audience by including the listener as an active participant in the imaginary scene.

So, I might have a lathe, and you might have a drill press. And when you needed power for your drill press you put that in a belt that connected up to the drive. Perhaps you've seen old pictures of these big belts going up to the drive shafts. As a matter of fact, it's widely thought that the phrase "knock off" is derived from the fact that when a worker was ready to quit for the day, he would knock his belt off the drive shaft.

Well, in the 1890s, electric motors were introduced. So, you could have an electric motor on your drill press and I could have one on my lathe. But, at first, things didn't change. I still passed the product on to you, and it went down the assembly line just like it had always done.

It wasn't until twenty years later, around 1910, that people realized that one of the things the electric motor gave them was the flexibility to reorganize work in the factory. Work no longer had to be aligned serially. They were no longer forced to be dependent on this single drive shaft that ran the length of the factory. They could now put in many separate stations powered individually by electric motors. So, output, production, and efficiency were all increased dramatically. But there was this gap of twenty years between the time the electric motor was introduced and when people, in fact, *took advantage of it* for productivity by reorganizing the work in the factory.

Well, that's kind of where we are today with information. That is, what we've done so far is to apply the information to do the existing process faster. However, getting computer power and telecommunications-shared data to the desk top allows us to *re-engineer* the work. So, *work, processes,* and *decisions* are made where they need to be made, not where they *had* to be made based on the old process.

Today, we still experience this lagging distance between the time new technology is invented and the time it becomes productive. So much of it, I think, is due to the natural human tendency to resist change. Over the years, we've made tremendous advances in information technology. Today's desktop computers have more power than room-size supercomputers had a decade ago. Communications speed and capacity have increased almost beyond comprehension, and there are many who claim that in just the last ten years, we've surpassed the magnitude of technology advances for the prior fifty.

And we're fascinated by all this. We herald every new technology development as another triumphant breakthrough for society. Somehow we get seduced by it. Yet, *as in the case of the old factories*, we often fail to notice that our ability to apply all this magnificent technology has failed to keep pace. While the rate of technology change has been accelerating at almost blinding speed, our ability to *apply* that technology has been growing ever so slowly.

This is a serious, growing gap between our ability to *invent* technology and our ability to *use* what we invent. It's what we at EDS call the Impact Gap.

SPEECH TIP: Having brought a concept to life with a clear, old-fashioned example, Sullivan now offers a shorthand term to describe the idea. This term will serve as a concise bridge between the concept's historical background and its contemporary manifestations, which Sullivan goes on to relate.

Why is the Impact Gap so troubling? Because it's only through the application of technology that we get the full impact—the real return—of our investment. We must be able to *apply* the technology that we develop, and not be developing new technology solely for technology's sake.

Let me mention an example of the Impact Gap in action.

Think about the bar codes you see on everything from stereos to groceries to express mail packages. They've been around for many years. But, when they first came out, all the bar code contained was a single number, and nearly all are still set up this way. The most significant data—the real information about the product—is linked to the number, but it's stored in a separate computer. By scanning the bar code, you read only the coded number, which then calls up specific information about the product. It's similar to the number on a license plate, which allows police to look up information about a particular car and driver.

Only recently have we been putting all the detailed information on the bar codes, as opposed to simply numbers. We can really bypass the central data bank, skip the checking by the number, and access the information right off the bar code. As a matter of fact, every word I'll say today can easily be placed into a small bar code.

Now, doesn't this sound a little like the situation when the electric motor was invented? For twenty years everything was kept in a straight line. In the case of the bar codes, we just made it work like the already established license plate system: Check the number against the data bank information. It took us years before we broke out of that mode. Still, we've probably only tapped some 10 percent of the potential applications for the current bar-coding technology. At our current rate of progress, this new technology will become outdated before we've used even 50 percent of its potential.

And so the Impact Gap continues to grow.

Well, how do we close this gap? Obviously, there are many barriers to tear down, but let me point out one major barrier.

We need better communication. It's that simple. Better communication between the *inventors* and the *users* of technology. One of our basic problems is that the user does not believe the inventor understands his problem, and the inventor believes he's already solved it!

On the one hand, you've got the people and enterprises that stand to benefit from the technology. They talk in terms of business need, speed to market, process re-engineering, and return on investment.

And on the other hand, there are the creators of the technology, who talk in terms of bits, bytes, VSAT, and RAM, using a language that usually doesn't connect with the rest of us. One group striving for scientific excellence, the other toward adding to the bottom line!

So, too often, we end up with these two factions, each in isolation from the other. One possessing the need, the other possessing the technology, and a large communication gap separating the two. It's a gap in communication, it's a gap in knowledge, and it's a gap in understanding. It cries out for true collaboration.

At EDS we place employees in our client's place of business. This practice eliminates the problem of isolation from one another. It facilitates better communication by *just being there*: one on one; face-to-face; shoulder-to-shoulder. It is basic human interaction. Systems engineers are often on the same floor as the client's front-line managers. Many times their offices are right next to each other. EDS people become part of the team, working together, striving together, winning together.

> *SPEECH TIP*: Rhythmic speech is a powerful tool for communicators. Harmonious repetition of like-sounding words or phrases—"one-on-one, face-to-face, shoulder-to-shoulder" and "working together, striving together, winning together"—has a soothing, even mesmerizing effect on the listener and creates forward momentum for the ideas that follow.

We find that when our people actually become part of our client's business team, they develop loyalty to the client. An emotional bond is developed, not to mention a financial bond. Our people are rewarded based on the level of customer satisfaction they create. Professional pride kicks in, and pretty soon they know just as much about the client's business as the client does. Then we start coming up with our own ideas about how to make money for the client, how to strengthen the relationship between our client and *their* customer. And, predictably, a successful long-term relationship is usually the result.

Let me give you one vivid illustration of successfully closing the impact gap. Recently, K mart (with the help of on-site engineers) implemented an innovative point-of-sale scanning system by combining bar-coding with radio frequency technology to improve the accuracy and flow of merchandise from vendor to distribution center. It bypasses the central data bank I mentioned earlier.

With an assist from satellite hook-ups, the retail giant now monitors—on a daily basis—sales data on 200,000 items in 2,300 stores, enabling them to identify and respond to shifts in customer buying patterns with unprecedented speed and accuracy. Instant data tabulation recognizes the fastest-selling items as they are sold, which allows K mart to keep popular items in stock. Several years ago, identifying such items required a sales manager spotting open spaces on the aisles, a couple of phone calls, filling out the paperwork. It took *weeks* to restock.

Today, it happens just like *that!*

The distribution center is instantly alerted that the store in Cranberry, Pennsylvania, is selling out of Barbies, and an order to restock goes out immediately.

Another retail giant, Walmart, has virtually the same process.

Walmart and K mart are the *leaders* in the retail industry, and two of the most profitable retailers. Other companies will be following in their footsteps with regard to implementing and *applying* new technology in this rapidly changing world.

What is the only thing that gives you the ability to embrace and take advantage of change?

It's leadership. Leadership that is at the very cultural core of an organization. Leadership at the top; leadership of the team; leadership from the inside on out of each individual employee.

In fact, I would go so far as to say that leadership is *the* strategic resource for success in the 1990s and on into the twenty-first century. It will be the chief catalyst in creating organizations that build and sustain the ability to deliver *value* to their constituency.

And, what is the value of leadership, anyway?

It's developing a strategic vision. It's rallying the rest of the organization around that vision. It's having the flexibility to *alter* that vision and move on to a new plan when circumstances dictate. And, it's renewing that vision as time passes, just as Lincoln did at Gettysburg.

Leadership is facilitating better communication—as that between *inventors* and *users* of technology. It's providing an atmosphere that encourages continual learning. It's the ability to *empower* people, lift them up to a higher level of awareness, achievement, and motivation. And, it's encouraging innovation.

That's another thing that Lincoln did during the Civil War. He constantly encouraged new ideas, new thoughts, new processes. In December 1862, he asked the Congress to open their minds. And this is what he said to them: "Still the question recurs 'can we do better?' The dogmas of the quiet past are inadequate to the stormy present. The occasion is piled high with difficulty, and we must rise with the occasion. As our case is new, so we must think anew and act anew."

Isn't that exactly what we, as an industry, need to do in these pivotal, changing times? Don't we need to be innovative? Don't we need to be creative? Don't we need to think of new ways of solving old problems?

Encouraging innovation is one of the key dimensions of leadership.

If you have a process that works, one that's proven and needs no changes, then you may only need mere managerial skills to execute that process. But, if you need to innovate, if you need to invent new processes, if you need to have new ways of doing things, if you need to have the people on your team acquire new skills, that requires more than just management. It requires leadership.

We're in a time, both in the public sector and the private sector, that requires everyone to "think anew and act anew."

> *SPEECH TIP*: Throughout his speech, Sullivan draws on a wide range of real-life illustrations to demonstrate his topic. While supporting his general assertions, Sullivan's examples also offer listeners concrete information that is interesting in its own right. Good speakers know that audiences value news as much as opinion.

Now, the good news is that this is happening in pockets around the country. It's happening in Chicago, for example, where just eighteen months ago the Chicago Parking Authority was faced with $420 million in unpaid parking tickets. And no wonder! Eleven thousand new tickets were being issued *daily*. There was a *year-long* delay in entering them into the system, a *two-year* delay in accessing ticket copies, and a lack of critical information for each of the 1,500 parking cases going to court each day. So they scrapped the entire system—completely redesigned it. They came up with a new process that combines hand-held computers with imaging technology that prints tickets on the spot and, later, loads them into a larger data base.

Today, the collection rate has increased 600 percent, ticket revenue is up $20 million, meter revenue up $6 million. And no more unpaid tickets. The City of Chicago did *more with less*—less people, more technology, more revenue, better quality enforcement.

It was a new process, generated by people who were "thinking anew and acting anew."

And it's happening in Los Angeles. In 1991, the Los Angeles County Department of Public Social Services installed what's known as AFIRM (Automated Fingerprint Image Reporting and Match), the first non-law-enforcement application of its kind in the United States. It is used as a deterrent to welfare fraud. Just six months after it was installed, it had saved the county $5.4 million.

Essentially, the county fingerprints all of its welfare applicants, compares the prints to a data base of those already on the rolls, and avoids any possible "double-dipping." Sounds simple, doesn't it? The amazing thing is that people simply place their fingers on a scanner for a moment. Five minutes later, the check is complete, *and* there's no paperwork.

The City of Los Angeles engineered a new process by doing *more with less,* created by people who were "thinking anew and acting anew."

And, it's happening on a national scale—at a Medicare office, for example, where *one* person thought of a new way to speed up the processing of claim forms in her department. So often innovation comes from the people who are intimately familiar with the problem. And that person's idea quickly spread through the entire system, saving Medicare thousands of hours of time and millions of dollars in revenue. One person doing *more with less.* One person "thinking anew and acting anew."

Right now, we are living in just as pivotal a time as that which existed during the Civil War.

Pivotal times require leadership.

Back then, Abraham Lincoln provided it.

Today, *we* must provide the leadership necessary for success!

But, it takes great courage to be a leader today. In these changing times, we find ourselves facing an entirely new set of pressures, pressures that didn't exist just a few years ago. They don't have to do with thermonuclear threats; they don't have to do with the ongoing threat of superpowers with great land forces and great arsenals that could threaten the existence of liberty around the world; they don't have to do with the Cold War.

They have to do with our competitiveness as a nation.

Today, we have not only the *opportunity,* but the *obligation* to lead. We can lead by building a country that has the capability to compete at the highest levels in a global economy, by building a country that has the ability to provide its citizens with the services that a first world country expects—and deserves.

We can lead by closing the Impact Gap, by facilitating better communication, by applying the technology we invent faster, by empowering our people, and by lifting them up to a higher level of commitment, cooperation, and caring.

In 1864, Abraham Lincoln ventured into the field to visit his battle-weary soldiers in an attempt to reinspire them, to let them know that neither he nor the nation had forgotten them, and to remind them of the importance of what they were fighting for:

> It is not merely for today, but for all time to come that we should perpetuate for our children's children this great and free government, which we have enjoyed all our lives.

> I beg you to remember this, not merely for my sake, but for yours. I happen temporarily to occupy this big White House.

> I am a living witness that any one of your children may look to come here as my father's child has. It is in order that each of you may have through this free government which we have enjoyed, an open field and a fair chance for your industry, enterprise, and intelligence; that you may all have equal privileges in the race of life,

with all its desirable human aspirations. It is for this the struggle should be maintained. . . . The nation is worth fighting for. . . .

Thank you for listening.

> *SPEECH TIP*: Sometimes the simplest expressions of courtesy provide the means for a graceful conclusion.

Beyond the Horizon:
The Pursuit of Goals

JAY VAN ANDEL
Co-founder and Chairman
Amway Corporation

Delivered at "Executive in Residence Day" ceremonies at Grand Valley State University's Seidman School of Business, Grand Rapids, Michigan, September 28, 1992.

SUMMARY: Recalling his entrepreneurial beginnings with partner Rich DeVos, Amway co-founder and chairman Jay Van Andel encourages today's business students to recognize potential in themselves and others.

Good morning and thank you for inviting me to be your Executive in Residence today. I'm also especially proud to receive an honorary degree from this esteemed university.

Grand Valley and Amway grew up together. We've become two of west Michigan's greatest success stories. GVSU graduates contribute daily to the economy and welfare of our community. More than 150 of your degreed alumni are Amway employees, contributing their skills to help us prosper.

> *SPEECH TIP*: At the very outset of his speech, Van Andel uses a specific numerical figure to establish a connection between the group he is addressing and the organization he represents. By "solving the equation" between speaker and audience, Van Andel settles the facts—and relevancy—of this relationship and frees himself and his listeners to proceed together, without further second-guessing.

I'm also flattered to be invited to speak about business to your business school, but I can't help feeling a bit like the man whose proudest accomplishment was being one of the few survivors of the great Jamestown flood. This man loved bending the ear of any listener with his story. After he died and entered heaven, St. Peter asked if he had any special requests. The man said, "Yes. I'd like to speak before a large audience about surviving that big flood in Pennsylvania in 1889."

St. Peter arranged a meeting and told the man he was scheduled to speak that afternoon on Cloud Nine. "But just one thing," said St. Peter. "I want to warn you that one person in the audience will be a guy named *Noah*."

I know there are many Noahs in the audience today, but I hope I can enhance *your* business expertise by sharing some personal experiences from nearly fifty years in business.

My message is simple. It's the foundation of every successful business person and business venture. Although simple, it's not practiced by many businesses, never learned by some, and forgotten by others. The key to Amway's tremendous success—and, I think, the success of any business—has been the continued commitment to the pursuit of ever greater goals: what I call "reaching beyond horizons." We've reached beyond each new horizon despite risks or setbacks, and regardless of our current level of success. Amway Corporation today is a $4 billion international company. We have ten thousand employees and two million distributors in nearly sixty countries and territories. Our facilities in Ada stretch more than a mile along Fulton Street. We produce four hundred diverse products.

And most of this happened within your lifetimes.

Amway is an unconventional business for many reasons. But one difference that sets us apart from many companies is our unfailing belief in the power of ordinary people to achieve the extraordinary. But I don't want to leave the impression that you recklessly drive toward your goals without planning. It's also important to look before you leap.

There's a story about a professor, a college student, and a dean riding in a small plane. The engine stalled, and their pilot announced they'd have to bail out. But he had only three parachutes for the four of them.

The pilot said he had a wife and children, grabbed a parachute, and jumped. The professor said he was one of the smartest men in the world, and his knowledge was too valuable to lose. So he jumped. The dean told the college student, "I've had a full life and yours is still ahead. Take the last parachute." The college student said, "That won't be necessary. We have two parachutes left. The smartest man in the world just jumped with my backpack."

SPEECH TIP: A good speaker knows the deadly peril of appearing pompous or self-superior. By poking fun at someone else's conceit, Van Andel acknowledges its folly and subtly assures the audience that he will forgo such airs himself.

When I began my business career, I was more like the student in that story than the smartest man in the world. Although I didn't know it at the time, my first major step as an entrepreneur began when I met my business partner, Rich DeVos.

Because my father owned a car dealership, I had a Model A Ford to drive to Grand Rapids Christian High School. Rich had a bicycle. So he offered to pay me twenty-five cents a week for transportation to school, and that was the beginning of our partnership.

Shortly after our high school graduation, America entered World War II, and I enlisted in the Army Air Corps. Training as an officer at the cadet school at Yale University was a great learning experience about human potential. The intensive training, in competition with some of the brightest students in the country, brought out qualities I never quite realized I possessed.

In the Amway business I see that happen every day. People who never realized their potential for success aim high and surprise themselves by hitting the target.

Rich's and my parents instilled the goal to be successful through owning our own business. After the war we owned several. We started a flying school—even though neither one of us was a pilot. But we hired a flight instructor, and Rich and I honed our sales skills by finding students and selling lessons. To serve the flight students, we started Grand Rapids' first drive-in restaurant. After a day at the air service, Rich and I would begin our evening of flipping burgers and waiting on customers.

We became successful, but we had our share of setbacks. When our air service was set to open, the airport runway wasn't finished. So we put pontoons on the plane and used the Grand River for our airstrip. On the night we were set to open our drive-in, the power failed. Rather than give up, we rented a gasoline generator.

We started other businesses—some successful, some not so successful. But we learned from our setbacks. We built our entrepreneurial foundation, learned the fundamentals of sales and marketing, and pursued the philosophy of reaching beyond the horizon.

The breakthrough came in 1949, when a second cousin of mine introduced Rich and me to the direct selling of Nutrilite Food Supplements. We had no direct selling experience. We weren't even familiar with the term. But it was a means of easily getting into a business of our own, and we saw the potential.

We started out and operated much like Amway distributors do today. We built a successful business that became a foundation for starting Amway in 1959.

The Nutrilite experience taught Rich and me a lot about sales and marketing and management. But, most of all, it showed us that our success depended on the success of people in our organization. If we could inspire them to be successful, we would be successful.

Amway was a dream with humble beginnings. We started the company from the basements of our homes in Ada. It flourished beyond our expectations by reaching for ever greater horizons and relying on ordinary people to achieve the extraordinary. The principle of the potential to be whatever you want to be has commonly been called the American Dream, but we've learned at Amway that the desire of people to realize their potential through their own initiative is an international dream.

> *SPEECH TIP*: Updating a familiar catchphrase—even a time-worn expression like "the American Dream"—can capitalize on its existing associations while reconfiguring its meaning and refreshing its value.

After I joined Governor George Romney in 1965 as a member of an overseas Michigan trade mission, Rich and I decided that it was time for Amway to go international. We opened our first overseas affiliate in Australia in 1970. Starting an operation halfway around the world was a real reach beyond the horizon. We chose Australia for our first overseas operation because it at least had a similar language. They say a person who speaks three languages is trilingual, one who speaks two languages is bilingual, and someone who speaks just one language is an American. Today Amway speaks many languages. We decided not to let differences in language and culture be barriers to our expanding horizons.

That was no truer than in Japan. Differences in language and culture—along with a perceived bias against U.S. products—could have been understandable excuses for staying away from that market. Our operation in Japan has been reported to be the fastest growing foreign-owned company in that country.

Another interesting success story has been Hungary. More than a decade ago, I was speaking across the United States as chairman of the U.S. Chamber of Commerce. My message was that the popular view of socialism was wrong and that free enterprise would prevail. I've had the satisfaction of watching that prediction come true with the fall of the Berlin Wall and the parting of the Iron Curtain.

Amway opened in Hungary about a year ago, and we're opening in Poland in November. We had no trouble meeting our projection of 50,000 distributors within a year of operation in the former communist country of Hungary.

Given a choice, people show they want to be rewarded in proportion to their efforts, to set their own goals, to reach beyond the horizon and be what they want to be. The free enterprise system is a proven success, and communism has proven to be a failure.

That's illustrated by the story of the man in the former Soviet Union who finally earned enough to buy a car, but because of slow production methods he was told he'd have to wait several years for delivery. When he pressed the dealer further, he was given an exact delivery date of June 30, 2002.

"Will that be delivered in the morning or the afternoon?" the man asked the dealer. The dealer replied, "What's the difference?" And the man said, "I have a leaky faucet, and my plumber is scheduled to come that morning."

My faith in the power of people to excel and the importance of reaching beyond horizons was renewed this year. In this quincentennial year of the voyage of Christopher Columbus, President Bush appointed me ambassador and commissioner general for the U.S. pavilion at Genoa Expo '92. That world's fair was held this summer in Genoa, Italy—the birthplace of Columbus. He was a man with a mission who literally reached beyond the horizon. Columbus was not only an explorer, he was an entrepreneur. Before refrigeration and rapid transportation, most food was spoiled by the time it got to the table. Spices were essential for food to be palatable, and some rare spices were worth their weight in gold. Columbus proposed that by sailing west and circling the globe, he could find a faster route to the Spice Islands. But, in seeking a sponsor, he was denied by those who were not as farsighted and adventurous. He spent ten years looking for support and was turned down by nearly every country in Europe before Spain granted one of his many requests.

Even the Portuguese—known for their sailing skills and discoveries along the coast of Africa—were content to hug the coastline rather than venture into the unknown open sea.

After weeks on the ocean, Columbus's crew nearly mutinied when he wouldn't turn back. He told his crew that if land was not sighted within forty-eight hours, they'd head home. Land was sighted the next day.

Columbus died without ever reaching the Spice Islands or realizing what he'd really discovered. As commercial ventures, his voyages were failures, but he doubled the size of the earth and opened an age of discovery that resulted in our being here today.

Five hundred years later, we can still learn from Columbus. Successful people don't hug the coastline. They sail beyond the horizon.

I know that you've been studying the writings of some of our best business minds and learning complicated theories and techniques of business management. But many times, experience is the best teacher. I hope that by sharing my business experience, you receive a basic message to help you succeed: Have confidence in your God-given talents, recognize potential in yourself and others, and keep reaching beyond the horizon.

CHAPTER 2

Research and Development

The topic of research and development presents both an opportunity and at least two challenges. The opportunity is the inherent excitement of sharing with others news of present innovations and innovations yet to come. The challenges are, first, to make the nature and significance of the fruits of R & D—of, say, a particular innovation—comprehensible to an audience that may or may not be thoroughly knowledgeable about the field in question. Indeed, the audience may be entirely uninitiated, or they may be a collection of technological gurus, or they may exhibit the whole range between these two extremes. It is a truism of speechmaking that the speaker should know his audience before he speaks. Obvious as this is, it is all too often ignored by speakers who feel that their only obligation is to know their subject. That, however, is only one side of the speaking equation. The effective speaker knows her subject *and* her audience and tailors her speech accordingly.

That leads to the second of the two challenges posed by the R & D speech. Unfortunately, in today's business climate, R & D is often treated as something of an orphan. To most business outsiders, R & D is like mom and apple pie—rather indisputably good. But, in many organizations, R & D is an emotionally freighted subject. The research and development personnel may feel slighted, frustrated, even threatened, while management may resent what they regard as a clique of prima donnas who see nothing but blue sky. For the speaker, therefore, it pays to be familiar not only with the audience, but with the corporate culture in which that audience partakes.

These caveats aside, the engine that makes an R & D speech run is enthusiasm, excitement, and even a touch of wonder. Second only to this is knowing how much to explain and how much context to provide. Above all, the speaker should avoid a tendency to abstraction. Make the subject of R & D real with real-world examples and vivid illustrations. How does X work? Why is it important? Now that we have X, what can we do that we could not do before? These are the gut-level questions to pose—and answer.

Technology Management: Transitioning to the Third Millennium

JOHN S. MAYO
President
AT&T Bell Laboratories

Delivered to the Eighth World Productivity Congress, Stockholm, Sweden, May 25, 1993

SUMMARY: *Telecommunications executive John S. Mayo believes that the divestment and restructuring of the Bell System ultimately strengthened the company by creating a more "nimble," customer-focused corporation. Sharing some of the lessons learned during Bell's transition process, he offers suggestions for developing and managing technology in the globally competitive marketplace of today and tomorrow.*

I'm delighted to be here this morning to discuss a topic of increasingly widespread importance: the management of technology. In the next twenty minutes, I will explore some of the lessons we at AT&T learned from our transition to a global competitive marketplace, and how these lessons apply to technology management in the third millennium.

Telecommunications in the U.S.A. must be viewed in the context of powerful interrelated thrusts in information technology, in competition, and in globalization. The U.S. telecommunications infrastructure today is the beneficiary of the powerful twin forces of information technology and competition, which are merging telecommunications, computing, and entertainment. The third force, globalization, is a powerful market driver, which also reaches strongly back into technology management. These forces are linked inseparably and drive the industry to meet the information needs of end users around the globe better than ever before.

Information technology is exceedingly rich. Until the latter part of the twentieth century, however, customer needs outstripped technology. The user willingly accepted whatever technological capabilities we were able to achieve. Thus, the telecommunications industry was supplier-driven, and the suppliers managed the evolution of the industry. But the technology became so rich that it made many more capabilities possible than the user could accept. That marked the transition from a supplier-driven industry to a customer-driven industry—from supplier push to marketplace pull.

The transition was also driven by the breakup of the Bell System and the increasing privatization of the PTTs around the globe. Let me briefly review this aspect of the transition.

Until about ten years ago, global communications developed according to the dominant suppliers' plans. But in the 1980s, competition began to be added to the mix. In the U.S. we trace the genesis of that competition to early regulatory decisions that finally led to the breakup of the Bell System.

The Bell System, as you know, was a highly centralized, regulated, dominant service provider and manufacturer in the U.S.A. for most of a century. It was divested into eight companies according to service and geography, but nonetheless eight independent companies. The Consent Decree agreement implemented in 1984, in effect, separated the monopoly parts of the Bell System's business from the competitive parts. And AT&T was permitted to enter other commercial markets, but remained under much tighter regulation than its competitors.

Today, except for local service, which is still a monopoly, competition is rampant in every facet of the U.S. market, and foreign companies are among the competitors. Choices proliferate among capabilities and innovative providers. Long-distance prices have dropped, and products and services have grown substantially in feature content. Quality of service is a competitive thrust, and AT&T quality surpasses that of the prior Bell System monopoly.

Today, the U.S. telecommunications industry is more attuned to customers than ever before. AT&T has become a stronger company over the past ten years. The marketplace has forced us to change, and the change has been for the better. We've worked hard at that transition, and it has been painful at times. So, we're rather proud of the results. And with the increasing privatization of PTTs, much of the world is now in the process of making a market-driven, competitive transition similar to the one we made.

Now, we're looking ahead to another transition—the transition into the third millennium. And critical lessons from our past will help with this next transition. We know already that it will require even greater emphasis on process, on customer focus, on quality and on intergroup or organizational learning.

Let's look first at key transitioning issues by examining the interrelationships among competitiveness, skill management, organizational structure, and corporate culture. I will focus on the lessons we learned in enhancing the competitive effectiveness of AT&T Bell Laboratories.

Very important are a clear vision, a sense of mission, stability of direction and constancy of purpose. R&D people, especially those at Bell Laboratories, have lofty goals and have always responded to a clear vision and a sense of mission. But the dynamic and changing environment of the competitive world requires a nimble organization that can indeed shift as necessary to meet user needs, and yet retain the stability of direction and constancy of purpose required for long-term success. It is the job of the leadership of an organization to see that the organization has a vision, a mission, values, and operating principles so carefully stated that they give strong guidance even under the most dynamic market conditions. Only then can the organization incrementally approach its vision and thereby avoid the trap of total focus on day-to-day crises.

> *SPEECH TIP:* Mayo's speech deals with issues and uses terms that all business people can understand. Rather than treating R&D concerns as uniquely special or arcane, Mayo emphasizes their connectedness to commerce as a whole.

At the heart of competitiveness is closeness to customers. And I refer to both internal customers associated with intra-company hand-offs and to external customers receiving our products and services. As we applied the thrust of quality principles, we quickly saw that allegiance to customers is more important than allegiance to function. We could no longer be satisfied with doing just a superb R&D

job. We could only be satisfied when the customer was totally satisfied. So we had to align R&D, manufacturing, and business management into small, highly focused, nimble teams. At the same time, we had to find ways to maintain and enhance functional excellence in each area of expertise.

That required Bell Laboratories to further cultivate its sense of professional community, a vital factor in R&D effectiveness. That sense of community is characterized by an ability to impact one's own destiny, by meaningful mechanisms for coupling within the community, by managing force imbalances across the whole community, by open exchange of information, and by being helpful to one another.

We also had to find ways to enhance the synergy between personal goals and company needs, so that both can be met in an optimal way. This is relatively easy to do for those of us in R&D, for we create exciting new products and services that enrich our society. Most of us delight in doing such useful things.

Excellence and diversity go hand-in-hand in building an outstanding R&D organization. That requires a lot of attention to the quality and diversity of its new hires. Attracting the best from around the world has been key to the success of organizations like mine. The new environment makes it even more so, but not so easy to implement.

Quality of technical supervision is among the most important factors in achieving R&D excellence, and the needs are changed somewhat by the competitive environment. A broader combination of excellent technical skills, people skills, and business sense is required. Also key to R&D effectiveness is a range of opportunities for self-development. An exciting and rewarding future must be available to everyone. That requires a wider range of education and training, greater diligence in career planning, and a good measure of job mobility.

The quality of the reward system is critical to competitive success. This includes a variety of recognition programs, but especially careful attention to incentive awards, performance evaluation, compensation, and promotion. This includes rewards that balance the opportunity to rise by excelling in one's function with the opportunity to rise by broadening into other functions.

Whatever the environment, the prowess of an R&D organization is closely tied to its mechanisms for intergroup learning, and especially for on-the-job learning in groups of more than critical mass that contain many stimulating co-workers. The organization that learns the fastest should eventually win. If you can't apply it competitively, you haven't learned it.

Finally, we must ensure that all employees have challenging work, that they are well-matched to their work, and that they have needed support and needed information. In short, we must ensure that all employees are utilized to the limit of their personal capabilities, and that those personal capabilities grow every day.

These, then, are some of the factors impacting technology development in an R&D community such as Bell Laboratories. Above all, technology leadership is dependent upon a first-rate R&D community—one characterized by excellence, by the excellence of people who are unmatched in their capabilities, and these unmatched capabilities must be highly focused on meaningful problems. But individual skills are not sufficient in the competitive environment. There must also be a high quality of teamwork to bring those individual skills to bear on complex projects and across multiple disciplines.

So far I have focused on human resources lessons that impact the competitive effectiveness of an R&D community, and that therefore impact the successful management of technology. In addition, there are other related lessons that deal with the very nature and purpose of an R&D community in the future. In part, these lessons deal with the relationships between total market sales for a technology and the cost of R&D for that technology.

If it is realistic to extend today's information-technology trends, we find that the technology becomes increasingly powerful, but the R&D increasingly expensive. Accordingly, the number of information-technology sources justified by a given market may decrease over time, with the most expensive R&D being conducted in fewer and fewer enterprises or in a few clusters of partnerships. I expect this to be true even though the recently decreasing cost of capital offsets the trend somewhat. If we reach the point, for example, where there are only a few sources of fine-line semiconductor technology in the world, what does that mean for technology management?

Assuming R&D continues to erode manufacturing as the high value-added content in a product, as is already the case in software and optical devices, we will need to change our mindset about technology management. The technical competence of a corporation would then become an ever larger part of the corporation's total assets. That technical competence would be a growing source of the corporation's competitiveness. Capital alone may eventually be of little consequence.

This is part of a very long-term trend. In the Industrial Revolution, the driving force shifted from people to capital. In today's information revolution, the driving force is shifting from capital to technical competence. Already, we have seen corporations throw billions of dollars at a technology and fail, while others with hardly any capital at all took over the customer base. Capital without competence is increasingly of no avail. Competence without capital is increasingly not a problem. To put differently, capital is having more difficulty in attracting competence than competence is having in attracting capital.

> *SPEECH TIP*: Having established "capital" and "competence" as basic forces in this field, Mayo now grounds their current interrelation in a formula as simple as it is clear. Such formulas help audiences grasp and retain key concepts over the course of complex discussions.

Now, we have learned that the new global competitive environment requires entirely new approaches for managing technology, and calls for the re-engineering—for the radical or discontinuous improvement—of all the processes that support the realization of new products and services. Let's look first at managing the process for identifying and exploiting emerging technologies.

At Bell Laboratories, we re-engineered this complex process. The first goal of the re-engineering was to achieve a greater customer focus, including a global focus. The second goal was faster time to market—to be achieved largely by shortening what we call the front-end process as well as the development and manufacturing intervals. And the third goal was to increase an already high rate of innovation.

Perhaps no other process is more critical to accelerating the conversion of emerging technologies into new products and services than the process for discerning and capturing the needs of customers, both domestic and international. That is a very difficult process, and I expect, in the third millennium, developers of technology will still be seeking better ways to ascertain customer needs. Corporate organization is at best only a partial answer to the challenge. Nonetheless, it is a powerful driver for a customer-oriented culture.

As you may know, AT&T is organized into a number of business units, each focused on particular types of customers. We at Bell Laboratories, in turn, support those business units with the technologies they need now and into the future. The Bell Labs development organizations are aligned with the business units they support. That structural arrangement enhances both our understanding of customer needs and our responsiveness to those needs.

Perhaps the most powerful driver for customer satisfaction is the pervasive application of quality principles, and that complements the organizational approach to customer focus. Our quality program is instrumental in our striving for customer satisfaction, because we have learned to define quality in terms of customer satisfaction. With today's quality revolution, we all speak of quality that is a strategic differentiator for products and services, of quality that is also a cost and time saver, and of quality that, above all, is the key to customer satisfaction. Because of its vital link to customer satisfaction, quality must ultimately be defined by the customer, both domestic and global. So across our industry, quality includes the features the customer wants, the timeliness the customer wants, and a price the customer is willing to pay.

These organizational and quality thrusts drive Bell Labs' alignment with both customer needs and business needs. These alignments extend through development and, for an entirely new product or service, extend all the way back to research or exploratory development. And the alignments are vital to the critical process of technology conversion, of moving emerging technologies to the marketplace in the form of new products and services. Technology sitting on a shelf or in a research lab is virtually useless. In the arena of global competition, the key is how *fast* technology can be moved to the marketplace.

Now let's turn to managing and optimizing the creative and innovative process within companies, because this process is absolutely central to the successful management of technology.

SPEECH TIP: Mayo carefully alerts his audience whenever he shifts his topic or focus. Like a convoy driver in heavy traffic, the speaker who uses such "directional signals" can keep followers better oriented—and better humored—while in tow.

Total quality management, as we have learned, is the modern methodology for managing the creative and innovative process as well as other corporate functions. It's the ideal methodology for managing this process in a global competitive environment, because it knows no geographical bounds. The worldwide goal is full satisfaction of customers.

As part of managing the creative and innovative process at Bell Laboratories, we have organized our research efforts around a series of key competencies that include fundamentals, photonics, electronics, computing, software engineering, networking, and speech and image processing. "Fundamentals" is a collection of various activities and a spawning ground for new competencies. Accelerating technology conversion within these competencies often involves concurrent development—that is, no serial hand-offs. But that is just a part of our re-engineering of product and service realization processes in order to shorten time to market. A very important part of this initiative is, indeed, our many applied research projects, where research, development, and manufacturing people are brought together in tightly knit teams to speed ideas to market.

This does not lessen our commitment to research. It simply means that good research and good development are often done concurrently. Research is still managed centrally and holistically. The Bell Labs vice president of research and the president of Bell Labs have the responsibility of setting the research program and aligning it with AT&T's strategic intent and the long-term technology needs of the AT&T business units. We have not reduced our commitment to basic research.

Over the past decade, we have enhanced our focus on architecture. Moreover, we have learned to pay as much attention to process architectures as we do to product and service architectures. A world-class innovation system requires a coherent, unifying family of core processes to identify customer needs, translate those needs into product and service specifications, and then produce designs that are manufacturable at competitive costs and intervals. We have been doing more and more development, even with the same resource level, because our process improvements are so powerful. An important aspect of this is the re-use of previously developed assets, such as previously developed and tested software modules and hardware platforms.

Now, as I noted earlier, intergroup learning, or organizational learning, has become key to technology management, and that is the collective learning among the people in the relevant disciplines who are physically present within an organization. Peter Senge of MIT's Sloan School of Management defines a learning organization as "a group of people continually enhancing their capacity to create what they want to create." This, of course, is central to competitive innovativeness. It is not easy to learn in a distributed organization, so we have to work very hard at it, and we are still inventing new mechanisms for dealing with intergroup learning across small customer-focused teams scattered around the globe.

One highly effective way to capture organizational learning has been through Best Current Practices, or BCPs. They are key to shortening development intervals and lowering development costs and, as such, represent a vital process for enhanced creativity and innovation. BCPs attempt to promote tried and proven approaches that are deemed to be "best in class" by people inside and outside AT&T. Each BCP represents a systematic or structured method for approaching one aspect of the development process. BCPs are based on the notion that great benefits come from analyzing successful projects in order to understand and apply whatever is being done right. BCPs have also been widely applied to manufacturing, but not so widely applied to marketing and business functions outside of financial accounting. I must stress that we do not view BCPs for R&D as a substitute for the creative and innovative processes so central to an R&D organization. Instead, we see them as a supplement to these processes—as a way to provide proven guidance without damaging creativity and innovation. Importantly, BCPs are broad, flexible guidelines, not rigid commandments, and that, of course, is because intergroup learning should not be legislated, but rather enabled.

In sum, AT&T has made the transition from a regulated monopoly to a globally competitive corporation. Key lessons we learned from the past transition are vital to our preparation for the next millennium. These lessons include an emphasis on both continuous process improvement and periodic process re-engineering, on intensive customer focus, on total quality management, and on the fastest rate of intergroup learning. Responding to these lessons has already led to an increasing number of innovations and to much more rapid conversion of emerging technologies into new products and services.

Our customers are happier, our shareowners are happier, we are happier. But, looking to the third millennium, it is clear that we have barely begun. All across our industry, there is much to do, and Bell Labs remains committed to leading the way.

Thank you very much.

Progress Through Innovation:
You Can't Have One Without the Other

ROBERT G. McVICKER
Senior Vice President, Technology, Quality Assurance,
and Scientific Relations
Kraft General Foods

*Delivered to the 1992 Leaders of the Future Engineering Conference, Pennsylvania
State University, University Park, Pennsylvania, April 3, 1992*

*SUMMARY: Sharing his insights with a group of engineering students, Kraft
General Foods executive Robert G. McVicker explores the nature and process of
innovation, which McVicker believes is fundamental to the course of human
progress. The senior vice president draws quotes and examples from throughout
history to demonstrate how invention has sparked innovation—or has failed to do
so, in the absence of other, non-technological prerequisites in a society, an organization, or an individual.*

Good evening . . . and let me say right off the bat that I'm delighted to be here with
so many of you leaders of the future. And I can hardly think of a more appropriate topic for tomorrow's leaders to be thinking about than progress and innovation,
because, let's face it, to some degree, you're going to be responsible for the
progress of the society in which you will *be* leaders. And so I thought I might help
you prepare for that role, by offering a few thoughts on just what innovation is, why
we need it, how we get it, and how you can help bring it about.

First, let's get some idea of what innovation is. Back in the late nineteenth and
early twentieth centuries, there was a great German chemist named Johann von
Baeyer. He made many contributions to science, and in 1905, he was awarded a
Nobel Prize. One morning, Baeyer came into his laboratory and found that his assis-
tants had built an ingenious mechanical stirring device operated by water turbines.
The professor was fascinated by the complex machine, and he summoned his wife
from their apartment next door. For a while, Frau Baeyer watched the apparatus in
silent admiration.

And then she exclaimed, "What a lovely idea for making mayonnaise!"

SPEECH TIP: McVicker's opening anecdote—and his subsequent assertion—employ one
of the most crowd-pleasing tricks of the speechmaking trade: the element of surprise.
Twists that confound expectation are necessarily interesting and frequently—especially to
younger audiences—delightful.

There's a basic distinction to be made here: the good professor's students were the inventors—but his wife was the *innovator*. As Peter Drucker says, "Above all, innovation is not invention. It is a term of economics rather than of technology. The measure of innovation is the impact on the environment." Innovation, according to Drucker, "allows resources the capacity to create wealth."

But invention and innovation don't necessarily happen together. In fact, if you look at the history of science, you find that very often the application of a new idea has lagged the idea itself, by many years, sometimes centuries.

One reason may be that the supporting technologies don't yet exist to make the invention fully functional. Five hundred years ago, Leonardo da Vinci envisioned a flying machine; an armor-plated tank, complete with firearms; a portable bridge; a cannon that worked like a modern machine gun; battleships; mechanically propelled armored cars; even an "ideal city"—but, of course, he never built them.

And let's say you do create a one-of-a-kind model. That doesn't automatically mean that you can turn it into a useful, functional, marketable device. It often takes someone else to do that, and perhaps with just one twist-of-the-wrist modification. The transistor was invented in Bell Laboratories in 1947. Yet Sony sold the first transistor *radio* in America in 1956. In that same year, Ampex, a U.S. company, introduced the first videotape recorder—but Sony improved its design and introduced its Betamax in 1975.

If innovation is to follow invention, the social and economic conditions have to be right, too. There had been many primitive calculating devices—going all the way back to Leibniz—before William Burroughs invented his adding machine in 1894. But by then, the time was right. Business and industry were getting pretty complicated, and Burroughs's invention was quickly commercialized and saved people from the endless toil of calculation, just as the inventor had intended.

But earlier in the nineteenth century, a genius named Charles Babbage had conceived—and even partially built—an extraordinary data processing device which he called an "analytical engine." At the time, few if any saw the implications of Babbage's work. It wasn't until the Second World War, when military people needed to rapidly calculate the trajectories of artillery shells, that the first true computers appeared—and in structure and function, they were remarkably similar to the analytical engine of Charles Babbage.

So we have invention . . . and we have innovation. And it's innovation that's essential to progress. In the words of Theodore Levitt, editor of *The Harvard Business Review*, "Just as energy is the basis of life itself, and ideas the source of innovation, so is innovation the vital spark of all man-made change, improvement and progress."

Why is innovation so critical to the success of countries, and even to the future of humanity? Because it's the raw material for the creation of wealth; everything else is just reshuffling and redistribution of what we already have. Just as a lever dramatically increases the amount of force you can exert, so does innovation raise pro-

ductivity, spur economic growth and increase wealth. In a world where everything
has its price, technological innovation—though it's not without its costs—is still the
closest thing there is to an economic free lunch.

And I'm not just talking about recent innovations like the automobile, the telephone, or the computer. The ancient Greeks gave us the lever, wedge, pulley, and
gear. (In fact, sometime in the first century, Hero of Alexandria even invented a
coin-operated vending machine to dispense holy water!) In the Middle Ages came
the horseshoe and stirrup, which revolutionized transportation and warfare, as well
as the chimney, which facilitated home cooking and allowed us to get presents from
Santa Claus. Islamic society gave us paper. And the Chinese invented matches, the
umbrella, and the toothbrush.

SPEECH TIP: From behind-the-scenes business history to "fun facts" about the ancients,
McVicker's illustrations are accessible and entertaining as well as relevant and informative.

My point is that many of what now seem to us to be the most mundane of
contraptions actually had a profound effect on human progress. The wealth, com-
forts, and living standards we enjoy today are built upon thousands of years of
innovations, many of which are now so common that it's hard to think that there
was a time when they didn't exist. But every generation makes its contributions, just
as you will make yours. And that's why, now that you know a little about what
innovation is, it's important to get some idea of how innovation takes place—in
societies, in organizations, and in individuals. I'll talk a little about the first two, but
I'm going to devote most of my time to the third, because while your influence on
organizations and on society are some years off, there are some things you can do
right now, as individuals, that can help make you the innovators and, yes, leaders
of the future.

The question of what drives innovation in a society is a tough one that
nobody has a definitive answer to. You need a supply of good ideas, plus an environment in which they can develop. So a society's level of education, its willingness to bear risk, the tolerance of its religion and its political structure, and its general openness to new ideas probably all have something to do with it. Even factors
as diverse as good nutrition and property rights may play a role. But when everything comes together, watch out! It's probably no coincidence that in ancient
Greece and the Renaissance, there was extraordinary innovation not only in science, but in literature and art as well.

Of course, war is a great motivator, a shock to the system, a forcer of innovation for survival. As I mentioned earlier, war helped bring about the first modern
computers. A few decades earlier, it was the First World War that drove the
Germans to find a new kind of marine propulsion system—an alternative to paddle
wheels. They came up with screw-driven, thrust-bearing propellers. The concept
had been known about for a hundred years (and the screw goes back to the ancient

Greeks), the lubricants and materials already existed, but engineers had never had such a powerful reason to bring them all together. And of course, the classic example is the Manhattan Project, which, in the interests of winning World War II, created the atomic bomb and changed the course of history.

The innovations that had the most powerful effect on living standards, including some of the ones I mentioned, are discussed in a very interesting book called *The Lever of Riches*, which was published last year. The author, Joel Mokyr, argues that there's no single set of conditions that guarantee technological innovation. And he reminds us that progress cannot be taken for granted, because there are such powerful forces that oppose it and enforce the status quo.

SPEECH TIP: Mentioning exciting resource materials by name does more than acknowledge your own debt to others' ideas; it gives your most interested listeners somewhere to turn when the presentation is over. Speakers who spark enthusiasm *and* provide a longer "fuse" can set wonderful things in motion—and be remembered long after they leave the podium.

Look at what happened in China. Before 1400, the Chinese were the most advanced civilization on earth. Before Columbus was even born, they were sending out huge "treasure ships," with crews of five hundred, all the way to the Persian Gulf and East Africa. One expedition brought back a giraffe, which was something of a culture shock to the folks back in Peking. The ships could have made it all the way to West Africa and Europe. And with all of their inventions and innovations, the Chinese may even have been within reach of the kind of industrial revolution that took place in Europe.

Then, suddenly, it was all over. And nobody knows exactly why. All we know is that the government was in charge of invention and innovation, and at some point, it lost interest in technological progress. The bureaucrats, the custodians of the status quo, got the upper hand. They decided that the wealth of the Empire was to be spent on public works projects that would improve the lot of the nation's farmers—and that was that. Leadership in technology began to shift to Western civilization, where it remains to this day.

Well, so much for what innovation is, and the kind of social environment that's conducive to it. Now let's narrow our focus and zoom in on business organizations, especially the science- and technology-based companies in which many of you will spend at least part, maybe even all of your careers. How can they be organized for innovation?

Let me begin my answer with a comparison. I'll ask you to think about the difference between basketball and football as a metaphor for differences in management . . . and by "management," I mean simply the most effective marshaling of human talent to get things done. Traditionally, American businesses operated like football teams, but it's the basketball team that's the model for the management style of the '90s and beyond.

You see, in football, we find narrow specialization of function: centers, linebackers, tackles, even special teams. The individual players at some positions tend to be interchangeable parts. But basketball puts a premium on generalized skills; though some players excel at scoring, playmaking, and so on, *everyone* must pass, dribble, shoot, play defense, and rebound.

In football, the players pause and regroup after each play, and one player—or the coach—decides what the team will do next. But basketball is too dynamic to permit rigid separation of planning and execution, which is what the football huddle is all about. And you can't rely on preset plays for every situation.

The point here is that to be the leading innovators in our world of rapidly advancing technology and global competition, we in U.S. industry have to learn to move quickly—to constantly improve our products and, most importantly, our manufacturing *processes*, within ever-shortening time frames.

And to do that, we have to be less like a football team—and more like a basketball team. We need to integrate specialist and generalist, managing and working, planning and doing. Specifically, we need to move people from one job to another to give them breadth. We need to make sure people have as much autonomy as they can handle, and we need to act as quickly as possible on what seem to be good ideas. In other words, we need to avoid paralysis by analysis.

But that's not the only way to organize for innovation. Another is to form cross-functional teams, the way they do in hockey.

I can give you one recent example from Kraft General Foods: the development of our fat-free products. Engineers played a key role in the development, not only of the processes that were fundamental to the product, but of the products themselves.

I can't overemphasize the importance of engineers like yourselves being team members with people from other disciplines. In any industry or organization, cross-functional teamwork is the mark of the innovative organization.

It's up to both the organization and the individual to make teamwork . . . *work.* The company has to see the importance of crossing the walls that naturally form between functions; it has to emphasize and promote teamwork. But you as individuals have a role in it, too. Your colleagues in other disciplines may not share your technical vocabulary—or even your view of the world—but you'll need to work with them, on projects to which each of you has a significant contribution to make.

When we developed our fat-free lines, product engineers worked with marketing people, with finance experts, with plant and operations people. It really was a basketball-team effort that got these innovative products to the marketplace so quickly.

To organize for innovation, we also have to stay as close as possible to our customers, because that's how we know which of our inventions has the potential to become a real—that is to say, a useful, marketable—innovation. And we have to keep our technology base strong, through a long-range commitment to science and engineering programs.

Cross-functional teamwork; a fast-breaking, basketball-style of execution; an understanding of the customer; and leading-edge technology: those are our four principles of innovation at Kraft General Foods. Other companies organize for innovation in their own ways. 3M has an excellent record, based on a few simple principles: they keep their divisions small (in fact, each division manager must know every staffer's first name); they encourage experimentation and tolerate failure (each division's goal is to get 25 percent of its sales from products developed in the past five years); they share internally developed technology throughout the company; and their researchers, marketers, and managers work with customers to brainstorm new product ideas.

Hewlett-Packard urges its researchers to spend 10 percent of their time on pet projects—and gives them 24-hour access to labs and equipment. Merck also gives its researchers time and resources to pursue high-risk, high-payoff projects.

My point is that there are lots of possibilities. And if you're in a company that consistently does any or all of the things I've mentioned, then you're in a place that's organized for innovation.

SPEECH TIP: Moving from the general to the personal, McVicker tells his listeners how to translate abstract ideas into positive actions—how to prepare *themselves* to be the innovators of tomorrow.

Now let's narrow the focus still further. Let's talk about you. Let's talk about innovation at the personal level, because when you get right down to it, it's not societies or organizations that innovate, it's people. So what can you, as an individual, do to train yourself to be an innovator?

First, I would advise you to cultivate breadth. Be a first-rate specialist—but be a generalist as well. Be like a doctor who's an excellent surgeon, but who also has the broad knowledge of a general practitioner. Of course, there is *no* substitute for strong functional expertise. But it's possible for engineers to become so functionally narrow that they don't have the capability for innovation. They may be great inventors—but poor innovators, just because they *are* so narrow.

So, even as knowledge increases exponentially, the key is to develop deep functional skills in your discipline (or sub-discipline) *while* you maintain a broad view of the world about you. To me, that's *critical* to the process of innovation—and to the progress that follows.

Why? Because in the world outside the university, the *application* of knowledge is far less compartmentalized than the *acquisition* of it. Finding an innovative solution to a problem may require you to employ concepts and insights from two or three or more different fields.

Time and again, innovation has come from crossing from one discipline to another, or from making a linkage between one branch of science or technology to another. In fact, the computer journalist Peter Borden, quoted in Roger van Oesch's 1983 book *A Whack on the Side of the Head*, says that "most advances in science come when a person, for one reason or another, is forced to change fields."

You could even argue that this is the *only* way that innovation takes place. Thomas Kuhn was the man who first described how and why it happens that, from time to time, scientists in one field or another adopt whole new paradigms, whole new sets of assumptions and ways of looking at things. And Kuhn said this: "Under normal conditions the research scientist is not an innovator but a solver of puzzles, and the puzzles upon which he concentrates are just those which he believes can be both stated and solved within the existing scientific tradition." In other words, the normal path to professional success encourages, even forces specialization. But nevertheless, the true innovator resists it.

So what can *you* do? Well, I would say that it's up to you, both during your formal education and afterward, to perform the synthesis—to look for ways in which the various disciplines complement and reinforce each other; to learn, as early as possible, to think in terms of *systems*; to find the "networks," the "connective tissue" between one discipline and another. And it's not only jumping from one branch of a discipline to another, or from one science to another, that helps you to grow into an innovator. It's a broad perspective on the world.

The problem is that too many engineers are happy to live within the confines of their little world of engineering, as opposed to knowing what's happening in Iraq, or up in space, or in a film, play or novel that has nothing to do with engineering. Carl Ally, founder of an advertising agency, once said that

> the creative person wants to be a know-it-all. He wants to know about all kinds of things: ancient history, nineteenth-century mathematics, current manufacturing techniques, flower arranging, and hog futures. Because he never knows when these ideas might come together to form a new idea. It may happen six minutes later or six months or six years down the road. But he has faith that it will happen.

It's impossible to say, right now, just what combination of stimuli and inputs will catalyze your individual personality and intellect and produce innovation, which is why it's so important for you to make the range of inputs as wide as possible: reading *Dune*, or *Time*, or *The Atlantic*; or listening to jazz or minimalist music; or playing tennis on Saturday afternoon. What's tennis have to do with innovation? Maybe nothing. Maybe it just frees up your mind for a while. Or maybe it gets you thinking about the infinity of possibilities within the simple, never-changing geometry of the court . . . or whatever.

SPEECH TIP: Reflecting on his own undergraduate years, McVicker relates how his views have changed over time. Insights gained through direct experience are the most valuable thing any speaker has to offer.

Thirty years ago, I wondered why they made me take English composition and English literature. Now I know why. And I wish I'd had more, rather than fewer, of them. The composition improved my communication skills, which I'll come to in a moment, and the literature introduced me to other people—to their lives, their values, their personalities, their interactions with the world around them—all of which are key considerations for the engineers who would be innovators.

Even the engineers who will go down in the annals of engineering as the world's best were not narrowly focused. Maybe that mysterious "X factor" that defines the real innovator came in some way from their other interests.

Examples? Well, the one I like is Antoine Lavoisier. He's best known as the founder of modern chemistry. But he also pioneered in physiology, scientific agriculture, and technology—and was *also*, in his time, a leading figure in finance, economics, public education, and government. Makes you wonder when he had time to sleep!

Of course, back in the eighteenth century, it was easier to know a lot about everything than it is today, when our knowledge is doubling every ten to fifteen years. But that doesn't mean we shouldn't try. In our time, we have innovative geniuses like Edison, a man of very broad interests, or Buckminster Fuller, who was into architecture, automotive design, city planning, education, and even the technological perfection of humanity—and that's only a partial list of his interests.

Lavoisier, Edison, Fuller, and dozens of others weren't just engineers. They weren't holed up in their pilot plants or their labs. They had other interests. They were out doing other things with their lives. And I hope you'll do the same.

Along with functional expertise and breadth, I would advise you to develop three separate but mutually reinforcing sets of skills: analysis/problem solving, persuasion, and vision.

You don't have to worry too much about analysis and problem-solving, because this is where American education excels. The training of engineers, accountants, financial people, systems analysts, and so on, all gears people for organizing, analyzing, and processing data; for finding solutions to problems; and for making decisions. So to develop yourself in this area, you simply need to acquire a solid technical background in the basic disciplines and analytic techniques. The better your foundation, the better you'll be able to solve problems under an ever-changing variety of conditions and an onslaught of new information.

The second major skill area is persuasion.

Back in 1865, Gregor Mendel made momentous discoveries in genetics—discoveries that had no effect for thirty-five years. That's partly because nineteenth-century anatomy and physiology didn't allow for the concept of discrete hereditary units; also, Mendel's statistical methodology was completely foreign to the biologists of his time. But that thirty-five-year time lag may also have had something to do with the fact that Mendel was a modest monk living off the beaten path in a monastery in Moravia.

Or consider Oswald Avery, who made the milestone discovery that DNA was indeed the genetic material—in 1944, twenty-one years before Watson and Crick discerned its exact structure and function. Why wasn't his contribution recognized at the time? Well, an article in *The Scientific American* points to his "quiet, self-effacing, non-disputatious" personality. Not exactly your high-powered Lee Iacocca type.

But if you're going to be an innovator, you *need* a little of Lee Iococca in you. Every innovator will encounter resistance, so every innovator needs to be able to sell his or her ideas—to influence, charm, persuade, arm-twist, compromise—do whatever it takes to get people to give his or her ideas a fair hearing.

What can you do to become better in this area? Put strong emphasis on your interpersonal and communication skills. Make sure you take some courses in language, rhetoric, writing, human behavior, or speech communications. And get involved in group activities, clubs, or organizations; put yourself in settings in which you have a chance to persuade people to put ideas into action.

Finally, to train yourself for innovation, you need to develop your imagination, your intuition, your vision. You've got to be a little like the entrepreneurs, the dreamers, the visionaries, the "ship captains" who know their destination even though no one can see it. These are people with a strong sense of purpose—and powerful beliefs about the way things should happen.

In business, these are people like Tom Watson, who founded IBM. Like Alfred Sloan, who created the framework for the modern General Motors. Like Henry Ford, who stated his vision very explicitly: "I will build a motor car for the great multitude . . . so low in price that no [one] will be unable to own one—and enjoy with his family the blessing of pleasure in God's great open spaces."

What can you do to become more of a visionary? Well, unfortunately, this ability is very hard to teach, and it isn't given much attention in school. The best way to get next to it is to expose yourself to examples: read biographies of successful visionaries in politics, business, and the arts; take courses in religious studies, philosophy, art history, and literature.

Now, I know that my comparing scientific innovators with poets and artists may seem farfetched, but it really isn't at all: both spend a lot of time in the world of the imagination, and both envision completely new arrangements of things. The leap to a new way of hearing or seeing, which artistic innovators make, really isn't so different from the scientific innovator's leap to a new way of thinking.

Well, I've covered a lot of ground tonight, so let me sum it up for you: Innovation is not the same as invention. Although we need both, it's innovation—the development of practical products and processes—that really drives economic growth and human progress. But neither progress nor innovation is guaranteed. That's why it's important that our societies promote it, that our companies organize for it, and that we as individuals—and you, as leaders of the future—train for it.

I hope it's clear, from all I've said tonight, that although no single field has a monopoly on innovation, the engineering mind and the engineering discipline are well-suited to the generation of innovative ideas. I think Isaac Asimov said it best: "Science can amuse and fascinate us all—but it is engineering that changes the world."

You have an opportunity to change the world. I urge you to make the most of it.

Remarks by Jerome B. York

Executive Vice President and Chief Financial Officer, Chrysler Corporation

Delivered at the Chrysler Patent Award Winners Banquet, Auburn Hills, Michigan, April 18, 1993

SUMMARY: Chrysler's CFO celebrates the spirit of innovation, invention, and the U.S. patent system.

Thank you, François, and good evening, ladies and gentlemen.

It's a real treat for me to be here tonight to help honor our patent award recipients. On behalf of Chrysler Corporation, I congratulate each of you.

You know, as I listened to François's introduction, I was reminded of a time when his English was *really* put to the test.

It happened a few months ago when François and myself and a few others found ourselves in a local pub that has a karaoke machine.

Well, as fortune would have it—or *mis*fortune, depending on your point of view—François was required to sing Harry Belafonte's old song, "Day-Oh." Ladies and gentlemen, you have not lived until you've heard a Frenchman singing a Caribbean song on a karaoke machine!

Now, as far as François's question about my mixed background, let me say this. As the head numbers guy at Chrysler, *most* of my time is spent making sure that our engineers, and designers, and manufacturing people, and everyone *else* at Chrysler have the financial resources they need to keep putting great products on the road. And—as a further answer to the question—my job also requires me to spend a fair amount of time speaking to financial analysts and investment bankers. It's not unusual for me to make a financial presentation from a script as thick as your arm, supplemented with a slide presentation that has fifty or sixty slides in it. Which can be deadly—even for me!

So, the invitation to speak to this group tonight is a rare opportunity for me, and I don't plan to abuse it. That's why I left all my financial presentations back at the office. And if there's a slide presentation in this room, it's not mine. Instead, I want to give honor where honor is due, and I want to do that by keeping in mind the words of Calvin Coolidge. He said, "No person was ever honored for what he *received*. Honor has been the reward for what he *gave*."

> *SPEECH TIP:* If, like York, you frequently deliver a different sort of presentation than the one at hand, don't hesitate to mention it. The fact that you are enjoying an unusual opportunity will help your audience enjoy it more, too.

That's what I want to do tonight: Help honor *all* of you men and women for what you gave: your inventions. Your inventions—and the patents you received for them —help not only to make Chrysler a better *company*, they also help make America a better *country*.

Now, who are these people we honor tonight?

Well, there are seventy-six of you who were granted patents last year. You're part of the class of '92, so to speak. In fiscal 1992, a record number of patent applications were filed with the United States Patent and Trademark Office—more than 185,000. Of those, nearly 110,000 patents were granted. That's also a record for any year. (By the way, the 128 patents *filed* by Chrysler employees in 1992 was a record for the company.)

> *SPEECH TIP:* Having offered his general congratulations to the honorees, York now establishes their number and begins to set their achievements in a larger context.

Seven of the seventy-six from Chrysler have retired since being granted their patents. Sixteen of you were issued more than one patent for your inventions in 1992, including six people who were issued *three* patents last year. I'm particularly impressed by that last group because it took me five *years* to get my three patents.

By the way, while we're on the number three, the *Big* Three made patent history last year. For the first time, we received a joint patent. It came through our research partnership, the United States Council for Automotive Research. In the not too distant future, we hope to use this patented technology to make parts from plastic composites instead of steel.

Tonight's honorees range from Lester Nelson to Tom Gale. Lester is an hourly employee at the Belvidere Assembly Plant in Illinois. Tom is Chrysler's vice president of design. Lester received a patent for a conveyor anti-runaway apparatus, while Tom received a design patent for the Lamborghini Diablo. He shares that patent with Marcello Gandini, an independent automobile designer from Italy.

By the way, the Diablo is the perfect car for the next James Bond movie. Not only because it's sexy and fast, but also because the last three numbers of the patent happen to be double- 0-seven.

All of you—Lester and Tom and the rest of you patent award winners—all of you are linked together to the wonderful process of invention. What's more, you are linked to each other, and to people like Thomas Edison and Alexander Graham Bell, to the Wright Brothers, Elijah McCoy, and yes, even to George Washington and Abraham Lincoln. And you're linked to people you may not have heard of—people like Francis Holton and Joseph Ledwinka and Mary Kies. Let me tell you how.

> *SPEECH TIP*: York's discussion of landmark patents starts with their very foundations in American history and law. This thoroughness not only grounds the issue firmly, it allows York to celebrate his topic as an expression of national ideals.

Of all the names I've just called off, only Washington did *not* receive a patent. But he got the ball rolling. On April 10, 1790, President Washington signed the bill that laid the foundations of the modern American patent system. Clearly, Big George and the rest of the founding fathers recognized an inventor's inherent right to have his or her invention protected by the government. They believed in it so strongly that they made it part of the U.S. Constitution. You'll find it in article I, section 8, which reads: "Congress shall have power to promote the progress of science and useful arts, by securing for limited times to authors and inventors, the exclusive right to their respective writings and discoveries." And because of this recognition that inventors and inventions ought to be encouraged and protected, men and women have been free to use their knowledge and their skills and their creativity to make life better for *everyone.*

Another founding father, Thomas Jefferson, once said that, "The issue of patents for new discoveries has given a spring to invention beyond my conception." If he were alive today, Mr. Jefferson would probably be astonished by the more than five *million* patents that have been issued in this country.

You know about the heavyweights of invention. I've mentioned some already—Edison, Bell, McCoy, and the Wright brothers. But did you know about Abe Lincoln? He was granted a patent in 1849 for a device for buoying vessels over shoals. Mark Twain, who is better known for creating great literature, found time to get *three* patents, including one he called, "An Improvement in Adjustable and Detachable Straps for Garments." (You would think that Twain would be the appropriate source for "a device for buoying vessels over shoals," but Lincoln beat him to it!)

I mentioned Mary Kies. She was the first *woman* to receive a patent. She got it in 1802 for an invention for weaving straw with silk or thread. And then there are those coincidences in history when patent milestones met the motor industry. For example, patent number one million was issued in 1911 to a man I mentioned earlier, Francis Holton. It was for a vehicle tire—designed for an automobile.

> *SPEECH TIP*: Exact figures are too often dull and dreary. York takes advantage of a chance to have *fun* with numbers.

Then there's Joseph Ledwinka. He received patent number *two* million in 1935 for vehicle wheel construction. Finally, I'd like to mention patent number five million, because it is also related to our industry. (There's just something about those big round numbers!) It went to the University of Florida in 1991 for a genetically engineered bacteria that produces fuel grade ethanol from agricultural waste.

How do you capture the importance of five million patents, stretching across more than two hundred years?

Well, the U.S. Patent and Trademark Office put it this way in one of its pamphlets: "Under the patent system, a small, struggling nation has grown into the greatest industrial power on earth." Now, if that sounds like the patent office was tooting its own horn, try this next quote, which was made by a *Japanese* official in the year 1900: "We have looked about us," he said, "to see what nations are the greatest, so that we can be like them. We said, 'What is it that makes the United States such a great nation?' and we investigated and found that it was patents, and we will have patents."

Wow! And here we thought the Japanese only *recently* started gathering intelligence on us!

Isn't that something? Ninety-three years ago, leaders of a tiny island nation thousands of miles away—a nation envious of America's strength and hoping to emulate it—came to the conclusion that at least *one* of the reasons for our greatness is our patent system.

And do you know what? They were right.

I mentioned earlier that I've been fortunate to receive patents for three of my inventions, all while I was at General Motors. The first two were for fuel systems, granted in 1967 and 1968. My last invention, an air supply pump, was patented almost twenty-one years ago on today's date, April 18, 1972.

Back in 1972, 31 percent of the patents granted in the United States came from foreign countries. The 1992 figures aren't out yet, but in 1991, 47 percent of the patents awarded in America were from foreign countries. Now, if I asked you which foreign country leads all others in *applying* for U.S. patents, what would you say? It's the same country that is *granted* more U.S. patents than any other foreign country.

Well, I guess the answer is obvious. It's Japan. In 1972, Japanese inventors were granted a little over 5,100 U.S. patents. The number quadrupled by 1991 to 21,000 patents.

We shouldn't be surprised by this. If you haven't figured it out by now, the Japanese are no dummies. They are smart, hard-working, competitive people who are not afraid of challenges, no matter how big. They've seen the value of invention—and the value of *our* patent system—and they have used them to their advantage. But, I wonder: Do they know what *we* know? Do they know our history? Sure, they probably know about Edison and Eli Whitney and George Washington Carver, and maybe they know about Harry Houdini. Yes, the great magician got a patent in 1921 for a diver's suit.

But do our competitors know about Lester Nelson and William Noble and Lynn Tilly and the rest of the patent class of '92 from Chrysler?

And do they know anything about the Chrysler inventors from the past who worked hard to help this company establish its renowned reputation for engineering excellence? I doubt it.

You know, around here, we talk a lot about the "Reinvention of Chrysler." That's all well and good. Sometimes you have to take a hard look at a process or a system—or, in this case, a company—and tear it down and "reinvent" it in order to make it better. But, let's not forget one thing: Before *reinvention* can take place, there must be *invention*. There must be a beginning. No one knows that better than you inventors.

> *SPEECH TIP*: Relating one's topic to a company slogan is a tried-and-true method for in-house speakers; it underlines the subject's importance to a company's greater goals.

As I told you folks earlier, more than a few years have passed since I received my patents. And, in my present job, I don't have much time these days to use my engineering training. Most of the engineering I do these days is so-called "financial engineering," such as our recent $2 billion stock offering.

Nevertheless, I'm happy to report that I haven't forgotten how rewarding it is to think through an engineering problem, to research it, to test it, to try some experiments, and to finally arrive at a solution that *nobody* else has.

Nor have I forgotten the thrill of seeing that solution evolve into an invention—an invention that is worthy of a United States patent.

So I encourage you inventors to keep at it. Keep on inventing. Not just for yourselves, but also for your company—and for your country.

I will close with the words of another great inventor and patent-holder. François, it's from one of your countrymen, Louis Pasteur. He is, of course, called the founder of the modern science of bacteriology. Here it is:

"Say to yourselves first, 'What have I done for my instruction?' and as you gradually advance, 'What have I done for my country?' until the time comes when you may have the immense happiness of thinking that you have contributed in some way to the progress and to the good of humanity. But whether our efforts are, or *not* favored by life, let us be able to say, when we come near to the great goal, 'I have done what I could.'"

To you inventors, thanks for doing "what you could." And to all of you, thanks for letting this old wayward engineer participate in this celebration of invention.

Good night.

CHAPTER 3

Education and Business

Where are today's business frontiers? The cutting edge? Are they to be found in the latest silicon confections? In fiber optics? In the "data communications superhighway"? In concepts like downsizing and outsourcing?

Maybe.

But, judging from the speeches in this section, as well as from portions of speeches found throughout this volume, the new frontier of today's business world is education.

Increasingly, business leaders are taking the long view and paying very, very close attention to education, not only as the means by which human beings, as individuals, may reach their fullest potential, but as an issue of commercial and economic survival in a highly competitive, technology- and psychology-dependent *world* marketplace. We all have a stake in education, and any speaker who feels at all passionately about the subject should not hesitate to address a business audience concerning it. That speaker will find a highly receptive audience.

As the best of North America's business speeches prove, the continent's commercial leaders have abandoned near-view, short-term business practices. As the business world—and, in particular, this hemisphere—has become more ecologically minded, realizing

49

that investment in the land *is* a genuine investment, which pays big dividends in the long run, so business on this continent has realized that it is only as strong as its people, and its people are, in turn, only as strong—as inventive, imaginative, and competitive—as they have learned to be. Education, therefore, represents a genuine business investment.

Of course, it is not necessary to frame a business speech concerning education in narrowly cynical or manipulative terms of profit and investment. As the speeches in this section illustrate, that point comes across in any case. But do not be afraid to emphasize the very real, very direct, and very immediate links between education and business.

Statistics—comparative scores on diagnostic tests, for example—can be used effectively in education speeches, as long as neither you nor your audience is smothered in figures. Even more effective, however, is vivid, firsthand, even personal information about specific educational programs—programs you may admire or in which your firm may be involved.

Education is one of those immense areas with vast implications, which is nevertheless also a very intimate subject that turns on a relationship of teacher and student—a one-on-one scenario multiplied many times. It is an immense field in which individuals do not make *a* difference, they make *all* the difference. Make an audience aware of this, and you have the ingredients of a most compelling speech on a vital topic.

The Role of Business in Education

LES ALBERTHAL
Chairman of the Board, President, and Chief Executive Officer
Electronic Data Systems (EDS) Corporation

Delivered to the Dallas Rotary Club, Dallas, Texas, March 10, 1993

SUMMARY: Education will be increasingly crucial to the global competitiveness of America's work force, says Les Alberthal, and the EDS chairman discusses innovative ways in which businesses—and individuals—can participate in teaching and training the employees of tomorrow.

I'm very pleased to be with you here today at the Rotary Club of Dallas—the first Rotary Club in Texas and the thirty-ninth in the world.

At first, I was a bit surprised to be asked to speak. I wondered what in the world I could say that would be interesting enough to such a cross-section of men and women from our community. Then Jim Smith sent me a pamphlet that reminded me of what Rotary Clubs are all about. The idea is to have an active representative from each line of business and profession in the area—to better serve society. You are professional men and women united in the ideal of *service*. You're a *service* organization. Well, coincidentally, I also am part of an organization that serves customers all over the world. So, I believe, we have similar interests.

I also understand that the Dallas Rotary is so well known and respected that, in 1991, Rotarians in Japan sent a TV camera crew here to shoot footage that was used in making a film on the establishment of Rotary. It's great, I think, that we can share things with our neighbors across the Pacific. They can learn from us. We can learn from them. And technology makes it all so much easier.

> *SPEECH TIP:* Acknowledging the host organization's international prestige, Alberthal also creates a lead-in for his opening anecdote and subsequent remarks on the role of education in global competition.

I was in Japan not long ago. And every time I go there I learn something that I didn't know before, something that usually causes me to think and reflect. I had a very interesting conversation with a Japanese gentleman, who just happened to be the chairman of a major corporation. He said that English is very difficult for the Japanese people to learn and speak.

"Because of all the words?" I guessed.

He thought for a moment and then responded: "Yes, but no."

So I said: "Well, it must be because of all the idioms. Americans have grown up with some unique idioms."

And he said: "Yes, that too. But, no."

So, I finally asked him the question: "Why, then, is English difficult for the Japanese people?"

"Because in English," he said, "90 percent of the burden of communication is on the speaker."

"And, in Japan?" I asked.

"In Japan, more than 50 percent of the burden of communication is on the listener. You must try to understand what I mean. The Japanese language is vague, and we like it that way. The listener must constantly engage himself with the speaker to try and understand what the speaker is saying."

Now, that got me to thinking. It's true, isn't it? It's true not only with someone in normal conversation, but it's even more true in normal teacher-student relationships in this country. Part of the overwhelming burden of teaching is that too much emphasis is placed on the teacher and not enough on the learner. It's true in public education. It's true in large companies. And it's true in the way we learn on national and global scales. The responsibility of learning needs to be shared—at least equally—between the teacher and the learner: the student, the employee, the future employee.

Well, since you are all business people committed to serving the community, I thought it might be appropriate to talk to you today about the role that business can play in education—not just kindergarten through grade twelve, but beyond that: education after high school, education in large companies, education within nations, education among nations.

The world is rapidly changing, as we all know. Technology, information, and geopolitics are all causing a rapid shift in how we do business. No longer is power going to be limited exclusively to individual countries. Rather, power is going to reside in *regional blocks*. As nations buy and sell less to themselves and more to each other, their economies become interdependent rather than self-contained. Free market trade agreements such as the European Community, the North American Free Trade Agreement, and the Association of Asian Nations will forever change world economics.

Within nations, proper education is fast becoming an economic necessity for survival. With the globalization of industries and economies, money, information, and goods flow freely around the world. The only thing that remains in place is the work force. Enabled by technology, most leading industries of the twenty-first century can be located anywhere, in any country, in any city. How are we going to get those industries to stay in the United States if they're already here, or move to the United States if they're elsewhere? We're going to be able to do it with a highly skilled work force. Those skills will be our most effective weapon as we compete for business in the future global marketplace.

SPEECH TIP: Raising—and resolving—listeners' most immediate potential doubts or objections helps clear the way for more deliberate consideration of a topic.

Now, you may ask: "Gee, don't we already have the best colleges and graduate schools anywhere in the world?" And the answer is: "Of course, we do." Our college graduates will be the people who come up with new ideas, new techniques, and new inventions. Well, that takes care of the top 25 percent of America's work force!

However, if we are to have skilled people who will turn those ideas into reality, who will produce products cheaper and faster, and of higher quality than the rest of the world, then we have to think hard about the other 75 percent of the future work force. We have to really concentrate on the students who graduate from high school and don't go to college. And, of course, we have to think about those students who don't graduate from high school at all.

I believe we can get some good ideas from other countries that seem to be pretty successful in these areas. For example, did you ever wonder why Germany is such a leading economic power, or how their high-tech workers became the envy of the world? Part of it has to do with their Apprentice System, which is an outgrowth of the guild system that began in Central Europe centuries ago. Government and business work together to make the program successful. Students usually have their first contact with the program at the age of fourteen or fifteen. Every ninth grader is encouraged to use one of the many Career Information Centers. On most days, these centers are filled with young people taking computerized tests, watching films that describe various careers, and reading other information that explains working conditions and salary ranges.

SPEECH TIP: As so many speakers in the *Almanac* point out, Americans know too little about life beyond U.S. borders. Listeners welcome a chance to learn more about how other countries handle the problems we all share.

About two-thirds of the students choose a career path when they are in the tenth grade. If they desire, and they are accepted by a company, they can start an apprentice program right away—and spend part of their time in school, part of their time with the company. This way, the kids get theoretical training and practical experience at the same time. When German kids are between sixteen and twenty, most of them are in a combination of school and career training. They know that if they do well, they will have good futures. They're motivated. They get a sense of orientation and meaning to their lives. They don't feel hopeless or drop out of society. This system contributes to making Germany's work force more competitive, and, the fact is that nearly every person entering the work force there has benefited from the program in some form or another.

What can we learn from this? Plenty. The success of any national economy rests on the high quality of its workers. Nearly everyone I know in business recognizes this fact. So, doesn't it pay off in the long run to invest a bit of money now in order to ensure a steady flow of highly trained workers for the future? It's really an investment: an investment in people; an investment in the future. It's like W. H. Pillsbury once said: "The businessman is coming to realize that *education* is to business what *fertilizer* is to farming." And believe me—as a businessman who's committed to education and as someone who grew up in the farming community of Comfort, Texas—I can definitely say that there's a connection between the two.

Now, I'm not advocating adopting the German system of apprenticeship in total. But I certainly like the idea behind it and maybe we can do something similar.

Now what about education at the enterprise level, education within companies?

The word "employee" is derived from the Latin word *implicare*, which means "to engage." Now, to me, that means not only to employ, but to stimulate, to win over or attract, to draw into, to involve. That's what we try to do with *all* our employees: to attract them, to stimulate them, to involve them.

Let me reemphasize that word *all—all* of our employees, including (and especially) top-level managers.

You know, conventional thinking is that managers, after they've attained a certain level, don't need development anymore. However, many companies have discovered that even their top managers are not prepared to deal with today's changing business environment. Why? Because they simply never got the right training. So, now, companies—either in-house or via consultants—are conducting learning sessions that include top-level executives, along with middle-level and first-line managers, whom the company has identified as having high potential. And what are they learning to do in these sessions? They're learning to manage—and take advantage of—change.

This just *has* to be done. The best executives of the future will be dealing in a much different environment. They won't be able simply to give orders as they used to. Teams and flattened organization are going to create an entirely new set of behavior patterns, attitudes, and methods of communication. Employees are going to have to understand such things as international competition, organizational versatility, and how to structure international teams and alliances, and yet still *understand* and *accept* accountability.

This strategy, of course, involves the key process of *continuous education* for everyone.

A major part of our corporation's infrastructure is devoted to employee development. We conduct "Global Awareness Programs" that teach our employees about global business issues, global market trends, political trade agreements, and trade barriers. We also use case studies to explore such things as cross-border components of team building, expatriation, legal issues, financial issues, and effective cross-cultural teamwork, and we learn subtle cultural differences that can make the difference between success and failure. For example, I'll never forget the mistake that the Mars company made when they first attempted to market M&Ms in Europe.

> **SPEECH TIP:** Backstage stories about corporate missteps in the global arena have a universal—and often humorous—appeal.

The European kids spat them out. They didn't even think it was chocolate. Why? Because it was too grainy. European chocolate is extraordinarily smooth. So, Mars went back to the drawing board to develop chocolate with less grit in it. And then there was the American floor wax manufacturer who entered the Japanese market. They did a great job selling their product, but they didn't think of one very important Japanese custom: the Japanese people take off their shoes when they enter a person's house. As sales of the floor wax went up, so did the number of injuries. People were sliding, skidding, and slipping on the newly waxed floors. Eventually, sales plummeted, and the company had to come up with a new product that had *more* grit in it.

So, how do you know when to use more grit—or less grit? How do you know when you have *True Grit*? (Sorry, I couldn't resist.)

The answer is simply that you've got to have people around who know these things. And, if they don't already know them, then they have to learn.

Our main focus is to try to give our employees a foundation of knowledge upon which to build an awareness of global issues as they observe and study global issues *on their own*. We try to spark their interest so that they'll continue the ongoing process of learning themselves.

Where employees are concerned, companies will also have to deal with a two-edged sword. If young people coming out of school today aren't properly educated, then we'll have to train them. And, conversely, if we are to find, attract, and retain the brightest, best-educated people we can find, we're going to have to realize that they will demand the very best of what new technology has to offer. So, we have to stay right up with it. And how do we do that? We do it through the process of continual education. And, let me tell you, that is not easy. Many of the kids coming out of school today are whizzes with new technology. My seventeen-year-old son is much more comfortable with a computer than I am, and that's been my profession for twenty-five years!

The world of knowledge and information is fast moving from a paper culture to an electronic culture. Let me give you an example. Every day, at the Illinois Institute of Technology law library, teenage workers rip out the pages and throw away the books. A computer scans the pages and stores them so anyone with a library password and a computer can retrieve them. The books will no longer be on the shelves.

Now, it will take decades before libraries become totally electronic. But already, many are starting to create what they call "limitless digital bookshelves." One reason it's being done is simply to save money. Columbia University's law library announced a plan to scan and store 10,000 deteriorating old books *every year* by 1996. That would provide enough shelf space for all the new, copyrighted material the library receives—at a far, far cheaper cost than their original plan, which was to build a $20 million addition to store new books.

When scholars go to the library in the next century, they won't actually go anywhere. The library will come to them, right to their desktop computers. Libraries of the future will probably be hooked up to some of the vast electronic networks (or highways, as they are being called) linking educational, government, and research institutions.

SPEECH TIP: A discussion of world-scale problems and solutions can be "brought home" to listeners via local examples. Such illustrations also demonstrate the speaker's awareness of and respect for progress and leadership within the region.

Just exactly what will the *classrooms* of the future look like? Well, we can get a pretty good idea by looking right in our own back yard, up in McKinney [Texas]. A few months ago, a federal grant was awarded to the McKinney school district to act on a bold new vision of the future of the American school. I was particularly interested in what they called this program. It's called ACT, which stands for Academic Competitiveness through Technology. The program calls for a curriculum that relies on interactive videos, laptop computers, and multimedia work centers to stimulate learning. In essence, it's going to be a technology-based curriculum. The new school is going to break the mold of conventional teaching strategies by using technology to deliver effective instruction that results in superior academic performance. The school will feature state-of-the-art technology, including telecommunications for distance learning, computers, learning stations, and CD ROM. And the teachers will also gain new support. There's going to be an aggressive training program that will move them away from traditional teaching strategies into the role of learning facilitators. In fact, that's what they'll be called: learning facilitators rather than teachers.

The training will stress not only facility with hardware and software, but will teach the teachers to develop their own multimedia materials for use in the classrooms. The plan is to make using technology as an instructional tool as natural for teachers as the chalkboard or overhead projector is now. What George Leonard wrote about in his book *Education and Ecstasy* is true. "Technology is preparing a world in which we may be learners all life long."

Students will be taught by using the most modern technological advances. They will learn from such real-time connections as weather imaging, wire service news groups like the Associated Press, and how the stock exchange works—as it's functioning. There'll be more distance learning in association with other schools, business, research centers, and libraries, just like the one at Columbia University that I mentioned previously.

High school students around the country are already finding out that technology changes the way they do research. Let me give you an example. A student in Washington was asked to do a term paper on the bombing of Hiroshima. He connected to a database in a university's computer. There he found a reference to a second computer database—in Hiroshima. Without leaving his classroom terminal, he obtained transcripts of eyewitness accounts of the atomic bombing from interviews with the survivors.

SPEECH TIP: Interest leads to inspiration, and inspiration leads to action. Having garnered the first and fostered the second, Alberthal now turns to the latter. As throughout, he points to concrete examples.

Now, what exactly can the business community do in helping out our public education system?

What companies have mostly done in the past is to give out hardware and scatter money here and there. But we're going to have to do more than that in the future. We're going to have to help teachers apply technology. We're going to have to lend people—provide the human touch—so that we can make ideas reality, so that we can make technology work.

When we started our Education Outreach program at EDS four years ago, we decided to approach it with the human factor. Only donating money, we felt, was the easy way out. If you want to make something work, you've got to be willing to get in the trenches. So, we decided to give schools resources that are much more valuable than money. We give them time—and people.

Our approach to Education Outreach is remarkably similar to the way we do business. Our employees sit down with the principal and the teachers of a school to determine a realistic list of wants and needs, and then they formulate a course of action. We draw up an agreement, sign it, and then we walk forward together, hand-in-hand with the teachers and students, to make things better.

EDS today has seventy school partnership programs nationwide, and, I'm proud to say that we have more than four thousand "mentors" around the country—all employees who have volunteered—from Buffalo, New York, to Los Angeles, California; from Southfield, Michigan, to Houston, Texas. They commit to spend three hours per month with a child. But what we find is that the majority of mentors give one to three hours per *week* with these children, and more than half of our mentors are now going into their fourth year with the same child.

Now, we all know that we're *not* going to impact education before 9:00 a.m. and after 5:00 p.m., when it's convenient for us. We made a commitment to get down to the level of the child, and that means going *to* the school, being *at* the school, being *in* the children's environment during working hours. I originally thought that many of our managers would object to people leaving work during the day. You know, work interrupted, things falling through the cracks, lost business opportunities—that sort of thing. But I never heard one complaint. The support was overwhelming, and our program continues to grow internally at astounding levels. I am so proud of our employees.

And you know it's all worth it when, before she is assigned a mentor, a nine-year-old girl is flunking all of her classes—and, one year later, with a mentor, she's on the honor's list. Or when a bright but troubled young man in high school, trying to survive a dysfunctional family, mired in debt, drowning in despair, two years later is awarded a full scholarship to Stanford University and is now studying to become a doctor.

Those are the kinds of rewards that you just can't quantify in dollars and cents. But, the fact is—and I want you all to believe this—the fact is that our Education Outreach program is good for business. Let me say that again: *Education Outreach is good for business.*

I know that many businessmen think that such a program is simply an extraneous extracurricular activity on which you have to spend money. It takes away from the bottom line of the company, which is to earn a profit. But I'm here to tell everyone that it actually *adds* to the bottom line, it *makes* money for the company. Now, EDS has been doing this for four years, and I know what I'm talking about.

This will come home to business people. It came home to me. It's what your employees do when they see you setting the example—that it's okay to leave the workplace during the day. It's okay to help people. It's okay to care.

That's really our top priority. People see that, and they swell with pride knowing that they are with an organization that allows it and *encourages* it. You feel good about yourself, you feel good about your company. And when you feel good about yourself and about your company, you're going to do better work. You're not going to be leaving in a year. You're not going to be doing a lot of complaining about your job. Along with that, I really believe that our customers, both present and future, appreciate the fact that—with EDS—they are dealing with a group of individuals who really do care about education: in the community, in the nation, and in the world.

Ladies and gentlemen, we must have concern for the future welfare of our children. We simply must. Remember what John Updike wrote in 1965: "If men do not keep on speaking terms with children, they cease to be men, and become merely machines for eating and for earning money."

We must become more involved.

In this country, we spend a lot of time discussing, cursing, describing, and debating education. But one good thing about Americans is that we not only talk about something, we also try to do something about it. We may not be as successful as quickly as we all would like, but we are willing to take it on. There are a lot of countries out there that won't do this.

The fact is that Americans *act!*

It's part of our tradition, part of our heritage.

It reminds me of the story of a young Harry Truman who, in World War I, during the heat of battle at the Argonne, took the initiative, acted, and made a critical decision for himself. While leading his 1,500-man artillery battalion in combat with ground troops, Captain Truman noticed an enemy battery pull into position on the left flank, beyond his assigned sector. He had been told not to open fire, and conventional wisdom told him to stick to his assigned area.

But Harry Truman did something unconventional that day. He ordered his battery to open fire, because it would save lives. What's more, he acted at the risk of an open court-martial, not to mention placing himself and his men at great personal risk.

Captain Truman did save lives that day—they knocked out that enemy battery—and, incredibly, he didn't lose a single man in his battalion.

Ladies and gentlemen, we, too, have seen the enemy. The enemy, in many cases, is an outdated education system. The enemy is a prevailing sense of hopelessness in the minds of our youth. The enemy is ignorance. And what's more, it's not just on our left flank—it is on all our flanks. It's all around us.

Now we, too, have a decision to make, and it is an unconventional decision. There are many people in business who say that this enemy is beyond our assigned sector. Don't mess with it. Leave it to those who are in charge of that area. We might lose men, we might be "court-martialed" by our bosses or our stockholders. But, my friends, *there are lives to be saved.* Let's take our cue from Harry Truman. Let's open fire. And let's do it now.

We need to adopt programs that better motivate children and enable them with the tools necessary to compete in a global economy.

We need to do so with more of a human touch—hand-in-hand, shoulder-to-shoulder, face-to-face.

We need to tap into the natural fascination with new gadgets, new gizmos, and new games. The innovations that are occurring in technology today interest everybody, especially children. Well, if that's what interests them, I say let's use technology to help our children succeed in the information age.

But the most important thing I can say to anyone about education is simply this: Just get involved. Somehow, some way, sometime. Just get involved.

We *know* it's the right thing to do.

It's up to all of us—*individually*—to find the right way to do it.

Thank you very much.

Remarks by Robert J. Eaton

Chairman and Chief Executive Officer, Chrysler Corporation

Delivered at the Arkansas City High School Commencement, Arkansas City, Kansas, May 23, 1993

SUMMARY: The CEO of a major automaker returns to his high school to deliver the commencement address.

Thank you, Superintendent Steinle. I appreciate the kind words.

Well, I want to begin by saying to the members of the Board of Education, to Mr. Gilstrap and all the Ark City teachers and administrators, and to the parents, students, and members of the Class of 1993: congratulations to all of you on a job well done.

To you graduates, let me say that it is a privilege for me to be asked to be here with you today, especially since I sat where you're sitting not too long ago.

At least, it doesn't *seem* very long ago.

This is your day, graduates. I am just about the last thing standing between you and your diplomas, and I promise not to stand in your way very long.

> *SPEECH TIP*: Speaking just before a much-anticipated event, Eaton assures his listeners that he will precede—not impede—their shining moment.

I'm here to give you some advice. That's my duty today. That's what commencement speakers are supposed to do, you know—give advice. And that's why they usually have a few miles on them.

We have to be old enough to have learned a few things about the road you're about to travel, and yet, it helps to be able to remember what it was like to be seventeen or eighteen—ready to take on the world—but not too sure exactly what's involved in taking on the world.

I remember the things that went through my mind back when I was graduating from Ark City High.

There was relief, of course, that graduation was finally here. High school graduation is the first big milestone in life. It's the one you have to pass on your way to anywhere else you want to go. There was also a lot of excitement about what would come next. For me, it was the University of Kansas to study engineering. I couldn't wait to get on with it.

And finally (although I sure wasn't about to admit it), there was some fear. It's a big world out there. How was I going to fit in? Did I learn enough at ACHS to be able to compete?

SPEECH TIP: Eaton's commencement address frequently speaks to the underlying fears that may accompany such a rite of passage. Offering the students reassurance that they will indeed find their way in the world, his personal reflections on the subject also emphasize the shared nature and normality of these anxieties.

I suspect those same things are going through each of your minds today.

Well, to begin with, this *is* a milestone. You *should* be relieved. You should be proud. Your diploma doesn't just say that you passed your courses, it says something even more important. It says that you persevered and succeeded in the first big challenge in your lives. Almost 20 percent of the youngsters across the country who were freshmen when you were in the fall of 1989 have dropped out along the way. So you have accomplished something. Pat yourselves on the back. You deserve it.

But there are other milestones ahead. You're not done with your education, for one thing. High school doesn't teach you all you need to know. It just gives you the tools to learn more. So far, all you've really done has been to *learn* how to *learn.*

Some of you are going to college, some to work, some to the military. Wherever it is, you'll find out that people won't care how much you know; they're only interested in how much *more you can learn*, and how *fast you can learn it.*

They'll help you, but probably not as much as your teachers in Ark City did. You see, high school graduation is also an important rite of passage into adulthood. From now on, how much you learn will be largely up to you. And you can never, ever, stop learning, because if you do, the world will zip past you and leave you in the dust or, worse yet, eating dust.

During junior high and my early high school years, I owned a 1935 Ford. In the course of three to four years, I took the entire car apart and fixed or replaced every major part. I learned a lot. By the time I was through, I knew just about everything there was to know about a 1935 Ford. But if I'd quit learning then, I probably wouldn't be able to change the oil filter on a car today. I probably wouldn't even be able to *find* it, in fact; that's how much cars have changed over the years.

And everything else has changed just as much and just as fast. Technology always advances faster than man's ability to use it. That's a fundamental lesson of history. The tools are always invented before we know how to use them, and often their main uses turn out to be something the inventors never envisioned.

Alexander Graham Bell thought the telephone would be a great business tool. The manager could call down to the plant floor without leaving his office. Bell didn't know that pretty soon every home would have one. And imagine what he'd think today if he saw one in a woman's purse!

When I graduated from high school, computers were mysterious machines that filled up huge rooms, cost millions of dollars, and were operated by a strange bunch of geniuses who were genetically incapable of speaking English. Today I've got one I carry in my briefcase that cost a couple of thousand and is more powerful than anything on the market back then.

And think of this: Many of the new cars we produce in Detroit have more computing power on board than the Apollo space ship that first took man to the moon.

> *SPEECH TIP:* Startling comparisons across time spans or distance—or both, as in Eaton's example—add drama and color to a speaker's remarks.

So no matter what field you go into, you will always be playing catch-up. You will never know enough. And as soon as you stop learning, you start falling behind. That's what makes our time so interesting and exciting. You know, up until just 150 years or so ago, everybody died in the same world they were born into. Over the course of the average person's lifetime, nothing changed very much. Back then, what you learned by the time you were seventeen or eighteen would do you fine for the rest of your life, because there wasn't anything new to learn.

Today, you don't know enough to get you through the next five years. (Neither do I, by the way.) And none of us can imagine what life will be like fifty years from now. But you've *learned* how to *learn*—and with that ability, the sky is the limit. You don't have to be afraid of the changes coming, because you've got the tools to adjust to them and to take advantage of them.

But, in a sense, those generations before us whose world never changed may have had easier lives. Certainly, *simpler* lives. They didn't have all the *options* we do. And as a result, they didn't have to make as many *choices*.

As I said, I was a little apprehensive about them when I was your age. I'll bet you are, too.

> *SPEECH TIP:* Pausing even briefly—at an appropriate juncture—can allow speaker and audience to marvel together at a wondrous concept or to reflect on the "big picture" as a whole. Such pauses unite speaker and audience and give both parties a short break from more focused attention.

All those choices!

What if you choose wrong?

Well, if you do, that just means there are fewer choices when you choose the next time, that's all.

But right now, you've got a world full of options open to you. You'll never have more than you do today. The important thing is to realize that, and not to waste them. You can't see them all yet, of course. They tend to show up one or two at a time, sometimes when you least expect them. And it's funny, but there's a direct correlation between how hard you work and how many options or opportunities suddenly show up.

I was unusual because I knew what I wanted to be when I was your age. Most of my friends who *thought* they knew ended up changing their minds—sometimes two or three times. And there's nothing wrong with that. There's nothing wrong with *changing* your goals, as long as you *have* some goals.

Many of you are going to find out that what you end up doing in life will be something that hasn't even crossed your minds yet. You still get to look forward to the excitement of discovering it, whatever it is. Just be sure it's something you enjoy. Don't just pick something because it looks prestigious or glamorous, or because it pays a lot of money. Find something you like to do, because, remember this: When you finally do settle into a job, you will spend most of the rest of your waking life doing it. If it's something you like—something that gives you satisfaction and pride—then it won't even be work. It will be fun. And you'll probably do it well.

But if it's something you hate—or work you can't respect—then you'll be miserable. And sooner or later, you'll fail at it.

Don't be afraid to explore. And don't be afraid to change your mind. It's not unusual today for somebody to change not only jobs but *careers* three or four times. As you begin to consider all the choices open to you, you're probably beginning to realize that from now on your decisions carry heavier consequences. You know that you're going to be held to higher standards: *adult* standards.

You're going to be held *accountable* for all the choices you make. That's part of the deal, too. That's what you get for growing up.

If someone gives you a job, you have a *responsibility* to do it well. If somebody sends you to college, you have a *responsibility* to do your best. In almost everything you do from now on, somebody is going to be holding you accountable for how well you meet your responsibilities. But more than that, you'll be judged by how willing you are to *accept* responsibilities.

Some people go through life ducking them. They think of responsibilities as burdens they want to avoid. Others spend their lives actively *seeking* them. They can never get enough. They see each responsibility as a new opportunity. They want responsibility and accountability, because they want the rewards that come with it.

They're usually called *winners!*

So, there's no use being worried about what's ahead. It's too late to turn back. And you don't want to, anyway, because all the excitement is up ahead.

Don't be afraid of it. Don't be afraid of the opportunities, or the choices, or the risks. Don't be afraid to fail now and then. Remember that it's okay to fail, but it's not okay to quit. And finally, be grateful that you grew up in Ark City. You may not realize it now, but this is a great place to grow up, and it's given you a better start than most people get.

And—Class of 1993—that's all the advice I have for you today. Work hard, have fun, keep learning, and grab all the responsibility you can.

I want to wish all of you the best of luck in the years ahead. And thanks a million for asking me to share this very special day with you.

Facing the Facts:
Reshaping the Academic Enterprise

JOHN T. HARTLEY
Chairman and Chief Executive Officer
Harris Corporation

Delivered at the 21st Century Conference, Palm Beach, Florida, December 8, 1992

SUMMARY: While affirming the essential role of higher education in American industry and society, the chief executive of Harris Corporation presents a candid view of the fiscal difficulties and reduced public confidence that challenge institutions of learning today. Offering specific examples and suggestions for improvement, Hartley urges college and university leaders to borrow the competitive techniques of contemporary business innovators to increase productivity and quality management.

Thank you, Gerry [Hillbrich], for that generous introduction, and my thanks to Fred Turk and KPMG Peat Marwick for inviting me to help keynote your session today. I am particularly pleased to share this platform with my friend and colleague from the Business-Higher Education Forum, Judith Albino, president of the University of Colorado.

By virtually any standard you choose—economic, political, social, or scientific—the United States today stands at a genuine crossroads. In many ways, the decisions we make in the next few years will determine what kind of nation we will be in the next century, and our nation's future depends heavily on the quality of the institutions represented in this room this morning. So, I stand here as a friend of higher education—a product of your institutions, a former engineering teacher, a current university trustee—and as the chief executive officer of a corporation with an enormous appetite for the products of your campuses: both your research and the trained, skilled, competent intelligence you develop.

It might help you understand our dependence on your campuses if I tell you that the Harris Corporation is a high-technology company with four core areas of business: electronic systems, semiconductors, communications, and office equipment. You may be using Harris's products without knowing it. When you switch on your television or radio, there is a very good chance that local broadcasters are using Harris transmitters and that your satellite weather map arrived via a Harris data-handling system. The copier in your office may well be one of our Lanier models, and you could be using one of our Lanier dictation systems. There's also a good chance that Harris semiconductors adjust your new car's engine speed or antilock brakes, and, when your automobile fails its emissions check, there is a faint possibility—so remote that I hesitate to bring it up—that a Harris chip has fallen down on the job!

High-tech industry is essentially knowledge work. Perhaps it would be more accurate to say it is knowledge*able* work, because the competitive technologies with which we're engaged today are not mature, not static, but dynamic and changing.

As you can imagine, a large proportion of our U.S. work force, about 30 percent, hold an undergraduate or graduate degree. Most of these people are scientists, engineers, or mathematicians. They focus on the very high end of advanced technology. So, we rely on you. Without your institutions, the Harris Corporation as we know it simply would not exist.

But I must tell you, as only a good friend can, that our institutions need attention if higher education is to prosper in the twenty-first century.

I will be candid in my remarks, since there is no benefit in minimizing the challenges we face. I will try to be direct, since there is no advantage in substituting euphemisms for straight talk or in kidding ourselves about the difficulty of the task before us.

Your conference program acknowledges that the 1990s dawned with higher education in perhaps its worst financial shape of the last fifty years. Following three decades of growth, higher education is on the defensive. Institutions are forced to justify every dollar, and student financial aid and private giving threaten to move in reverse, the victims of federal budget deficits and donor concerns about the economy. The best indicator of these troubled times has been identified by the *Chronicle of Higher Education*: Last year, total state appropriations for public higher education fell below the level of the year before for the first time in thirty years.

In the midst of this financial crisis, America's colleges and universities are also undergoing a crisis of public confidence. Public opinion analyst Louis Harris reports that people's dissatisfaction with higher education has been increasing at a remarkable rate. He reported earlier this year:

> For three decades I have been measuring the levels of confidence that people have in the major institutions of U.S. society. When I began in the mid-1960s, 61 percent of Americans said they had a great deal of confidence in the "people running higher education." By 1990 that confidence level had dropped to 35 percent. This year, 1992, the level has hit an all-time low of only 25 percent.

The criticism from within academic ranks is even more damaging. I wonder how many of you have been able to read Martin Anderson's new volume, *Impostors in the Temple*, without considerable misgivings.

The curriculum has been politicized, these insiders claim. The "canon" has been turned inside out. Most undergraduates, and practically all lower division courses, have been abandoned to the care of students—graduate students, to be sure, but still students. Tenure has become a sinecure. Too many scholars, once the drive for tenure has been satisfied, ignore productivity, abandon significant research, and content themselves with trivial teaching loads.

In the face of this growing financial pressure and public criticism, there are at least two ways we can respond. One is to curse the darkness, dig in our heels, and resist any proposal or inclination to alter the status quo. This approach can only lead to frustration and failure for all of us.

The second is to face the facts, lead the effort to change, get out in front of it, and help formulate new constructive approaches. This approach makes more sense to me, because it recognizes that the facts are always our friends, however unpleasant they may occasionally seem.

Which approach will higher education take? I think the jury is still out on that. Some experiments to support the second are under way, and I want to return to them later, because they seem to me to be the best hope for the future. But too many leaders appear to have adopted a siege mentality, digging in their heels behind the campus bunker while cursing the darkness.

I promised to be candid. I believe academic defenders of the status quo are ignoring reality, and the reality is that this country can no longer afford an open checkbook in financing higher education. There are too many competing claims for scarce tax dollars: claims such as the plight of our inner cities, the need to improve our public schools, the problems of health care coverage and the alarming spiral of health-care costs, to mention but a few. Don't misunderstand. I place a very high priority on continuing investment in education, but I also believe that our institutions of higher learning can and must find ways to increase productivity in the same manner that we in industry are being challenged to do.

U.S. industry is in the process of a *wrenching* transition toward increased international competitiveness. American companies suffered in the 1970s and early 1980s at the hands of astute overseas competitors. We had grown complacent and had taken our eyes off our customers, and we suffered the consequences in the form of lost market shares both at home and abroad. U.S. businesses learned some very hard lessons from that experience, and since the mid '80s we've been getting our act together. We had to to survive. While we've still some way to go, I believe we're on the right track. We now have a success mentality and momentum for the future.

This transition has not been without pain. Using Harris as an example, we have had to reevaluate everything we do throughout the company, discarding activities that add relatively less value and find more efficient ways to serve our customers. Making hard choices of this type are among the most difficult decisions faced by managers. The most painful part was the reduction in employment associated with this transition. Downsizing hurts. It hurts the individuals affected, their families, and the communities in which they live and work. And I can tell you from personal experience and from experience shared by other chief executives, that the feeling of profound grief lingers in the executive offices where these tough decisions are made.

But these are the kind of decisions that have to be made for the survival of an organization. To remain competitive globally, we at Harris had no choice but to reduce operating expenses by more than $200 million. Our employment has been reduced from a high of more than 34,000 in 1989 to a little above 28,000 today, while maintaining around the same level of revenues.

The Harris experience is indicative of the sweeping changes taking place throughout the U.S. industry. Almost daily you see headlined in your newspaper another major work-force reduction plan, and the moral of this story is that I believe that higher education in this country is faced with a similar far-reaching challenge. But that challenge will not be met if we simply wring our hands and wish and wait for better days.

If we at Harris had tried to continue with "business as usual," paring a little here and there in token recognition of the new realities, we would have been history. We knew that we had to get back to basics, refocus on our customers, and dedicate all of our operations and activities to best serve our customers' needs.

I think most of you are familiar with the concepts of Total Quality Management—TQM—pioneered by W. Edwards Deming and Joseph M. Juran. These concepts are helping to revitalize American industry, and I believe they have equally important application to American higher education. You should understand that TQM is not a program at all. It is a process of continuous change and improvement, and that change is not just the incremental, 10-percent-per-year variety. It is often *revolutionary change*.

At Harris, our name for TQM is Quality First—and that's Quality with a big "Q." We have a vision of being a company of the highest quality in everything we do, and our goal is nothing less than world-class performance. Quality First is our strategy for achieving that goal. In its broadest sense, Quality First is a culture change that involves everyone at Harris. It focuses all of us on recognizing that customer satisfaction is the paramount purpose of all company activities, and that the customer is the one who sets the standards by which we are measured. *We don't get to vote.*

Quality First also helps us to recognize that improvement in quality and productivity must be continuous: a race without end. This involves building an environment in which all Harris people are trained, encouraged, and given the freedom to focus on ways to improve the value and effectiveness of their activities.

SPEECH TIP: When transferring a set of principles from one discipline to another, it's a good idea to show how the principles work in the original arena, as Hartley has done. Only then can an audience appreciate the potential value to be had in a new or different application.

I believe that these core TQM disciplines of customer focus and continuous improvement are just as important to higher education as they are to U.S. industry. The reality of today's world is that educational institutions need to refocus their missions, accomplish high-priority tasks with less, and eliminate lower priority activities.

In terms of customer focus, too often the primary customer of higher education—the undergraduate—has been given a back seat. In the words of Dr. Shalala, chancellor of the University of Wisconsin, Madison: "The needs of our undergraduates are sometimes an afterthought at many of our universities." I might add that Dr. Shalala is a strong supporter of TQM at her university.

I believe there is also a very real need—and room—for productivity improvements in our educational system, particularly in the current environment of reduced funding. This is not a particularly popular recommendation among those anxious to maintain the status quo. But the fact is that a significant portion of the increased funding for education over the past three decades has not been directed to the classrooms, but to various layers of administration. A 1990 study financed by the U.S. Department of Education indicates that between 1975 and 1985 the number of four-year college students increased by 7 percent and the number of full-time faculty members increased by 6 percent. But, in that same period, administrative budgets grew 26 percent faster than faculty budgets. The result: the number of administrators increased by 18 percent and the number of "non-academic professionals"—

accountants, lawyers, information specialists, and public affairs officers—grew by a staggering 61 percent.

Here in my own state, Florida TaxWatch has pointed to precisely the same phenomenon in the public schools and argued, "The education of students takes place in the classroom, not in the district office."

It seems to me the same argument applies to higher education. In a period of austerity, we need to think about increasing productivity by redirecting scarce resources to where they will best serve higher education's customers—its students.

I am delighted to learn that a number of institutions of higher education are beginning to apply TQM to their operations. Most of these efforts address the administrative side of campus operations, but a few pioneers are also thinking about applying TQM to instruction. For example, I understand that Oregon State University has used TQM to produce dramatic improvements in administrative productivity: time required for remodeling buildings down 23 percent, time for development of a budget report reduced 50 percent, and errors in accounting vouchers chopped by 94 percent. The university's next targets are academic areas, including faculty evaluation, and faculty and student involvement in TQM.

I hear Northwest Missouri State University is on the same track. Its "Culture of Quality" plan relies heavily on two major principles: benchmarking—that is, comparing your own operations with best practices elsewhere—and parsimony—the administrative application of an old engineering axiom that the perfect design is associated with assembling the fewest parts. Northwest Missouri has consolidated seven colleges into four, flattened its administrative hierarchy, and re-allocated $1.9 million from administration to instruction. To me, that's putting first things first.

So, I think these examples give us some cause for optimism. But if our hopes are to be realized, more and more campuses will have to follow suit. Here are a few suggestions that might make the transition a little easier.

> **SPEECH TIP**: Hartley's speech concludes with step-by-step suggestions for improving educational quality. Constructive recommendations are the best—perhaps the only—way to close a thorough or unflattering critique.

First, face the facts. It really is a truism that one cannot solve any problem without first acknowledging its existence. Our nation's budgetary difficulties cannot be wished away. As I mentioned earlier, higher education's claim for public support competes with equally important demands in other areas of our national life. James Whalen, president of Ithaca College, had this to say about facing the music at this conference last year: "Failure comes only when we refuse to face up to facts and fail to exert leadership in making hard choices in the long-term interest of our institutions." Dr. Whalen said it well.

Next, rethink who you are and what you stand for. In business parlance: What is your strategic plan? The new economic realities should force university leaders to refocus on their mission and consider re-inventing their institutions to pursue that mission most effectively. Some hard questions need to be asked: "What values sustain this institution? Can we continue to be all things to all people? With fewer resources, how can we do more with less? Is tenure essential to academic freedom, or can academic freedom be maintained without it? Is excellence what we always thought it was, or do our customers and other stakeholders have a different definition of excellence?

A key element of this rethinking must be a renewed emphasis on undergraduate education, which appears to have become a foundling on many large campuses. Three-quarters of American adults do not hold a bachelor's degree, yet all Americans provide tax support to the institutions awarding the degrees. If the American people ever become convinced that institutions of higher education have ignored or de-emphasized their basic obligation to undergraduates, the response is likely to be a very strong public outcry.

Finally, identify lower-value activities and eliminate them. Given the reductions of the past few years, you may believe that there are none left. But undoubtedly there are. Cuts have been made, but were they the right ones or simply the easy ones? My guess is that the hard choices lie ahead.

Higher education amounts to a $165 billion enterprise, accounting for nearly three percent of Gross Domestic Product. Any corporate finance officer would probably believe he or she could cut 10 percent from that total and hardly anyone would notice the difference. Is it conceivable that senior faculty could be persuaded to teach six hours or nine hours routinely every semester? Are you sure administrative bloat has been eliminated? Universities should find the fat now before someone else decides to cut it for them.

Earlier this year, the American Council on Education asked the public to "Imagine an America without its colleges and universities." In such an America, opportunity, the engine of a free society, would still belong to the well-born. Medical science would be in its infancy. The quality of American life and the standard of living of our people would be impoverished.

Your campuses make an enormous difference in people's lives; with your help, young people create their futures; entire communities are dependent on academic payrolls; corporations such as my own depend on your graduates; and the nation benefits immeasurably from academic research. In short, our society depends increasingly on quality education, spearheaded by vibrant, adaptive, and responsive centers of higher education.

In closing, I am reminded of the words of our old friend Pogo: "We is confronted by insurmountable opportunities." It often seems that way, I'll admit. But higher education has overcome even greater challenges in the past and will continue to do so in the future.

CHAPTER 4

In the World Market

In the 1960s, when Marshall McLuhan told us that the world had shrunk to a "global village," he was referring to the effects of the ongoing communications revolution. That revolution continues today, and McLuhan's observation has proven true—as far as it goes.

But it does not go far enough.

Today's world is smaller not just by virtue of digital communications, satellites, fax machines, and the like, but because of the steady growth of a truly global economy, which, far more thoroughly than any weapon of war, is tearing down political barriers that, a short time ago, seemed absolute and unbreachable. It is not surprising, then, that many of the speeches the editors reviewed for this volume address issues of competing, surviving, and prospering in the world marketplace.

Well, McLuhan and a flock of trend forecasters and economists can *tell* us that we are functioning in a world marketplace, and it is almost certain that we can pick up any number of items we use daily in our own homes only to find that they were manufactured in places we once considered exotic or even hostile: Japan, China, Malaysia, Singapore, and so on. Nevertheless, psychologically, the world still *seems* to most of us a very *big* place, and, faced with the

71

task of discussing your company's place in the world can seem daunting—the province of politicians and diplomats, not a sales manager for a toaster manufacturer.

The speeches included in this section, useful and stimulating for the factual information they contain, are also valuable as lessons in how to make a very big subject very real and very comprehensible to your audience.

Assigned a large subject, don't feel that you have to begin with sweeping generalities and "profound" theoretical statements, as if only these could encompass the breadth of your theme. In fact, it is almost always better to *avoid* such an approach. As the old Chinese proverb goes: "A journey of a thousand miles begins with but a single step." In tackling a big subject, start with the points at which that subject is tangent to *your* area of expertise, to *your* life, to the business of *your* company or department or division. Seasoned writers—the greatest philosophers, poets, and novelists—have always known that, to be most universal, one must be most personal. Don't take on the big assignments feeling that you must now talk about *the* world. Take them on in the knowledge that you are responsible for discussing *your* world.

A vivid example of this is Carole M. Howard's speech about how her company, Reader's Digest, set up branches in Russia and Hungary. Here are nations caught up in the most momentous struggle of our century, nations undergoing tremendous changes and faced with titanic challenges, nations with whom world leaders are continually engaged in complex and delicate negotiations. And here is a very large and sophisticated publishing/media organization coming to do business with these nations.

The prospect for the speaker who must deal with such themes is daunting indeed. But Howard approaches the task by showing how her company took those first steps on the great journey. Did those steps involve abstruse issues of international law and complex formulas of world economics? No. They concerned such issues as how you get a telephone line installed in financially strapped Moscow. Or how you keep your stapler supplied with staples. Or what you can do with a burned-out light bulb in the former Soviet capital. Howard deals with the daily details of doing business in today's Eastern Europe, and what she has to say is clearly born of real-life experience—the most valuable commodity a speaker can share with an audience.

The reader of this section of *The Business Speaker's Almanac* will find a variety of approaches to a very large subject. All have one feature in common: They make their subject comprehensible by imparting individual perspective and individual experience.

Global Alliances and Joint Ventures . . .
Or, How to Avoid a Dangerous Liaison

JOSEPH E. CAPPY
Vice President
International Operations
Chrysler Corporation

Delivered to the International Law Section of the State Bar of Michigan, Dearborn, Michigan, February 25, 1992

SUMMARY: A veteran architect of international joint ventures discusses their profit potential and liabilities.

Thank you, Logan [Robinson], and good afternoon to you all.

Although I was happy to accept your speaking invitation, I had to admit to laughing when I saw my assigned topic: "Global Alliances and Joint Ventures." As you know, global alliances and joint ventures are often referred to as "marriages" between companies. So, I guess if you want to hear from an expert on marriage, you invite Liz Taylor!

It's no coincidence that the marriage analogy is the one most frequently used to describe international business alliances, because, in *theory*, an international business alliance, like a marriage, should be a great partnership. But in *practice*, it can be a lot of hard work—and can lead to occasional disappointments. (Just ask Liz!)

I recently read an interesting study on strategic partnerships, which was published by the Nomura Research Institute. In the opening paragraph, the author,

Isao Yamamoto, discusses a phenomenon in Japan called the "Narita divorce." I'll paraphrase the story for you because I think it draws a good parallel between international ventures and human relationships.

SPEECH TIP: A term or catchphrase from another country's popular culture can do two things simultaneously: frame a conventional topic in a new and interesting way, and appeal to your listeners' curiosity about unfamiliar social worlds.

The name "Narita" comes from the airport outside of Tokyo. Apparently, Narita divorces occur in two instances. The first is shortly after older couples see their children off for their honeymoon at the Narita airport. And the second is when some younger couples return to Narita *from* their honeymoon!

The moral of the Narita divorce story is that when a shared vision is lost—be it holding together the marriage "for the kids," or whatever—or if it fails to change to reflect some new realities—a long-standing partnership can fail. Also, if expectations in a *new* partnership are made that won't or can't be met, the partnership may never really get off the ground. And, if either of the above is the case, a divorce isn't necessarily bad.

This lesson applies to international business as well as to matters of the heart. By no means do I intend to discredit the value of global alliances. Just as couples will continue to marry in spite of the high divorce rate, companies will continue to seek alliances with international partners with no guarantee of success, because when an alliance *does* work to the mutual benefit of the partners, the rewards can be great!

SPEECH TIP: Acknowledging his listeners as experts in the field of global agreements, Cappy is able to outline the basic benefits of such alliances without appearing to underestimate the audience's knowledge.

As international lawyers, you're all familiar with the benefits of global alliances. In *theory*, they allow for access to technology; access to markets; increased economies of scale; the sharing of investment costs and financial risk; as well as access to management skills. Those are all opportunities well worth pursuing. However, if an alliance lacks that common vision I spoke of earlier, or if the expectations on either side are unrealistic, then the relationship in *practice* will be rocky at best.

I can support this theory by offering up some examples from Chrysler's own experience in the international arena. And I thought I'd throw in some "war stories" for illustration. (By the way, Logan advised me that telling lawyer jokes or mentioning Dan Quayle would be in poor taste, so I won't do either!)

I'll begin with an alliance that is working very well for Chrysler, and has for more than *twenty-one years*—and that's our global alliance with Mitsubishi Motors Corporation of Japan.

(By the way, *Business Week* recently featured what I consider the *second* best strategic automotive alliance: the thirteen-year Ford-Mazda relationship. Chrysler and MMC's overall scope and volume of business rivals that of Ford-Mazda, and has been in place *eight years* longer!) Now, some people are surprised to hear that Chrysler, due to our somewhat outspoken stance on U.S. trade policy with Japan, has the longest-standing American partnership with a Japanese vehicle manufacturer. But we do—to the tune of over a billion and a half dollars of business a year today, forecasted to double to over three billion dollars of business by 1995. The reason that this relationship has remained productive for so long is that it has served the interests of both Chrysler and Mitsubishi, and has evolved over time to reflect the changing needs of both companies.

> *SPEECH TIP:* Having begun with a current overview of the Chrysler-Mitsubishi alliance, including a forecast for its continued growth, Cappy firmly establishes the relationship's productivity—and audience interest—before detailing its origins and development over time.

The Chrysler-Mitsubishi relationship began back in 1970, when Chrysler and Mitsubishi Heavy Industries signed an agreement giving Chrysler the U.S. distribution rights for MMC cars and trucks. (Mitsubishi was just beginning to produce cars at this time.) This original agreement gave Chrysler access to low-cost small cars, and gave MMC access to Chrysler's nationwide distribution network. Over the next fifteen years, the Chrysler-MMC relationship evolved to include MMC's own U.S. distribution. It also grew to include mutual technical assistance, and an agreement for Chrysler to purchase engines from MMC. Then, in 1985, Chrysler and Mitsubishi agreed to build the Diamond-Star Motors plant in Normal, Illinois, to assemble the jointly developed Plymouth Laser and Mitsubishi Eclipse sports coupes. Production was launched in November of 1988.

We've since worked together on the development of other vehicles. Perhaps the flashiest example of this cooperation is the Dodge Stealth, which was designed by Chrysler and was developed and is assembled by MMC. (The Stealth's a great car for red-hot international lawyers, by the way.)

> *SPEECH TIP:* Teasing the audience in a flattering way, Cappy lightens up his narration; even better, he manages it with a good-humored—even slightly tongue-in-cheek—pitch for his company's products.

Last October we agreed to a major restructuring of our Diamond-Star joint venture with the sale of our equity share to MMC. Many people incorrectly interpreted this restructuring as the makings of a "divorce." But that's simply not the case.

In reality, our new agreement gave each party more of what it needed in a changed business environment. For their part, Mitsubishi gained full ownership of the Diamond-Star plant, which gave them a highly visible U.S. presence. We got our original investment in Diamond-Star back, and were relieved of current and future financial obligations. However, we *retained* the right to half of Diamond-Star's current and future production. Furthermore, we have an agreement to sell Chrysler-built engines and transmissions to Diamond-Star over the life cycle of the next-generation Diamond-Star cars. In other words, you'll be able to walk into a Mitsubishi dealership in the mid-'90s and find a Chrysler engine under the hood. And that's a helluva switch!

So, our relationship with MMC continues to be "win-win." But we're no Ozzie and Harriet. We have our share of difficulties and misunderstandings. (Just like a *real* marriage.)

Now and again, we've encountered some unique, and even humorous, situations in our cross-cultural business relationships with MMC.

One of my favorite stories is one that Lino Piedra, the former Chairman of the Board of Diamond-Star Motors, likes to tell. According to Lino, the American managers thought it would be a good idea for the Japanese managers at Diamond-Star to use "anglicized" first names. So, the public relations manager suggested to Osamu Itoh, the assistant general manager of human relations, that he might like to be known as Sam. "No," Itoh replied, "I think I would like a different name."

"What would you like to be called?" the P.R. manager asked.

"Awesome. I think Awesome Itoh is a very good choice," was the response.

They had a similar problem with Mr. Watanabe of MMC International Corporation. He chose the name "Handsome," remarking that he had always wanted to *be* handsome. In the end, our Japanese counterparts at Diamond-Star did not receive their colorful names.

Nonetheless, the Chrysler-Mitsubishi alliance has provided strong mutual benefits over the years—evolving as our respective needs have changed—keeping the relationship in balance.

My second story is of an alliance that, unfortunately, *hasn't* panned out as well: Chrysler-Renault. In this case, I think both Chrysler and Renault would agree that, like the Narita newlyweds, we failed to share a common vision and expectations from the beginning. Chrysler and Renault came together, of course, as a result of Chrysler's acquisition of Renault's interest in my former company, American Motors. As a part of that deal, Chrysler took over the new AMC plant in Bramalea, Ontario, built for the production of what became the Eagle Premier. In addition, Chrysler turned to Renault for Jeep distribution in Europe.

SPEECH TIP: Cappy shares lessons from company mistakes as well as successes. His candor is refreshing in itself, and by recounting Chrysler's less-than-perfect unions with Renault and Fiat, he is able to continue rounding out his discussion of global alliances without sacrificing his emphasis on specific, "homegrown" examples.

The next logical step for the Chrysler-Renault alliance seemed to be the establishment of a joint venture. And that joint venture became the now defunct ARCAD, which was formed to build a small, entry-level sport-utility vehicle code-named the Jeep JJ. The JJ joint venture project was conceived as an efficient way to build a new Jeep vehicle—positioned *below* the current Jeep Wrangler—for both the U.S. and European markets. The idea was to have a plant in Spain assembling JJs for Europe, with an existing Chrysler plant here assembling JJs for the North American market. Although there were contractual commitments from the outset concerning JJ, indicating agreement on the direction of the project, neither side, in retrospect, was in full agreement as to the final product.

Chrysler's concept of JJ was an entry-level sport-utility. Renault's was that of a somewhat more upscale version. Each company had its own powertrain and wanted option combinations that were popular in their respective home markets. Chrysler was also interested in a four-door version for young families, which would have been positioned below the Jeep Cherokee. However, both Chrysler and Renault *were* in agreement that both the venture and the vehicle had to be very low cost.

Unfortunately, that single, overriding expectation just couldn't be met, because complexity in this business comes at a cost. And to have developed a vehicle that would've met the *product* expectations of both Chrysler and Renault, plus having production and administrative functions spread over the U.S., Spain, and France, just added too much cost.

There were other factors compounding matters, too. While the JJ project was moving forward, the world market for small sport-utility vehicles was becoming increasingly competitive. The U.S. market for small sport-utilities, in particular, wasn't growing as originally projected. Later, Renault began to focus its attention on its new European partnership with Volvo. Chrysler began looking at other partner possibilities as well. (Call this a case of wandering eyes!)

Ultimately, the ARCAD joint venture was terminated because the risks and rewards were no longer balanced. No common vision. No shared expectations.

Although we called off the engagement, Chrysler and Renault have remained friends. And I'm happy to see that David Syed, a former Renault attorney during the JJ project, is one of your speakers today.

Then there's the big deal that just couldn't be put together: Chrysler-Fiat. As you may know, Chrysler and Fiat spent several months in negotiation in the latter half of 1990. These negotiations explored a variety of business opportunities. Nothing was ever "off the table," so to speak. Both sides were looking for all of those great global synergies. In theory it made a lot of sense. Fiat is very strong in Europe, but has no significant North American presence. Chrysler, on the other hand, could have provided a North American outlet for some Fiat products, while gaining access to Fiat's well-established distribution network in Europe.

But it just wasn't to be.

For one thing, the timing was bad. While we were negotiating with Fiat, both of our home markets began to deteriorate. Fiat's share in Italy was being seriously challenged by its European competitors. Our sales in the U.S. were going under with the recession. Then came the war in the Gulf, and the whole world held its breath! All of this made us both a bit leery about putting something together.

However, I believe that one of the major stumbling blocks to building an alliance was that Chrysler and Fiat just didn't have a history of working together. And, just as in the realm of human relationships, an international business relationship is best built on familiarity, and, ultimately, trust. Chrysler and Fiat simply didn't have the experience operating together that would've provided that critical foundation of trust. You might say that we were contemplating a move for the altar after having shared just a few cups of espresso!

Sometimes the best deal is the one you walk away from.

Well, that's a thumbnail sketch of three major global alliances at Chrysler: one that works, one that didn't work, and one that we just couldn't put together.

But we've met with more consistent success with *joint ventures* at Chrysler. And there are two in particular that I'd like to mention that are doing quite well.

The first is our Beijing Jeep operation, officially known as Beijing Jeep Corporation. This venture is one we began back in 1984 at American Motors, and have continued since AMC came to Chrysler in 1987. For both Chrysler and the Chinese parent company, Beijing Jeep has proven to be a sound investment. In fact, the venture was recently ranked by the Chinese Government as one of the top ten of over 20,000 joint ventures operating in China today. The Chinese have benefited from our manufacturing and vehicle technology, and management development, while we've benefited from the sale of kits and components to a market that's otherwise closed to Western companies.

But dealing with a culture as foreign as China's, as many of you know from first-hand experience, can be difficult. And the magnitude of difficulty increases with the disparities in the cultures. Beijing Jeep is no exception. Especially when it comes to negotiations. Our annual board of directors meeting at Beijing Jeep stands as testament to the Asian art of negotiation. This is one case where it really pays off to be the *Vice President* of International Operations. That's because I can get away with sending our people in for the heavy negotiations, and I only need to show up for the signatures!

We know from experience that the Beijing Jeep board meetings tend to drag out. So, our people do a lot of work in preparation. This past year, the pre-meeting work lasted six very full work weeks. (Bear in mind that it's not uncommon for our negotiators to labor an entire *day* over a single word!) In spite of the heavy preparation, our '91 board meeting lasted thirty-one hours. That's thirty-one hours of non-stop bargaining at the table. In total, some forty resolutions were passed in that period. However, at the twenty-hour mark, only two resolutions had been approved—and they were doosies. The first formal resolution levied a fine of twenty-five yuan, or about $4.50, on any board member who fell asleep for more than one minute during the negotiations. Now, that's actually a very steep fine for the

Chinese, because it represents about one-eighth of a month's salary per snooze. (And one drowsy Chinese board member *did* ante-up nearly an entire month's wages!) The second formal resolution banned smoking during the negotiations, which, as you can imagine, added a little extra tension to the smokers on both sides of the table.

Our Chrysler negotiators discovered in the course of this board meeting that a marathon session had been well-anticipated by their Chinese counterparts. They tipped their hand by suggesting a "surprise noodle break" at 4:00 o'clock in the morning. And the noodles were ready.

Those of you who've been to China know that there's no such thing as a twenty-four-hour fast-food restaurant. Obviously, our Chinese counterparts did some pre-planning of their own!

Of course, sometimes the joke's on us. One of our delegations to Beijing Jeep was invited to attend a dinner banquet. Each table setting included three glasses: one full of orange soda, one full of plum wine, and one full of a 160-proof liquor. Our Chinese hosts insisted on several toasts, explaining that tradition dictated that their guests participate. After a few toasts, our people noticed that only we and the Chinese toasters were drinking the liquor, while the rest of the Chinese toasted with their orange sodas (and enjoyed watching their Western counterparts get blasted). So, our people insisted that the Chinese all toast with the liquor. They obliged. But they only took tiny sips while our people kept downing their drinks at each toast.

Chuck Busch, now our managing director of operations in Venezuela, then introduced a "new" American custom. He stated that it was customary for Americans to down their drinks at each toast, and then hold the glass upside down over their heads to prove that the glass is empty.

That did it. Everyone got sloshed.

But the story doesn't end here. Three weeks after this event, another one of our people went over to Beijing Jeep for some follow-up meetings. He returned from the trip recounting an *ancient* Chinese drinking custom he'd been taught by his hosts—turning the glass upside down over your head after a toast!

> *SPEECH TIP:* With an admiring tip of the hat to the other invited speakers of the day, Cappy delivers a friendly compliment to his hosts as well.

Another of our joint ventures that is quite successful is Eurostar in Austria. In fact, Wieland Schmid-Schmidsfelden, our outside counsel for Eurostar, is another one of your speakers this afternoon. (You've really got an all-star cast!) Eurostar is a joint venture with Styer-Daimler-Puch (SDP), assembling minivans in Austria for the European market. SDP is an experienced and highly regarded manufacturer of four-wheel drive systems and vehicles. The Eurostar plant began assembling minivans for Chrysler last fall. We chose Styer as a joint venture partner for four convincing reasons. First, the national and local governments were eager and willing to work with us to help get Eurostar up and running. Second, we found the Austrian work force to be skilled, well-educated, disciplined, and conscientious. Third, Austria is situated in the geographic heart of Europe, within a six hundred-mile radius of 75 percent of the European car and truck market. In addition, Austria's pending application for EC membership (not to mention the recent EC-EFTA trade agreement) enhanced its attractiveness. And, finally, Styer had a reputation for engineering excellence and high-quality assembly. Styer, in fact, was already familiar with our minivan because they had helped to engineer the superb all-wheel drive system.

Perhaps the nicest single feature of Eurostar for us is that it is a pure *assembly* agreement—which suits Styer just fine. We're not entangled in distribution rights or other agreements, which Chrysler wasn't ready to make with our crown jewel minivans.

While we're *very* pleased with our overall progress at Eurostar, I must admit that our experience in Austria hasn't been entirely problem-free. Specifically, we've had some difficulty dealing with the local Graz bureaucracy. And that's led to some unnecessary delays, costs, and frustrations for us. In fact, I'll give you an example that's downright ridiculous!

The underlying problem in this instance is that there are no comprehensive building codes or procedures in Graz for a project of the scope of Eurostar. Nonetheless, we designed and built the Eurostar plant to provide the safest possible working environment. The plant is open and well lit. It has state-of-the-art fire detection and fire-control facilities. And there are large exit doors close to each work station. However, after inspecting the facility, the local fire officials decided that we needed to add "*flucht*" (or escape) tunnels leading out of the facility. Now, why anyone would want to run down into a tunnel during a fire instead of running straight out the door is beyond me! Nevertheless, we complied and built the *flucht* tunnels. Then the fire officials returned to inspect our *flucht* tunnels. They decided that our sprinkler system was so extensive and effective that it might flood the tunnels. So, the officials mandated that we build a pumping system for the tunnels. Again, we complied. Then the fire officials returned and told us that we would have to have several large fire ponds in order to supply the sprinklers. So, we constructed fire ponds. Then the officials came back and said that the ponds could freeze in winter—so we'd have to do something about that. We're still trying to figure that one out!

I guess this is a case in which the marriage is fine . . . we're just stuck with this nagging mother-in-law!

Now, I've covered a lot of ground this afternoon—without one lawyer joke, mind you—but, if nothing else, at Chrysler International I think we've learned a few things about global alliances and joint ventures that might have some application to all of you.

In international business, as in romantic courtship, it's still best to start small, build some mutual trust, and then expand. Each alliance and joint venture must have a common vision and a very well-defined (and mutually understood) set of expectations. And, like a healthy marriage, the relationship should be allowed to evolve to meet the changing needs of its partners.

Take it from me, the Liz Taylor of international liaisons, if you can pull all of this off—despite the additional challenges of the multi-cultural international business environment—your business stands a good chance of surviving the treacherous Narita airport.

Thank you.

Dominion Textile's Financial Outlook

CHARLES H. HANTHO
Chairman, President, and CEO
Dominion Textile, Inc.

and

KENNETH J. DOEL
Vice President and Treasurer
Dominion Textile, Inc.

Delivered to the Toronto Society of Financial Analysts, Toronto, Canada, May 6, 1993

SUMMARY: Top-management representatives of an important Canadian textile firm use well-chosen facts and figures to explain to a group of influential investment analysts the nature of their business, how it weathered a recession, and how it is now poised for growth.

Thank you. I'm pleased to have this opportunity to bring you up to date on Dominion Textile.

There's a lot of ground to cover. In less than five years, the company has undergone a swing of the pendulum from roaring expansion to a wrenching recession and restructuring and then back to profitability. It's been tough, but we are breathing the fresh air again. Dominion today is in an excellent position for a focused approach to profit growth and building sustainable shareholder value.

> *SPEECH TIP:* Hantho's opening remarks will in themselves cover a lot of ground: sketching out the most dramatic lines of Dominion's "story", assuring listeners of an eventual happy ending, introducing a co-presenter; and stating the structure and planned length of the joint presentation.

Sharing this microphone with me today will be Ken Doel, who is Vice President and Treasurer of the corporation. I will start with a profile of the corporation today and then Ken will briefly run down our five core businesses and present the financial highlights. I will then come back to comment on our strategic thinking and our expectations. This should take just under thirty minutes, after which Ken and I will do our best to answer your questions.

I should mention at this point that there will be copies of my remarks, including pertinent data, available on the way out.

> *SPEECH TIP:* If you plan to distribute a printed version of your presentation, mentioning this fact at the outset will save your listeners from taking any unnecessary notes, a double courtesy they are sure to appreciate.

Let me start with a quick snapshot of the company. We are one of the top twenty primary textile manufacturers in the world. From a head office in Montreal, we serve the apparel and industrial markets in fifty countries and operate thirty-five manufacturing plants on three continents. We are organized under five autonomous product groups. The distribution you see is based on 1993 sales estimates, and denim fabrics today is our largest group, accounting for 37 percent of total volume. Yarns account for 22 percent, followed by Technical Fabrics, Apparel Fabrics, and Industrial Products.

Although we are far from abandoning the Canadian market, we have become increasingly international in our approach. In 1993, 76 percent of our sales will come from outside Canada, as compared to 50 percent five years ago. Roughly 80 percent of our assets are now outside Canada.

> *SPEECH TIP:* Organizing presentation material is certainly a speaker's duty, but choosing the organizational method and sequence is also a speaker's prerogative. Rather than interrupt the momentum of his introductory overview, Hantho opts to postpone certain details until later in his speech, when their discussion will be more germane.

I'll review our strategic positioning later, but let me summarize our present situation quickly: From an operational perspective, the portfolio restructuring has been carried out, and we are clearly focused. We are in businesses with strong market positions in North America and Europe, we are on the ground with great potential in the Far East, and we are reviewing our options in Central and South America.

From a corporate viewpoint, we are making money again. We have had eight straight quarters of growth, operating cash flow is strong, and our balance sheet ratios are steadily improving.

Our mission statement reads as follows: "The mission of Dominion Textile, Inc. is to serve worldwide markets profitably with quality textiles and textile-related products. The fundamental goal of the Corporation is to attain and sustain leadership positions in selected market segments on an international basis, concentrating on total value to customers."

The challenges in this statement are not insignificant, but I think we're doing a good job of meeting them. I'll ask Ken Doel at this point to summarize where we are with the product groups and supply financial highlights.

DOEL: The new Dominion Textile has a balanced portfolio of strong core businesses in various markets around the world. I'll review our product groups in the order of their contribution to total sales, starting with denim.

We're the largest denim producer in the world, despite recent claims to this effect by Cone Mills, one of our U.S. competitors. We operate under the Swift trade name with manufacturing facilities in the United States, Canada, and Tunisia. Denim is one of the truly global operations in the portfolio, and our objective is leadership in denim apparel on a world basis.

Sales last year totaled $415 million, an increase of 33 percent. Volume is still building at 20 percent this year, and we are estimating $497 million for fiscal 1993. Swift has a dominant 22 percent share of the North American market.

Denim has been described as the fabric of North America. The current surge in denim popularity is founded in a back-to-basics lifestyle and the ability of manufacturers to make jeanswear stylish and comfortable for aging baby boomers.

It's also tied to increased use of denim in shirts, shorts, and other apparel as well as non-apparel applications such as home furnishings and car interiors. The result is twenty-seven straight months of growth and, for Swift, the highest plant utilization in five years.

Swift is seen as a market innovator and has played a major part in this market renaissance. It has also made substantial progress in the past three years toward reducing the cyclical vulnerability of the business. Swift has done this in three major ways:

- by expanding the customer base and increased focus on value-added, unique product offerings
- by gaining some geographical balance through increased exports, and
- by partnering with customers to ensure the highest levels of quality service as well as inventory and process control.

Exports to South and Central America have been growing steadily. A North American Free Trade Agreement would expand trade with this region still further by encouraging the finishing of domestic fabrics into garments that could compete with import price levels.

In the Far East, we have established a marketing office in Hong Kong, and we plan a distribution and service center in Singapore. In Europe, our product mix has helped to counter the poor market conditions, and operations there are profitable. There are strategic opportunities opening up in Eastern Europe. However, we don't expect any major developments until there is a sustained European economic recovery.

Sales yarn, in contrast to denim, is a continental portfolio. We're a major producer in North America, with operations in both Canada and the United States under the Dominion trade name. Our yarn operations are segmented according to market need into Commodity and Specialty Yarn groups. Management of the Group has been realigned to consolidate our plants on both sides of the border along these two market orientations.

Our objective is to sustain our position among the leaders in the yarn business on a North American basis. The Yarn Group has played an important role in our cash-flow recovery, as these figures indicate. The group enjoyed a record 19 percent increase in sales last year, and margins also firmed up significantly after a period of depressed prices and high cotton costs.

As you know, we evaluated a potential disposition or IPO of the Yarn Group earlier last year. We concluded that shareholder interests would be best served by retaining the unit. Both the 1992 figures and our projections for the current year support that position.

Commodity yarns are generally long-run, low-cost yarns used in the knitting industry for T-shirts, sweaters, underwear, sweatshirts, and hosiery. Investments of over $22 million in the past three years have made Dominion one of the lowest-cost, most efficient producers of commodity yarns. Commodity yarn represents over 70 percent of Group production, and this industry sector is growing at 6 to 8 percent per annum. Our plants have been at or near capacity since March 1991, and the North American market remains strong, driven by continued good demand for activewear and knitwear.

> *SPEECH TIP:* Doel's reports on the Dominion product groups are lean, concise, and assertively phrased. By joining numerical figures with active verbs, the speaker conveys sense as well as statistics.

Specialty yarns are generally short-run, custom-made products and require a quite different manufacturing and marketing approach. The Specialty Yarns unit achieved an 18 percent increase in sales last year after a shift to higher value-added products and a strong export focus. Exports now extend to a dozen countries. The domestic Canadian market remains subdued, but the outlook is strengthening with the overall recovery in North America.

The Technical Fabrics Group operates on a global mandate, with the bulk of activity currently in Europe and the Far East. There are two distinct segments to the group.

Under the DHJ trade name, we are the world's largest producer and distributor of woven shirt interlinings. Subsidiary and associated companies operate fourteen plants in ten countries. Our objective here is to develop leadership positions in shirt and garment interlinings on a global basis.

Under the Nordlys trade name, we produce and distribute nonwoven products for apparel and industrial uses in Europe as well as Southeast Asia. Our objective in nonwovens is to achieve leadership positions in selective market segments on both continents.

Total sales for the Group slipped slightly in fiscal 1992 and have been impacted by both the European recession and currency fluctuations in 1993.

DHJ's business is traditional interlinings, and the company distributes an extensive product range. These are the substrates that go into collars, cuffs, lapels, and other parts of shirts and garments that require stiffening or support. Demand in Europe in 1993 has been uneven. DHJ has kept pace with the migration of garment manufacturers to less developed regions and has experienced particularly strong growth in the Far East.

Interlinings can be made from woven or nonwoven fabrics, and Nordlys supplies the majority of the nonwoven fabrics to DHJ in both Europe and Asia. The parent facility is located in France, where Nordlys is also a major player in industrial nonwovens for products ranging from protective apparel to underground cable wrap.

Nordlys has steadily increased volume each year, and with strong growth in the Far East we estimate a 38 percent sales increase in fiscal '93.

Our Apparel Fabrics business is now exclusively in Europe, where we operate under the Klopman International trade name. We're the largest European producer of career apparel fabrics and hold a 40 percent share of the poly-cotton workwear market. Our objective is to build on this leadership position.

Klopman's career apparel business has suffered from the recessionary market conditions in the U.K. and Germany, where its major customer base is situated. This has been offset by improvements in workwear markets. and total sales are up 7 percent in the first nine months of fiscal '93.

Klopman has undergone—and is still undergoing—stringent cost cutting and has been successful in differentiating its products and services from the competition. Although the market remains subdued, there is attractive upside potential. At 80 percent capacity, Klopman is break-even at the operating level, and a 5 to 15 percent increase in demand will produce significant returns.

I'm going to break the pattern here and present the sales of the Industrial Products Group first, because it shows you very quickly how the composition of this group has changed radically.

This is where much of the strategic restructuring has taken place in response to two realizations:

1. Included in this group were market segments where we could not realistically expect to attain leadership.

2. The industrial sector has proved slow to recover from the recession.

The restructuring began in 1991, and last year the Group was further reduced from four business units to two. Dominion Industrial Products produces traditional woven industrial fabrics, and our objective is to make this Canadian-based company a North American supplier of value-added fabrics to selected industrial markets.

Poly-Bond is on the cutting edge of industrial nonwovens. Its technology positions it in the diaper coverstock, hygiene, and protective apparel markets, and our objective is to develop a leadership position in these segments.

DIFC's manufacturing base was consolidated and upgraded in '92. An example of its value-added focus is the company's development work in flame-resistant fabrics, which produced good results in the last fiscal year. DIFC competes in a tough marketplace, however. There's aggressive competition on a continental basis, and reduced demand is forecast for 1993 due to a slow rebound from the North American recession.

Poly-Bond, on the other hand, is experiencing solid growth, with sales increasing 29 percent last year. It is in the top three in spun-bonded technology—the fastest growing sector of the nonwovens business, which is itself growing at 6 to 8 percent per annum in North America.

A new composite production line will play an important role in this strategy and came on-stream in the third quarter. Poly-Bond has developed new technology for bonding different substrates to form new characteristics without sacrificing or altering the values of the original elements. Composite barrier fabrics, for example, can protect health-care workers from the HIV virus while still allowing the body to breathe and remain comfortable. The successful commercialization of the new composites line gives Poly-Bond a technical edge on the competition.

Let me turn now to our financial performance and steadily improving financial position.

The results—as measured in sales, operating and net income, and resources from operations—reflect the steady overall improvements the corporation has experienced over the past two years. Total sales, restated for operations sold or discontinued, for the third fiscal quarter increased to $343 million versus $302.3 million last year, a 13 percent increase. We are expecting the fourth quarter to show continued good performance on a year-over-year basis.

Operating income at $34.2 million for the third quarter reflects a margin of 10 percent of sales and shows the steady improvement in overall results. Cash flow remains very strong, as reflected on this graph of resources from operations. Active management programs are in place to control and reduce working capital through cycle time reduction. Cash conservation efforts have created a keen awareness of the importance of cash flow.

Our net debt/equity ratio at March quarter end has reached 50:50 from a level of 61:39 at 1992 fiscal year end. The corporate target is a level of 40:60, and we feel that this level is achievable within the next three years.

HANTHO: You will have got a feeling for elements of our strategy from Ken's review of the Product Groups and where they find themselves today. I'd like to expand on that: first with a look at our current situation, and then by sharing with you some expectations.

Our new organization was shaped by two principal forces. One was responsible reaction to a serious situation caused largely by the recession. The second was a review of our strategic thinking and clarification of where we want to be within a rapidly changing industry.

Let me deal quickly with the first part—management's response to the recession. I say quickly, because many of you may already know most of the details. For those who don't, these actions played a major role in defining our current position.

Briefly, Dominion embraced a global policy back in the mid-eighties and, by the end of the decade, had amassed many new interests, often at premium prices. The general economic recession that followed contained within it the worst textile industry recession since the thirties. The pressure on our financial structure was overwhelming, and Dominion entered into seven straight periods of net loss.

Management's response was to focus our resources on fewer core businesses and to raise cash to reduce corporate debt.

This resulted in the following corporate priorities for the past two years:

- focus on improved earnings and operational cash flow
- strengthen strategies and operational management in businesses with good long-term potential
- improve, divest, joint venture, or shut down underperforming businesses
- curtail capital spending, reduce head office costs, and sell non-strategic assets
- strengthen the balance sheet and prepare to restructure debt.

As you saw from the financials, the results achieved include a substantial improvement in earnings and cash flow. We have fewer core businesses, and they have strengthened management teams.

We have acted on underperforming businesses:

- we closed Fiberworld, the Canadian carpetbacking plant
- we closed Dominion Fabric Company, which was in apparel fabrics in Canada
- we consolidated and rationalized Dominion Industrial Fabrics
- we sold Mirafi and got out of geotextiles
- we sold Wayn-Tex and exited the U.S. carpetbacking business
- we reduced capital spending, cut dividends, reduced overhead, and sold the Montreal head-office building.

SPEECH TIP: After itemizing a group of individual decisions, Hantho uses a single before-and-after comparison to show their collective impact on company sales.

The resulting, leaner organization can be seen in this comparison. Two years ago we had eleven production units contributing $1.3 billion in sales; this year we have seven units expected to produce roughly $80 million more.

Finally, we are closer to the goal of revising our debt repayment schedule. Negotiations are currently under way to refinance our debt with the objective of extending maturities and normalizing amortization schedules as well as reducing the size of the banking group.

The second force shaping our current path was an in-depth analysis of our industry and Dominion's role within it. Here is our outlook of the industry changes taking effect that impact upon our operations.

If we take our three major markets, the most exciting change for Dominion is the turnaround of the North American textile business. In as little as three years, we have gone from looking inward to looking outward. I'm talking about the emergence of a superior, world-competitive textile industry here in North America.

The 807A legislation in the U.S. has been an important stimulant. Under that legislation, American fabric can be shipped offshore to the Caribbean basin, cut and sewn into finished garments, and shipped back into the States with tariff only on the value-added portion. We welcomed this initiative two years ago, and it's working well; it recaptures a lot of what otherwise would have been imported from Southeast Asia.

NAFTA simply builds on this. Yes, it will support the North American garment-making business and dislocate imports through access to relatively low-cost labor. But, equally significant, by keeping the whole chain on "home" territory, we can best serve the needs of "quick response," which is a main driver in the retail business today.

International competitiveness begins with leadership in strong domestic markets. As the North American textile market builds global strength, so do we, as leaders within that market.

Our denim operations are world class. We are building on the strength of our domestic market position and resources to export our leadership capabilities in selected parts of the world. Besides our established presence now in the Far East and Europe, we are increasing our exports steadily to Central and South America.

The North American market is also positive for yarns. Although our orientation is continental, leading North American yarn producers are cost competitive on an international basis. This is reassuring in terms of the future of both the domestic industry and the yarn group.

In fact, the fundamentals of the North American market and our position within it appear strong and robust. Cyclicality has not been eliminated, but our competitiveness against global competition has never been better.

The short-term outlook for Europe remains subdued due to the poor economy, but, when it does recover, our businesses are well positioned for substantial profit growth. This growth will start with the recovery itself—with apparel generally the first industry to benefit. It will continue as our fabric and interlining businesses follow the migration of their customers and garment manufacturing generally to Northern Africa and Eastern Europe. And it will be enhanced by cost improvements in our sourcing and by new product development for selected markets in denim, career apparel, protective garments, interlinings, and industrial nonwovens. Eventually, as the newly emerging economies of Eastern Europe gain economic weight, we are well positioned for the enormous growth potential that will be created.

The Far East continues to be the highest growth-rate market for primary textiles and apparel. Our strategies for the area are focused on two emerging trends: the need for higher quality, more differentiated product to meet the standards and style requirements of global brands, and the development of larger, more sophisticated domestic markets as the individual economies grow and prosper.

The technology and know-how we have developed in North America and Europe in denim, interlinings, and industrial nonwovens is transportable and can develop a competitive advantage. We have been in the area in interlinings for many years, and in 1992 we commenced the manufacture of nonwovens in Malaysia. Also, last year we took the first step in our Asian denim strategy by opening up a sales and distribution facility in Hong Kong and will soon establish a technical service facility in Singapore.

Given these global opportunities and challenges, and given Dominion's recent history, our current Strategic Action Plan continues to reflect two preoccupations: the final phases of corporate consolidation and the pursuit of our vision of international competitiveness. Here are the main elements of that plan:

1. We will maintain our focus on earnings improvement and strong cash-flow performance. The short-term outlook for the company is positive, and we hope to reinstate the dividend in fiscal 1994 (commencing July 1, 1993).

2. We will continue to improve our balance sheet ratios and normalize debt. By fiscal year-end, we anticipate a debt:equity ratio of 50:50, improving to a target of 40:60 over the next three years.

3. We will continue to invest in strengthening our internationally competitive businesses with strong market positions. We have recently announced a $20 million expansion of our denim facilities in Georgia and a $30 million modernization and expansion investment in our two nonwoven plants—Poly-Bond in the U.S. and Nordlys in France.

4. We will expand our businesses outside of North America and Europe on a selective basis, where we can establish a position of strength through competitive advantage. I have already mentioned our new nonwoven plant in Malaysia and our beach-head in denim in Hong Kong. Southeast Asia will be a particular focus for growth opportunities.

5. We will continue to press for profitability improvement in businesses performing below the corporate target. We have aggressive action plans to improve the returns from our Dominion Industrial Fabrics business in Canada and our Klopman operations in Europe.

6. Lastly, our plan calls for building enduring shareholder value. The key word here is *enduring*, and it is a logical outcome of our present strategic positioning. Through careful positioning in developed markets, selective expansion into new markets, and a clear focus on industry sectors with lasting growth potential, we will build that value on a long-term basis.

These are exciting times. There may have been a tendency in the past few years to write off textiles as yesterday's industry. But the period we are entering could be one of the most stimulating and rewarding yet. We see the potential. And we are among the leaders in pursuing it.

Thank you for your attention. Now, if you have any questions, Ken and I will do our best to answer them.

Perestroika from Pleasantville: Lessons Learned Launching **Reader's Digest** in the Soviet Union and Hungary

CAROLE M. HOWARD
Vice President, Public Relations and Communications Policy
The Reader's Digest Association, Inc.

Delivered at the Conference Board's Corporate Image Conference, New York, January 28, 1992

SUMMARY: A publishing executive shares in practical detail her firm's experiences in profitably expanding capitalist enterprise into formerly communist Eastern Europe.

This past summer, there was a story going around Moscow that the most popular item at flea markets was a used light bulb. Yes, a *used* light bulb. Here's why: You buy a used light bulb for a few kopecks and take it to work. You then unscrew the good light bulb from your office lamp and replace it with the blown-out bulb. You tell your boss you need a new light bulb because yours is out—and you take the original good bulb home. If you are lucky, you can also take the dead bulb home after it has been replaced, sell it at a flea market—and start the cycle all over again.

SPEECH TIP: Howard's lively opening anecdote serves as an immediate attention-getter as well as the symbolic parable she goes on to explain.

This story symbolizes for me what it's like to launch a new product in the former Soviet Union, now known as the Commonwealth of Independent States. On the one hand, you have consumers faced with horrendous shortages, endless lines, outrageous inflation, and a work force that doesn't seem very interested in working. On the other hand, however, you have an ingenuity and entrepreneurial spirit that even seventy years of communist domination could not completely crush.

The entrepreneurial spirit and enthusiasm is even stronger in Hungary. In fact, after private businesses became legal in 1989, thousands of people turned their cars into taxis. I'm told that today there are as many taxis on the streets of Budapest as there are in New York City—because anyone who had a car could immediately take advantage of the new free enterprise system and go into business for himself.

During 1991 we launched two new editions of *Reader's Digest*—a Russian-language edition in July and a Hungarian edition in October—and set up operations in Moscow and Budapest. I am pleased to be asked to share our experiences with you. We learned many lessons as we planned and implemented our public relations and promotions for these launches. I hope they will help you as you expand into new markets in Eastern Europe and the former Soviet Union.

The first lesson we learned is that you can't get to the communications issues until you have solved the business issues. And you can't solve the business issues until you have a good understanding of the local market, culture, and business environment.

For example, many Russians don't arrive at work until 9:30 or 10 in the morning. This can be discouraging, especially after you learn that the Russian proverb about work translates to "Work isn't a wolf; it won't run into the woods." Or, put it off if you can because it will be there to do tomorrow.

It's not that Russians are inherently lazy. It may well be they've been up since 5 a.m. standing in lines for food. Three hours for butter. Another two for milk. Yet another three hours for a scrawny chicken. Western stores in Moscow also have long lines—two hours for McDonald's, Pizza Hut, and Baskin-Robbins; three or four for Lancôme and Estée Lauder. Even admission to many big department stores is rationed—you can shop only when it is your district's turn, and even then you must line up for hours. The largest children's store in Russia was across from our hotel. The line-up began before six every morning and stayed at several thousand all day. During one of our visits, the famous GUM department store on Red Square had so little merchandise that it was open only three days a week.

One of our editors quit because we required her to work a forty-hour week. She said she couldn't spend that many hours on the job—and certainly couldn't come in every day—because she had no *babushka* to stand in lines for her.

All this has incredible ramifications for companies doing business in Russia, of course. It's not only non-productive, it's debilitating. Basic office conditions we take for granted are non-existent, so productivity expectations cannot be too high. For example, in our Moscow office for several weeks there were no pencils. Everyone locks their offices, even if they're stepping out only for a few moments, because thefts are rampant—and on the increase.

After one trip to Moscow, we returned with a long list of supplies our editor-in-chief needed to do his job—supplies ranging from fairly sophisticated equipment like light tables and layout boards to basics like pads of paper, pens, pencils, pencil sharpeners, Scotch tape, Post-it notes, typewriter ribbons, a three-hole punch, and manila folders. He needed his own copier, because it took two days to get copies made in the central copying center, and he reminded us not to forget lots of paper and toner as well. One is useless without the other two, of course, and all three are virtually impossible to find in Moscow. He also asked us to send lots of staples. The only way to get staples is to buy another stapler—*if* you can find a store that has any for sale. Those are not the kinds of problems that would wake up your average American business person in the middle of the night!

In the Budapest office, supplies are not a critical issue—but office space is. We were told there were 3,200 joint ventures launched in Hungary in 1991 alone, so acceptable office space is almost nonexistent. What is available is very expensive and usually needs extensive renovation. Even more scarce are phone lines. In fact, many companies choose an office not for its location or amenities but because it is available—and has a phone line. We consider ourselves very lucky to have three lines, a radio telephone, and a FAX for our staff of fifteen in our Budapest office. And yet they still spend wasteful hours bucking endless busy signals as they try to make local and international calls. And telecommunications often cease in rain storms. In July, when we were in Budapest, a two-and-a-half hour storm knocked out all lines into Parliament for four hours.

> *SPEECH TIP:* Because it follows such a vivid depiction of the radically different business conditions her company encountered in Russia and Hungary, Howard's next point comes as a fresh surprise: some things worked the same. The order in which these business "lessons" are presented increases the impact of each.

The second lesson we learned is that most of the public relations and promotions techniques that work well in the U.S. also work well in Russia and Hungary. Some are even more successful than they are here, because in those markets they're unique. But, in Hungary, advertising and promotional activity is relatively sophisticated, with most Western techniques practiced to some extent. We used direct mail very successfully in both countries. We sent out several thousand complimentary advance copies of the magazine with a letter signed by our CEO at world headquarters in New York and our editor-in-chief in Moscow or Budapest. They went to VIP lists that included journalists, business and government leaders, post office and kiosk distribution companies, advertising agencies, and libraries. The result was a great deal of word-of-mouth publicity, requests for subscriptions, and a flurry of news articles. We also sent a special mailing to 100,000 households with above-average demographics in Kharkov, an industrial city in the Ukraine, which attracted attention because no company had ever done such a broad consumer mailing.

A few words of caution about using direct mail in these markets, however.

In Russia it's best to send your material registered mail and in a plain brown envelope. Attractive packages tend to get "lost" in the postal system—like pretty postcards that never reach your family at home. Registered mail is very cheap—and payable in rubles—so cost is not an issue. In Hungary, direct mail is virtually unknown. That can give you a great marketing advantage if you're experienced in the field, but can be dangerous if you're not.

Be wary of the quality of existing lists. We saw some in Russia that seemed padded with names not even close to our target audience. It's best to try to build your own list to meet your objectives and target audience. Then guard it carefully for proprietary reasons and use it for future mailings.

We also used large hot-air balloons and billboards in both launches. The balloons drew a crowd, and the Moscow one made the front page of *Advertising Age.* Our Moscow billboards were unusual enough that Tom Brokaw mentioned them on the "NBC Nightly News." He'd seen them on his way from the airport into Moscow to cover the Bush-Gorbachev summit the week after our launch. It was great timing and gave us a second round of media coverage.

At kiosks we used point-of-sale displays (it's called "spot of sale" in Russia). These are inexpensive tools, which can be updated easily if you have a new message every month, as we do when a new issue of the magazine comes out. And we gave calculators and pocket alarm clocks to our distributors to encourage them to answer questionnaires on delivery and sales results. Basic premium ideas here—but unusual there, so the returns were excellent.

If you're in the advertising business, it won't take you long after arriving in Budapest to notice the traffic jams and think, "Ah, drive time radio!" And it's true. Our research told us that, generally speaking, Hungarians listen to the radio more than people in Western Europe, and they watch television less—concentrated in the evening, when they watch the news and films. Almost all households have a TV. About 300,000 Hungarian households now have satellite dishes, one-fifth of them have a VCR, and one-quarter of the population watches cable TV.

Interestingly, radio is a weak advertising medium in Russia, because of the lack of car radios and the fact that in the evenings people prefer to read or watch television.

So we did some advertising in both markets. But the vast majority of our publicity efforts concentrated on media-relations techniques. These are much more cost-efficient and effective over the long term.

That brings me to the third lesson we learned: to trust your own instincts and professional knowledge, especially if you have international experience.

In Moscow, we were told repeatedly by local business colleagues that the only way we could expect coverage of our launch was to buy advertising. I've been told that in scores of countries. It simply isn't true. You may well be asked to advertise or get involved in a business venture by journalists. There is no clear separation between business and editorial, as we're used to at home. But professional news media relations work around the world when they are based on *real* news announcements and practiced with respect for journalists' needs as well as your own company's objectives.

We hosted news conferences for both launches. The Budapest event followed our Western format very closely. In Moscow, however, presentations are expected to be significantly longer—forty to sixty minutes rather than our more normal twenty—and if you can incorporate a historical perspective about your company and product, so much the better. Most reporters ask their best questions at the news conference, not waiting to do so in private after the general Q and A session, as is true in the West. On the contrary, as soon as the news conference is over, everyone rushes to the food—traditionally a full meal consumed at record speed. Russian journalists have learned from experience that if they don't get to the meal quickly, it will be gone—and food is a major enticement to attend a news conference.

So are giveaways, and it's worth your while to make them special. Knowing the long lines that Russians must endure, we gave each journalist a very large tote with a shoulder strap, featuring our logo in English and Russian, of course. Inside was a "traveling office"—a wide variety of office supplies in a leather case, also featuring our logo—just the items that are so hard to get in Moscow.

In Hungary, our giveaways also matched the market: another tote, with our logo in Hungarian and English—plus a business card holder, again featuring our bilingual logo. We were told executives are now getting and giving business cards for the first time, and have nowhere to keep them.

Our bilingual invitations to the news conference were also special. We engraved them, pictured both countries' flags, and individually wrote in the reporter's name. We were told these touches made our event stand out in journalists' minds.

At The Reader's Digest Association we have an advantage when it comes to generating global news coverage: We have eighteen international companies around the world. They released our launch news materials to their local media simultaneously with the news conferences in Moscow and Budapest, and that significantly increased our coverage worldwide.

I mentioned trusting your instincts and professional judgment. In Moscow we got great pressure from suppliers to invite government officials and others to the news conference. We refused, saying the news conference was strictly for working journalists, and its objective was solely to generate media coverage. You lose focus when you begin to mix messages and target audiences.

I believe the one hundred-plus journalists who attended appreciated our concentrating on them alone, and the extensive positive coverage about the new magazine and our company around the world reinforced our belief that we'd made the right decision. In fact, media coverage was so extensive and our magazine so popular in Russia and the Ukraine that we sold out within a few days. So we scaled back plans for significant additional promotions, relying primarily on mailings of each issue of the magazine to key journalists every month.

Which brings me to the fourth lesson—and probably the most important one of all: A "back to basics" approach is essential to success.

People may have little or no knowledge of your brand or your company. Take time up front to work with your operations colleagues to develop detailed business and marketing plans. Do your market research early, so you have time to recover from surprises. Think through your positioning carefully. Then pick one or two simple messages and repeat them over and over again.

Ours was "*Reader's Digest Válogatás*: World's most widely read magazine now on sale in Hungary"—and the same with our Russian magazine name. You saw the brand name and this phrase in everything we produced: our ads, news materials, promotional and point-of-sale pieces, VIP mailings, billboards, everywhere. It was played back in the media coverage.

Never miss an opportunity to picture your product and your logo. Frequency, focus, and consistency are key to making them familiar to your potential consumers.

A "back to basics" approach is closely related to the fifth lesson—and that is a relentless attention to details. Mies van der Rohe once said, "God is in the details." He was speaking of architecture, but his point is equally valid when it comes to product launches, especially in new markets.

Create a master list and update it often, sharing status reports with everyone involved in the project. Who *exactly* is responsible for printing and mailing the invitations, handling followup RSVPs and interview requests, arranging for translators and name plates on the head table, hiring photographers, writing and translating the news materials, seating people according to the correct protocol at banquets, making sure your video plays in the host country's technical format, having signage at the press coverage site so it's *your* logo that appears in photographs, not the hotel's. The list is endless, and important. Many a key message has been lost at a news conference because no one checked the microphone or arranged for coat racks and umbrella stands.

> *SPEECH TIP:* Once again, as throughout, Howard's enumeration of highly specific details serves to sharply focus her listeners' imaginations. No doubt audience members planning to do business in Russia or Hungary carefully noted her words of wisdom; perhaps some even thanked their lucky stars for a reminder about particular items they themselves would otherwise have been likely to overlook.

Make sure your translations are impeccably accurate. We're lucky, because we have our own editors to cross-check translations. Be sure you find someone you trust—and someone who understands the local idiom. Also, watch for misunderstandings when you are working in the metric system. Thank goodness one of our bright people actually took out his ruler and measured: the *Izvestia* ad we thought was a half page had shrunk to less than a quarter that size when the specs came, in centimeters, for our final approval.

Which brings me to lesson number six—communications.

During the three days of the failed Soviet coup in August, we saw the dramatic power of instant global communications. When you have FAXes and cellular phones and computer bulletin boards—not to mention unjammed broadcasts of the Voice of America, the BBC, and CNN International—communicating to Soviet citizens and the world *what* is happening *as* it happens, you realize the long-term ramifications of perestroika. In fact, Gorbachev credited the BBC with his ability to follow news, during his capture, of the coup's progress and Yeltsin's efforts to resist. And I was able to talk by phone with our editor-in-chief in Moscow the very day of the coup, as he was watching the tanks through his office window. He told us he received several FAXes from us the next day as well.

As one observer put it, the very technologies that George Orwell once feared would be the tools of totalitarian control helped ensure the coup wouldn't succeed.

But it's all a matter of degree.

Today, there still are only one hundred international lines going into Russia. For months, our editor-in-chief had five phones on his desk, none of them his. To make an international call he had to go two floors down to the FAX room and dial the rotary phone for hours before getting an international line. Further, the Russian post office is not always reliable or secure. So we rely on overnight courier services.

These communications problems are exacerbated by the fact that most of the people you are dealing with will be listening and speaking in a second language. I don't think the problems of the language barrier can be overestimated. Each conversation in an international country takes place on two planes. You are thinking and speaking in English. But your colleagues probably have to do the translation in their heads before they can comprehend and respond. I think people sometimes pretend to understand, not wanting to interrupt the flow of the conversation for clarification. Or maybe they think they *do* understand, but subtleties are lost. It's important to state things as simply as possible and be crystal clear in your communications. Get agreements in writing to see if your expectations match theirs. And talk frequently to be sure there's an easy avenue for questions.

On the other hand, be wary of business people who have traveled in the West saying they speak no English. Even if they require a translator, they may understand more English than they let on, and you should be careful not to discuss your negotiating strategy with colleagues in asides, thinking no one else understands.

The seventh lesson is to allow much, much more time to accomplish each activity than you would here at home. It's important to be realistic in your expectations. After a period of frustrating inaction and delays on our Hungarian launch, I went for advice to one of my colleagues, a Hungarian who now lives in New York.

"It's the culture," he said. "Over the years they've learned: 'I don't have to do it. First, it may not happen. If it does happen and it's that important, someone else will do it.'" Of course, he's right. Former General Secretary and KGB Chief Yuri Andropov called it an "accumulated indifference." Desire and envy are backwards in the republics of the former Soviet Union—not *keeping up* with the Ivanovs but *tearing them down.* Brezhnev's grandson Andrei put it in an epigram: "In your country you struggle so the poor will be rich, and in ours we struggle so the rich will be poor."

For generations people have been denied access to the rest of the world, penalized for showing initiative or making a profit, and taught that capitalism and private ownership are evil. Indifference replaced initiative because that was the best way to survive.

Yes, there are problems with bureaucratic inefficiency, shortage of technology and equipment, manual systems, and lack of experience. But there also are severe cultural obstacles—legacies of the communist rule. For years people waited for orders and responded to the demands of a grandiose central plan. There were no choices; Moscow did the thinking for everyone. Now their beliefs are shattered, the state is collapsing, and there is no order in their lives. Many are frightened and wish that order could return.

Overcoming that numbness and encouraging individual initiative may take generations. So will attention to deadlines, the ability to be flexible and adaptable, and the desire to work around obstacles that come up in any major project as a matter of course.

At a recent public relations seminar, a Swiss executive talked about his company's entry into Eastern Europe. He said it would be at least two years before one could assume local people would understand the professional standards we take for granted. He also suggested spending more time doing the work yourself than you would think you needed to. In Budapest, for example, all the proposed press conference sites initially shown for our approval were much too small and had no provision for translators or television. You can't manage a project like this from a desk in the United States. Nothing beats on-site knowledge.

Be prepared for the phone calls and FAXes that start out, "I am very sorry to inform you again of the problems we face in ..." whatever, or "I wanted to ask you once again about . . ." such and such. And be equally alert to the questions that *don't* come when they should. Remember Sherlock Holmes's best clue came when the dog *didn't* bark.

I have been speaking here as if the former Soviet Union and Hungary are similar in this regard—but they are not. There is a world of difference between seventy and forty years.

In Hungary, there are people alive who remember how it was before 1945. They are helping others relearn the old culture. It happens in small ways, such as when our business manager in Budapest asks his mother where to find a street. In both the new Commonwealth of Independent States and Hungary, they are busy returning cities and streets to their pre-communist names, Leningrad reverting to St. Petersburg being the best-known example. So maps and street signs rarely match. And it happens on the major issues of values and culture and the work ethic.

On the other hand, in the new Commonwealth, very few people have memories of freedom. Fewer still have any feel for business. The tradition of the merchant class in old Russia was never very strong, and Stalin eliminated the best of them when he wiped out the independent farmers who opposed communalizing agriculture. Even today, the word "biznessmen" is derogatory; it most often means speculator. The average citizen believes there is little difference between business and mafia; both are about accumulating wealth at the expense of others.

So keep pushing—but try to be tolerant. And remember that, as you work to fix the problems, you should have a tremendous sense of satisfaction that in some small way you are helping to build a knowledge infrastructure and put in place systems that will help those countries develop a free market economy.

And speaking of help, don't hesitate to ask for it yourself. That's lesson number eight: Take advantage of local resources to help you achieve your objectives.

Our decision to hire Burson-Marsteller to help with our Moscow launch was clearly the right one. The U.S. head of the office speaks fluent Russian and understands both the news media and the Russian culture. He's backed by a superb team, many of them Russian citizens.

That's key. You probably don't need any more North American eyes and ears. You need *local* help—so fluency in the local language and sensitivity to the local culture are essential. You need someone who'll catch you if your ad looks like it was created from an American perspective. Or help you do some local research on your brand knowledge and perception. Or remind you that in Hungary last names come before first.

They might also help you sleep more easily at night if, only twenty-four hours from the news conference, you still don't have a menu—or even know which restaurant will cater your lunch for the journalists—even though you've been negotiating for two months. This is apparently normal and nothing to worry about, but it helps to have someone you've learned to trust tell you that!

Another valuable contact is the U.S. Embassy—especially the press attaché at the United States Information Service. They have daily dealings with journalists and are pleased to give you advice and practical counsel on how to conduct business in their countries.

Lesson nine: You'll want to pay attention to money even more than usual. If you're able to negotiate contracts in Russia so you pay most of your promotion and public relations bills in rubles, as we did, you'll save a great deal.

This is a key point. For international business purposes the new Commonwealth is essentially without a currency. Don't be surprised if there's an ulterior motive to generate hard currency when some of your suppliers or partners make recommendations. Be prepared for some tough negotiating. *Izvestia* held up our ad, first demanding hard currency and then saying we had to change the wording to comply with some law. We held firm. The ad ran—and we paid in rubles. But no one seems to care much what a contract says. The laws are changing so fast and inflation is such a factor that you sometimes will feel like Alice after she stepped through the Looking Glass, where the words mean whatever someone chooses them to mean.

You also have to be flexible. You may have to agree to inflationary increases in your contracts. Inflation is 35 percent in Hungary. It's virtually unmeasurable in the new Commonwealth republics, where prices seem to go up almost every day. You should remember the valuable advice an experienced Sovietologist gave me: not to make them lose face. In that way Russians are more Asian than the Asians.

In Hungary there's a 25 percent value-added tax on any services ordered by an American company. If you have established a Hungarian company—as The Reader's Digest Association has—services should be ordered and paid for by your local subsidiary. You won't save the VAT on car rentals, taxi services, and entertainment, but you will on everything else. Twenty-five percent can be a lot of money, so it's well worth your time to investigate the legal and financial details.

In the former Soviet Union, as the laws change, you may be asked by your suppliers to change the entity to which you pay your money—or the country in which it is paid. This can be complicated, and you'll want competent counsel to be sure you comply with their laws.

Lesson ten: Don't forget your employees. Product launches in new markets can be a source of immense pride if you publicize them internally. In addition to newsletters, video tapes, and Russian food in our cafeterias, Reader's Digest offices around the world celebrated the launch of the Russian-language edition with a variety of special events. In South Africa, each employee received a vodka glass carrying the Russian logo and participated in a contest about the new magazine. Our British company arranged for a parade of Cossacks from the Moscow State Circus, which was appearing in London, to ride around Berkeley Square mounted on horseback, holding up large covers of the Russian-language edition. Our Swiss company placed ads in the leading business paper promising a copy of the new magazine to the first hundred people who called. In Hong Kong and the United States, employees celebrated with free cakes picturing the Russian edition.

Indeed, there is much to celebrate. Of course, there are difficulties, but there is also cause for optimism and hope.

There is a highly educated work force in these markets. One third of the world's engineers and scientists live in Eastern Europe and the former Soviet Union. In Moscow, they have a clean, fast, and very inexpensive subway system. They also handle airport parking problems more efficiently than anywhere I know. If you over-park, they'll take your license plate off your car, and you don't get it back until you pay a forty-ruble fine on the spot. Somebody ought to tell that to the folks at JFK or La Guardia! Many people care about quality and are willing to learn. Our Russian magazine, printed in Moscow, ranks with some of the best of our forty-one editions around the world.

Our Hungarian editor-in-chief put it well when he warned that pessimism is the real enemy. Declining living standards, increasing crime, and political squabbling result in a natural preoccupation with the negative aspects of the changeover. But, he reminded us, traditionally on Wall Street, the peak of pessimism is a signal for a new bull market.

At The Reader's Digest Association, we are investing our money and time because we believe that, over the long term, we can develop profitable businesses in Eastern Europe and the new republics. That's been our history ever since 1938 when we started our first international company in the United Kingdom and rapidly expanded throughout Europe, Scandinavia, and Latin America in the '40s, right after the war. We are willing to invest, to become a part of the local culture, to build businesses that will be profitable in the future. Most recently, only a few weeks after the Berlin Wall came down, we were in East Germany distributing free copies of our German magazine. Today, we have over 400,000 paid subscribers in the eastern part of Germany alone—and these customers also are buying our books and music collections.

So we want to be there now, encouraging the entrepreneurial spirit and being part of the rebuilding of a free market economy.

And we know we can't fail when—as one columnist observed—today it's possible to sit in a Moscow or Budapest McDonald's eating a Big Mac, reading the local edition of *Reader's Digest*, and griping aloud about the fools in the Kremlin!

Thank you for your attention. And good luck as you enter these exciting new markets.

Economic Assistance and Business Opportunities in the Independent States of the Former Soviet Union

LAWRENCE M. LESSER
Adjunct Professor of Business and Management
University of Maryland

Delivered to the Ninth Annual Washington Consortium of Schools of Business Faculty Research Forum, Washington, D.C., April 17, 1993

SUMMARY: Warning of financial hazards in the turbulent states of the former Soviet Union, a business professor cautions U.S. policy makers against risky lending policies and expensive debt forgiveness. Lesser recommends grand barter transactions as a more fiscally prudent, mutually beneficial system for official aid and private investment in the new Independent States.

My presentation today deals with economic assistance and business opportunities in the New Independent States (NIS) of the former Soviet Union.

The great nineteenth-century French historian and political philosopher Alexis de Tocqueville observed in his famous book *Democracy in America* that the futures of the United States and Russia are bound tightly together by history. He spoke of "two great nations in the world which . . . have suddenly taken their place among the leading nations, making the world take note of their birth and of their greatness almost at the same instant." But, he added, "Their point of departure is different and their paths diverse; nevertheless, each seems called by some secret design of Providence one day to hold in its hands the destinies of half the world."

Now, of course, communism has been cast aside, and freedom and democracy are on the rise in these NIS. And, in keeping with de Tocqueville's observation of a century ago, the United States, as the sole remaining superpower, has a unique opportunity to nurture this transformation so that it will continue along its present course.

In seeking public support for aid to Russia, President Clinton recently outlined America's values and priorities. He said, "We support democracy, we support free markets, we support freedom . . . it is essential that we act prudently but urgently to do all that we can to strike a strategic alliance with Russian reform."

The economic and political transformation of the former Soviet Union, which Ronald Reagan once called an "evil empire," is a slowly evolving process that is mysterious to outside observers and painful for those directly affected.

At the recent meeting of the seven major industrialized nations in Tokyo, the Group of Seven agreed upon a $28 billion package of aid to Russia. They also agreed to reschedule $15 billion of Russia's debt to the West.

For several years now, American businesses have been at the forefront in creating new markets in the countries of the former Soviet Union and in assisting with restructuring the economies of these New Independent States. A few figures will illustrate the commercial importance of Russia and the other NIS to the U.S. During 1992, for example, the United States exported $3.6 billion of goods and services to the NIS. Over the past two years, U.S. exports of manufactured goods increased by 65 percent and now exceed one billion dollars. American companies are the largest foreign investors in Russia today, with some $400 million. And more than 300 American companies now have offices in Moscow. Many are establishing a base in other cities as well.

> *SPEECH TIP:* Having opened with quotations and a philosophical tone, Lesser now shifts to a very straightforward presentation of actualities. He lays out important facts and figures that will serve as a foundation for his arguments throughout.

Russia and the other NIS possess many valuable resources. For example, Russia grows more wheat than any other country in the world. The NIS also represent one of the largest sources of strategic metals and minerals, including aluminum, gold, nickel, and platinum. And, most important from an American perspective, Russia is the largest oil producer in the world, larger even than Saudi Arabia.

> *SPEECH TIP*: Turning his discussion from NIS resources to NIS needs, the speaker continues to build a strong case for the possibility of mutually beneficial economic exchange.

But Russia and the other republics also have critical needs that American companies are particularly well suited to meet. These include the need to enhance their oil production output, which has declined as a result of massive breakdowns in equipment. Other needs include a more efficient food distribution system, improved safety at nuclear power plants, financial and technical assistance in dismantling nuclear weapons and converting defense facilities to peaceful commercial purposes, housing for the returning Russian military, and modernization of the telecommunications and transportation infrastructure.

If progress toward a market economy can be sustained and if some of these priorities can be met, millions of new jobs would be created, productivity would grow, and the NIS could become the fastest growing market in the world by the end of the decade. However, the continuation of economic reform and the transition to a market economy has not been a smooth one and it will not be easy in the future. For many obstacles lie ahead that pose grave political and financial risks both for the United States and for American companies that seek to do business in this part of the world.

SPEECH TIP: Now Lesser "lowers the boom": he highlights figures and points to conditions that spell danger for American investors—and American taxpayers.

Since December, Russia has failed to meet its required interest payments on $4.2 billion of U.S. agricultural credit guarantees, which it has used to purchase American grain. It is now in default on more than $600 million, and the total is expected to grow to more than a billion dollars shortly. International lenders have started to file claims with the U.S. Department of Agriculture, which already has paid out about $180 million. Over the next several years, American taxpayers may have to ante up an estimated $4.5 billion to cover these losses.

I might note parenthetically that this $4.5 billion potential default is more than double the losses already incurred by the U.S. Government as a result of similar agricultural credit guarantees the Bush Administration extended to Saddam Hussein prior to Iraq's invasion of Kuwait. Now it appears that the Clinton Administration is compounding the problem by continuing the prior administration's policy of extending food credits and other export credits through the Export-Import Bank to non-creditworthy borrowers. These mounting losses will be borne by American taxpayers. It should be noted that Russia also has failed to pay debts of more than $200 million it owed to fifty-seven American companies.

Another serious obstacle to foreign investment in the NIS is the lack of a reliable legal system. Moreover, it is difficult to establish title to property. And there is an inadequate banking system, as well as excessive regulation and taxation imposed on foreign businesses.

One of the most egregious examples, which is slowing investment by major oil companies, is a $5.50 tax per barrel on oil exports. This export duty eliminates the large profits American and other foreign oil companies say they need to compensate them for the enormous risks of investing in Russia at a time of great political and financial uncertainty. If the tax is not repealed, the companies will hold back, unless they are able to negotiate exemptions from it.

Conoco, the first American oil company to make a major financial commitment in Russia, was able to win an exemption from the onerous export duty. But it got burned anyway. Last year, Conoco reached a preliminary agreement with Russia to develop a major oil field. And it invested $20 million along with its partners. The Russian government, however, turned around and awarded the rights to a Russian consortium instead.

At their recent summit meeting in Vancouver, President Clinton and Russian President Yeltsin agreed to a U.S. proposal to establish a joint commission to sort out the problems that are holding back American petroleum investment in Russia.

Winston Churchill once described Russia as "a riddle wrapped in a mystery inside an enigma." As we look to the future, we hope that Russia will continue its march toward economic and political integration with the West and the adoption of Western values. On the other hand, the ongoing political turmoil could perpetuate the deadlock in policy-making or, worse, degenerate into anarchy or dictatorship. The potential rewards for American and other foreign companies are enormous. But the risks are also huge.

> *SPEECH TIP:* Harking back to the speech's opening citations, Lesser's use of this Churchill quotation marks a turning point in the speech, signaling the renewal of a more optimistic tone.

One possible solution to this dilemma is barter. The United States rightly wants to extend a helping hand to Russia and the other NIS. American business wants to expand investment there. Barter is a concept that the people of the former Soviet Union are very familiar with, since they bartered goods for years with their former Eastern European allies. Barter also was widely used between producing and consuming regions of their own country, and among individuals. Barter can provide the NIS with goods and services they need while at the same time offering the U.S. government and American firms a way to minimize risk.

Under barter, the U.S. could provide managerial and technical assistance, along with food aid, to encourage the development of competitive food markets in the NIS. Perhaps U.S. energy producers could share their technological expertise to help Russia and the other NIS overhaul their outmoded energy production facilities and distribution systems. In return, given the NIS's lack of hard currency, American companies could receive payment in oil.

On April 6, a serious accident occurred at a nuclear weapons complex in Siberia when a tank of radioactive waste exploded and burned. It was the worst nuclear accident since the Chernobyl nuclear plant disaster in 1986. In the aftermath of this latest incident, which is just the most recent of many at Soviet-built nuclear power plants, the United States should provide technology and equipment to improve safety at the many aging nuclear power plants in the former Soviet Union that have been identified by the International Atomic Energy Agency as unsafe.

Since the U.S. already is helping the Russians store surplus plutonium that has been dismantled from nuclear warheads, we should offer to take their plutonium as well as their uranium in payment for our assistance. By doing so, we will also lessen the likelihood of nuclear proliferation, since Russia has sought to sell its surplus plutonium and weapons-grade highly enriched uranium on the open market in order to gain hard currency.

> *SPEECH TIP:* Lesser offers many innovative, yet solidly practical suggestions for strategic cooperation between the U.S. and the NIS. By presenting his ideas one after another, without excessive elaboration, he conveys to listeners that many more such possibilities exist for exploration and consideration.

A barter deal also could be structured around construction of housing for the Russian military, which is returning from Eastern Europe and the non-Russian republics of the former Soviet Union. American and other Western companies could build housing complexes both for the Russian military and for civilians. The construction companies could be paid in oil. Or, Western developers could be given title to land and other assets controlled by the military, as has been suggested by the Heritage Foundation. The private developers would be free to build housing and develop the land and other assets for commercial and private purposes.

Unfortunately, the United States has been slow to grasp the enormous potential that grand barter deals offer. In fact, the Internal Revenue Service and the Bureau of Customs have gone out of their way to discourage international barter transactions involving American firms.

Meanwhile, several of our trade competitors already are bartering goods with Russia. For example, Canada has bartered wheat for timber and cotton and is negotiating a three-way swap of wheat for Russian diamonds. In another example, Australia recently traded one-and-a-half million metric tons of wheat for aluminum.

Let me conclude with the following observations. First, I believe that it is in our interest that the political and economic transformation now underway in Russia and the other NIS succeed. And we should help. But I also have doubts about the wisdom of the United States proceeding with additional large-scale financial assistance to the NIS in the form of cash grants, loans, and credit guarantees when so much debt already is piling up and the Russians have shown no willingness to repay what they already owe us.

And while the United States and the other G-7 countries consider restructuring Russia's existing debt, President Clinton should refuse to write off both the $84 billion in debt to us that Russia inherited from the former Soviet Union, as well as Russia's own new and growing debt to the United States, as several members of Congress have suggested.

Instead, we need creative alternatives today in international finance, such as barter. And now there is fresh evidence that President Clinton may be warming up to the idea. In a written response to Senator James Exon (D-Neb), who is one of the leading Congressional proponents of barter, the President said, "American companies need greater access to countertrade and other trading methods." Secretary of Agriculture Mike Espy and Commerce Secretary Ron Brown also have expressed interest in using barter with the former Soviet republics. And by the end of next week, an interagency task force is expected to report to President Clinton on the feasibility of expanding American use of barter in trade with the NIS. The report, which was prepared pursuant to an amendment sponsored by Senator Exon last year, may help to get President Clinton's attention as well as to focus public attention on the merits of barter.

Grand barter transactions, such as a large-scale food-for-oil deal—and others like it—make sense for several reasons.

First, the use of oil and other resources as collateral for Western loans and as payment for goods and services would enable American and other Western firms to minimize the risks of doing business today in the NIS and protect American taxpayers against default.

Second, they would advance U.S. economic and political relations with Russia and the other NIS.

And finally, agreements of this kind would further America's national security interests because they would enable us to diversify our energy resources and reduce our reliance on oil from the volatile Persian Gulf.

Global Competitiveness:
Five Steps to Failure

RICHARD J. STEGEMEIER
Chairman, President, and Chief Executive Officer
Unocal Corporation

Delivered at the CEO Night of the Financial Executives Institute, Los Angeles, California, February 20, 1992

SUMMARY: The head of a major oil company analyzes the major forces that inhibit America's competitiveness in the world marketplace.

This is a pivotal year for America. We're going to elect a president and a Congress. We're going to see if we can pull out of a deep and painful recession. And we're going to see if the other military superpower—the former Soviet Union—can begin to move toward political freedom and a market economy, or if it will fall into darkness and dictatorship once again.

Because it is a pivotal year for America, I wish we were off to a more promising start. In early January, we watched the president and a group of 18 corporate executives travel to Japan to lobby for more favorable trade relations.

"It ain't fair!" they said.

That's the kind of complaint I hear from my grandchildren when they're squabbling over their toys.

I lived and worked in the Far East for thirteen years. In my view, the Japanese are doing exactly what we've asked them to do—selling us high-quality goods at reasonable prices. The Japanese succeed because they work hard. They are well educated. They are committed to quality. And their government does not burden the productive economy with unreasonable regulations and misguided tax policies. I'm sure it is tempting to bash Japan in an election year, but America is starting to behave like the crybaby of the Western world. Not to be outdone, some Japanese politicians decided to retaliate. American workers are lazy and unproductive, they said. Such comments are totally unrealistic.

American workers—at least those I know in the petroleum industry—are as good as any workers in the world. Remember, it was Americans who put out the hundreds of oil-well fires in war-torn Kuwait. And we did it more quickly and efficiently than anyone dreamed possible.

Americans can do the job. I don't doubt it for a minute. We're intelligent, hardworking, and ambitious. So why can't we compete?

SPEECH TIP: Stegemeier's opening remarks establish a tone that many listeners will recognize as "tough talk." Right from the start, the speaker makes it clear that he does not intend to mince words in his discussion of American competitiveness abroad.

I believe the answer goes much deeper than Japanese trade practices. Several decades ago, America became the most affluent society in the history of the world. Before long, we started taking our success for granted. We created a myth—that big business or big government can do it all, and the average person won't have to pay. And we began to pursue an impossible dream—the dream of a risk-free society.

We became obsessed with what seemed wrong with America, and we ignored everything that was right. Instead of working within the system, we started to play against the system. Instead of saying "can do," we started saying "you do." Instead of joining hands, we started pointing fingers.

It's no surprise, then, that some Americans have started pointing fingers at Japan. We'd like to blame others for problems that are largely our own. We see this happening every day in our Congress, in our courts, and in our communities. In reality, we've been following what you might call a five-step path to competitive failure. Those five steps are

SPEECH TIP: The speaker's "five steps to failure" will form the structural skeleton of his presentation. This numbering of topical material helps unite and clarify diverse subject areas, and the "sum total" numeral sometimes helps listeners review and recall each element even long after the speech is over.

Number 1: Regulation

Number 2: Litigation

Number 3: Confiscation

Number 4: Taxation, and

Number 5: Education.

These are not economic problems per se. Ultimately, they are political, social, and legal problems, involving deep-seated attitudes and expectations. But they entail increasing levels of government control, administration, and subsidy. In other words, bureaucracy. And, as the saying goes: "The nearest thing to immortality in this world is a government bureaucracy."

Here in the United States, we have created the largest, most intrusive government bureaucracy outside of the old Soviet Union. It's ironic that as the Soviet republics struggle to establish free markets and economic liberties, we're moving steadfastly in the opposite direction, all in the name of fairness and equality. As economist Milton Friedman recently observed, "Why should we be any better at socialism than the Soviets?"

Let's review these five steps to competitive failure one by one. First, regulation. Some regulations are necessary, but all regulation comes at a stiff price. Regulation distorts economic incentives, it raises costs to business and consumers, it builds meddlesome bureaucracies, and it creates opportunities to "game" the system. For these reasons, the most competitive economies try to keep regulation at the essential minimum. Otherwise, we run the risk of tangling up our economy in costly, complex, and counterproductive sets of rules and regulations.

I fear we are losing the battle. Despite periodic efforts to deregulate, America today has more rules and regulations than ever before. The *Federal Register* is the Bible of federal regulations. In 1954 it had 10,000 pages. In 1991 it had about 60,000 pages. That's 160 pages per day to read, understand, and implement. Failure can mean substantial fines or even jail sentences. It's a textbook of "gotcha's."

We have to ask ourselves, is all this rule-making really necessary? This tidal wave of regulations absorbs financial capital and human resources that could otherwise be used to improve productivity and stimulate innovation. Economist Thomas Hopkins estimates that federal regulations are costing American consumers about $400 billion every year.

How much is $400 billion? It's about ten times the size of our trade deficit with Japan. It's about double the annual cost of public education in America, from kindergarten through the twelfth grade. It's about 33 percent larger than our entire defense budget. It's enough to give every household in America $4,000 every year.

SPEECH TIP: Not only are quantities in the millions and billions inherently difficult to grasp, most citizens of a nation as huge and prosperous as the United States have grown thoroughly inured to their mention. Here and elsewhere in his speech, Stegemeier "translates" large figures into practical comparisons, the better to convey their values and meaning.

These costs are going up. Environmental costs in particular have been rising steadily for the past fifteen years. Data from the Environmental Protection Agency show that mandated compliance expenditures reached $99 billion, about 25 percent of our total regulatory burden. It's estimated that the new Clean Air Act and other environmental regulations could cost the petroleum industry another $20 billion or more a year by the end of the decade. That's equal to the entire earnings of the twenty largest energy companies in America last year. And that's just for one industry.

Some costs cannot be measured—at least directly. For years, the U.S. petroleum industry has been blocked by moratoria from drilling for new oil and gas reserves in the most promising places in America—offshore California and the North Slope of Alaska. A slew of other regulations and tax policies has inhibited drilling and development in many other places. In response, major American oil companies feel they have little choice but to focus their exploration efforts overseas. Some people complain about oil companies "leaving" the United States. But as one petroleum executive put it, "We're not leaving, we're being thrown out!"

As a result, U.S. oil production continues to decline. In the fourth quarter of 1991, production fell to less than 7.3 million barrels a day, the lowest level in thirty years. Since 1982 the industry has lost more than 350,000 jobs. Imports of crude oil and petroleum products provided 45 percent of our needs last year at a cost of about $50 billion. That's nearly 80 percent of our total trade deficit for 1991, substantially greater than our import cost of Japanese cars.

Few seem to care that the petroleum industry has learned over the years how to drill and develop energy resources safely. And few seem to realize that imported oil is brought to this country by tanker and that tankers pose a much greater risk of spills than offshore platforms and pipelines.

But the implications go far beyond our coastlines. We fought a vicious war against Iraq last year, in good part because of the strategic value of the oil resources threatened by Saddam Hussein. That war added tens of billions of dollars to our oil import bill, not to mention the tragic loss of human lives. That war was the ultimate environmental disaster. Now I see that the Iraqi dictator has told his people that he plans to rebuild his military capability. According to the *New York Times*, Saudi Arabia has been pushing the Bush Administration "to organize a large covert action campaign" in order to topple Saddam's regime. Some say that the CIA has gotten the go-ahead to do it.

Like it or not, if we don't want a domestic energy industry, the Middle East is our problem, and it will not go away. You can see how our government's domestic energy policies weaken our strategic position overseas. More than a century ago, William Gladstone, the prime minister of England, said, "Here is my first principle of foreign policy: Good government at home." His words are as true today as they were then. An effective energy policy for America would reduce our demand for imports and help stabilize the world petroleum industry.

To the degree we can diversify petroleum supplies, develop alternative energies, and improve energy efficiency, the strategic importance of Middle East oil reserves will be diminished. Obviously, the lesson here is not to abolish all regulation. Our goal must be to ensure that every regulation is truly needed and cost-effective.

Now let's consider step number 2: Litigation. The profession of law enjoys a long and distinguished tradition in the United States, particularly as the champion of our personal rights and liberties. But sometimes you can have too much of a good thing. It's become a truism in recent years that we live in the most litigious society on earth. Last August, the Vice President's Council on Competitiveness estimated that Americans spend as much as $380 billion on the direct and indirect costs of litigation each year. Only 15 percent of that $380 billion is believed to go to the clients. The rest goes for attorneys' fees and other costs and expenses in an endless search not for justice but for deep pockets.

These expenditures support an army of attorneys. According to recent data, California has about 58,000 scientists and engineers with doctoral degrees. We have about 92,000 actively practicing attorneys—58 percent more. But if you're really looking for lawyers, go to Washington. The nation's capital has more than 15,000 attorneys in private practice alone—one attorney for every forty people, by far the highest ratio in the country. Who knows how many more attorneys work in the federal government—churning out 160 pages of new laws and regulations every day?

What do scientists and engineers do? They produce VCRs, autos, and computers. What do lawyers do? Lawyers produce laws, regulations, and court cases. The net result: Americans are fighting each other in court while others are competing in the global marketplace.

Now let's turn to step number 3: Confiscation. This could be the key business issue of the 1990s. It is based on the Fifth Amendment to the Constitution—the so-called "Takings" clause. Everyone believes that the Fifth Amendment is our protection against self incrimination. That's true, but the second half reads as follows: "No person shall be . . . deprived of life, liberty or property, without due process of law; nor shall private property be taken for public use without just compensation." That last phrase, "without just compensation," is critical. It is the constitutional foundation of our economic system. Let me give you an example from the petroleum industry—one that I've already touched on in my earlier comments. Over the years, the industry has spent about $500 million for the exploration rights to 127 leases offshore Florida, North Carolina, and in the Aleutian Basin area of Alaska. We've invested as much as $2 billion more for geologic work in these areas. Now these lease blocks are locked in moratoria. We cannot drill, nor can we get our money back. Our property has been confiscated.

Unocal property has been taken only five times in the last 101 years—in Mexico, Argentina, Venezuela, Iran, and now in the United States. Naturally enough, the petroleum industry has turned its attention to new exploration and development overseas. It's estimated that the industry will spend about $14 billion in foreign countries this year. That's more lost jobs and investment for America.

Once again, we have to wonder about a government that tries to open trade doors in Japan, while closing economic doors in the United States. Is our system truly the economic model for the world? Or is it becoming a copy of the failed economic policies of Eastern Europe?

Step number 4 is Taxation. Taxes are a necessary cost of business. They also provide important economic incentives and disincentives. America is not one of the most heavily taxed countries. But state, local, and federal taxes represent almost 40 percent of our enormous GNP.

Also, you have to question how our tax system is structured. Take capital gains, for example. In most industrialized countries, the long-term capital gains tax is either relatively small or nonexistent. In Germany, for example, it's zero. In Japan, it works out to about 1 percent. In the U. S., of course, the long-term capital gains tax rate is 28 percent.

The tax on corporate dividends is another example. Dividends are taxed twice in this country. If a company earns a dollar for dividends, it is first taxed at the corporate rate—reducing it to as little as 61 cents. Then it is taxed to the individual, reducing it to about 40 cents or less here in California.

Occasionally, U. S. business faces punitive taxes. Ten years ago, the petroleum industry paid a windfall profits tax, which took as much as 90 percent of every dollar above a certain level of income. Punitive taxes punish success and help spread the misconception that profits equal greed. They discourage investment, innovation, and the creation of jobs.

Profits are not evil. Profits are not buried in the back yard. They are reinvested in new jobs and products.

A small capital gains tax rate is an economic signal that tells investors to put their money into new private businesses that create jobs and wealth for the community. A high capital gains tax and double taxation of dividends are strong disincentives to invest in companies. In the global arena, such tax policies help create competitive disadvantages.

The fifth step is Education—or perhaps I should say the lack of it. The U. S. educational crisis is well documented. I don't plan to spend much time on this subject.

I'd just like to make one key point: Educational quality is not just a problem of more money. In California, we spend on average about $5,000 of state, local, and federal money per student per year in our public schools or about $150,000 per classroom. The average teacher salary is about $35,000. That's a big difference. Subtract the teacher's salary and another $5,000 or so for books and supplies, and the overhead cost of running that classroom is about $110,000. In other words, the classroom overhead is about three times its direct cost. No business could run that way.

Here's another thought. Students in Japan go to school about 220 days per year. Students in the United States go to school about 180 days per year—80 percent as much. We're either very foolish or very arrogant to think that our kids can learn as much as Japanese kids in just 80 percent of the time.

Let me make one more point. The most recent issue of *Scientific American* includes a fascinating study of the academic performance of refugee families from Indochina—the so-called "boat people." When they arrived in the United States these people spoke virtually no English. Often they came with nothing more than the shirts on their backs. Nonetheless, these students have excelled in our public schools, scoring above the national average on standardized tests. Their parents played the critical role in their success. After dinner on a typical weeknight, the family cleared the table and all the children sat down to do their homework. Older children helped younger children. This probably accelerated learning for everyone, which may be why children in large families tended to do better than children in small families. Although the parents didn't know enough to help with the homework themselves, they set the standards of study and monitored progress.

> *SPEECH TIP:* Although too much sarcasm might alienate an audience, speakers with a light touch can occasionally dip into irony or satire, especially if the presenter takes care to include himself in the joke. Stegemeier subtly assures his listeners of a shared affiliation in the colorful statement he makes next.

Compare this picture to the typical American family. After dinner, the table is cleared and the television set is turned on. Everyone sits down to a stimulating evening of "Cheers," "Three's Company," and "The Golden Girls."

No wonder the Japanese are, as they say in sports, "cleaning our clocks." We can't compete if we don't have a highly trained, well-educated work force. As the researchers point out, the U.S. educational system can still teach. Unfortunately, we've asked it to do too many things besides teaching the "Three R's."

We want our schools to prevent teenage pregnancy, stifle drug use, inhibit gang violence, and generally instill values, morality, and a respect for the law. We expect teachers to serve as proxies for parents. It's unrealistic to ask our schools to be everything to everybody. Once again, we're abdicating our responsibility.

Ladies and gentlemen, we live in a great country. Somehow, in recent years, we've begun to lose our way. To get back on track, we must ask ourselves some hard questions and squarely face our responsibilities.

We must learn to value our economic rights as well as our political rights. Together, they made America the envy of the world.

U.S. Investment in the New South Africa

PATRICK J. WARD
Chairman, President, and Chief Executive Officer
Caltex Petroleum Corporation

Delivered to the National Foreign Trade Foundation Council Conference, New York, New York, September 27, 1993

SUMMARY: Evaluating both the risks and rewards for American business enterprises in a climate of political change, a petroleum company executive advocates investing in South Africa's transition.

Good morning! I appreciate this opportunity to be with you this morning to open this conference. Since 1914, the National Foreign Trade Council has focused business attention on important issues in the international market, and I applaud their decision to hold this conference. The subject is vitally important not only for its impact on companies, but also for its effect on the lives of tens of millions of people.

To invest or not to invest in the new South Africa?

Represented here today, no doubt, is a wide range of viewpoints on that subject. We all have followed events in South Africa. Probably all of us already have formed certain conclusions. Possibly, each of us has a slightly different view.

SPEECH TIP: By acknowledging that audience members may already have strong and differing opinions on the subject of his speech, Ward signals his respect—not only for his listeners, but also for the complexity of the topic itself.

As investors we all ask ourselves: Do the rewards outweigh the risks?

So that you know where I am coming from when I tell you my conclusions, let me say that Caltex has had a stake in South Africa for eighty years. Among American corporations doing business there, we are the largest employer. Caltex has made an economic commitment and a moral commitment to South Africa.

> *SPEECH TIP:* Ward shows further respect and consideration for his listeners with an "out front" statement about his company's longstanding investments in South Africa. Speakers who attempt to gloss over their own corporate affiliation or over their company's vested interests not only invite suspicion, they insult the intelligence of their audiences.

Our investment policies further social aims as well as our business objectives. For example, our 50-50 partnerships with black South Africans in owning and operating retail service centers promote economic opportunity. We also feel that, through the Sullivan Code and related activities, we have played a part in the political changes now taking place.

The fact that Caltex has a large and growing investment in South Africa reflects the confidence that we feel concerning the future of that country. Our confidence is grounded, first, in the fundamentals of the situation. South Africa is a land rich in many ways. As an industrial nation, South Africa satisfies important requirements for foreign investment. You can find world-class infrastructure, varied entrepreneurial opportunities, a modern financial and legal system, mineral wealth, raw materials, plentiful and rich agricultural land, and a talented work force. South Africa also offers a rapidly broadening consumer class and an excellent distribution point to other countries in southern Africa.

Of course the risks exist. They include:

> *SPEECH TIP:* When your speech must detail the potential risks or "downsides" of a given proposal or argument, sooner can be better timing than later. Tackling such issues early in a speech allows you to deal with them and move on to more positive material. In the end, you will leave your audience with optimism and incentives rather than pessimism or doubts.

- Uncertainty regarding the outlook for a political settlement.

- The potential for further violence.

- Problems in training, education, productivity and cost of labor.

- Ambiguity currently concerning the investment code and economic policies, including taxation and foreign exchange.

Nevertheless, the potential is good for sustained economic growth. Provided a political settlement can be achieved soon, South Africa should experience sustained growth of 4 to 5 percent per year.

Most expert analysts on South Africa are optimistic. We recently asked a wide range of these observers inside and outside of South Africa about the probabilities of different scenarios. In a nutshell, they said the following:

- The likelihood of a favorable constitutional settlement is good.

- Forecasts also are favorable for a market-oriented economy with lower taxes and reduced inflation.

So, on balance, we are cautiously optimistic that a stable political environment and an internationally attractive economic management program will eventually be achieved.

Others, also from a business perspective, may not feel as positive about this equation. No doubt you have read or heard many stories about violence and recall the angry rhetoric of the extremists. I don't want to minimize the tensions nor the violence that has taken place. At the same time, however, it's important to maintain a perspective that rises above day-to-day events.

The daily events during the period of the American Revolutionary War must have provoked pessimism and despair in many minds about the prospects for independence. Many colonists sided with the Crown. Patriots argued among themselves. Indeed, the so-called "smart money" may have been on King George. Washington's army at Valley Forge was so poorly provisioned that the feet of his troops were shod only in rags. At that time, the worldly wise or the cynical might not have invested their confidence, not to mention their money, in leaders such as Washington, Jefferson, and Franklin. Despite the many obstacles, however, democratic government did come into being.

> **SPEECH TIP:** By striking a parallel with the early days of the American Revolution, Ward creates a potentially new—yet venerable—context for his listeners' perception of South Africa's political conditions today.

For certain, the situation in South Africa is far from settled. Negotiations are still in their early stages to achieve a constitution for a multiracial government. The Inkatha Freedom party and the Conservative Party have been boycotting the talks. The National Party is suffering splits, and the ANC is learning about the difficulties of becoming a political party. No party is completely satisfied with the draft constitution. Both white South Africans and black South Africans are divided among themselves. Moreover, bloodshed has been appalling, and there are those who threaten more violence if their demands are not met.

Furthermore, it stands to reason that there will be jockeying going on during the process of negotiating a constitution, and elections next year will conclude only the first of a two-stage transition process. That election will select the members of a constitution-making body or constituent assembly, which will devise and adopt the final constitution. A two-year deadline has been set for this process. This intervening time could well be marked by continued violence. We all know that political differences have, in the past, resulted in violence, and at least until there is a negotiated settlement, we should probably not expect to see real peace.

Of course, political stability is essential to general economic prosperity and corporate profits. I believe a workable constitution and political stability are likely to be achieved for two reasons: First, these things will be achieved because they must be achieved; if we as foreigners can easily see that the wounds must be healed, the need for reconciliation must be even more apparent to the people of South Africa. To people weary of the strife in their land, the electoral process and the rule of law offers a way toward civil debate and the beginning of the healing process.

In a news story about political violence in Tembisa, a township northeast of Johannesburg, it was reported that Joseph Nkuta, thirty-seven, was hospitalized with a leg wound. The armed attack in which he was shot apparently was designed to disrupt the transition to democracy and to deter residents from voting. When asked, Nkuta said, "Of course I'm going to vote. Maybe if you vote, some things will get better in this country. Maybe the killing will stop."

> *SPEECH TIP:* Not all effective quotations come from historical or other "celebrity" sources. Journalists routinely include man-or-woman-on-the-street quotes in their news articles, and Ward makes good use of this content, as well as the technique.

When such visions become shared beliefs, reality must change. I think we can all understand that people everywhere will resist injustice, and that some people resort to violence because they feel they have no better way of defending their interests. The ballot box and the political process offer peaceful alternatives. Even if the outcome fails to satisfy everyone at once, a fair process can offer hope for future progress. Where that hope exists, people tend to regard their government, constitution, laws, and social values as legitimate and, thus, are willing to work within the system.

So I believe that the imperative for a settlement and a successful transition to multiracial government is overwhelming. Even if extremists try to sabotage the transition, the more moderate center, made up of earnest people of all parties, can still exert the will to keep the transition on track and bring it to success.

Imperatives shape history. Like preservation of the Union and the elimination of slavery during the American Civil War, like the defense of England during the Battle of Britain, like the resolve of the United States throughout the Cold War that finally was vindicated, and, last but not least, like the release of Nelson Mandela, some things happen because they must happen because enough people believe in them.

Most people of South Africa want the transition to succeed.

Another intangible that seems to be leading South Africa to a brighter tomorrow is the spirit of the times in which we live. With long hindsight, the spirit of a period of time is easy to assess. It's not as easy to understand the opportunities available today that didn't exist as recently as ten or even two years ago.

In 1983, stalemate was the overriding factor in international relations. The United States and the Soviet Union were in their Cold War standoff, and around the globe, including in South Africa, there didn't seem to be much hope of resolving long-standing differences.

Something changed. The Cold War ended. The Soviet Union dissolved. The Berlin Wall fell, and Germany was reunified. North and South Korea began talks, and dialogue opened up in the Middle East.

Some situations haven't improved, but if we needed any conclusive evidence about the direction of things, it certainly came with the "handshake felt round the world" between Israeli Prime Minister Rabin and PLO Chairman Yassir Arafat. Stalemate, for the most part, seems to be over. In its place is rapid change. Boundary lines have changed so frequently that map makers are putting out revisions that are already out of date.

In that same spirit of change, stalemate in South Africa was broken. Following the government's release of Mr. Mandela from prison, talks began toward a multiracial government. Thus, the prevailing dynamic of change seems to be injecting a momentum into the affairs of South Africa that wasn't possible just ten years ago.

As business executives, we seek all the relevant facts about the market before forming important decisions. Likely rates of return, statistics on economic growth, production, distribution, and marketing are all important. We also want to know the background of potential business partners, the business culture, and the preferences of our customers. But there is a level of information that transcends factual data. That level of perception relates to the confidence we have in the times in which we live. It has to do with our sense of whether the tide of our fortunes is ebbing or is on the rise.

The existence of a process for change and accommodation suggests that South Africa's tide is rising. The struggle by no means is over. Violence still is a serious problem. Nevertheless, a goal has been set, and the widespread acceptance of that goal is a strong driver for a positive eventual conclusion.

As the political situation improves and basic agreements are reached on a constitution, the economic situation should also improve. As called for by Mr. Mandela, the removal of all remaining international sanctions would be greatly helpful. The focus of the country also needs to shift to the further improvement of the economy in order to meet rising expectations.

To sum up, I believe there are many reasons to conclude that the gains from investing in South Africa will outweigh the risks.

Finally, in all our concern about politics, about economic facts, about expectations, we shouldn't forget the individuals involved. An American company, when it invests in South Africa—with its philosophy, values, and skills—also makes its own special contribution to the economic and social health of that country and to its people.

The South African people, like people everywhere, have hopes, dreams, and aspirations. Caltex shares these. Our aim is that, through activities that enhance profitability, we will simultaneously improve the lives of all the people of South Africa. Our desire is for a South Africa where, in the famous words and vision of Dr. Martin Luther King, Jr., people will be judged by the content of their character and not by the color of their skin. When we can make business investments that earn for us and also enhance the lives of others, we are doubly blessed.

Thank you.

CHAPTER 5

Competing Today and Tomorrow

There was a time when the topic of competition would evoke belli-cose speeches liberally laced with analogies from sports—especially football. Such an approach was born of a one-dimensional view of competing seen almost exclusively in terms of *selling* a product or service to someone before your competitor could get to him. In recent years, however, most leading-edge businesses have been looking at successful competition in more holistic terms, and the concept of "Total Quality Management" (TQM) was born. Whereas old-style managers saw competitiveness in terms of *getting*—getting more business, getting more money—managers influenced by TQM and similar philosophies place the emphasis on *giving*: giving greater value, giving better service, giving more personal attention, and so on. It is no surprise, then, that the speeches in this section avoid cheerleading and aggressive rhetoric. Instead, they take inventory of the competitive challenges of the 1990s, and then they suggest ways in which those challenges can be turned into opportunities: opportunities to *give* more in order, ultimately, to *get* more.

A speech on competing runs the risk of becoming strident and stale. The way to avoid that is to seek surprise and revelation. For example, William A. Brewer III, of the law firm of Bickel & Brewer, tells an audience of lawyers that clients are demanding far greater value for their money than ever before—and, in a nation glutted with lawyers, they are getting it. Does Brewer bemoan this fact and pine for the good old days? Not at all. He has identified a reality, a challenge, and the freshness of his speech is in turning that challenge into an opportunity. Another speaker in this section, James F. Orr III, finds his surprise—makes his revelation—in a discussion of untapped assets: "learning to learn."

The Breakdown of the Monopoly of the Bar Card: The Game Is Over

WILLIAM A. BREWER III
Bickel & Brewer

Delivered to the American Bar Association Annual Meeting, Washington, D.C., August 10, 1992

SUMMARY: "Law firms that prosper into the next century will be firms that do not chafe and struggle against economic and social change but rather view it as an exciting business opportunity." A senior partner in a major law firm offers strategies for billing, accountability, and efficiency to meet the challenges of an increasingly competitive—and glutted—market for legal services.

The suggestion was put forth in a newspaper article last year that to solve the problem of the oversupply of attorneys, the government should pay lawyers $500,000 each to turn in their bar cards. It was proposed as a sort of a "farm subsidy" program, whereby the government would pay lawyers *not* to practice law. So instead of say, wheat, the uncultivated crop in the fallow north forty would be litigation. The suggestion was only *slightly* tongue-in-cheek.

Of course, farm subsidies are used *to keep prices high*.

Oddly enough, what the lawyer bashers have overlooked is that the current oversupply is having some very positive effects; among these are increased *competition* and *efficiency*. Although these are not typically words used to describe lawyers or those in the legal profession, maybe they should be. And that, I might add, is perhaps a more radical idea than paying lawyers not to be lawyers—that is, increasing competition and efficiency in our profession.

Having inherited and protected a business with numerous barriers to entry and restrictions on competition, lawyers have for years enjoyed a monopoly. As every monopolist knows, the ability to achieve monopoly profits is dependent upon the ability to restrict competition. To restrict competition, the players themselves create the rules of the game, which limit admission or entry, by enacting rules of conduct and arcane rules of procedure.

The point is—like it or not—the lawyer glut is one of the significant factors changing the face of the legal profession today. Clearly, we are experiencing a time of dramatic change. It's a buyer's market for legal services, and the oversupply of lawyers is the main catalyst for change. To be sure, billing abuses have provoked outrage over the way some law firms conduct business. Public and media scrutiny of the law firm business has never been greater. Clients are paying increased attention to the quality and cost of legal services, because they have an obligation to do so. And all this portends a shift in the balance of power between clients and law firms.

Inevitably—as Bob Dylan told us—the times, they are a-changin'. The first sign of change: the hourly fee system.

It's interesting to look at the origins of the hourly fee, because although the billable hour has for the past two decades been something of a "sacred cow," it is of relatively recent vintage. In fact, during the Roman Empire lawyers performed their services for no fee at all. In this country, billing practices have tended to reflect the kind of work most lawyers were engaged to perform at the time. In days gone by, when the majority of lawyers were engaged in handling *personal* matters, rates of pay tended to be *personally* negotiated.

SPEECH TIP: When times are a-changing, it can be helpful to reflect on the changes of times long past. Brewer may have startled his audience with this reference to ancient Rome, but his discussion of the profession's more recent history places current market conditions in perspective.

It was not until the postwar years that a significant percentage of lawyers began serving almost exclusively for corporations. In the 1960s, lawyers began keeping time records, and by the 1970s time-based billing was universally adopted. Ironically, it appealed to corporate clients because it was based on something tangible rather than the more elusive "value of services." For the '90s, however, the hourly billing system is an anachronism in today's changed profession. It is inherently problematic. Billing by the hour creates a conflict of interest between the client, who almost always wants the matter resolved quickly, and the lawyer, who knows that the more time spent on the case, the more he or she receives in fees. It rewards inefficiency.

Studies show that clients believe outside counsel pad their hours and perform unnecessary work in order to bill for it. What's worse, most lawyers admit it. One survey of lawyers showed that, for economic reasons, lawyers engage in all kinds of deceptive billing practices—estimating hours instead of keeping accurate time logs, knowingly performing unnecessary work and billing for it, inflating the chance of success in order to encourage continued litigation, billing two clients for the same work, and billing hours not worked in order to meet law firm requirements.

SPEECH TIP: Despite its implications about the very audience he is addressing, Brewer faces a potentially "hot" subject squarely, without euphemisms or evasions. Commendable in itself, this straightforward approach also recalls an old saying: "Never kid a kidder."

The demise of the hourly fee system was inevitable. Clients distrust the billing methods of lawyers who bill by the hour, and with good reason. Hourly billing abuses have led clients to hire investigative companies to review their legal bills and identify inequities. Perhaps even more significantly, clients have taken more and more legal work in-house to cut costs and maintain greater control.

The fact that investigative companies that monitor legal bills even *exist* today illustrates the wholesale deterioration of the relationship between clients and law firms.

Corporate clients are doing what anyone should expect a business to do: They are responding by initiating changes that make bottom-line business sense and getting out from under what has been a frustrating relationship with outside counsel. Corporations are doing a number of things to reduce reliance on outside counsel and increase productivity of in-house lawyers. They are increasing law department salaries, particularly for those in supervisory positions. More and more, it is becoming the *exception* for a corporation to hire a law firm when it needs legal services. And, when they do, control is maintained by the client. The "senior" role of outside counsel is changing. Many of the services they historically provided have now been assumed by in-house general counsel. Law firms today are increasingly relegated to providing specialized services or high-volume work.

Legal services are a means to an end. Clients ultimately want results and, not surprisingly, they do not want to pay excessive legal fees to obtain those results. Clients seek predictability, accountability, and productivity.

To deal with the changes of this new age, law firms have two options. They can continue clinging to hourly billing and what is left of the monopoly, or they can offer innovative billing alternatives to meet their clients' growing demands and reap the benefits of the evolution of their profession.

Some have chosen the former. Rather than address the inherent problems with the billable hour, some firms merely have lowered or decided not to raise their hourly rates. The problem with this approach is that it ignores both the conflict of interest between the client and the lawyer created by the hourly fee and the client's demands for predictability, accountability and productivity. Lowering or holding the firm's rates is an unimaginative compromise, which does not eliminate the real problem. It's a Band-Aid solution for a situation that requires surgery.

Still, examples of innovative billing alternatives abound. Among the alternatives are the fixed fee, value billing, premium billing, unit billing, split-fee billing, and contingency fees.

And before implementing any billing procedure, the lawyer should determine the goals of each client with respect to the case as well as the client's billing preferences and aversions. The lawyer should outline the alternatives and review the chosen billing method in detail with the client.

Those best suited to this new age will be firms offering specialized services and a few megafirms, which will provide garden-variety services to clients. The remaining needs of corporations will be more efficiently satisfied by their own legal departments. The law firms that will flourish under this new-found victory for clients—and, arguably, the profession as well—will be those organized efficiently and with well-thought-out objectives and the means to achieve them.

This means offering clients the quality of service needed to meet their specialized needs, such as litigation consulting groups qualified and able to work with lawyers in complex litigation and dispute resolution matters. This means that law firms will—or should—compensate their lawyers at a rate commensurate with the quality of their work and the results achieved for the firm's clients. This also means that firms will have to price legal services differently than they have for years.

I'd like to offer three suggested alternatives to conventional billing that provide clients with the greatest assurance of predictability, accountability and productivity.

> *SPEECH TIP:* Problems are always a dime a dozen; solutions are worth much more. Here Brewer begins to offer some practical suggestions for eliminating the dilemmas he has raised.

First, the *fixed fee.* A fixed-fee arrangement can offer the client, especially a first-time client to the firm, a high degree of predictability. The client knows at the outset what the legal fees will be and can budget accordingly. The risk shifts from the client to the law firm. The law firm shoulders the burden of performing the necessary legal services, even if the firm ends up exceeding the estimate. The client does not bear the burden of the law firm's miscalculations in estimating the costs of resolving the dispute. On the contrary, the law firm assumes the responsibility of anticipating problems that may arise.

Second is the *fixed fee with performance bonus.* In complex cases, a fixed fee combined with a potential for a bonus can offer the same advantages, while creating further incentive for the lawyer to achieve the client's desired results. The possibility of a performance bonus encourages the lawyer and client to be *partners* in resolving the dispute and eliminates the conflict of interest inherent in billing by the hour. This type of arrangement can benefit clients whether they are on the offense or the defense of a dispute. For example, if the law firm saves a defendant from having to pay damages over a certain dollar amount, the bonus would be earned. Conversely, a plaintiff might agree to pay the law firm a bonus if the law firm secures a judgment above an acceptable level.

Another alternative is *volume pricing*. That is, if the client agrees to provide a certain amount of business to the law firm, the client receives what is essentially a volume discount. This makes particular sense because part of the law firm's job in representing a client is to know its client's business—not just pertaining to an isolated legal issue. In knowing the client's business, the firm can offer innovative legal solutions in tune with the client's business goals. The firm's ongoing familiarity with the client's business means not having to "get up to speed" each time the client intermittently returns to the firm with legal business. The firm's time, effort, and resources are saved, and this savings can and should be passed onto the client in the form of a volume discount.

> *SPEECH TIP:* In his closing remarks, Brewer defines and emphasizes a hypothetical "law firm of tomorrow." Everyone knows that the best endings are new beginnings; good speakers also know *how* to leave their audiences with a positive vision for the future.

The law firm of tomorrow will not have the option to bill its clients without carefully considering the interests and needs of the clients and communicating with them about the method of billing.

The law firm of tomorrow—with few exceptions—will not bill by the hour. Those law firms that survive this changing era and flourish into the next will be those who want to restore integrity and credibility to the business relationship between the firm and its clients.

The law firm of tomorrow will be reinvented as an efficient organization able to pass along those efficiencies to clients. They will attain this by compensating their own members according to their abilities to achieve results for clients; by actively seeking non-lawyer professionals to assist them in meeting their clients' combined business and litigation needs; and by being flexible, innovative, and genuinely concerned about the client's value for the dollar.

The balance of power has shifted. The game of monopoly law firms have been playing with clients is over. And the normally change-resistant legal profession will have to not only adjust, but *embrace* this change with enthusiasm and innovation. Law firms that prosper into the next century will be firms that do not chafe and struggle against economic and social change but rather view it as an exciting business opportunity.

The Challenge of Change:
Building a New Competitive Spirit for the 21st Century

RALPH S. LARSEN
Chairman and Chief Executive Officer
Johnson & Johnson

Delivered to the Executive Club of Chicago, October 23, 1992

SUMMARY: In order to survive and compete in today's world marketplace, American business has radically changed. The CEO of Johnson & Johnson asserts that revitalizing our public institutions will require similar change.

Thank you, ladies and gentlemen, for inviting me to be here with you today.

I come here with a message to deliver, and it is not one of business as usual. Instead it is a message of *challenge* and *change*. It is a message about the fundamental need for American business and its institutional counterparts in the public sector to become more effectively involved in shaping the future course of this nation.

Let me begin by stating up front my strong personal belief that *at no time* in our history have so many events conspired simultaneously to impact on private and public institutions. *At no time* have so many voices of social and economic discord been raised, so many competing agendas advanced, and so many dollars put at risk chasing so many elusive solutions.

> *SPEECH TIP:* Here and throughout his presentation, Larsen repeats certain phrases—"at no time," and later, "challenge and change"—both for emphasis and for their rhythmic value. This periodic "ringing" of key words—as in a chorus or refrain—can add an almost musical element.

And *at no time* has there been less clarity to our purpose, less sureness in our direction, and less confidence in our power to command people and events—not just in our own country, but in the radically changing world in which we live.

During recent months I have spent many hours with colleagues, customers and others in the health care industry, discussing a major problem we face—the rising cost and pricing pressures on pharmaceutical drug manufacturers. And I have wrestled with how to place that issue in the broader context of the ever higher costs of technology-driven research and development.

What I have said to them—in part—was this: to gain some measure of the degree to which accelerating change impacts a company like Johnson & Johnson, you need only realize that fully one-third of our more than $13 billion in world-wide revenues comes from products, including pharmaceuticals, that simply didn't exist five years ago. And the cost of developing these new medical products—and moving them through an increasingly complex and burdensome regulatory process—is enormous. As a corporation, we will spend approximately $1.1 billion this year in research and development—up more than 60 percent from just five years ago.

> *SPEECH TIP:* Larsen is right: these figures do speak volumes. Some numbers—like some pictures—are worth a thousand words. The speaker's challenge is to seek out and recognize the figures that do tell.

New scientific knowledge is opening additional research opportunities every day—opportunities ranging from the exciting possibilities of gene therapy in the treatment of disease to the remarkable advances in less invasive surgery, which reduces the pain and trauma of surgery, dramatically accelerates recovery, and shortens the number of days that people must spend in the hospital.

As we enter our second century of service to health care it is reasonable to project that Johnson & Johnson will change more over the next decade and a half than in all the previous years of our history combined. This is not, in our thinking, just another remote academic assumption. It is a real and distinct probability, a probability that engages us every morning of every day as we attempt to absorb the impact of change—and assemble the strategic framework of our response.

And as we do so, we remind ourselves that in the five years just past, 143 companies have disappeared from the *Fortune* 500. Not quite one-third, but near enough to deliver a powerful message: Change now or be changed forever.

Now, as formidable as this task may seem to us from the vantage point of our headquarters in New Brunswick, New Jersey, it is but one measure of the greater burden that our private and public institutions must assume during this unprecedented period in America. And it is to that broader need—to face squarely the *challenge of change*—that I want to address the balance of my remarks.

I think that most of you here today will agree that this has been an unusual election year, a period dominated by the politics of frustration and by the awesome ability of television to shape the national agenda. But overall, this quadrennial exercise of the American political ritual has served to sharpen our focus on social fundamentals and economic choices. It has confronted us with difficult questions: questions of how we are going to live in the next century, what price we are prepared—or able—to pay, and who will pay for the choices we make. It also has helped to crystallize the debate over America's place in the world and to begin the process of seeking a new equilibrium between the enormous task of redesigning our society on the one hand and exercising a new global role in world politics and in business on the other.

When the Berlin Wall came down, we knew that it symbolized the end of an historic struggle for people's minds and a triumph not only of freedom, but of free markets as well. What we were slower to realize is that it also signaled the end of an era—the end of the world as we knew it—just as surely as the funeral of Queen Victoria did in another time nearly a century ago.

And so we now find ourselves in the throes of a transition between the kind of country we have been for the last fifty years and the kind we will be—or want to be—for the next fifty and beyond.

The twentieth century will no doubt go into the history books as one dominated by wars and the politics of conflicting ideologies. The twenty-first century we are about to enter is more likely to be dominated by the total globalization of the planet, with:

SPEECH TIP:: Slowing your pace with an outline-style list gives the audience a little extra time to absorb the weight and implications of farther-reaching ideas.

▓ Less sharply defined political boundaries

▓ An economy driven by fiercely competitive regional
alliances

▓ A shared responsibility for the environment, and

▓ New demands on our ability to maintain human health and well-being as people throughout the world lay claim to their right to good and affordable health care.

One of the questions we have to address as we work through the long agenda of our changing world is whether or not our institutions, both public and private, are equal to the new tasks that lie before us.

In short—can they meet the *challenge of change?*

SPEECH TIP: By posing even a minor riddle to the audience, as Larsen does here, a speaker can break through the potentially glazing effects of straight monologue and engage the listeners in a more participatory, imaginative way.

Ten years ago, if I were to describe a particular institution as being top heavy, with unresponsive management and uninterested employees, and one that delivered poor quality products at high prices, you'd probably have thought I was referring to any number of U.S. companies. I don't think most of us would use those terms to characterize the average American business organization of 1992. The beginning of the turnaround of the private sector in this country has been substantial, and if the job is not yet done—and it isn't, by any means—then, at the very least, we have divined that there is a way out and a way forward.

Today, unfortunately, I think the description of a bloated organization—one out of touch with its constituency—more aptly describes our institutions of government. You only need to look around and listen to the people to know that rarely, if ever before, has government in this country been under such pressure to change.

There is no question that the impact of serious divisions in our social, political, and economic structure is being felt everywhere. And how could they not be? From the visible decline in the standards of public conduct and responsibility to the explosion of our national debt; from the failing promise of public education to the vacillation in public leadership and public purpose, we are every day witness to an erosion in the foundations of our traditional government institutions. I believe the message from the public is quite simple: "Enough is enough."

Americans are demanding change and they are willing to consider a wide range of options—to "roll the dice" if necessary. Just as they were willing to take a chance on those first cars from Japan or televisions from Korea. Why else would a relatively unknown business executive—and a billionaire to boot—so captivate the people that even as an undeclared candidate last spring he could command—sight unseen—the support of one out of five of the nation's voters?

The question that all this public discontent raises in my mind (and I'm sure in the minds of many of you here today) is, "Where are we headed?" Unfortunately, we cannot declare Chapter 11 on the public problems of this nation or the world. We cannot simply walk away with our assets protected and our creditors at bay and begin to trade our way out of the problem.

But we can begin to take a serious look at the lessons we have learned in business over the past few years—in the last decade—and begin to address solutions that have some common ground between our own private experience and the public mess that seems poised to engulf us all.

The current unresponsiveness of our public institutions did not happen overnight, nor is it the result of any one individual, administration, or party. We must all share the responsibility. In part it occurred because the American political system has been historically geared to the principle of "more is better"—irrespective of war or peace, prosperity or recession. We have become a nation without limits—a limitless society. Whenever there has been a choice between resolving a problem through efficiency or numbers, the numbers have won: numbers of people, numbers of dollars, or both. It's a trap many large corporations fell into and suffered dearly for as a result.

There is no question that we in business have faced our share of serious problems over the past ten years:

■ The globalization of markets, which seriously eroded our competitive advantage and threw the balance of payments into a tailspin

- The problems of size and structure, which increasingly isolated the top, over-expanded the bureaucratic middle, and demotivated the essential, productive employee at the bottom

- The decline in productivity and product quality that eroded our customer base and gave rise, first, to foreign competition, and then, inevitably, to foreign ownership of our nation's business assets

- And finally, the problems of absorbing a rising tide of health and social obligation costs, including the long overdue closing of the gender gap, the reshaping of our educational system, and meeting the special needs of two-income and single-parent families

I would suggest to you that how we in the private sector are beginning to respond to these fundamental challenges may well help to provide a new blueprint for public sector survival.

The long and the short of it is that a great number of companies in this nation were fat, happy, and arrogant. They'd lost touch with their customers, their employees, their communities and, in some cases, their shareholders. It took corporate raiders, activist public pension funds, advocacy groups of every stripe—and competition from every corner of the globe—to shake American business out of its lethargy. To paraphrase a famous Johnson (from another century), "The prospect of a hanging in a fortnight concentrates the mind wonderfully well."

And so, the threat to our very survival forced the necessary change in our thinking. To those that survived, fundamental change did occur. At Johnson & Johnson and at hundreds of other companies, we realized that it wasn't enough to play better by the old rules: the game itself had to be changed.

As a result, we are becoming more cost effective by improving productivity, leveraging our physical and human resources, and reducing the size of our managerial bureaucracy. We are creating new opportunities by becoming more customer-driven. We are becoming more quality conscious and more aggressively competitive—not only in our traditional markets but in new markets as well. We have consciously rejected the conventional, hierarchical command structure in favor of moving responsibility and authority to the office, factory, and laboratory floors.

As a result, we are engaging our people more directly, recognizing them more quickly, and rewarding them more adequately. And the results have been more impressive than we ever would have dreamed. We have learned, once again, what we all intuitively know: Trust—well placed—liberates creativity, encourages and motivates, and brings out the very best in good people.

We have brought forward our agenda of company values. And we have reinforced their social and ethical foundations—giving our people a vision of the standards by which we want to live, of what we want to become, and the basis for getting there.

We are reinvigorating our commitment to entrepreneurship, by broadening the participation base and giving a new sense of active ownership in the process—from which we are generating growth and profitability.

Above all, we are in the process of redefining the role of the corporation from one of passive compliance to one of active leadership in our industries and in our communities. And we are working more closely with our employees and our customers alike in tackling head-on the changing issues that face them. In short, because we had to change, we *did*, and we are continuing to change on a daily basis.

American business today—while still not over the goal line—is, by any measure, leaner, more agile, more global in its view—and frankly, more competitive than at any point in my lifetime. We in business have made enormous progress against the serious competitive threats facing us.

Now, I know some of you may be thinking that a threat of this magnitude to our government institutions is a bit farfetched. The United States government, after all, is not Silverado Savings & Loan, Eastern Airlines, or American Motors.

Well, I go back to the phenomenon of Ross Perot—not to the individual so much as the chord of response he initially struck with millions of Americans. Almost overnight Perot became the lightning rod of disaffection, the messenger of public frustration over the inability—or unwillingness—of government to face the issues that seem to threaten the very foundations of this country. The clear message to our government institutions is: *Change or be changed.*

I believe the lessons that we have learned—and the solutions we are attempting in private business—have some application to the public sector. It may surprise you to find that many of the lessons and solutions have a distinct, grassroots political base.

First and foremost, the success we have achieved so far at Johnson & Johnson—even as we are becoming larger and more diversified—is the result of a relentless drive to get closer to, and better understand, the needs of people. We realized that by stressing the essential value and dignity of each individual and by giving each of them a stake in a common goal, we could grow our business through a shared commitment to its success. We could produce higher-quality products, earn a better return for our shareholders and, at the same time, enrich the quality of life for our employees, our customers, our communities, and society as a whole.

It is my view that the American people, if called upon, have a tireless spirit and an infinite capacity to respond to challenge—and to adjust to demanding change. They will do so, however, only if there are institutions and individuals prepared to lead them out of the wilderness—not deeper into it. The lesson of Ross Perot is not that he emerged by design—but that he emerged by default. And the lesson of our public institutions is not that they are terminally bankrupt, but that they have lost touch with the basic values that drive this country. They are out of touch, out of sync, and dangerously close to being out of time.

Now, I am not suggesting, as an executive did long ago, that "what is good for American business is good for America." Far from it. But I am suggesting that what is working for American business can work in the public sector as well.

Ultimately it comes down to an exercise of courage:

- To downsize the bureaucracy, through privatization and other mechanisms;

- To move authority and responsibility down the line, creating opportunities for individual enterprise and a system of rewards and incentives to encourage it;

- To improve the quality of government service by paying attention to the needs of the customer—in this case, the taxpayer—and by becoming more efficient in every phase and facet of exercising the public mandate.

It took business an entire decade to get the message. It will probably take our public institutions that long, or longer, but there is no better time to begin than now, and no better source of inspiration than the voice of the people, the customers of our public institutions.

I am very optimistic about our future and I believe that our progress over the next few years will take us to the threshold of a new century, one which promises both unprecedented challenge and enormous hope. But it is critical that the badly strained fundamentals of this country work well once again. And for that to happen our basic business systems must perform both *competitively* in the world economy that will unite us and *compassionately* in addressing the social imbalances and economic grievances that threaten to divide us.

I think we would all agree that to have 37 million people without health insurance in a nation like ours is simply not right. But if we are going to deal with this and similar issues, we need to revolutionize and revitalize our public institutions. And we need to insist that they learn from and work cooperatively with the private sector so that the creation of wealth is not siphoned off by the size and inertia of an unresponsive bureaucracy.

Business *cannot* be a spectator on the sidelines of unfolding events. Neither can government and its institutions be oblivious to the signs that are so obvious—and so repugnant—to the people it serves. Clearly, we need to renew our competitive spirit, sharpen our focus, revitalize our institutions and re-engage the great entrepreneurial drive that engineered America's once dominant leadership position.

In closing, may I say the tasks we face in both the private and public sectors will not be easy and it will take a nation of broad shoulders to make it work. But confronting the *challenge of change* is what created the supremacy of American enterprise in the first place, and, in the final analysis, it is what will help us regain that position, which is so critical to the future of this great nation.

Thank you so much for allowing me to be with you today.

Learning to Learn

JAMES F. ORR III
Chairman and CEO, UNUM Corporation

Delivered to the Seventeenth Annual LIMRA International European Regional Meeting, Edinburgh, Scotland, June 25, 1993

SUMMARY: Learning is the key to competitive effectiveness in the coming century, and learning to learn (rather than merely impart and receive training) is a vital first step.

Looking out the window here at the walls and turrets of centuries-old Edinburgh Castle, you might feel that time has stopped for a moment. And you can get the same feeling walking the Royal Mile and throughout the old town of this beautiful ancient city. But, appearances aside, change has swept through Edinburgh and all of Scotland much the same as it has through the rest of the world. In fact, even timeless Edinburgh Castle has been through much change over the years.

> *SPEECH TIP:* Orr opens his speech with a lyrical tribute to the gathering's immediate surroundings and locale. Like a storybook prelude that describes setting and scene, this form of introduction allows listeners to—literally and figuratively—"settle into place" for the main event.

The chapel of St. Margaret, the highest point in Edinburgh and the oldest surviving castle building, may date from as early as the eleventh century. David II's tower was built in the fourteenth century, and the cliff-hanging ramparts of the castle were built mainly in the eighteenth century. And, seeing the monument to Edinburgh's own Sir Walter Scott in the foreground here, I'm reminded of the effects of change, because many of Scott's novels can be seen as a lament for the passing of simpler times.

Well, we might do the same ourselves, except that the pace of change in today's world and in our industry doesn't allow for such luxuries. So, rather than lament the past, I'd like to talk about the future, specifically about learning to build a more successful future for us all. And I'd like to start by taking a quick look at more recent history.

As students of history know, World War I began seventy-nine years ago, almost to the day. And if you're one of those students, you know the so-called "War to End All Wars" officially ended five years later on the same day, June 28, with the signing of the Treaty of Versailles. But, of course, the wars did not end. In fact, there have been so many conflicts since then that it makes you wonder what—if anything—we've learned along the way. And this wonder is compounded by the fact that today is the second anniversary of the start of the Yugoslavian civil war—the day Croatia broke away. Now, this coincidence is doubly ironic, because, as we all learned in school, World War I also started in Yugoslavia, and because today's war fracturing the former republic comes just when its neighbors are working to unite more fully throughout Europe.

All of this is a long way of saying that learning dates and other historical data—conventional learning—doesn't necessarily help us understand history, and it certainly doesn't help us change or adapt to change. Indeed, for the modern business, learning encompasses a range of activities, not the least important of which is human behavior. In fact, it's the behavioral element of learning that will drive the difference between winning and losing in our industry and virtually every other between now and the year 2000. And it's the role of personal behavior in learning that I'd like to specifically address today, because behavior, more than any other factor, will determine whether we shape our future or our future is shaped for us.

If we as an industry are to build and shape a successful tomorrow, we must begin today with learning, true learning, which transcends the old ways of doing business and positions us to adapt and prosper in a world of continuous change.

First, let's recognize the difference between the old view of learning, which is really more like conventional "training," and the new view of learning: Training implies that there's a formula for every problem, that all you have to do is memorize the formula, or know how to find it and apply it. Learning implies, and requires, greater flexibility. Employees who are learning don't just react to the world; they shape it.

> *SPEECH TIP:* When a speech's key concept involves a term that is very commonplace or familiar (such as "learning"), the word—and by extension, the speaker's message—will be pre-loaded with associations and assumptions. Refining one's meaning, as Orr does here, may be essential to lessen the catch-all burden and free up communication.

I suspect that two great sons of Scotland would agree with this distinction. One hundred years ago, thirty-seven-year-old Scotsman James Keir Hardie helped form Britain's Labour Party.

Keir Hardie worked as a miner from the age of ten to twenty-two. He went on to organize a labor union among his fellow miners, and he was later elected to Parliament. It's doubtful his little bit of schooling contributed greatly to his success. But, based on his ability to shape the world around him, we can be certain that he mastered the art of learning, and that he was able to overcome the dominant logic of the time and help create a completely new view of politics—a new logic.

SPEECH TIP: Orr again makes reference to the heritage of his host country. Such remarks are appreciated by most audience members, local and foreign alike: the former bask in the glow of national pride, and the latter enjoy a brief tour through unfamiliar terrain.

Two hundred years ago, another Scotsman produced perhaps an even more remarkable example of the power of learning. It was 1793 when fur trader Alexander Mackenzie, twenty-nine, became the first European to cross the North American continent. Employed since age fifteen by the Northwest Fur Company, he sustained himself on his 3,000-mile journey by eating a mixture of shredded game, melted fat, bone marrow, and wild berries. It almost makes haggis sound appealing, doesn't it?

Well, you can only imagine how this was but one of countless examples of his flexibility and adaptability in the face of continuous change. And, as with his countryman Keir Hardie, it is an illustration of the power of learning, as he transcended the accepted logic of his time in traversing the continent.

What Keir Hardie and Mackenzie proved is that no matter what your business, learning is the key to getting the most out of yourself and out of your greatest competitive advantage: your people.

Maybe that's why Dr. Stan Davis, author of *Future Perfect* and *2020 Vision*, predicts that learning in the work place will increase from a day a month to a day a week by the end of this decade. This is especially important when you consider the increased competitive, regulatory, and consumer pressures that have moved many of us to revisit and—in some cases—re-engineer the way we work.

And this work almost always begins with learning, as in:

- learning to better meet customer needs
- learning to improve the efficiency of our processes and systems, and
- learning to compete more effectively, both domestically and internationally.

Learning to compete more effectively is the most complex of these pressures, first, because it means you must learn both to better meet customer needs and improve your efficiencies, and, second, because even if you're not competing in a foreign market today, you may well be soon. Even if you don't, odds are you'll be facing foreign competition on your own turf. Certainly this has been true in the U.S., where we've seen some sixteen billion dollars in merger and acquisition activity by foreign insurers between 1987 and 1992. Cross-border M & A activity by European insurers totaled more than fifty billion dollars worldwide over the same period. And all the while, the U.S. share of world insurance premiums has been dropping, from 65 percent in 1965—when they totaled 280 billion dollars—to 35 percent of 1.4 trillion dollars in 1990.

So, the trends are clear. The world market is developing rapidly, and more and more insurers are pursuing premiums around the globe. Consistent with this global growth are global-sized risks in each of the three major trading blocs for those who do not focus greater attention on learning:

> In North America—and the U.S. especially—we risk losing more control of our business to legislators and regulators. The push for a national health care program in the U.S. underlines the enormity of this risk.

> In the Pacific Rim, we risk losing any chance of gaining a foothold in Japan, one of the most promising but, in many respects, one of the most difficult markets in the world to enter.

> And here in Europe, established insurers risk losing current and future market share to greater competition from banks and —in the U.K.—building societies, as well, as many develop their own insurance operations. As in the U.S., we face the risk of greater regulation.

But for all the risks facing those who do not take up the learning challenge, the greatest is losing the trust on which our business is built, the trust—the promise—of every policy and contract we write. Protecting that trust today depends on our ability to make learning a higher priority.

So, I think it's fair to say that our future—individually and as an industry—depends on our ability to learn. Which brings us to the question: What, precisely, is the new logic of learning?

Well, let me start to answer that with another question: Did you know that the people you might assume are the best learners—the smartest, the most successful people—often are the worst learners?

That's what Chris Argyris says. Professor Argyris, who teaches at Harvard's graduate schools of business and education, argues that highly skilled professionals generally have never learned how to learn. Because they're usually successful in what they do, they don't have many opportunities to learn from one of life's most effective teachers: failure. But even when they do fail, successful people often become defensive, screen out criticism, and blame everyone but themselves. "In short," he writes, "their ability to learn shuts down precisely at the moment they need it most."

Well, now that we've covered all of you—successful people—what about the rest of the world?

Not to worry. They face behavioral challenges in learning as well. And if you have any doubt of this, consider Winston Churchill's observation that "success is often nothing more than moving from one failure to the next with undiminished enthusiasm."

SPEECH TIP: It's easy to see why Churchill is one of the most often quoted public figures of our time. If you rule out slapstick dives over tangled microphone wires, then dry wit or wordplay—two Churchill fortes—may be the surest method of raising an audience laugh.

In fact, we all face essentially the same challenge in learning: overcoming what professors Rene Bouwen and Ronald Fry, writing in *International Studies of Management and Organization*, call "dominant logic," that is, the logic that dominates our personal behavior and the collective behavior of our organizations. Now, Harvard's Professor Argyris has coined two terms—"single-loop" and "double-loop" learning—which help explain this phenomenon and its relationship to our reasoning. He defines them by way of analogy: A thermostat that automatically turns on the heat whenever the room temperature drops below a certain level is a good example of single-loop learning. A thermostat that could ask, "Why am I set at this temperature?" and then explore whether another temperature might achieve the goal of heating the room and do it more economically, is double-loop learning.

In single-loop learning, which is so popular among so many managers, the focus is on identifying and solving problems. And while that's important, Argyris argues that, "if learning is to persist, managers and employees must also look inward. . . . They need to reflect critically on their own behavior, identify the ways they often inadvertently contribute to the organization's problems, and then change how they act."

If there's any question about why identifying and solving problems isn't enough, and why we must learn continuously, remember this: The basics of management today consist more than ever of "guiding and integrating the autonomous but interconnected work of highly skilled people," according to Argyris. This is especially true for our business and other knowledge businesses. But, remember, those highly skilled people are not generally good learners themselves, so your responsibility is, automatically, doubled.

Why? Because while we're all born learners, our enthusiasm for learning decreases as we gain experience. Ultimately, learning becomes a burden, an addition to all the responsibility we've gained throughout the years, responsibility that is, if you examine it, often more about maintenance than creation.

It's more about maintaining and improving on the logic that dominates our organizations than considering new ways to work, new logic.

Even as many of us re-engineer our operations, we're going about it in the context of our old view of the world. But the old logic can't withstand today's pace of change. Consider this: of the forty-three companies listed as "excellent" in the 1982 best seller *In Search of Excellence*, fewer than half retained this status five years later. No doubt, many of those who slipped had become so focused on one set of circumstances that they couldn't adapt to change.

More recently, we've seen the same thing happen in the computer industry, among such companies as IBM and DEC; in the automotive industry, with the problems of General Motors' North American operations; and even in our own industry, with the solvency problems that swept under a number of insurers just a couple of years ago.

In each case, these problems resulted largely from the inability to learn new ways of doing business and a determination to simply fine tune the old ways.

Opening our organizations to learning—to new logic—demands that we first open ourselves to it, and this is where your double responsibility comes in. As much as participative, bottom-up action is essential to developing a more flexible, more responsive organization—one able to keep pace with change—senior management must model this behavior, because your employees won't invest the time and energy necessary to learn—and take the risk of embracing new logic of any kind—unless it's clear to them that you will support them, unless it's clear you're doing the same. Only you and your other senior managers can make this clear.

So, the first and most important step toward learning is to examine your own behavior. And when you do, you'll probably find it's defensive. That is, your reasoning is defensive. The number of heads I see shaking in protest only serves to confirm this.

In fact, most of us are wired for defensive reasoning. It's our way of retaining the knowledge—and, therefore, the control—we've worked so hard to acquire. Indeed, knowledge is power. But knowledge shared is all the more powerful.

Once you've identified this defensiveness, the next step is to see how open-minded you think you are, but how closed-minded you are in your actions. In other words, just how dominant your dominant logic is. Finally, you can move on to identifying how others in your organization reason defensively, and you can help them move beyond this through the same process of examination—providing behavioral modeling and support along the way.

As G.E. Chairman and CEO Jack Welch has said: "We have to undo a hundred-year-old concept and convince our managers that their role is not to control people and stay on top of things, but rather to guide, energize, and excite." Now, as much as you have a double responsibility in this, each of your employees has his or her own personal responsibility to learn, as well, because, of all the things you can't make people do, making them open their minds to new ideas is among the most difficult. You can help them, but ultimately they have to get there themselves.

There's no magic formula for this—no prescribed amount of funding or hours or materials. True learning transcends any such patterned approaches. That's why at Unum we've created what we call the "Learning Framework." Introduced last year, it's a document that details how learning occurs at our company, what competencies we are working to build to help us better meet the challenges we face, and what opportunities for learning are available. It's designed to help our employees develop to their fullest potential, which is one of our corporate values. It's designed to help leverage our disability knowledge, which is one of our core competencies. And it's designed to help our people work more effectively in teams, which is an approach we're applying increasingly to all our work. But the most notable element of Unum's Learning Framework design is that it places the bulk of responsibility for learning on the individual. It makes clear that learning is experiential, that it's about taking risks, and, again, that it's more than simply attending formal training programs.

Yes, we still provide these programs and support of all types. But, ultimately, it's up to each of our employees to learn and, collectively, to build the knowledge of our institution. And this is especially important to us with the 1990 addition of operations here in the United Kingdom, the expansion of our operations in Canada in recent years, and the opening last year of a Unum office in Tokyo, among other strategic developments around the world.

The political pioneer James Keir Hardie and the explorer Alexander Mackenzie clearly were exceptional people, exceptional in their ability to adapt, learn, and shape their world. What we're trying to do at Unum—and what I encourage you to do—is to help foster those skills for all of our people. Help them become exceptional in their ability to learn. Help them learn to

- serve customers better

- improve the efficiency of processes and systems

- compete more effectively, both domestically and internationally

- and, most importantly, learn to better protect the trust on which our business is built.

In other words, learn so that we can shape our future rather than have our future shaped for us. Today, more than ever, knowledge is power. To maintain power, business leaders often protect their knowledge—even from their associates. As a result, they rarely learn, because to learn is to admit not knowing something, which our dominant logic tells us is unacceptable. But what's really unacceptable in these times of continuous change is putting your business—and our industry— at risk over what amounts to a behavior that you—and only you—can work to change.

So, as LIMRA's primary mission is to help us learn more about our business, I think it's appropriate to use this gathering as a time to begin learning more about ourselves.

The Work Force

It will quickly be apparent to readers of the speeches in this section that, as management styles have changed among North America's leading companies, so the attitude toward "the people" has evolved. Absent from the speeches in this section is all trace of the traditional adversarial relationship between management and labor or between the corporation and the individual. Indeed, in our speakers' view, employees cease to be *employees* and emerge as *assets*, the sources of an organization's strengths.

But there is an additional dimension here. Having the right people is not merely a matter of *seeking* the most gifted or most experienced, but also of investing in a corporate culture that encourages growth, learning, and a flexible, creative approach to problem solving. All of the speeches in this section look at the oldest relationship in business—employer to employee—in a new light. We are accustomed to thinking of the dutiful employee making an investment of time, talent, and effort in the company for which he or she works. Our speakers are in the rhetorically fortunate position of being able to take this cliché and stand it on its head. For them, the emphasis is not on the employee's investment in the company, but on the employer's investment in the employee.

The speeches in this section are stimulating in their own right, but they also offer valuable lessons for the business speaker. Don't avoid the tried-and-true and the overly familiar, but do take your listeners on an unconventional tour of these subjects. The only thing that will leave a more lasting impression upon an audience than showing them something new is showing them something new in a subject with which they are all too familiar.

Sharing Power:
New Paths for the Saskatchewan Power Corporation

CAROLE BRYANT
Executive Vice-President
Saskatchewan Power Corporation

Delivered to the Canadian Public Personnel Management Association, Regina, Saskatchewan, April 20, 1993

SUMMARY: A changing marketplace, with changing technologies and changing needs, requires a flexible, broadly educated work force.

Thank you.

As people who work in the personnel management field, you are all well acquainted with the rapid pace of change in today's working world. Every organization has to prepare for the abandonment of everything it does. Managers need to question each process regularly. If ever there was a consensus among human resource managers, it is the initial resistance to any change. Change strikes at the comfort zone of both individuals and corporations. Change represents the unknown. That is why it is often clouded in suspicion. Professor John Kenneth Galbraith once noted: "Faced with the choice of changing one's mind and proving that there's no need to do so, almost everyone gets busy on the proof."

SPEECH TIP: Pithy in itself, Bryant's quotation of Galbraith may conceivably forestall—in the audience—the very effect it describes.

At SaskPower, the monumental changes taking place in all aspects of our operations are already having a profound effect on the way we deploy our human resources. Utilities *were* protected monopolies. Now, they must face the realities of the marketplace and be prepared to re-think the basics.

Non-utility generation—where private developers build and operate their own generating facilities, and then sell the electricity back to SaskPower or to other customers—is about to end SaskPower's sixty-year monopoly in Saskatchewan.

In both Canada and the United States, utilities at the provincial or state level are increasingly less likely to build new generation within their own service area. There will be much more competition, which will include the loss of traditional customers. On top of this, energy efficiency and conservation programs are encouraging people to use less, instead of more, electricity.

Managing this change, and ensuring employees do not become overwhelmed by the speed or extent of these changes is one of the biggest challenges facing our corporation.

It will not be an easy task.

Here's a glimpse of the environment employees have worked in for years—and one that is now beginning to change. Imagine you're a SaskPower planning engineer. For twenty years, it has been your job to plan big energy megaprojects to meet the rapidly escalating electrical needs of the province. Suddenly, it all stops!

You're told to work with private developers and integrate their facilities into SaskPower's provincial electrical system.

Now your job is to find ways to *avoid* building new megaprojects. The new buzzword is *conservation*.

You question the change in direction that relies on private developers. Megaprojects have been an effective way of serving the province for years. Saskatchewan has one of the best records in North America with respect to electrical service, reliability, and cost of electricity. All of this was accomplished through a large centralized generation, transmission, and distribution system.

In other words: If it's not broken, why fix it?

Although the old way of doing business is still as effective as ever, there's now more than dollars and cents to be considered in today's business world. People are asking for a chance to participate in the decisions that are being made at all levels of government and industry. The days where corporations used to impose decisions on their customers, without any consideration or consultation as to how these decisions might affect their lives, are over.

That relates directly to utilities, particularly when we see public opinion polls telling us that people are growing more opposed to new energy megaprojects. This shift in public opinion was on full display during a series of town hall meetings along the route of a proposed 225-kilometer transmission line beginning at Condie, just north of Regina, to SaskPower's Queen Elizabeth power station at Saskatoon.

SPEECH TIP: Bryant paints several before-and-after pictures during the course of her speech. And as any artist can tell you, the closer the juxtaposition of different hues or values, the greater the contrast that will result.

A few years ago, the public involvement strategy for most large corporations, including SaskPower, was to inform people of project plans when the contractor arrived on their land to do the work. Now we are inviting people to give us their opinions on all aspects of the line: its route, any environmental concerns they might have, or questions about cost and need. We are committed to listening to the options they might propose, ones that include not even building the line.

We need to be open and accountable so we can provide customers with the answers to their concerns. But openness, if it is to be lasting and sincere, has to start inside the corporation. We have to look beyond the edges of our desks, and see what the rest of the corporation is doing.

This represents quite a switch from the somewhat myopic job focus that has prevailed within SaskPower and most other corporations for the last quarter century: A mentality that says, if I'm educated as an engineer, that's what I'll do. If I'm an administrator, I'll administer. If I'm an accountant, I'll work on the balance sheet. Sticking to that narrow course only ends up depriving the corporation of new ideas.

I know that administrators think about more things than just spreadsheets. We need to view our human resources as more than merely employees. They're also citizens of this province, with a vested interest in its long-term future. They have concerns about the effect of power plants on the environment, or making sure that public money is spent efficiently.

We need to tap into that knowledge, and give serious consideration to their opinions. That starts by encouraging a more interdisciplinary approach to the way we do business. Collaboration—interactions based on a common purpose, with a focus on teams, individuals, and organizations—is the direction we are taking in the corporation.

In collaborative organizations, top management groups are strongly committed to breaking down departmental and functional barriers that limit internal competition. The collaborative organization maximizes diversity of opinion, experience, and expertise. It also provides an information system that supports interdependent achievement.

This interdependent and interdisciplinary approach is also part of a larger issue society must confront. For years, we've been encouraging our children to pursue a narrowly defined path through high school and university that will culminate in a lifetime of employment. The days are passed of being employed for thirty years or more with one corporation. We need to place a new priority on producing—and hiring—employees who have a more general training—training that will allow them to pursue a number of job options during their working lives.

Adopting this generalist approach means these new employees might not have the specific skills to crunch numbers or draw a specific set of plans on the day they arrive at your office.

What they will have developed is critical thinking skills and a level of confidence that can be adapted to a whole variety of tasks.

The traditional bias in favor of "technically trained" employees is particularly noticeable at SaskPower. This is reflected in the few women holding senior positions within the corporation. Undoubtedly, being a corporation that relies on engineers and technical expertise more than many other entities of government, SaskPower has no choice but to hire employees with a high level of specific skills. Another obstacle is that engineering programs at Canadian universities are still not attracting significant numbers of women. SaskPower is working to change that. We are looking at shifting the emphasis on the university scholarships we sponsor to encourage more women engineers at the University of Regina and the University of Saskatchewan.

SPEECH TIP: Bryant draws full attention to one of her company's weaknesses—and lingers there a moment—before describing the impressive efforts that SaskPower is making to change that condition within the company and in the community at large. Like the pause at the apex of a roller coaster hill, her approach makes the delivery more powerful.

But change must begin long before university. That's the motivating factor behind SaskPower's new Empowering Girls in Science and Math program, which will see women in non-traditional positions at SaskPower serve as role models and mentors for grade eight female students attending St. Catherine School in Regina.

Our long-term goal is not limited to improving employment opportunities for women only. We want to develop a human resource pool at SaskPower that is as diverse as possible, one that is truly representative of all citizen groups in the province. Not all these people will be interested in careers in engineering or hard science. Tradespeople will always be responsible for a large amount of SaskPower's work. That's why SaskPower has joined forces with the Saskatchewan Department of Education to develop the Building Futures for Students Program. The programs educate high school students on everything they need to know about a career in the trades. The program has been spearheaded by Martin Nowakowski, a SaskPower employee for thirty-three years, who saw a desperate need for trades education in our high schools. So far, Martin has visited close to fifty schools, speaking to over two thousand students. The ultimate goal is to take the message—one that, above all else, emphasizes the need to complete high school—to all eight hundred high schools in Saskatchewan. And while we continue to develop better trained tradespeople, we will also need generalists to determine how their skills can be best utilized, and who make sure they don't become compartmentalized in one particular job function.

Human resource managers at SaskPower also face the less defined, but more challenging task of changing attitudes within the corporation—specifically, the belief that engineers make the best managers. Or the belief that men make the best recruiting officers, since they're the ones selling the corporation's merits to a group that is still predominantly male. In this sort of environment, it is a revelation that a well trained administrator—one with proven decision-making and problem-solving skills—is capable of managing a group of engineers, even if the administrator has no technical background.

Our job is to convince senior managers that knowing the trade or the formula for calculating the minute details does not automatically make you a better manager. Interpersonal relationship skills must be given the same weight as technical skills when it comes to selecting new managers.

A recent survey by Robert Half International showed that interpersonal skills are the most admired trait in supervisors, managers, and senior executives. Interpersonal skills are increasingly becoming one of the prime factors in hiring decisions. The importance of interpersonal skills has much to do with the new types of corporate organizations that have emerged from decentralization and globalization of operations. Because of these trends, companies are putting greater control into the field, and, in turn, this is altering the traditional chain of command. A manager with a non-engineering background does more than bring a new perspective to the decision-making process; he or she also forces the engineers, computer programmers, or designers to explain their work projects in plain language.

That ensures better decisions and improves accountability by removing some of the mystery surrounding the technical work carried out by corporations like SaskPower.

That's good news for our customers.

It was a lot easier to sell people on the merits of the Condie/Queen Elizabeth transmission line at seven town hall meetings when we were speaking in language and terminology they could understand.

By advocating for the increased use of non-technical managers and clear language, I'm not dismissing the importance of these details. What I am saying is that we need to refocus the direction of our corporation so that our customers, and not our own internal interests, are the top priority.

SPEECH TIP: Bryant follows up theory with example. No principle of public speaking is more important.

The work done by the coordinator of our public safety program is a perfect example of what I'm talking about. The coordinator is a woman with no technical or electrical background. I remember her telling me when she first started in our Safety Division that she had to begin by studying the basic rules of electricity. In the end, that turned out to be in her favor. Because she had to start from scratch—and force others within the corporation to explain in plain English how things work—she can do a better job of communicating our safety message to our farm and urban customers, along with their children. She succeeds at her job because she communicates in a language people can understand.

We've made other breakthroughs in the area of human resources. Our recruiting department is now completely staffed by women, proving that you don't need male recruiters to hire for male-dominated positions. You hire people with good interpersonal skills. To get where they are today, these women had to challenge some long-standing stereotypes about women in the work place: stereotypes that say women can't work long hours, can't handle stress on the job, or aren't as willing to travel because of their families. We can't be afraid of deviating from the norm when it comes to hiring our employees, or repositioning them within the current structure.

I recently heard about one large American corporation that put as much emphasis on an employee's extracurricular activities as it did on a résumé in choosing a new director. And if I remember correctly, it was the person who skydived on the weekends who was given the job.

SPEECH TIP: Of course, the only thing better than a good example is a good and *colorful* one.

Now, I'm not suggesting that we all run out and sign up for skydiving or bungie-jumping courses. What I think this story represents is an open and honest attempt to take the blinders off, or at least loosen them a little, when it comes to how we have traditionally viewed our hiring and training practices at corporations like SaskPower. People who skydive possess a sense of confidence and adventure that will serve as an asset to any corporation.

We will need people with diverse backgrounds if we're going to adequately address the diverse technical and socio-economic issues that are facing the corporation in the future. I very strongly believe we already have those people, and those skills, within SaskPower. Our biggest challenge now is to take down the barriers that have prevented them from being used in the past.

And even by taking on that challenge, by agreeing to work together to develop a corporation that is not afraid of diversity, we are taking an important first step.

Thank you.

Keys to Profitability in the 1990s

STEPHEN FRIEDMAN
Senior Partner and Chairman
Goldman, Sachs & Co.

Delivered to the Securities Industry Association 1993 Trends Conference, April 14, 1993

SUMMARY: The chairman of a major investment firm suggests that we look within our own organizations—especially to personnel and corporate culture—to find the keys to profitability in the 1990s.

Good morning. The topic for my talk is "Keys to Profitability in the 1990s." In the short time we have to spend together this morning, I will try to identify some of the basics by which we try to run our firm. We will not have time to get into the details, so I will try to point to what we at Goldman Sachs view as the philosophical issues.

Our basic question is: "What matters in the long term?" Our answer is, again and again: "People and culture, culture and people, people and culture." A small dose of vision helps, but if we get the right people and culture, they will provide what is necessary.

> *SPEECH TIP:* Speakers needn't shy away from singsong or other playful effects. Friedman's repetition and inversion of "people and culture" here introduces and reinforces the keynote of his presentation.

What does that mean in practice? Foremost, it means building and believing in a tight core of immutable principles. It means spending tremendous energy investing in our work force. It means continually designing and reworking our evaluation and compensation schemes to make them flexible and fair. We believe in subjective compensation schemes that do not have room for people to "game the system" as they might with rigid incentive formulas. It means keeping the firm balanced, especially as between the execution side and the operations side. It means keeping the channels of information open and flowing. It means encouraging people to think big, to take controlled risks, and to keep a creative eye on cost control. But before we can go on to anything else, it means "people and culture."

Ninety percent-plus of a business is the quality of the people and culture. No doubt, we can spend loads of time figuring out where our business is going, but if we do not have the right team, it won't get us anywhere. A strong culture attracts and breeds good people. Maintaining and nourishing a strong culture is, foremost, the job of the firm's leadership. At Goldman Sachs, we try to defend a tight core of immutable principles from generation to generation:

1. The client comes first.

2. An emphasis on team work.

3. We consider our most valuable assets our people, our capital, and our reputation. If any one of these three is lost, our reputation would be the most difficult to recover.

This tight core of absolutes gives us a point of reference. It makes us comfortable when we address those aspects of the business that must change to keep up with the times. The old adage, "If it ain't broke, don't fix it," leads to complacency and can put us behind the innovation curve. So we ask: "What makes sense under the circumstances?" What businesses are we really in? The answers are not necessarily tied to the past. I will elaborate on this point later when I talk about "Big Ideas."

There are three central issues regarding people in our firm: getting them, keeping them, and helping them improve. We invest heavily in recruiting. We dedicate our key people to it, for both M.B.A.'s and lateral hires. Our investment in people is time-consuming and costly. But the cost of turnover, and the cost of having the wrong people, is even higher. We value our people, and we invest in them through training, mentoring, and motivation programs, and through continuing education.

Our compensation system plays a crucial role. We have found that rigid incentive formulas provide "false objectivity." Rigid formulas invite people to spend time and effort "gaming the system" by figuring out how to advance their own particular self-interest or their business unit's interests rather than the interests of the firm overall. Instead, we operate under a "subjective" compensation system.

The key point is that compensation must not only be fair, it must be perceived as fair. To that end, we have a career review process at Goldman Sachs that we work hard at getting people to understand and consider fair. It is based on months of peer appraisal, and anonymous upward and downward evaluation all the way across the firm's hierarchy. In the last few years, we have revamped our career review process to make it more detailed, and a better foundation for subjective compensation. This intense analysis allows people to get better feedback and motivates them to do good work.

We spend much time these days focused on growing and motivating our people. I am not sure if we are doing a great job, but we spend more time thinking of how to re-pot individuals, to grow their careers, while at the same time fulfilling the needs of the firm.

We try to think in terms of the value we get from these two: people and culture. We can spend our time talking about which niches we should be in, or which part of the capital markets will be most successful in the nineties. If we don't have the players, we will not be very effective or competitive. I am not much of a basketball coach, but give me personnel like Michigan's and North Carolina's, and give

North Carolina's coach Harvard's personnel—and I suggest that you bet on me because I will have the talent.

We have been noticing that departments once considered in the background have become crucial in the nineties. As our businesses mature, we learn what armies have known for centuries: logistical support wins wars. Strategic logistical activity can spell the difference between success and failure in our business. It is no longer just the front line that makes or breaks a deal or a trade. Today we need balance.

There used to be a somewhat supercilious term: the "back office." Implication: the firm's operations departments did not have quite the cachet of the execution departments. The volatile, complex international business trends of the nineties require analysis, creativity, and vigilance. It is perfectly obvious, however, that failure in the operational side of the business can kill you.

> *SPEECH TIP*: Presentations offer welcome opportunities to deconstruct and dispose of outmoded or otherwise noxious clichés. Like "exploding" preconceptions or "debunking" myths, such linguistic and conceptual demolition seems to have a certain, perhaps gladiatorial, audience appeal.

Quick disasters can come from weak risk management, compliance problems, bad credit assessments, liquidity problems, operational snarl-ups, and so forth. Processing systems go down. We had a fire a few weeks ago at our main office—and it is crucial that people can respond quickly, with determination. We have been investing in ways that were traditionally not a practice at our firm. We infused some of our best people from the execution area into our operations side. We found that when our execution people—our traders and senior sales people—felt there was effectual parity on the operations side, that they were dealing with people of equal firepower to them, people of equal experience in handling complex derivative instruments, people with comparable exposure to international markets—then we began to see better collaboration and teamwork. Without teamwork, we were not going to get an understanding of problems.

We found an inhibitor to our ability to do new business in new geographical areas was if information systems and operations couldn't keep up. So we altered our policy regarding internal advancement. Some of our best people and some of our best career paths are now in what used to be called the "back office."

The world of compliance has become increasingly complex. Think about how many people regulate your respective firms; for us, it is more than twenty regulatory agencies and exchanges around the world. The legal area is an area where we have said we need absolutely top-caliber people. The amount of time, money, and psychic income firms in our industry can lose, the amount of energy consumed by compliance problems is staggering. So this is part of "building a balanced firm."

We think of ourselves as being in an information-processing business. More to the point, we are in an information channeling business. For us, in today's world, the profits from intermediation are relatively small. We are trading for our own accounts and providing advisory services for our clients. These activities depend on our skill in processing and channeling information. We would not be happy competing with a major German bank if we only operated intra-Germany, head-to-head. We could be competitive, but it would not be the field we would most want to choose. Rather, our advantage would lie in being better than the domestic German bank at taking German clients into China or the United States. That means managing the information flow. When we make a bid for a merger assignment in Fort Worth, Texas, we must be able to tell the entrepreneur who owns that business we can identify and do business with the best buyers in Japan, Asia, and Europe. We believe smooth information flows are as crucial in our business as they are in any high-technology business.

Ask yourself, what is it that stops information from flowing easily? We think the answer is internal bureaucracy. Internal bureaucracy, "Jello walls," is the enemy of the free flow of information.

> **SPEECH TIP:** Friedman's use of a lively and descriptive colloquialism no doubt raised an audience chuckle. Whether the expression was brand-new or already familiar to listeners, the speaker's quick shift to a funkier, less "official" vocabulary adds an unanticipated spark to a serious discussion.

I start out with the article of faith that people in the trenches know everything that is going on in our business and in our competitor's business. They know what the clients want and so they know what product we should be serving up. When their ideas begin to percolate up vertically in the organization, we need to energize the flow because the ideas may meet with bureaucratic resistance.

We work at trying to make people feel comfortable being gadflies—in feeling that they have access up. Are we perfect? No. Far from it. But we do know how valuable such information is, and we are better than we used to be. If you consider the advantages of being the first mover, if you look at people in our industry who have innovated a product, you will find the advantages are significant. Creativity has a substantial payoff. We know that we will not always be the most creative. None of us always is. However, if you can't be first, there is no excuse for not being a fast copycat. People in the trenches know when clients are happy with products one of our competitors just served up. There is little excuse in my view for slow reaction time. We work hard at developing our channels of information upward.

Horizontally and laterally we are just starting to tap into cross-selling opportunities. We emphasize to our equity people, our bond people, our investment banking people, that making each other aware of the opportunities with our clients—cross-selling—is good for the firm overall. We are not as good, by any means, as we ought to be. Still, we have moved beyond the stage of ignoring this area, to the stage where when the merger person closes an assignment for an entrepreneur with a large amount of liquidity, he or she will automatically try to bring our money management, or stock brokerage, or other part of the business into it. We have a way to go with all of this, but now that we recognize the opportunity, the incentives tend to work in our favor.

Internally, these are win-win situations.

Next, I would like to talk about one of my favorite topics, "big ideas." "Big ideas" brings us back to the spirit of creativity in organizations. It's always possible for any organization, for a while, to live off the big ideas of the past. Business and industry in New England was stifled in the last century because of the way trust funds were set up. People for generations had just lived off the income their entrepreneurial families had generated. All of our businesses are susceptible to that danger. I have seen it at our firm. Just living off the income of past great ideas, and eventually dipping into principal.

One of the conventions of modern, high-powered industrial managements is the scorning of meetings. Personally, I think this is a mistake. True, if it is a big bureaucratic meeting, they are right to scorn it. I have discovered from my own experience, though, that the way to generate big ideas, those ideas future generations can live off of, is to have people in your organization get together in small groups—small, interactive groups meet and huddle together—and brainstorm. I would love to see more such meetings in our firm, more meetings of the right kind.

We get so much mileage out of two of our people riding together in an airplane, and after finishing with the trip's specific business, just brainstorming together. I encourage people occasionally to stop whatever they are doing, to sit for a while—and think! There is a certain macho culture that says we always have to be out on the road trying to get the next piece of business or the next assignment. I do not think that is productive. I get excited when our people generate a list of big potential ideas. Maybe only one out of five clicks—but those are the ideas that build you one heck of an annuity.

I have developed a simple test of whether we are active enough in generating big new ideas. Big ideas come at a big price in terms of opportunity costs. You don't take an individual from one area and put him or her in another without first having a sense of a big prospective payoff. And unless there is a fair amount of that traffic going on, it probably means we are stagnating. When I hear squeals from our managers that we are taking this competent person away from them and that it is tremendously painful, the decibel level of those squeals tells me we are probably on to something. That is a kind of rough-and-ready test.

SPEECH TIP: As Ross Perot can attest, people respond well to an informal, even folksy approach in the description of executive decisions.

Cost control is an important philosophical keynote to making money in the nineties. I know this subject is old. Still, it is easy to get complacent here.

As a firm, in early 1985, we had about 7,500 people; a few years later, we had 6,200 people. We downsized largely for cultural reasons. We were not at that time happy with our ability to select, train and bond our people at that larger size. In the aftermath, we discovered ourselves to be more efficient, culturally stronger, and it was very positive for the P & L. This was not just a process of headcount reduction. It was a process of introspection, of self-accountability—an ending to complacency. We improved as a firm because we started to examine the premises by which we had been living. We discovered we really could run leaner. We invest a great deal in finding and training our people. They are hand-picked. We do not let any one of them go without careful thought and self-searching. But, once we started to put pressure on ourselves, we discovered other things.

The single best investment we ever made—it is almost embarrassing to say it, except it is kind of unusual and it was highly profitable—was when some genius in our operations area came up with a bold new idea: If you have people just sit a little bit closer together you could save a lot of space. This meant that from the cubicle areas in which our people sat, you would take out the extra unused chair. This was not like the work conditions at some sweatshop; it was still a perfectly comfortable work space. It just did not have an extra chair, where the people would put their raincoats or their folders. I don't think I ever saw anyone sitting in one of those unused chairs. We ran a present value number on this change, and the value turned out higher than any leveraged buyout. It was incredible. And the cost savings meant not only more profits, but a much bigger bonus pool for our employees. We discovered dozens of these little cost-saving ideas floating around, once we could tap them. It was always a matter of working smarter, not necessarily harder or cheaper.

Up to that time, whenever we talked about cost savings, someone would always say, "Well, let's not have people fly first class." So we wouldn't have them fly first class. That meant they would often tend to fly three hours earlier in the day and lose a full day in the office. They would have to book an expensive hotel, have an expensive meal—and we would be net behind a few thousand dollars a trip. The space optimization idea, in contrast, resulted in real savings. So one philosophical thing you get when you put some of your best thinking and agonizing into the operations area is that you start coming up with some surprisingly cost-effective moves.

The last thing I was going to say, and I can't speak for your respective businesses, is that we have found that taking controlled risks is crucial to our profitability in the nineties. We love the agency business; we are going to be in it forever; we take pride in our leading market shares. We have found, though, that we do better in our agency business when we are controlled risk-takers on a diversified basis. Any firm attending this gathering, given sufficient capital, will have ample opportunity to move into this area, because you will have a priceless ingredient:

expert knowledge of your particular areas. You will have venture capitalists who will be close to you; you will have LBO opportunities. That is a source of gold worth thinking of mining in the nineties.

Those are my philosophical thoughts on "Keys to Profitability in the 1990s." We can meet here a decade from now and see how well they worked.

Thank you.

SPEECH TIP: Friedman ends on a wry, self-parodying note. Not all closings require fanfare, pomp, or ceremony.

The Workers' Compensation Dilemma: An Insurer's Perspective

DOUGLAS W. LEATHERDALE
Chairman and Chief Executive Officer
The St. Paul Companies

Delivered at the Alexander & Alexander Workers' Compensation Seminar, Bloomington, Minnesota, October 15, 1992

SUMMARY: Insurance executive Douglas W. Leatherdale discusses rapidly increasing costs and other problems in the state-regulated workers' compensation system, and he offers examples of how employers can work with insurers for better and less expensive risk management.

To get a sense of the impact of the workers' compensation issue, you need simply to look at the current edition of *Business Week*. An article entitled "Workers' Comp Goes Under the Knife" looks at ways employers and states are trying to contain the increasing costs of workers' comp. Measures discussed in the article include managed medical care, return-to-work programs, and medical utilization review. In the same issue, an editorial urges the nation to "try a new approach to workers' comp." The magazine calls the current system an "adversarial nightmare." It praises cost-containment efforts and promotes a system that compensates injured workers fairly.

Business Week is on the right track, but it's important to realize that there's no one magic solution to today's workers' compensation problems. There's no cure-all for what has become an ailing system. The remedies will include concerted measures by employers, insurers, and brokers—and long-term decisions by society as a whole.

SPEECH TIP: There are many advantages to quoting a published critique. Like a ventriloquist, the speaker can use the vehicle of another voice to project a different, perhaps riskier sort of message: a bald truth, a worst-case scenario, or simply a pungent but popular opinion. Then, as Leatherdale does here, the speaker can establish a moderate stance in precise relation or opposition to the quote.

As you study workers' compensation, three things become clear: The picture isn't pretty. The issues aren't simple. The answers aren't easy. But they merit our attention, understanding, and action.

As an old American proverb states, "The surest way to mishandle a problem is to avoid it." So let's roll up our sleeves and get to work—and address the workers' compensation issue from three perspectives:

- First, let's take a look at the scope of the problem, and how serious it is.

- Then, we need to understand forces beyond our immediate control. In several states, these factors make it difficult for insurers to provide workers' compensation coverage, and make coverage both very expensive and very hard to find.

- Finally, I'll close with some examples of steps you can take to minimize the risks and reduce the costs of workers' compensation.

My message is this: In many ways, workers' compensation is a management issue, and employers can take various steps to manage it. But additional bigger issues also affect the workers' comp system. As noted in the *Business Week* article, the nation's total annual tab for workers' compensation, since 1980, has nearly tripled, to a staggering $70 *billion* a year. Over the past five years, workers' comp insurance costs are up more than 90 percent. If you're in the construction business, the increase has been even *higher* than that.

From the viewpoint of an insurer, the major problems with the workers' comp system are skyrocketing medical costs, excessive litigation, inadequate rates, and a growing residual market. Let's look at some figures that illustrate the costs of this line of insurance.

In 1991, the insurance industry's combined ratio for workers' comp hit 123. The combined ratio compares premiums to losses and expenses. It is an accepted, basic measure of the profitability of lines of insurance. A combined ratio of 123 means that, for every dollar of premium, insurers paid out $1.23 in claims and claim expenses. Remember: that's an average; some insurance companies did better, others did worse. But it indicates that, from an insurer's perspective, workers' comp is *not* a profitable line of business. Today, workers' compensation has the poorest results of any line of insurance.

The picture isn't any better for employers. For many businesses, workers' comp costs account for 10 to 30 percent of total labor costs. For every dollar you spend on a work comp claim, it's estimated that you pay about two dollars more in non-insurance costs, like lost productivity.

Some recent trends show how costs have risen steadily for employers countrywide. Between 1980 and 1990, medical costs per workers' comp case rose an average 14 percent per year, peaking at almost $7,000. Compare that rate of increase—14 percent—to the medical consumer price index for the same period: 8 percent.

For company owners and managers, here's where the costs can *really* mount: in lost work days due to occupational injuries. Lost work days are a good indicator of the *number* and the *cost* of workers' comp claims. The rate of lost work days has increased steadily, from about *60* lost days per 100 private sector employees in 1983, to *84* lost work days in 1990.

It's easy to see how costs have risen, but costs alone have not created the problems in the workers' comp system. Here's why: One way to view insurance is as a *pass-through mechanism*. An insurance company charges a premium to cover losses and expenses, plus make a profit. Rates needed to cover costs are filed with state regulators. But, in many states, workers' comp insurers can't charge rates that are adequate to cover costs. Where rate *regulation* leads to rate *suppression*, the availability of coverage begins to dry up, driving more and more policyholders to assigned risk plans, the "residual markets" of last resort.

> *SPEECH TIP:* Throughout, Leatherdale uses vocal emphasis to stress important facts, to introduce new concepts, and to distinguish between like-sounding terms. This helps guide his audience through sections of dense or tricky material.

The result is a system that's out of whack, and that hurts both employers and injured workers.

This brings me to my second point: The workers' comp system is out of balance because of forces beyond our immediate control. We must do what we can to contain day-to-day costs. Insurers also need to be able to charge adequate rates to cover the costs of accidents and illnesses, which can't be avoided and which *will* occur.

Here's an example of how rate *in*adequacy is manifesting itself nationwide. I want you to use your imagination for a moment. Imagine that you've reached one of the highest career goals in U.S. business today—the pinnacle of one of the most exciting industries in the world—an occupation in which, every day, you make monumental decisions affecting the lives of thousands of people.

Imagine yourself as—the president of an insurance company.

> *SPEECH TIP:* Leatherdale asks his listeners to step into the shoes of an insurance company executive; then he walks them through an imaginary, ultimately disastrous scenario. A projected visualization needn't be entirely pleasant to be effective, especially since audience members can enjoy a little sigh of relief once the fantasy is over.

Oh, yes: there's a catch: Your company writes *only* workers' compensation insurance. In fact, all of the operations in the United States that write workers' comp—insurance companies, self-insurance groups, government pools and other entities—have been rolled into one company. *Your* company.

You begin operations in 1984. You start with capital of $7 billion. You plan to charge premiums, pay claims, and invest your holdings wisely. Most important: You plan to base your rates on the losses you expect over the course of the policy. If rates are adequate, you'll at least break even, if not make money.

So far, so good. Sounds pretty easy.

You track your results year by year, but instead of going *up*, your capital gradually, steadily, goes *down*. You followed the rules and thought you did everything you were supposed to, *except* for one other catch: In many states, as your losses increased, you *weren't* allowed to charge the rates needed to cover losses. Over time, your losses ate up your surplus. By the end of 1991, that seven billion dollars had turned into a one-billion-dollar *deficit*.

So much for your insurance career.

The president in my story is imaginary, but the problem isn't. That's what *actually* happened to workers' comp insurers in the 1980s.

The point is: You can't underwrite insurance without adequate rates, but in many states, workers' compensation rates have been held down artificially. As an insurance company, if we don't have a reasonable expectation of a profit in this line of business, we'll allocate our capital elsewhere.

How can you determine if rates in any given state are adequate to cover costs? One way is by looking at what is called the "residual market burden" in different states. That sounds like insurance jargon, so let me explain. If a factory, service, or other operation or business can't obtain insurance in the open market, it's placed in the residual market. A common type of residual market is an "assigned risk pool." All insurers writing workers' comp in a state are assessed a fee, the residual market "burden," to cover the market's costs. Insurers pass that cost along to their customers. A low fee indicates a low residual market burden. It means there's competition in the marketplace, insurance is available, policyholders can obtain it, and insurers can charge what's needed—for example, in these states: Connecticut, with a 7 percent burden; Illinois, with 2 percent; Iowa, 5 percent; Michigan, 4 percent;

and Oregon, 8 percent. There are other states with similar rate levels; I've selected these only as random examples.

Now consider the workers' comp assessments in four other states, where rates are *not* as adequate, insurance is *not* as available, and more and more businesses must resort to the residual market for coverage. The fee assessed on top of a workers' comp premium in Kansas is 24 percent of the policy; 28 percent in Tennessee; 34 percent in Florida; and 49 percent in Arkansas. And there are other states where the assessment is even higher—*much* higher.

These high assessments are symptoms of an ailing system. As I noted earlier, the system is functioning better in some states than in others, but overall, the burden has increased, from a countrywide average assessment of 4 percent in 1983, to 16 percent in 1991. What's more, an unprecedented number of employers are buying coverage in these residual markets. In 1991, the workers' compensation premiums written in the residual market totaled *25 percent* of the total workers' comp premiums in the United States. That compares with about 5 percent in 1984.

It reflects a broken system that's putting pressures on insurers and employers alike.

One additional comment, on our own state. The residual market load in Minnesota is determined by Minnesota companies, who file the level of assessment with the state commerce department. The assessment for Minnesota's workers' comp residual market is estimated at less than 5 percent. That indicates our state's system is in relative balance: rates can cover costs. But, as you all know, the costs *are* high. Legislation enacted earlier this year may go a long way to reduce the cost of some very expensive claims.

The law—addressing such areas as managed care, medical fee schedules and treatment protocols—appears to have the potential to streamline the costs of the system.

I've outlined some of the problems, issues, and pressures that confront our system. In states where the system is out of balance, those who want to fix it will need to decide to lower costs, raise rates, or choose a combination of the two.

SPEECH TIP: With just a few words, Leatherdale sets a pivot to swing the focus of his speech.

In the short term, there *are* steps employers can take to minimize costs. One is to select loss-sensitive insurance programs, in which policyholders—especially *large* policyholders—share in the risk. One way to do that is through large deductibles. Selecting a large deductible can lower a policy's premium. It also provides an incentive by the company to work to lower the number and cost of workers' comp claims.

At The St. Paul, we work with customers—in particular, large policyholders—who are committed to reducing their workers' comp claims. We view workers' comp as one part of a customer's total protection package. That package also includes loss prevention, to keep claims from occurring and for lowering claim costs. Medical cost containment programs, for example, are geared to getting injured workers the best and most cost-effective medical care. Our medical claims staff review billings and utilization patterns to cut claim costs. Other St. Paul efforts examine the "human factors" that contribute to losses among employees: alcohol and drug abuse, stress, lifestyle. We also provide tools to pre-screen job applicants.

These innovative efforts, along with *other* services such as safety programs and ergonomics, can pay off for employers in reduced workers' comp costs. Consider, for example, one policyholder, a midwestern service company with one thousand employees. We surveyed employees and found that stress and wellness issues—not the traditional work safety problems—were driving the company's losses. The survey showed the need for employee assistance, counseling, stress management, and similar programs. The programs were introduced. The result: the frequency of workers' comp claims was cut in half, and the average claim cost dropped from $14,000 to $3,750.

In another example, a boot manufacturer was experiencing major increases in workers' comp costs. Our risk management people looked at problems with cumulative trauma claims, back injuries, inappropriate work assignments, and the lack of a program to return injured workers to the work place. The company implemented the recommendations. Three years later, the company's annual workers' comp costs had fallen from $3 million to less than $400,000. The average cost of a claim had decreased by 92 percent.

These are some examples of how employers, today, can directly address their own workers' comp losses. Firms that are effectively managing the workers' comp exposure are seeing more success than those that are only looking for the lowest premium. Those managers who manage the risk well will be positioned to compete effectively in the '90s.

Your insurer should work with you to address workers' comp and other liability issues. Your broker must work with you to maintain a viable, controllable insurance program. Insurers and brokers, along with the policyholder, form the insurance quality chain to address the day-to-day workers' comp risks. But, at the end of the day, for the system to function, workers' comp must be profitable. That's not the case in every state, nor for every customer group.

For the long-term issues—the balance of the system, the level of overall costs, the fairness of compensation—effective answers require a full and fair understanding of the system. We've worked in that system, and we've been involved in efforts to improve it.

For those who want to participate in that effort—an effort of change and reform—we're ready to help, to share our own experience and understanding.

Thank you.

Charting a Leadership Course for Management

JOHN LYNCH
Chairman and CEO, Towers Perrin

Delivered at Town Hall, Los Angeles, January 13, 1993

SUMMARY: "The message I want to share with you today is about people, and it's as simple and straightforward as this: People are our best source of long-term competitive advantage today. But if we want to realize that advantage, we've got to manage our people resources very differently than we have in the past."

Although this talk is officially titled "Charting a Leadership Course for Management," I might more accurately retitle it: "Managing Your Investment in People for Competitive Advantage." The message I want to share with you today is about people, and it's as simple and straightforward as this: *People are our best source of long-term competitive advantage today. But if we want to realize that advantage, we've got to manage our people resources very differently than we have in the past.*

> *SPEECH TIP:* Sometimes speakers have to forestall knee-jerk or stereotypical assumptions by the audience based on the presentation's topic or title. Here Lynch makes clear that concern for human *resources* is business pragmatism, not social idealism.

This is not a humanistic message. Rather, it's a hard-nosed, bottom-line, dollar-and-cents message, and it's as important a message for senior line management as for human resource (HR) professionals.

More important, actually.

In my view, unless line management embraces this philosophy wholeheartedly, real change cannot take place.

While the message itself is simple, executing it is very, very difficult, especially in the current economic climate. I know how tough things are in Southern California right now. And, you know, California is not suffering alone. Although the recession hit here fairly recently and more severely than in many other places, the rest of the country and, increasingly, the rest of the world are struggling too. With all of us so busy putting out the day-to-day brush fires, it's no surprise that people issues are easily overlooked.

But even in the best of times, maximizing the investment in people is challenging. After all, there are no cookie-cutter solutions. People are too dynamic a resource. Unlike machinery, they don't always behave in ways you can anticipate or easily handle. You have to expect mistakes—and I stand here as living proof of that. Any one of Towers Perrin's five thousand employees will be glad to tell you about the mistakes I've made in the last two years. And I'm going to make some more. It's part and parcel of managing an organization and the people that breathe life into the organization. So I know how tough it is to deal with people issues. I also know our long-term success depends on it. Let me tell you why.

> **SPEECH TIP**: A *mea-culpa-first* approach tells audiences not to worry—their speaker has parked his ego at the door. Up-front admissions of human fallibility are music to the ears of anyone who has ever had to endure a long and windy display of complacency and braggadoccio. (More's the pity: almost everyone has.)

Traditionally, our sources of competitive advantage have included proprietary technology, access to capital, raw materials and information, and a superior cost structure. These are all extremely important and will continue to be important. But in my opinion, they are no longer sources of *long-term sustainable* advantage. Today, for example, a company's competitors can very quickly reverse-engineer virtually any technological development. Some years ago, the major computer firms used to say they got a two-year market advantage from a technological advance. Now, they're lucky if they get a six-month advantage.

> **SPEECH TIP**: In the course of his general statement about trends in competitive advantage, Lynch zooms in briefly to view strong effects in a particular industry. His example is so apt that it needs no further elaboration or fine detail, and the speaker carries on with his broad-based introduction to the main section of his speech.

With access to financing, raw materials, and information also increasingly available to everybody on a global basis, these sources of market advantage are eroding as well. As for the cost factor, virtually every organization today is addressing its cost structure. We've seen tremendous emphasis on streamlining and reducing costs, and we'll continue to see organizations making cuts. But there is a point of diminishing return, and most of us know that companies can't simply cut their way to success in the long term. So, low cost, too, no longer serves as a source of long-term competitive advantage.

Although we are fast losing our traditional means of differentiating ourselves in the market, we are more than ever in need of sustainable sources of competitive advantage. Today, we're all operating on a much more level playing field than in the past. We are facing competition from new sources. We're continuing to see the expansion of global companies in local markets. So it's especially vital that we find new ways to differentiate ourselves and maintain and build our customer base. .

I believe the way to do this is to focus on three key, interrelated areas:

- Quality

- Customer satisfaction

- Efficiency—not just cost efficiency, but operational efficiency, including identifying new products and getting them to the marketplace quickly.

The common thread in all three is *people.* You've got to have your people behind you to truly make good on these goals. And that's as true for the small, start-up entrepreneurial venture as it is for the large, well-established company. Let me touch on each goal briefly.

There's been a lot of talk about quality in recent years, and we're all familiar with the buzz words. Companies have tried various kinds of quality programs, and while some have succeeded, many have failed. Why? Because they approached quality as a separate, stand-alone activity.

To really create and sustain quality, it must become part of the culture and fabric of an organization, not just another mandate from the CEO or a program of the month. Employees must understand and accept the need for quality improvement in everything they do. They must understand how to improve quality, and they must drive the effort. Otherwise, you won't succeed.

That's why Corning Glass involved employees at all levels when it developed its strategy for quality improvement. Corning's goal wasn't to win the Malcolm Baldrige award. It was to win in the marketplace. Motorola is another company that has had great success in this area. It makes quality an integral part of its culture and the way it operates. As a result, Motorola has reduced its defect rate more than 99 percent over the last five years and is still looking for further improvement. It has reduced costs almost $900 million in 1992 alone and over $3 billion cumulatively over a five-year period. Clearly, quality can pay off when it's more than just the management fad of the hour.

SPEECH TIP: Whenever possible, speakers should consider the use of illustrations from a diverse range of industries, as Lynch has done here and elsewhere in his presentation. Principles that are shown to apply across conventional business categories are the most compelling, and variety adds natural interest to the proof.

Quality is only part of the success equation, however. As an example, suppose you've purchased the best software package on the market for your home computer. When you get it home, you find the manual is written in a way only a rocket scientist could understand. Great as the program itself might be, you're not going to be a satisfied customer if you can't use it properly. The next time you make such a purchase, you may feel you're better off with the second- or third-best software package on the market, so long as the instructions are clear. The point is, you can't overlook any of the tangible and intangible elements that, along with quality products and services, help create satisfied customers. Customers have to feel they're getting full value from your product or service. They have to feel they're being treated fairly and responsibly. They have to feel confident that you will stand behind anything they buy from you.

There's not much doubt about the role employees play in driving customer satisfaction. In service businesses, front-line employees have the most obvious impact on satisfaction. But even those behind the scenes have an impact. After all, you'll never see the people who write software manuals, but their work forms an impression of the company in your mind and influences your buying behavior.

SPEECH TIP: Here Lynch gets double use—and value—from an excellent example.

The effect employees have on customer satisfaction explains why an organization like Marriott has such rigorous recruiting standards. It's also why the hotel chain invests so much in training all its employees. Marriott wants every aspect of a customer's visit to be first class.

Finally, we come to the third area I mentioned: efficiency. You cannot optimize operating capacity without employee support. You can't reduce waste, reduce costs, develop and get products out to the market quickly unless your people are willing to work differently than they have in the past. Consider these two examples from the auto industry.

In 1985, Ford made it a priority to get employees involved in increasing productivity. Again, not for humanistic reasons, but to ensure it met its key business objectives. As a result of this effort, a press operator at a stamping plant in Cleveland discovered a way to conserve four inches of sheet metal on every part he made, saving the plant $70,000 a year. Now, if you multiply that example by thousands of workers, you can see the power of getting people involved in trying to improve your business operations. And, indeed, that's far from the only result the Cleveland plant achieved from employee involvement. Since 1985, it has reduced labor and overhead costs over 3 percent a year. Ford's now-retired Chairman, Philip Caldwell, who started the involvement program, pulled no punches in explaining his rationale. He said: "It's stupid to deny yourself the intellectual capacity and constructive attitudes of tens of thousands of workers."

Another example of the power of people involvement comes from Chrysler. This automaker found that its people were indeed the key to greater efficiency in new product development. Because it used small, cross-functional work teams to develop the Dodge Viper, it brought the new car to market sixteen months earlier than is typical in the auto industry, and for a much-reduced cost. Chrysler empowered this work team to make decisions, and that's exactly what the team did—with great success.

Inspiring as these stories are, they're easy to push aside at a time of such pressing financial concerns. Many organizations are struggling with tremendous debt and are continuing to lay off workers. Virtually all are under tremendous cost pressure. Employee health-care costs are just one example. Many of you know this first-hand. How can an organization absorb 20-percent increases in health-care costs when its revenues are essentially staying flat?

Cost is not the only obstacle to capitalizing on the people advantage. Employers also have to come to terms with the dramatic changes in the composition, abilities, and needs of the U.S. work force. I'm sure you are all aware of the trends we refer to as Workforce 2000. But let me touch briefly on two areas that are having a major impact on our ability to manage our investment in people.

The first is the alarming projected increase in the so-called skills gap—the gap between the skills you're going to need to be successful in the future and the skills new employees will bring, or fail to bring, into the work place. The Department of Education currently estimates that we have about 27 million functionally illiterate adults in this country, and that's projected to increase by about 2.3 million a year for the next several years! So, just about the time you are going to need certain kinds of skills to drive your company forward, you're going to have a harder time finding people with those skills.

Part of the answer lies in a closer partnership between business and education. But another part lies in increasing the investment in worker training. Many employers will say: We can't afford to train. But I question whether any of us can afford *not to train*. The cost of illiteracy to business in errors, lost productivity, and down time is staggering.

The other trend I want to touch on is the increasing racial, ethnic, and sexual diversity of our work force. This diversity presents us with a tremendous opportunity to capitalize on different ideas, different ways of thinking, more creative problem solving, and so on. Companies that successfully tap the rich array of talents inherent in a diverse work force will benefit in many ways. But doing that requires a very different style of management. We can't continue to try to fit everybody into the same pattern, as we have in the past. That management style is part of the reason many employees today feel insecure, increasingly demoralized, and disenfranchised.

To turn things around economically, we need to turn things around in the work place. We need employees to contribute materially to our organizations. We need their help, their commitment, their talents, their energy.

> *SPEECH TIP*: Parallel organizational elements within a presentation can help convey an overall sense of clean and powerful structure. Earlier, Lynch outlined three areas of importance in global competition—quality, customer satisfaction, and efficiency—and here he offers three proposals for creating a corporate culture that can successfully compete.

What must we do to meet this challenge? I believe three things are required:

- First, a new social contract in the work place.
- Second, complete integration of business and human resource strategy
- Third, a supportive work-place structure and environment.

In the past, the employer-employee relationship was paternalistic. In return for an employee's loyalty and time on the job, the employer provided security, generally in the form of lifetime employment and clear direction on what to do and how to do it. That relationship is dying, and the contract that defined it—loyalty for security—is virtually gone. We need to forge a new contract based on participation and shared responsibilities. The new contract must clearly acknowledge the employees' ability to contribute to the business and to take responsibility for themselves and their futures. This means giving people more authority to make decisions on their own. It means having people share in both the risks and rewards of the business in direct and meaningful ways. And it means fully involving people at all levels in the business.

The new social contract should reflect the fact that both employers' and employees' expectations have changed:

- Employers now expect employees to work harder and faster, to be more customer-focused, to deliver higher quality at a lower cost, and to contribute breakthrough ideas.

- Employees now expect more balance between their work and personal lives. They want more flexibility in their work arrangements and a clear return on the time and energy they put in on the job, not just financially, but in personal satisfaction, growth, and recognition.

Both employer and employee must continually evaluate whether they are fulfilling their respective parts of this contract and, if they are not, must be willing to make necessary changes.

This sharing of responsibility does require something else from employers: increased employee education. To be fully contributing business partners, employees need to fully understand the business: its mission, goals, financial structure, and so on. To accept greater responsibility for their futures, employees need education and support in planning for the future. At Towers Perrin, for example, we are implementing an approach to retirement planning that clearly communicates it is a shared responsibility. We're helping employees evaluate their long-term financial needs. We're giving them financial planning tools and as much flexibility as possible in investing their benefit dollars. We believe this allows them to make informed decisions about how best to plan for their future.

The second critical area has to do with integrating human resource programs and operations fully into the fabric of the business. We've all talked for years about linking HR and business strategy, and most companies do connect the two on some levels. But few have accomplished the kind of total integration necessary to move business forward today. That's because total integration requires a major change in the relationship between line management and human resource staff. Both must be accountable, but I believe that line managers have to drive the human resource strategy in our organizations to make it really work. HR staff have to act as counselors and partners, advising business and line managers about the kinds of initiatives and programs necessary to achieve their goals.

Last year, Towers Perrin conducted a worldwide survey for one of our clients and interviewed both senior line management and HR staff around the world. Both groups noted the importance of a linkage between line management and HR, and both groups saw the linkage as critical to their mutual future success.

It's already starting to happen. Allied-Signals' CEO views this linkage as so important, for example, that he himself is getting personally involved in a number of so-called traditional HR areas. He is spearheading efforts to reorganize work and improve training. He is involved in executive recruitment, development, and performance management. This new direction stems from his philosophy that you can't focus just on cuts, but must also prepare the company to grow and add jobs in the future. And he wants to be right in the middle of this effort.

Simply put, the days of the standalone, isolated HR department are over. The new HR function must work closely with the line and understand the line's needs. That means HR people have to ask questions like: What kind of skills do we need to drive our business in the future? Do we have those skills? If not, how do we develop them or acquire them?

The third area critical to capturing the people advantage is a supportive work place. Employers must build the kind of environment that reinforces efforts to improve business performance. That sounds almost too obvious to bear mentioning, but I wonder how many of our organizations would pass that test.

Creating the right environment has to start with eliminating unnecessary layers of management and developing leaders who are committed to removing barriers and supporting employees. Unilever, for example, a major worldwide company, competes in many different markets. It provides a great deal of autonomy to local operations, allowing local managers to make whatever decisions best meet their market's needs. Unilever also provides rigorous training for its managers worldwide. Its CEO was recently quoted as saying, "We have a consistent and long-standing policy when it comes to one thing, the importance of managing people rather than simply analyzing problems."

Going forward, we must all continually test the effectiveness of the support structures in our organizations. We need to look at every aspect, from reporting relationships and work assignments to compensation and benefit programs and evaluate everything against this basic standard: *Do programs and policies foster or impede our business goals?* When we find that they impede progress, we must also have the courage to follow through and make whatever changes are necessary to create an open, participatory environment.

At the beginning of these remarks, I outlined my view that people are our best source of long-term competitive advantage, and I've presented what I believe are the three key steps business must take to capitalize on that advantage: a new social contract; integrated business and human resource management; a supportive work place. Collectively, these will be very powerful stimulants to competitive success.

Making appropriate changes is going to demand the best of all of us in this room, but I think our efforts will help create a much more dynamic and exciting work place. Even more, I think our ability to create and sustain change over the next several years will effectively separate the winners from the losers in the new global marketplace.

The winners will be those that stop treating their people resource as a liability to be reduced and, instead, view employees as a valuable asset to be carefully managed and optimized. We must stop thinking of people as units of production and start viewing them as sources of creative ideas.

When people understand your strategic direction and goals, when they see where they fit in, when they're trained, empowered, and rewarded for helping achieve business goals, you'll see a dramatic change in the quality of your products and services; in customers' level of satisfaction; and in the efficiency with which you operate. Then, and only then, you'll begin to see the kind of bottom-line results you need to compete successfully in this tough marketplace.

Thank you.

Learning to Compete:
Developing Canada's Human Resources

C. E. RITCHIE
Chairman and Chief Executive Officer
The Bank of Nova Scotia

Delivered to the Canadian Association of University Business Officers, Winnipeg, Manitoba, June 14, 1992

SUMMARY: Banking executive C. E. Ritchie calls for significant improvements in the preparation and training of Canada's work force. Emphasizing that a lifelong commitment to learning will be essential to employment in the global marketplace, Ritchie offers provocative suggestions for upgrading and streamlining the nation's educational system.

It is an honor to have the benefit of this platform to address you on a subject of increasing concern to all of us. I will speak of the need to create in Canada a society that is committed to *lifelong* learning.

This audience needs no reminder of the paramount importance of education, from cradle to grave. You are already committed in your professional lives to the excellence of higher education in Canada, committed to providing value for money and to ensuring that the highest standards of efficiency and accountability are maintained in our colleges and universities. Many of you are also parents. So you share a deep concern for the educational preparation of your children, a preparation that must equip them to find prosperous and satisfying careers in an increasingly competitive world. And all of us in this room are citizens and taxpayers. We thus share a common concern for the continued economic health of our country. Today, the economic prospects of Canada depend as never before on the quality and relevance of our human skills.

> *SPEECH TIP*: After denying any need for such reminders, Ritchie does gently review for his listeners the many ways in which education concerns them. The fact is, people do appreciate fresh acknowledgment of their daily roles, their shared beliefs, and other important characteristics that are too often taken for granted.

In a sense, this is hardly a novel insight. It was in 1874 that Prime Minister Disraeli said of Britain: "Upon the education of the people of this country, the fate of this country depends." But as we approach the twenty-first century, the truth of Disraeli's statement has taken on even greater significance.

It has become a cliché—but nonetheless true—that ours is a knowledge-dependent economy. This means that economic value and the potential for greater productivity depend on the generation of ideas, on the manipulation of information, and on the ability of workers continuously to upgrade their skills. To succeed in such an environment, one must be capable of lifelong learning and great vocational flexibility.

The present recession has only accelerated the inevitable process of adjustment, in which businesses are forced to shed the hundreds of thousands of jobs that cannot survive Canada's cost structure in the face of more open competition. But to understand the human face of this abstract adjustment, think of the unemployed auto parts worker with twenty years' experience and still far too young to retire. What is he going to do with the next twenty or thirty years of his life? Have we equipped him with the *basic* learning skills needed to embrace complex new computer-based technology—skills that will have to be upgraded repeatedly throughout the balance of his working life? In far too many cases, I fear that we have not. That is no longer tolerable.

The importance of education obviously goes well beyond its purely economic dimension. A well-educated population is also a prerequisite for social and cultural vitality. Recent studies have even highlighted a positive linkage between one's education and one's health, irrespective of income level. So, by virtually every measure, the quality of our lives reflects the quality of our learning environment, from cradle to grave.

Today, I would like to share with you some personal thoughts as to how we might create a *superior* learning environment in Canada. My own life experience has been primarily in the business sector, so you will forgive an emphasis on the economic dimension of our education challenge. Mind you, I don't think such an emphasis is misplaced. Without economic success, there is little chance that the social and cultural goals of our society can be achieved.

SPEECH TIP: Here Ritchie very gracefully acknowledges the particular angle of his own viewpoint, while at the same time affirming the value of such an outlook on education.

Obviously I am not a professional educator. I must therefore rely heavily on the conclusions of those who have studied the issues deeply. But I am not entirely without first-hand experience. Scotia Bank is in business around the world and in all facets of the economy. This has afforded a practical perspective on what it takes to compete today, and it has given me some insight into how well the Canadian education and training system is measuring up to the task.

Both my reading and my experience have convinced me that we need to reform Canadian education in fundamental directions if we hope to make our way successfully into the twenty-first century. But before suggesting an agenda for reform, some diagnosis is in order.

Let us first ask how well Canadians are being served in return for the annual expenditure of more than $40 billion of public funds in our schools, colleges, and universities.

The good news is that virtually every young Canadian has access to basic education. Furthermore, we rank second only to the United States in the proportion of our population that goes on to college or university. And while we may wring our hands over poor performance on international tests in science and mathematics, a closer look at the numbers shows that in the *early* grades Canadians are right up among the best. So there is nothing wrong with our raw material. Unfortunately, our scores deteriorate as our students advance through higher grades. But even here, our *top* students are equal to the best in the world.

SPEECH TIP: Here and throughout, Ritchie takes pains to give credit where credit is due. This lends greater credence to his specific criticisms of Canada's educational system, and it maintains a measured, supportive foundation for his discussion overall.

Where we North Americans fail to do a good job is with the *average* performer. But it is precisely the education and training of the average performer that counts most in creating the broad base of skills for a modern competitive economy.

There is a great deal to be proud of in Canada's education system. It is a system that has reflected our society's commitment to equal opportunity as well as to respect for the differences among individuals, and, until fairly recently, it is a system that has served our economy well. But, the truth be told, education in this country is no longer doing the job that Canadians expect and require. The symptoms of failure have become all too evident and familiar. For example:

- Thirty percent of our young people fail to finish high school.

- Thirty to forty percent of adult Canadians cannot read or calculate well enough to function effectively in the modern workplace.

- Fewer than one-quarter of senior high school students take mathematics and science. Consequently, university enrollments in these critical subjects have been declining.

- Our system of vocational education is widely recognized as inadequate, particularly when compared with competitors in Europe and Asia.

- Workplace training in Canada is notoriously poor by international standards.

- And—as this audience knows better than anyone—our universities are facing a financial crisis that is eroding the quality of higher education and research in Canada.

Based on detailed analysis of such trends, the Economic Council recently warned that failure to correct the serious ills of our education system would mean that Canada's schools will graduate a *million* functional illiterates during the next decade. This would be a social and economic catastrophe. It must not be allowed to happen.

Unfortunately, there can be no quick fix. This is the wisdom of an ancient Confucian proverb, which says: "If you think in terms of a year, plant seed; if in terms of ten years, plant trees; and if in terms of a hundred years, *teach the people.*"

SPEECH TIP: Because it is equally apt as summary and as introduction, this quotation of Confucius creates a smooth transition between two sections of Ritchie's discussion.

For our impatient society, perhaps the biggest difficulty is to set our minds to a task whose payoff is measured in decades, not in days or weeks. Moreover, the barriers to fundamental reform in education have been very well constructed. Public education is fragmented among provincial jurisdictions and often among too many school boards. We face powerful institutional resistance from a system that is dominated by unions and bureaucratic administration. It is a system where seniority, more than merit, is too often the criterion for advancement. Those in control have, therefore, evolved remarkably effective tactics of self-preservation.

But, at a deeper level, we must acknowledge that the fundamental problems facing our education system—and many of the reasons why it has gotten off track—are rooted in the very nature of our society. Should we be surprised that Johnny can't read when he spends more time in the TV room than in the classroom? And when both parents work, there is less time and energy to provide the necessary encouragement and supervision at home. The problems of child poverty and the single-parent household only complicate matters further.

In short, many of the traditional disciplines and support systems of the family have been eroded, but our society has failed to face squarely the consequences of this reality. Instead, we have implicitly foisted far too many social responsibilities on our schools. In the process, we have compromised their educational objectives and exceeded their professional competence.

But in spite of the deeply rooted nature of the problems, and despite the enormous conservatism of our education industry, we really have no alternative but to tackle the issue of reform head-on. Fortunately, the public willingness to do so is building every day. Parents are increasingly dissatisfied. Employers are demanding change. And educators and administrators themselves recognize that reform is overdue, even if they cannot agree on the shape it should take.

The public school system has been the focus of most would-be reformers. This is because it presents a defined institutional target that, in theory at least, is subject to political control. But to create a learning society—a society in which education is a *lifelong* process—we must address *every* phase of human development from infancy through old age. The earliest childhood experience can be most critical, since this is the time when the biological and psychological foundations for learning are established. Without adequate care and feeding of mind and body during the first five years of life, a child's prospects will be permanently stunted.

Similarly important is the crucial transition out of grade school. If this is poorly handled, the result can be the student who is drawn by peer pressure and family expectations into a university program for which he or she lacks aptitude and motivation. In either case, there is a tragic waste of resources, both of the individual and of society.

The final critical component of the learning system, and probably the most important in narrow economic terms, is the process by which on-the-job skills are created and upgraded. By and large, this has been a haphazard process in North America. The advanced countries in continental Europe and Asia spend at least five to ten times as much per worker on training as do Canadians. For some reason, we have developed an attitude that formal education and training are "front end" investments. We have left it almost entirely to schools and colleges to provide a stream of fully prepared entrants to the work force.

Contrast this with the attitude of a company like Toyota. They see the fresh engineering graduate as almost entirely devoid of *directly* relevant knowledge. Of course the new recruit is well-equipped to *learn*, thanks to the rigors of the Japanese school system. But Toyota accepts it as their responsibility to provide an extended period of intensive training to equip the newcomer for production responsibility. And thereafter, throughout his career, the company will provide frequent intervals of formal training to continuously deepen and broaden his base of skills. The result in Japan, and in much of Europe, is a work force that views continuous training and retraining as the lifelong norm.

I have suggested that the learning process must be viewed as a *system* extending from infancy until the end of one's life, and it is a system in which each phase creates the conditions for success or failure at subsequent stages. To create the learning society that Canada needs to prosper in a world where knowledge rules requires a clear statement of the primary goals. I think it was Yogi Berra who said: "If you don't know where you're goin', you'll probably end up somewhere else." So we must begin with a sense of direction. I would propose three broad objectives:

- First, our education system should prepare young people for lifelong learning.

- Second, it should launch them into careers for which their aptitude, ambition and skills are well matched.

- And finally, it should continuously develop the potential of the individual—both intellectually and vocationally—throughout his or her adult life.

While these broad goals may seem self-evident, the fact is that Canada is falling far short of their achievement. These basic goals must nevertheless be addressed within financial constraints that have become critical. Public expenditure on formal education—more than 6 percent of our GDP—is among the highest in the world, ranking just behind the Scandinavians. Our spending per student, relative to per capita GDP, is already well above levels in the United States, Germany, and Japan. This suggests to me that Canadians will *not* have to dig deeper into the public purse to finance a superior education system. But, obviously, we will have to spend much more effectively.

Part of the answer is to eliminate *wasteful* spending that has been too readily tolerated in the past. For example, the cost of administration as a percentage of total school board expenditures has more than doubled since the early 1960s. I am skeptical that this has added much value to the educational experience.

There is ample evidence that greater education spending is *not* necessarily the key to better outcomes. For example, during the past three decades, Canada's expenditure per student has gone up more than 230 percent in real terms, and the student-teacher ratio has declined from 26:1 to approximately 16:1 today. But actual classroom results—as measured by thirty years of standardized tests—have deteriorated.

These are puzzling trends that call out for much deeper understanding of what is going wrong. Obviously, they prove the need for really fundamental reform. Fortunately, a great deal is already known about what works and what doesn't. But that wisdom has been confined to research journals and crusading editorials. Rarely has it found its way into widespread practice. That has got to change.

Many years of observation and experience have identified the common characteristics that define truly effective schools:

▨ Effective schools have high *expectations* and high standards for both achievement and behavior.

▨ Class time is overwhelmingly devoted to teaching rather than to discipline and administration.

▨ A significant amount of homework is assigned, and it is carefully marked.

▨ And, inevitably, the best schools have top-notch principals, who have been given the authority to set and enforce these high standards.

So we are not flying blind. Much of what needs to be done to achieve the broad objectives outlined above is already known to those who examined the issues closely. The missing ingredient is the will to act in the face of a group of well-entrenched interests intent on defending the status quo. But our biggest mistake would be to give up the ghost because the opposition is implacable or because we can't solve all the problems at once. The vain search for the perfect, all-encompassing solution must not be allowed to postpone improvement *today*, one step at a time.

> *SPEECH TIP:* Many speakers cite time limitations as a constraint to more in-depth discussion of the chosen issue; few are candid, modest, aware, or—paradoxically—confident enough to acknowledge the boundaries of their own expertise. The result is distinctly refreshing.

In the remainder of my remarks, I will suggest some elements of a reform agenda. Limitations of time and competence prevent me from addressing all of the critical components of our learning system. I will confine myself to a few proposals—some modest, others somewhat radical—that would put Canada on a course to create the human resources we will need to succeed in the decades ahead.

Let me begin with the grade school system. Here, the objective of reform is to reverse the deteriorating outcomes that have so alarmed parents and employers. I believe the following measures would go far to reverse the trend.

First, regarding the school curriculum: I think it should be streamlined to focus on a smaller group of basic compulsory subjects. In particular, there must be far greater emphasis on mathematics and science to prepare students to function in this technological age. It is especially important that female students receive much more encouragement to continue with mathematics through senior high school.

More generally, the qualifications of science and math teachers in the elementary grades need significant improvement. One study found that in Japan, for example, these teachers are drawn from university graduates whose mathematical skills rank in the top quarter, whereas in North America, elementary school math teachers—notwithstanding many exceptions—tend to come from the bottom quarter. No wonder we have problems. Without skillful teaching in mathematics and science in the earliest grades, most students have great difficulty with more advanced material and will give up the subjects at the first opportunity.

Second, regarding the time spent in school: North American children simply don't spend enough. Fifty years ago, every able-bodied young person might have been needed to help out on the farm, but those are bygone days. Yet the typical school year in Canada is only about 180 days, and even of that, as much as 10 percent is lost to professional development of the teaching staff. Compare this with the school year in Japan of more than 240 days or in most European countries, where 225 days is typically the minimum. The longer school year in most countries outside North America means their young people get almost one-third more basic education. Small wonder that so many Canadians now see a college degree as a minimum preparation for the workplace. It is simply the extra time required to bring the student to the level that their Dutch or German counterparts have achieved coming out of high school. For those Canadians who are unable or unwilling to go on to college, the fact that they have been short-changed in grade school means they lack proper preparation for modern vocational and on-the-job training. It is a shortcoming that haunts them the rest of their lives.

So I would suggest that the school year be lengthened to at least 200 days. Probably 225 would be better. That would still leave students and teachers with *seven weeks* of holidays.

Regarding the contentious issue of testing: I confess to being a hardliner. I can see no reason why there should not be common testing, at least province-wide, in the core subjects of the high school curriculum. It is a basic fact of human nature that the prospect of examination creates, in the vast majority of people, greater motivation to master the material. A comprehensive test also provides the opportunity to consolidate what you have taught. And a common set of tests, preferably nationwide, would provide the objective data needed to evaluate the performance of individual schools and of entire school systems.

We have all heard the counterarguments. Teachers will gear their instruction to passing the test, students will experience anxiety, which will diminish their enthusiasm for learning, cultural differences will not be taken into account, and so forth. But the truth is that rigorous, broadly based testing is the norm in many countries, just as it once was in ours. The hard facts of the matter are that once students face the world of work, they are required to meet standards of performance that are now being set by the best global competitors. And the penalty for failure in this examination is *unemployment* and *permanently* diminished prospects. So we do our students no favor by shielding them from the reality of competition and high standards of performance.

Finally, a word on changing the incentives in our school systems: It is probably unrealistic to expect that the public schools will reform *themselves* to the extent required, despite the best intentions of politicians and administrators. This is why there is increasing interest in putting some real competition into the system. One way is to give parents much freer choice of the schools their children will attend. I understand that Vancouver and Edmonton, and no doubt other communities, have had some positive experience in this regard. With freedom of choice, schools that succeed in attracting more pupils would be given greater financial support. Of course, the exercise of parental choice will only be really effective if there is enough public information, including broad-based test results, by which schools can be evaluated and compared.

Turning now to the crucial transition from school to work, one of the most significant shortcomings of our system, particularly compared with its counterparts in Europe and Asia, has been a failure to connect the grade school experience with the requirements of the workaday world. Too often, the school drop-out is simply the unmotivated student who can't see the relevance of the classroom to workplace realities. The sad truth is that our public school system pays far too little heed to the 70 percent of students who are not bound for college. The real test of the success of our schools will be the preparation and the motivation they impart to this majority, not to the academic stars. The best students will succeed in virtually any system. But what about the less *academically* inclined? I would emphasize that we're not talking here about basic intelligence. If properly motivated, those not bound for university are just as capable of developing the habits of lifelong learning as their more studious counterparts.

Surely the way to engage this majority is to provide vocational education alternatives that are *rigorous, relevant,* and *respected.* The anti-vocational cultural bias in North America must somehow be overcome.

The German system of apprenticeship is justifiably renowned, but it is certainly not the only model. For example, about one-third of Dutch students enter vocationally oriented schools at age fourteen. Employers of young people in Holland are required to grant two days of leave every week to permit part-time attendance in colleges. And the standards of performance in mathematics and language skills are high. Careful studies, carried out at the factory level in Holland and Britain, have demonstrated the significantly greater productivity and flexibility of Dutch production workers as compared with their U.K. counterparts. This superior competitive performance translates into higher earnings and, ultimately, into the prestige of what we would call "vocational careers."

I realize it will not be easy to erase the cultural bias in North America against those who choose not to take a college education. But we could start by boosting the quality of grade school education so that a university degree was no longer needed simply to provide an adequate base of intellectual skills. The vocational system could then be made challenging and equipped with sufficient resources, as it is in Holland and Germany. Then no one could brand it as a "second best" alternative.

It is also essential to expand the growing contacts between businesses and schools. These are giving students *and* their teachers a close-up look at the realities of the modern workplace, and the contacts will also give business people a realistic appreciation of the challenges in today's classroom. Progress has been impressive. Already there are about 100,000 high school students enrolled in government-assisted co-op programs. This is building on the enormously successful university co-op movement, in which Canada has been a pioneer and now leads the world in per-capita participation.

The recurring theme of my remarks is that education must be a *continuous* and lifelong endeavor. Global competition has demonstrated the need for continuous upgrading of products, of services, and especially, of people. It follows that there must be far greater commitment to training and skills upgrading by *employers* in Canada. The present shortcomings are particularly acute in smaller businesses, though certainly not confined to that sector.

Much of the reluctance of North American firms to undertake more training is a fear that the investment will be lost if the employee leaves, particularly if he leaves to join a competitor. Personally, I think this concern is overblown. It has certainly not inhibited large training investments by firms in continental Europe. More to the point, those companies that gain a reputation for excellent training will inevitably attract many more high-potential employees than the average, and they will end up keeping a good proportion, particularly if continuous training is part of an integrated program of career development.

Despite this logic, the fact remains that Canadian business, on the whole, continues to under-invest in formal training. Some extra incentive may be needed to get the ball rolling. One possibility would be to provide government-guaranteed "training loans." The *employer* would be obligated to repay the loan, *except* if the trainee quit before his employer had a reasonable time to benefit from the training investment. In that case, the *trainee* who left voluntarily would bear the obligation to repay. Of course, this obligation might then be picked up by a new employer to reflect the training benefit being inherited.

Much has been said lately about the need to build a stronger economic union in Canada. Interprovincial barriers abound in the areas of apprenticeship and professional licensing. The result is a much less efficient labor market and system of skills development. These are self-inflicted costs, which Canada can no longer afford.

So if we are serious about strengthening the economic union, we should insist that provincial governments establish compatible, *nationwide* standards in virtually every skilled area. And once those standards were met by an individual in any one province, they would be recognized throughout the country. To date, despite repeated statements of good intentions, there has been little progress. A firm nudge in the right direction is evidently needed. The present constitutional negotiations provide the ideal opportunity. If the federal government is prepared to vacate the field of manpower training, it should at least insist, as a *quid pro quo*, on common provincial standards and mutual recognition of credentials.

I would like to conclude with some observations on the subject of greatest immediate interest to this audience: our colleges and universities.

I start from the fact that our universities and colleges, to whom we entrust the education of one and a half million people, are in dire financial straits. This has persisted to the point where the quality of education and research has already suffered significantly. Too many of our brightest students have concluded they must go abroad—usually to the United States—to maximize their educational opportunities. This is an unacceptable state of affairs.

Partly, the fault lies with the universities themselves, since they have remained stubbornly isolated from the economic realities of the world around them. Among other torments, unyielding faculty demands have made university administration one of society's most thankless tasks. Your role as administrators is nonetheless all the more important, and I sense that the business end of our colleges and universities is changing significantly for the better, thanks in large part to the efforts of those of you here today.

But there is only so much economizing that can be accomplished without tackling the larger structural questions. For example, scarce university resources are being squandered by students who lack serious commitment to their studies and eventually either drop out or take far too long to complete a degree. Can we honestly say that universities have accepted their responsibility to minimize this kind of waste?

Our institutions of higher education must also face up to the consequences of those bygone days when the government gravy train was under a full head of steam. We ended up with more colleges and universities than we need, or can afford. I fear that some institutions will have to be wound up and converted to other purposes, perhaps to fill the need for more vocational facilities, as I mentioned earlier.

There is also an urgent need to rationalize many overlapping programs in a multiplicity of institutions. I am personally familiar with the situation in Nova Scotia. I would be surprised if there weren't similar opportunities right across the country. In concentrating our resources, the objective would not only be to save money. A small country like Canada—with fewer people than the state of California—also needs to concentrate academic talent in each subject area in order to build the critical mass that is needed to achieve world-class standards of excellence. In this regard, Canadians can be very proud of the Centres of Excellence programs established by Ottawa and some provinces, and I would particularly commend the outstanding initiatives of the Canadian Institute for Advanced Research. The CIAR has shown us how to pool the best research talent across Canada into focused programs that are tackling many of the most important economic, scientific and social questions of our age.

SPEECH TIP: When urging widespread reforms, speakers do very well to draw attention to efforts already underway. This helps listeners feel less thoroughly overwhelmed by the prospect of attempting such massive overhauls from scratch. And helping to publicize progressive programs promotes further study—and perhaps imitation or adaptation—of useful existing models.

When we come down to the bottom line, the *number one* challenge facing institutions of higher education in Canada is simply to obtain the revenue needed to deliver what is expected of them. Obviously, it would be easier if Canadian universities enjoyed the same philanthropic support as their counterparts south of the border. For example, the annual income per student at Stanford University from gifts and endowment exceeds $20,000. This dwarfs, by a factor of ten or more, the amount from comparable sources in Canada. For some reason, the pools of significant individual wealth in this country have never equaled the generosity toward universities that the Americans have. But now that excellence in education and research is increasingly seen as a key for economic success, I would hope that philanthropic support of universities might increase significantly.

But what about *tuition*? Why do we Canadians leave this largest and most appropriate source of university revenue almost untapped? In 1990, student tuition covered only about 15 percent of the cost of the average college education, a proportion that has declined significantly over the years. In the early sixties, tuition covered almost a third of student cost. When we consider that the majority of university students come from the wealthiest quarter of the population, the public subsidy implied by ludicrously low tuition appears to be socially inequitable. Yet, in the convoluted logic of politics, we have somehow concluded that tuition must be kept low in order to protect universal access to higher education opportunities. This is nonsense. Experience in many countries has proven that access to university education is largely unrelated to the tuition that is charged. Disadvantaged students are frequently seen on the campuses of private U.S. universities despite tuition levels of more than $15,000.

The explanation is simple. Those universities have set aside a portion of their ample revenue to fund generous scholarships for academically deserving but financially disadvantaged students. There is no reason why tuition in Canadian universities should not cover as much as 50 percent of the cost of education. Even at that, the fee would be considerably less than the rates charged by many U.S. institutions. Furthermore, students (or parents) who *paid* more would *demand* more—another healthy spur to excellence.

Being realistic, it is probably too much to expect any one university—or even a provincial system of universities—to take such a bold step alone. The courageous pioneers would likely end up with *no* students and *no* revenue. So we need some leadership and concerted action from every province and every university.

Let me conclude with one final thought about the future. We now live in a world where economic prosperity and personal fulfillment depend on the ability to master and to create knowledge. Canadians must therefore either develop high skills or accept low wages. The geometric growth in the amount and sophistication of technology demands a learning culture. Fortunately, the march of technology is also creating the opportunity to equip every citizen with the *means* to learn throughout their lives.

Consider television. It may be the bane of parents and educators. But, for better or worse, TV is a medium of enormous power to impart ideas, particularly to the younger generation. Social critics have expressed alarm—and rightly so—at the prospect of proliferating television signals emanating from so-called "death star" satellites, which will beam hundreds of channels into virtually every home. On the other hand, what an opportunity to impart skills and knowledge throughout one's lifetime! In an endless variety of subjects, and from the most talented tutors.

But to seize this opportunity, the *appetite* for lifelong learning must first be stimulated. That, ladies and gentlemen, is our challenge.

CHAPTER 7

Government and Regulation

Business people generally have strong feelings about the relationship between business and government, and speeches on the subject both generate and address some very strong feelings. Emotionally charged subjects make for high-profile speeches that can be exciting to hear and quite gratifying to the speaker's ego. The problem, however, is to avoid, on the one hand, mere demagoguery or preaching to the choir, and, on the other hand, deliberately provoking a possibly hostile audience, thereby generating more heat than light.

How do you walk the line between these two extremes?

The most effective strategy is to balance appeals to emotion with relevant facts and figures. These should be carefully chosen to illustrate your point, and they should be made as vivid, immediate, and *real* as possible. All the speeches in this section have at least some element of combativeness. Certainly, it is always clear just where the speaker stands. But, passionate as these speakers are, they all support their feelings and assertions with verifiable facts.

The chief lesson these speeches offer other speakers is one that is as difficult to put into practice as it is simple to understand: The more emotionally charged your subject, the greater the amount of rational, intellectual homework you need to do.

While you must not let the fruits of this homework smother the passion and conviction that originally motivated the speech, you should not be too afraid that an audience will be bored by facts. Think of the tremendous quarter-century success of a television program like *60 Minutes*, which is a skillful blend of emotion and fact. Careful preparation will mean that you may well convert—or at least induce thought among—a hostile audience. Perhaps even more important, the information provided in a well-researched speech will *empower* a friendly audience, an audience with whom you are essentially in agreement. Instead of merely commiserating with such an audience, you have the opportunity of educating a highly motivated group and even directing them to action.

International Aviation at the Crossroads

ROBERT L. CRANDALL
Chairman and President
American Airlines, Inc.

Delivered to the Economic Club of Detroit, November 10, 1992

SUMMARY: American Airlines president Robert L. Crandall recounts the evolution of postwar international aviation agreements and discusses their continued effect on the global competitiveness of U.S. carriers today. Sharply criticizing the American government's past and present policies when negotiating bilateral route rights with foreign countries, Crandall also warns against the long-term impact on the national interest of a proposed transaction that would integrate the networks of British Airways and USAir. Crandall calls instead for a worldwide, multilateral open skies agreement.

Thank you, Chick, and good afternoon, ladies and gentlemen. I'm pleased to have this opportunity to talk with you about the airline business, which is one of our country's most interesting, most important, and most troubled industries. As you all know, our industry seems to be in a state of perpetual turmoil. Since we were deregulated back in 1978, the pace of change has been fast and furious:

> *SPEECH TIP:* Like the changes he describes, Crandall sets a snappy pace right at the outset of his presentation, showing that preambles needn't amble.

- Carriers have reshaped their route systems to revolve around more than twenty hubs throughout the country.

- Consumers have been presented with vastly expanded choices of carriers and services in virtually every origin and destination market.

- Computerized reservation systems, which offer every prospective customer complete information about every airline's prices and products, have become the mainstay of the airline distribution system.

- The inherent conflicts of our business, which create nearly irresistible incentives for every carrier to offer seats for any price higher than out-of-pocket cash costs, have stimulated extraordinary price competition and tremendous growth—but produced little profit.

In this intensely competitive environment, some have failed, others have succeeded. In general, the market has awarded victory to those carriers that have been most successful in fashioning carefully integrated route networks, which serve a large percentage of potential customers.

These changes to the domestic industry have had important effects in the international arena as well. While international aviation remains heavily regulated, the key to success there, as in domestic aviation, is a comprehensive route system offering service in many origin-destination city pairs. Unfortunately, the U.S. government has not paid as much attention to the competitive importance of international route structures as have foreign governments, and unless that deficiency is soon corrected, competitive parity may become permanently out of reach.

International aviation is governed by the provisions of an agreement crafted at a conference held in Chicago in 1944 to plan the world's postwar aviation system. The United States advocated a multilateral agreement, which would have given all carriers the ability to serve all markets—a true open-skies approach. However, because most nations at the time felt that the overwhelming economic strength of the U.S. would allow its airlines to use open skies as a route to permanent dominance, the conference chose instead to regulate international aviation by means of bilateral aviation agreements between pairs of countries.

> *SPEECH TIP:* Crandall serves his later arguments well by taking time to review the regulatory history of international aviation. What may be old hat to an industry's insiders is often big news to audience members from other business backgrounds.

In the years since, most nations other than the U.S. have given the interests of their airlines a high priority during bilateral discussions. As a consequence, most bilaterals limit, rather than encourage, competition. The restrictive instincts of most of the world's governments—and the unwillingness of the U.S. government to exert its negotiating leverage—have denied U.S. carriers not only dominance, but even the level of leadership, which should be the natural benefit of being based in the world's largest aviation market.

Unhappily, international aviation is but one area of trade in which our government has handicapped U.S. producers. For many years, the U.S. approach to trade negotiations has been shaped by several unique perspectives:

> *SPEECH TIP:* Sketching out the larger influences of postwar culture and politics, Crandall situates aviation regulations in the context of American trade policy as a whole.

- The first is the sense of *noblesse oblige,* which arose from the nation's posture at the end of World War II. Our shores were untouched by the ravages of war, opportunity was everywhere, and a sense of obligation to help those less fortunate than ourselves was deeply engrained in our national psyche. In economic terms, these views translated into an inordinate willingness to give market access to every country that passed our political litmus test.

- A second factor bearing on U.S. postwar trade policy has been our government's abiding belief in the superiority of U.S. producers. That view, which matched reality at the end of World War II, has made it easy to argue that any agreement that increases trade opportunities, even if that agreement is imbalanced in favor of foreign producers, is likely to increase economic activity, advance the cause of free trade and—theoretically—broaden the market for U.S. goods and services.

- Third, our trade and economic policies have been predicated on the premise that consumer benefit should be the primary focus of trade policy. In most other nations, governments believe that improving production, service, and distribution opportunities for their companies—and thus, increasing jobs—should be the paramount goals of economic diplomacy. Most governments recognize, more clearly than the United States, that workers and consumers are simply the same folks in different roles.

- Finally, all our trade negotiations since World War II have been conducted in the shadow of our focus on national security issues. For many years, advancing U.S. economic issues has been secondary to achieving our geopolitical objectives.

As a consequence of all these factors, we have often given considerably more than we've gotten in trade negotiations—but our trading partners, virtually without exception, have taken a more mercantilist point of view, focusing more than we on creating competitive advantage for their producers. While few United States companies can blame all their international problems on U.S. trade negotiators, I think it's fair to say that U.S. trade policy has contributed to our worldwide competitive difficulties in virtually every industry.

That is certainly the case in international aviation, where the last twenty years have been a long tale of missed opportunities. Although U.S. airlines are willing and able to compete worldwide, the United States has failed to use its negotiating leverage either to secure as many route rights as it could have or to assure U.S. carriers of full opportunities to optimize the use of the rights they have. As a consequence, U.S. carriers operating abroad must deal with a host of non-tariff barriers, including inadequate airport facilities, non-competitive arrival and departure slots at foreign airports, prohibitions on the use of proprietary computer systems, and even, in some countries, requirements that we hire our competitors to provide customer services.

Moreover, the U.S. has been reluctant to hold its aviation partners to the agreed terms of bilateral agreements. For example: When American attempted to launch service between Miami and Madrid in 1991—a route provided for in the existing agreement between the United States and Spain—we were denied the right to do so until the U.S. government agreed to provide substantial new opportunities for Iberia, a carrier wholly owned and heavily subsidized by the government of Spain.

Our agreement with Japan, negotiated in 1952, permits either side to designate multiple airlines for U.S.-Japan service, but the Japanese, for many years, have simply ignored the agreement. Thus, my own and other U.S. carriers anxious to tap the Japanese market from our major hubs in the United States and to participate in burgeoning intra-Asian markets are prohibited from doing so.

Worst of all, perhaps, is the United Kingdom. Our first bilateral with the U.K., negotiated in 1946, was known as the Bermuda Agreement. In 1976, deciding that they did not wish to honor that pact's provisions, the British simply renounced the agreement and persuaded the U.S. government to accept, in its place, "Bermuda 2," which is far more favorable to U.K. carriers and far more limiting on our own. As a codicil to that agreement, the U.S. even agreed to give Britain veto power over which U.S. carriers we may designate to serve Heathrow—an expensive mistake, which came home to roost last year, when the U.S. decided to designate United and American to fly to Heathrow in lieu of TWA and Pan Am. Believe it or not, just to gain the right to substitute two U.S. airlines for two others, the U.S. was persuaded to grant U.K. carriers an extraordinary package of new authorities, and allowed the U.K. government to subject American and United to even more onerous frequency restrictions at Heathrow than had previously been in effect.

SPEECH TIP: Having offered compelling evidence of things gone awry in days gone by, the speaker is now well-positioned to discuss his views about policy planning for the future.

Unfortunately, the lost opportunities of the past twenty years pale by comparison to the consequences we may suffer in the next twenty years if we fail to understand—and respond to—new forces now reshaping international aviation. In international, as in domestic aviation, consumers generally prefer, if given a choice, to travel on a single carrier. A carrier that serves more markets than its competitors thus has a great advantage. This phenomenon—and our government's inattention to it—was instrumental in the failure of Pan American World Airways, long the premier U.S. international carrier. For many years, U.S. government policy denied Pan Am the right to build a domestic system to collect traffic to support its international services. During those same years, Pan Am's European and Asian competitors built strong hubs in their own countries and used those hubs to transfer cargo and passengers from other points in their countries—and other countries around the world—to and from the U.S.. Hubs like BA's at Heathrow, Air France's at Paris, KLM's at Amsterdam, Lufthansa's at Frankfurt, and JAL's at Tokyo gave the foreign carriers great advantages relative to Pan Am. While Pan Am's demise cannot be blamed exclusively on this factor, I think most knowledgeable people would agree that if Pan Am had had domestic rights during the '60s and '70s, and had developed a full-fledged hub-and-spoke system, it would likely be a vigorous global competitor today.

Be that as it may, the U.S. domestic carriers that have grown the most since 1978—American, United, and Delta—have done precisely as Pan Am might have done, but in reverse. Each of us has developed powerful domestic hubs and used them to support a growing network of international services.

Our collective ability to compete more effectively—and our enthusiastic desire to do so—has sparked a growing hue and cry from our international partners for access to the large domestic market from which U.S. carriers derive their strength. This effort should be seen for what it is: an attempt to create a unique advantage by gaining hub strength on both sides of the oceans over which they fly.

The major transaction now under consideration—a real watershed whose resolution will shape global aviation for many years to come—is the proposal that British Airways be allowed to acquire effective control of USAir. This transaction, advertised as a foreign investment likely to promote enhanced competition, is about neither investment nor competition. Rather, it is about the creation of a global network structured to prevent effective competition by U.S. carriers.

The BA transaction, and others like it, if permitted, will tilt the playing field forever in favor of foreign carriers. With hubs in both the United States and overseas, such carriers will have access to the 50 percent of the world's aviation market represented by U.S. traffic—as well as the other half, which they are already able to serve.

The worst element of the proposed transaction is that the combined BA-USAir network—and others like it—will be immune to effective competition from U.S. carriers. The two route networks, on the day they are combined, will give British

Airways the ability to serve twelve thousand U.S.-to-foreign-city markets. While U.S. carriers are willing and eager to compete, we will be precluded from doing so in about two-thirds of those markets.

I have little doubt that, within short order, British Airways, which is run by a very capable management team, will optimize the scheduling of the combined BA-USAir fleets to create more than twenty thousand U.S.-to-foreign-city markets, most of which will be closed to U.S. carriers.

Unfortunately, U.S. carriers will not be able to respond, for several reasons.

First, U.S. carriers are not permitted to fly beyond most foreign hub cities to the many points in other nations served by our foreign competitors. The right to fly, say, from the U.K. to Thailand, or from the U.K. to Kenya, or from the U.K. to Greece requires the consent of our own government, the government of the United Kingdom, and the government of the third country to which a U.S. carrier proposes service. Such rights are unlikely to be granted.

Second, even if the needed route rights could be secured, the United Kingdom is unwilling to provide the takeoff and landing slots and facilities required to compete effectively with British Airways at Heathrow. Nor are slots and facilities available at other foreign hub cities—Frankfurt, Paris, Tokyo, and others.

Third, the deregulated character of the U.S. market has created a unique opportunity for foreign airlines. Only the United States has a fully deregulated industry, which includes multiple substantial carriers that can be effectively mated with foreign airlines to create global networks. American—or United—or Delta— cannot buy a European carrier with which to mirror the BA-USAir transaction because there are no substantial European carriers to buy! Few small privately owned airlines exist, and none have had the resources with which to establish an effective presence at any international hub. This means that the only way to create a global carrier will be for foreign carriers to own or control U.S. airlines. The inevitable consequence—ten or fifteen or twenty years hence—is that all U.S. carriers will be either foreign owned or, alternatively, will be effectively excluded from international competition.

Now, before you chuckle to yourself and write me off as an alarmist, ask yourself: "How many in this room would have predicted, twenty years ago, that Pan Am would not exist in 1992?" Ladies and gentlemen, unless the U.S. government chooses the right course, international aviation will be yet another industry in which both primacy and parity will be lost.

What must be done?

Our government must set aside its past paradigms and modify its past practices. We need to develop and apply an aviation trade policy consistent with the long-term national interest.

As a first step, the U.S. government should set aside its long-held belief that Uncle knows best. Incredibly, the Department of Transportation, which has no one on its staff with any substantive airline experience, refuses to permit our country's major airlines to participate in international aviation negotiations. In the current talks with the United Kingdom, the U.K.'s negotiators are joined at the table by representatives of British Airways. United, American, and Delta are unrepresented. Even more incredibly, the United States government has never performed an economic analysis of the proposed British Airways-USAir transaction. *We* have, and we have told the D.O.T. that the transaction, if approved, will divert more than $500 million of revenue annually away from U.S. carriers and into the coffers of the new British Airways. Washington's reaction has been a combination of indifference and lack of interest.

Second, the U.S. must find a way to come to grips with the unique policy problems presented by having the world's only truly pluralistic airline industry. In most countries—the U.K., Germany, France, Japan—governments and aviation interests speak with a common voice. In the United States, because we have a deregulated, competitive industry, and because competitive airlines inevitably have different interests, it is up to the government to shape divergent advice into coherent public policy. To date, its focus has been almost exclusively on the short-term consumer implications of alternative decisions. Continuing that focus will inevitably produce a nation whose aviation industry employs many fewer than today's, whose consumers are poorer, and which is served primarily by foreign-owned carriers.

Unhappily, some bad decisions have already been made. The open skies agreement recently negotiated with the Netherlands—which, believe it or not, gave KLM unrestricted rights within the U.S. in exchange for unrestricted U.S. carrier rights within the "enormous" borders of the Netherlands—will strengthen KLM at the expense of U.S. carriers. Similarly, the proposed British Airways transaction will strengthen BA at the expense of U.S. carriers, and both transactions will encourage other foreign carriers to bid aggressively for other U.S. airlines—again, at the expense of the remaining U.S. carriers.

Many will contend that the short-term benefits of these transactions are good for U.S. consumers. In my view, those benefits are a grossly inadequate tradeoff for the long-term competitive disadvantages that their realization will impose on the U.S. airline industry. Unless the tradeoffs are recognized and measured soon, our government seems likely to make the wrong choices.

Third, America's airlines need our government's help when confronted by exclusionary commercial practices. While U.S. law entitles U.S. carriers to equal competitive opportunities vis-a-vis foreign carriers, our government has ignored its obligation to enforce its bilateral agreements. Thus:

- U.S. computerized reservations systems, the best in the world, are excluded from France and Spain

- U.S. airlines are denied adequate facilities in London, Milan, Paris, and other cities around the world

- U.S. airlines are forbidden to use their proprietary computer systems in the battle for service supremacy

- And U.S. carriers are competitively disadvantaged abroad in a host of other ways

These matters are readily addressed. We require only a government with a resolve equal to its resources. Unless we soon exercise that resolve, rethink our policy options, and give greater weight in our negotiations to the importance of U.S.-owned producers, there simply won't be a U.S. international aviation industry twenty years hence.

Since that would be a poor result, I think it's time—past time—for the U.S. to call again, as it did in 1944, for a worldwide, multilateral open skies agreement.

If the United Kingdom and other nations truly believe in competitive, free-market solutions, they will support us—and we can turn all the world's airlines, U.S. and foreign alike, loose to work the magic of competition in every market. But if other countries are not willing to support new opportunities for all, they should not be allowed to buy their way into U.S. markets to the detriment of U.S. producers.

Thank you very much.

Flash: The Sky is **Not** Falling!
A Call for Balance

EARNST W. DEAVENPORT, JR.
President
Eastman Chemical Company

Delivered to the Downtown Rotary Club, Knoxville, Tennessee, June 30, 1992

SUMMARY: Eastman president Earnst W. Deavenport, Jr. speaks with pride of his chemical company's environmental efforts as well as its contributions to the Tennessee economy. Stating that good business policy makes good environmental policy, Deavenport warns against emotional decision-making and policy "imbalance" in the allocation of America's national resources.

Thank you, John, and good afternoon, ladies and gentlemen.

It's good to be back in Knoxville. I was here in April to participate in the Europe Business Outlook Conference, but since then, I've been on the road. I've just returned from the former Soviet Union, where Eastman announced a joint venture with two Belarus companies and Pepsi-Cola to produce resin for plastic soft drink bottles.

I'm pleased to report that capitalism is alive and well there. Little boys were running around peddling Soviet Army hats and medals, but I didn't see anybody selling missiles in Red Square!

I *did* buy a hat. I'm going to put it on when things aren't going well in a meeting and announce that I'm making a command decision!

Seriously, though, I plan to keep the hat in my office . . . not for command decisions, but as a reminder of what can happen when things get out of balance. That's why the Soviet economy collapsed, and then the government. The guns and butter equation got out of balance. Too many guns and not enough butter.

Whenever extremists on either side of an issue have too much input, the inevitable result is the misallocation of resources.

Today, I want to talk about keeping things in balance, keeping environmental issues and economic issues in perspective. In that regard, I have good news for you. Despite some of the doomsday predictions made at the Earth Summit in Rio earlier this month, *the sky is not falling*. And, if we can strike a balance between the allocation of resources and preserving the environment, we can, indeed, accomplish what the folks in Rio set out to do: *save the planet.*

But I'm getting ahead of myself. Let's talk, first, about the home front: Tennessee.

> *SPEECH TIP*: Deavenport's introductory remarks deal with far-flung places and even embrace the planet as a whole. But the speaker really gets down to business when he "homes" in on the home state.

We've read a lot in the newspapers lately about Tennessee being near the top of the EPA list of toxic waste producers. Other headlines shout that the state of Tennessee is ranked second worst in air pollution. Using EPA's measuring criteria, the headlines are right. But headlines don't tell the whole story. The rest of the story is that air emissions were down by 11 percent here in Tennessee during the most recent reporting period—the third straight decline. That's progress.

Tennessee should be proud of its economic and environmental progress. We're certainly proud to be a part of it, a large part. Eastman is Tennessee's largest industrial employer and one of the largest chemical complexes in the United States. Over 12,000 work in our Kingsport facility. We have 391 buildings located on an 850-acre site. Last year, in East Tennessee, we pumped more than $1.1 billion into the local economy for salaries and benefits, materials and services, freight, and local taxes.

And we're not standing still. We're growing.

We spend $200 to $300 million each year on capital projects in Kingsport. That's like having several multimillion-dollar companies move into Tennessee every year. Our sales last year were around $4 billion. That's a considerable economic impact for the state.

But, so what? So we're big. What good do we do?

> **SPEECH TIP:** Speakers who ask *themselves* the rudest, most unsympathetic questions any audience member could conceivably raise provide themselves with the chance to answer such questions successfully.

Well, we're a supplier to other industries: automotive, housing, aircraft, agriculture, textiles, pharmaceutical, and many, many others. We supply these industries with chemicals, plastics, and fibers—raw materials for products that enhance the quality of life for millions of people around the world, and, in the process, we generate air emissions, we generate solid wastes, and we require a great deal of water during the course of daily operations.

So, what are we doing about it? How are we treating the environment?

I am well aware that we in the chemical industry have a poor public image when it comes to the environment. Some players in the industry made some bad mistakes in the past, and history has a habit of following you around.

But a lot of things have changed.

Technology, especially. Eastman's operating procedures and monitoring systems are state-of-the-art. In 1991, we spent almost $200 million on environmental protection and improvements. That's 5 percent of sales; as a percentage, that's more than any other major chemical company. And we've become more environmentally sensitive. We're the energy behind a recycling effort like nothing else in the country.

Several years ago, Eastman and Waste Management teamed up to build a Recycling Center in Kingsport to provide the entire Northeast Tennessee-Southwest Virginia region with a place to recycle glass, aluminum, paper, and plastics. It's been a huge success. In fact, last year, the Recycling Center received a national award from Keep America Beautiful. It's the first industry-community project of its kind in the country.

We're making progress in other areas as well. Our new waste water treatment facility is a good example. It's built off the ground on concrete pillars so inspectors can walk underneath to check for leaks. Innovative stuff.

We're making good progress. That's why I take exception when I hear that the threat of appearing on an EPA toxic list is an incentive for manufacturing plants in Tennessee to "clean up." To paraphrase President Eisenhower: "Hitting someone over the head isn't leadership. That's assault."

The incentive for reducing waste is the bottom line on a balance sheet, not the top line on an EPA list.

Waste costs money. It hurts when you make it, and it hurts when you have to get rid of it. So the incentive is not to make waste in the first place. That's just good business sense. Good business policy makes good environmental policy, not the other way around.

The chemical industry is proof that good business policies translate into good environmental policies. The industry provides some of this country's highest paying jobs. Obviously this increases our standard of living. In terms of the nation's balance of trade, the chemical industry puts something on the plus side: $19 billion last year.

But, let's face it. Manufacturing chemicals can be a risky business. We know how to manage those risks. Is it worth it?

Ask the farmer who relies on herbicides and fertilizers. The U.S. can feed the world because of chemicals. Ask the terminally ill patient suffering with pain. Chemicals make life bearable. Ask the parents of a child with a life-threatening disease. Chemicals make life possible.

SPEECH TIP: Here Deavenport uses a tried-and-true rhetorical technique: he refers his audience to people whose vested interests in an issue are even more compelling than his own.

The notion of a zero-risk society, touted by some environmental extremists, needs close scrutiny. Risks are inherent in life, but risk assessment should be based on reasonable probability and scientific knowledge—not emotion. Even government agencies disagree on what constitutes zero risk. The Food and Drug Administration, probably the most conservative agency in federal government, figures that a risk of one-in-a-million equals zero.

Not the EPA. A one-in-a-million risk factor often drives environmental policy, such as Superfund or RCRA cleanup standards. This kind of risk assessment often results in a gross misallocation of resources—resources that could be used in other areas of our society.

The American people agree. A CNN/*Time* magazine poll showed that more than half of those surveyed feel that some people go too far in their environmental demands. Take the Earth Summit as an example. Clearly, the threat of global warming is an issue that can't be ignored, and we should continually pursue the whole truth about it. But to treat climate change as the most critical issue facing the human condition at this time, as some claim, is like the tail wagging the dog. It's out of perspective. It's out of balance.

For the United States, the Earth Summit amounted to international "greenmail"—an attempt by many nations to extort money from the American public. I applaud President Bush for taking a stand in Rio against costly measures to limit carbon dioxide emissions through heavy energy taxes. The Department of Energy calculates that the cost of such policies would double the price of electricity over the next ten years.

Is the earth in serious jeopardy if we do *not* spend the money? The George C. Marshall Institute—a Who's Who of science—estimates that a five-year delay in limiting carbon emissions will make the world warmer in the next century by no more than one-tenth of a degree. Now, listen to this quote from the Marshall Institute: "An additional warming of one tenth of a degree in the twenty-first century is a very small penalty to pay for better information on government decisions that, if taken unwisely, can be extraordinarily costly to the U.S. economy."

As columnist George Melloan observed last week in the *Wall Street Journal*: "The sky is not falling, so let's not play Chicken Little with billions of dollars of the American public's money." And while we're at it, let's you and I not be silent when others refer to this country as "Uncle Filthy."

The United States has done more to protect the environment than any other country in the world. The facts speak for themselves. The United States spent more than $115 billion on environmental protection in 1991; that's more than 2 percent of Gross National Product. More than any other country. More than Japan. More than Canada. More than Germany. Yet we're being bullied into believing we have done little.

This is not to say that we don't face some challenging environmental problems. We do. But is the environment the only pressing problem?

The World Bank's 1992 *World Development Report*, published just last month, suggests that there are other global issues that deserve our resources and attention.

Drinking water is one. The report says that two million people, mostly children, die each year as a result of dirty water due to poor sanitary conditions. The report states that providing sanitation and clean water to the world's poor would be the single most effective means of alleviating human distress.

Another critical issue is world trade. The World Bank report says that a 50 percent reduction in trade barriers by Europe, the U.S., and Japan could raise export earnings from developing countries by $65 billion by the end of the decade—money that could provide critical resources needed to address the environment and other problems. Again, good business policy makes good environmental policy.

Still another difficult and sensitive issue is world population. Another is world peace. The Cold War may be over, but shooting wars aren't.

I could go on, but you get the idea.

When this country is spending 2 percent of GNP on environmental protection at a time when America is ranked twenty-first in the world in education, and there is an urgent cry for adequate housing for the poor and homeless in the country, and medical researchers are begging for money to track down killers like the AIDS virus and heart disease, I say that things are out of balance.

Remember the Alar scare? How about Chilean grapes? These were scare stories that cost fruit growers, retailers, and freight haulers millions of dollars before the apologies could be printed.

Something even more devastating could take place right here at home. There's been talk about building an imaginary fence around the Smokies—120 miles out from its boundaries—to keep industrial development out. Such a proposal, if adopted, would be economically devastating to the states of North Carolina, Tennessee, and the [Great Smokies National] Park itself. It's poor business policy, and poor environmental policy as well.

When some activists in the National Park Service objected to Eastman building its new power-generating plant in Kingsport, we used an EPA analysis model to see what the fuss was about. Their model showed that emissions from our new coal-fired boiler would be about the same as driving one car each day continuously through the park. Put another way, our emissions will be equivalent to one inch in a million-mile journey.

Now, ladies and gentlemen, I'm no rocket scientist, but I believe that's about as close to a zero impact as I know.

Environmental risks should be assessed by the proper use of scientific data, not emotion.

Many of the world's leading scientists and intellectuals—including more than thirty Nobel Prize winners—believe so, too. They said it best in a petition called the Heidelberg Appeal, sent to the heads of state who attended the Earth Summit. Here's what they said:

> We are worried, at the dawn of the twenty-first century, at the emergence of an irrational ideology which is opposed to scientific and industrial progress and impedes economic and social development.

> We fully subscribe to the objectives of a scientific ecology for a universe whose resources must be taken stock of, monitored, and preserved.

> But we herewith demand that this stock-taking, monitoring and preservation be founded on scientific criteria and not on irrational preconceptions.

At Eastman we use scientific criteria to guide our business decisions, especially on environmental matters. We believe in balance in all things. That's the nature of our business. But we also want the allocation of our national resources put in perspective. We don't want some visiting industrialist, years from now, taking one of our army hats back home as a reminder of what can happen when things get out of balance.

SPEECH TIP: Deavenport's twist on his opening reference to Russian army hats creates an unexpectedly symmetrical closing for his speech.

The Future Energy Policy: Cooperation Is the Key

CHARLES J. DIBONA
President and Chief Executive Officer
American Petroleum Institute

Delivered to the Annual Meeting of the American Petroleum Institute, Washington, D.C., November 9, 1992

SUMMARY: A week after the November 1992 national elections, American Petroleum Institute president Charles J. DiBona expresses his concerns about the future direction of U.S. energy and environmental policies—and their impact on the oil industry—as these policies undergo the combined influence of the incoming Clinton administration and the newly elected Democratic Congress.

Today, this industry and the country stand at a crossroads—a crossroads created by great pessimism over the nation's economic future. The electorate has put into office a new president and vice president who have sharply different ideas from their predecessors as to how to lead the country back to a rising standard of living.

The question is: What will this change mean for our industry?

The general consensus is that it will mean more—and worse—trouble, although some might wonder how things *could* be worse. After all, as an industry, we have lost nearly 450,000 jobs in the last decade—72,000 just in the past year. We have not been permitted to open the most important prospecting areas in the country for development. And we are confronted with the prospect of spending upwards of $20 billion annually to comply with environmental mandates that, in many cases, may produce only marginal benefits.

Nevertheless, at this crossroads, we are understandably concerned that a new Democratic administration, assisted by a House and Senate controlled by the same party, could put in place interventionist energy policies that would force our domestic petroleum industry and the American consumer farther down the road of economic hardship. It would be foolish not to worry—and yet, things may not be as bad as they seem. It may be, in the immortal words of Yogi Berra, a case of "*Déjà vu* all over again."

> *SPEECH TIP:* Churchill was certainly wittier, and Lincoln was more profound, but Yogi Berra remains a favorite with speakers because his malapropisms exemplify the "just folks" wisdom that many people enjoy.

Once again, as in 1976, we are confronted with a leadership that seeks to wean the nation *away* from oil. But the Carter administration soon learned that other national objectives can, and do, get in the way of simplistic solutions—objectives like the need to encourage strong economic growth. And the lesson for us should be the same now as then. It would be a great mistake simply to hunker down. We need to be proactive, to come forward and make our case that available, low-cost energy is essential to job creation and to a robust economy. We need to do so in a spirit of cooperation, to demonstrate that we want to be a part of the solution, not a part of the problem.

Today I'd like to review some of the challenges in our immediate future, look at the economic and political constraints that might mitigate them, and encourage all of us to make our positions—unpopular and politically incorrect though they may be—heard at all levels of government. We have a strong case. We need to make it clearly.

Of course, our challenges are substantial. First, there's the matter of the new president's appointments. So far, he has selected as his vice president a true believer in government activism, particularly in the environmental area. If President-elect Clinton makes similar appointments for key energy and environmental positions in his administration, we can be prepared for an avalanche of legislative and regulatory proposals that would dramatically increase bureaucracy and the costs of regulation.

Second, there's the matter of a Democratic Congress. Many of their initiatives have been thwarted over the years by Republican presidents. A poll of Senate candidates taken in October shows that the new Senate will be noticeably *more* liberal on energy and environmental issues, and a changed House has been profiled as younger and more environmentally activist, though it also may be more fiscally conservative. So, we can probably expect House and Senate members to re-introduce previously defeated proposals that would make it more difficult for us to operate here at home.

Third, there's the very tangible matter of the Clinton campaign's energy policy. Simply put, it argued that massive reductions in energy use, combined with mandated use of alternative fuels, could reduce the need for oil, and thus justify placing the Arctic National Wildlife Refuge and most offshore areas permanently off limits.

Campaign platforms, of course, are not necessarily policy blueprints for a new administration. Nevertheless, the intention of this one could not be plainer: It is to diminish the role of oil.

So what are the constraints that could moderate these intentions?

Above all, there is the matter of the *meaning* of last Tuesday's election. This election was not a mandate for the interventionist government view, nor was it a referendum on pump-priming versus supply-side economics. Instead, this election was clearly an expression of exasperation, and a call for action, not talk, about jobs and economic growth.

The American people were angry with policy makers who, among other things, wouldn't or couldn't get the economy moving. So they shook things up. To powerfully underscore the message of change, fourteen states voted to limit the terms of their legislators.

Clearly, the American people are serious about not accepting a stagnant economy and about wanting leaders who will be more aggressive in finding ways to give them, and their children, the enhanced economic prosperity and security they have come to expect. And this puts tremendous pressure on government to take actions that will end the prolonged economic slowdown and put us on the track for another long period of solid economic growth.

Four years from now, President-elect Clinton, the beneficiary of some of this year's protest votes, will either have succeeded by doing some sensible things with the economy, or he himself will be the victim of a protest vote. The election results and the imperative for economic growth should also dampen the enthusiasm of the Democratic Congress for extreme, anti-growth legislation, because they, too, will be held responsible for the results. Without an opposition president to blame for unwise policies, Congress must be—and has in the past been—more careful of the legislation it sends forward. When President Carter took office in 1977, a Democratic Congress declined to pass a number of measures that previous Democratic Congresses had sent to Republicans Nixon and Ford for their certain veto.

The imperative for growth should play a major role in the policies the new president will advocate. He is going to start from behind the economic eightball, facing a record deficit, a budget impasse, and growing health-care costs, among other serious domestic concerns. Despite talk of bold "first 100 day" plans, President-elect Clinton will have to be careful that his spending and taxing policies do not alarm financial markets and cause stock prices to fall, interest rates to rise, and confidence to ebb. And he will have to factor in the global economy, and deal with the fact that the United States cannot remain globally competitive if it moves massively away from abundant and low-cost oil and natural gas.

The proposals in the Clinton campaign's energy platform, if implemented, could substantially raise the cost of doing business and cause the economic situation to worsen significantly. This is the heart of the matter.

The Clinton campaign's major energy plank was a promise to cut oil consumption by nearly two million barrels per day by the year 2000. This would be accomplished by adopting an aggressive program to substitute natural gas for oil, primarily through incentives for natural gas use in homes, businesses, electrical generation, and transportation. Initially, mandates would convert the enormous federal vehicle fleet to natural gas. And, soon after, *all* fleet vehicles—public and private—would be forced to use some alternative fuel.

No one can doubt that there is an important and growing role for natural gas in U.S. markets, but a realistic and effective policy must focus on supply and demand. Domestically produced gas, which accounts for a quarter of our energy supplies, *cannot* substitute for a significant portion of the 40 percent of our energy that is supplied by oil *and* at the same time satisfy the growth in the nation's energy demand that will accompany a growing economy. That is simply wishful think-ing. When, on top of this, you also *prevent* new offshore and Alaskan oil and gas production and yet expect to reduce dependence on oil imports, then you have to believe in fairy tales.

What *could* happen if the campaign strategy is tried? If oil imports were, in fact, restricted, demand would surely increase faster than supply. Domestic energy prices would skyrocket above world rates. American consumers and businesses would be stuck with higher energy costs. The price of goods and services would rise. U.S. products would be less competitive in global markets, and, ultimately, jobs would be exported overseas.

That could happen. But what is more likely is that the strategy will fail—imports will not be restricted—and, rather than falling, imports will rise far more quickly than if realistic policies had been followed. Interventionist government poli-cies will only create havoc in energy and export markets, with consumers and workers paying the bill. I don't believe that *this* is what the American electorate voted for on Tuesday, and I don't believe that the new Clinton administration would persist for long in pursuing such policies.

The Clinton campaign also advocated an ambitious energy conservation tar-get: reducing energy consumption per unit of gross national product by at least 3 percent annually. Such a target would mean holding energy consumption constant or reducing it, while maintaining normal economic growth.

We have been through this before. Projections show that in a normally grow-ing economy, even with extensive gains in energy efficiency, total energy con-sumption will increase by around 1 percent per year through the year 2000—or a total of about 7 percent. If the country actually tried to hold aggregate U.S. energy consumption *constant* through the year 2000, the overall price of energy would have to rise, in real terms, two to three times its current level. *Reducing* aggregate consumption, of course, would mean even higher energy prices than that. These kinds of price increases would only hurt the economy, wiping out the very growth that is being sought. Again, that's not what the public voted for.

I know that many environmentalists argue that energy efficiency steps are cost-free, that cuts in energy use could be achieved painlessly if American busi-ness only had the will to implement them. But they are mistaken. Mandated changes in industrial processes will only encourage industries to move their oper-ations—and jobs—overseas to avoid being at a competitive disadvantage. Also, contrary to unfounded assertions by some, environmental regulations—even those that provide important benefits—do not, on net, create jobs. The immedi-ate jobs created by regulations are a cost to business and, on average, destroy more jobs than are created. Once again, that's not what the public voted for in this election.

It seems likely that unless the economy begins a quick recovery—which can-not be ruled out—President-elect Clinton would soon be forced to reevaluate his economic and energy strategies. The value of allowing this industry to do its job of providing the energy needed to support a growing economy would be apparent.

> *SPEECH TIP:* Having laid out the ramifications of a given government policy, DiBona now begins to temper his cautionary scenario with reasons for greater optimism.

Given President-elect Clinton's past record, there are reasons to think he will be willing to adapt to economic imperatives. His work as chairman of the Democratic Leadership Council demonstrated an inclination to support moderate, pragmatic, and sometimes conservative policies. And as Governor of Arkansas, he not only worked for robust job growth, but he also took a balanced approach to environmental problems.

There is another factor that may also come to bear. Despite the strong support of his candidacy by environmental organizations, it is likely that, as president, he will only enjoy a brief honeymoon with them. The marriage won't last. Because these organizations depend on criticism of government to generate the several hundred million dollars of annual contributions that finance their activities, many will soon find fault with the new administration. Then President-elect Clinton will have to choose between trying to satisfy environmental organizations that cannot appear pleased, or recognizing the impossibility of that situation and focusing on the economy.

I do not want to understate or underestimate the challenges this industry will face in the United States, particularly for the short term. They *will* be formidable. And if the economy finally begins its long-awaited recovery, that could temporarily make the impact of unwise energy policies less obvious. Or, as we saw in 1976, the new administration could plunge ahead with wrong-headed policies, regardless of their consequences to the economy, and only reverse course later, as experience and wiser heads prevail.

> *SPEECH TIP:* However, as the speaker now explains, oil industry efforts will be necessary if its interests are to remain secure. The sequence of DiBona's remarks provided incentive first, then reassurance, and now a rallying call to action.

Nevertheless, as I have said, we cannot afford to sit on our hands. We need to be proactive, to demonstrate to the new leadership and to new policy makers at all levels of government the central importance of reasonably priced, efficiently produced energy—and of oil and gas in particular—to a dynamic society competing in world markets and, specifically, to creating jobs.

We should have time to make our case. Energy and environmental issues are unlikely to be among the issues resolved during the first hundred days of the new administration.

We need to emphasize that we are not running out of oil. In fact, a new Department of Energy study indicates that, at current rates of U.S. production, we have thirty-five to seventy-five years of potential reserves. We need to emphasize that anti-oil energy policies send jobs overseas. In fact, restrictions on access over the past six years have resulted in the migration of an estimated $20 to $25 billion of capital investment and the jobs they would have created. We need to emphasize that we are making tremendous strides in our environmental performance and in providing cleaner-burning fuels. The long-term commitment we have forged in STEP—our "Strategies for Today's Environmental Partnership"—is demonstrating through *actions* that we are serious, and skillful, in protecting the environment and human health.

To make ourselves heard, we will need unity in our own industry and among all energy producers. We will need to work constructively with the president-elect and his administration, with the changed Congress, and with the new state legislatures, and we will need to step up efforts at the grassroots level.

We need to show that our industry can help to move the economy quickly into times of growth and prosperity. And that's what was on people's minds when they went into the voting booths last week.

Corporate Strategies in a Global Economy

ROBERT J. EATON
Chairman and Chief Executive Officer
Chrysler Corporation

Delivered to the Greater Detroit Area Chamber of Commerce 1993 Mackinac Conference, Mackinac Island, Michigan, June 4, 1993

SUMMARY: How to make a region hospitable—or inhospitable—to world-class business and industry.

Thank you, John, and good evening to all of you.

It's great to be on Mackinac Island again. I was a little worried when I saw the agenda, though. I don't want to sound ungrateful for the opportunity to speak to this august gathering, so don't get me wrong. But this is a Friday night. The bar's been open for hours. We just had a great meal. And the coffee is going right to your kidneys. Now, would you like to try to hold a crowd like this with a speech entitled "Corporate Strategies in a Global Economy"?

SPEECH TIP: What an opener!

Then somebody reminded me that the ferries have stopped running, and there's only one TV set in the hotel.

So you've got nowhere to go and nothing to do. And that's good, because I timed my speech on the way up, and it will run about an hour and a half!

About that speech title, by the way: that's what you get when you call the office seven months ahead of time and insist on knowing what the speaker will talk about. Obviously, I didn't have the foggiest idea what I was going to say way back last fall, so we sent in one of our generic speech titles—something that sounds kind of high-toned and cerebral but is actually so broad that it'll cover almost anything. We have one, for example, called "Looking Back and Looking Ahead." That works just about anywhere. But tonight you get "Corporate Strategies in a Global Economy." Which means that I'm going to talk about how disappointed I am that Proposal A was defeated on Wednesday!

SPEECH TIP: It takes a flair for comedy to pull off an introduction like this. But if you've got it . . . flaunt it.

Don't laugh. Believe me, it's not that big a stretch at all!

One of the strategies of corporations trying to compete in the global economy is to locate facilities in the most hospitable places. Proposal A would have made Michigan a little more hospitable to business. It was another missed opportunity for the state, I'm sorry to say. But I want to congratulate Governor Engler for his personal leadership on that issue. It was a tough sell from the beginning, but he did an outstanding job.

The campaign focused on property taxes, sales taxes, and education. Not much was said about the impact on business, but Proposal A would have had a positive impact on Michigan's business climate. The over-reliance on property taxes in this state to fund education and government in general isn't just a problem for homeowners; it's a problem for business, too.

Taxes are obviously one of the first things you consider when you're deciding where to locate a business. And today, businesses have lots of options about where to locate. Technology is portable and transferable. So are skills. For a lot of products today, particularly high-tech products, you can build them just as easily in Singapore as you can in Saginaw.

So Michigan just sent the world business community a bad signal. It means that the state still has a long way to go to be recognized throughout the country and the world as a great place to do business.

There was a time when the Law of Comparative Advantage applied only to things like geography and natural resources. That's not true anymore. Today, when you're looking to build a plant and you ask about "climate," it has nothing to do with rainfall. It has a lot to do with tax rates, however. And infrastructure. And workers' comp laws. And environmental regulations. And a host of other factors that all add up to whether or not it's a good place in which to do business.

Michigan doesn't rank very high, I'm afraid. And I'm not telling you anything you don't know.

Dave Cole talked to you this morning about the study his group at U of M recently completed. I'm sorry I missed his presentation, but I'm familiar with the study and its conclusions. It says:

- That the DNR needs to work closer with business. (We're not the enemy. We live here, too.)
- That Michigan is a relatively high-tax state, and that doesn't help its competitiveness.
- That unemployment insurance and workers' compensation costs also hurt the state.
- And, of course, the study says that you should never let yourself get sued in Wayne County!

That's too quick a pass, of course. I'm not doing the study justice, but it was a good warning to all of us that Michigan has a lot of work to do if it's going to keep the auto jobs it has, and if it hopes to attract new jobs of any kind. Again, Governor Engler deserves credit for getting the Commerce Department and Dave's group together on this research. It's not all pleasant reading, but it tells it like it is. It tells us where we have to go and what we have to do.

The study that really bothers me, though, is the one completed in March for the State of Ohio by researchers at Cleveland State University. The object was to compare Ohio's competitiveness in attracting and keeping businesses and jobs to that of a number of other states. I was mainly interested in how Michigan stacked up. In a word, "Not well."

The researchers looked at a number of areas from state fiscal and tax policies, to employment and labor regulations, to how well the states had adjusted to the changing global auto industry. In area after area, Michigan was near the bottom of the list. If I could take some liberties and characterize the study, I'd say that one of Michigan's key competitors doesn't consider Michigan much of a competitor.

That's embarrassing. It's also an opportunity. If there's anything that Chrysler's recent history proves, it's that the best time to make your move is when everybody else is writing you off.

I think it's time for Michigan to make its move.

And, in spite of the defeat of Proposal A, there are some encouraging signs.

- There's a new team at the DNR that seems more interested in working with the private sector on environmental issues.

- The budget is balanced, and that's more than they can say in Washington.

- *Financial World Magazine* this spring jumped Michigan from the 34th to the 24th "best managed" state in the country. We're still in the middle of the pack, but that's a big move in one year.

- And we're out soliciting new business. Governor Engler took a hundred business people to Mexico in March to explore opportunities that could be even more significant if the North American Free Trade Agreement is approved.

So we're moving ahead in Michigan. But we've got a long way to go. If there's one thing that makes me optimistic, it's that business and government are talking together—at least more than in the past. I see more of it here at the state and local level, and also at the national level.

As you may know, I was in Europe with General Motors for four years before coming to Chrysler. I noticed a big difference there. Business at all levels and government at all levels always seemed to try to work their problems out before they became divisive public issues. You didn't see one side or the other injecting politics or running to the news media at the drop of a hat. There weren't a lot of threatening speeches. Problems were there to be solved, not to be *exploited*.

It wasn't like that here before I left, but I've been back for fifteen months now, and I honestly do see a change. Or at least the *beginning* of one. And that's healthy.

One thing you tend to find in Europe is that the labels fall off when it comes time to solve a problem. It doesn't matter much whether you're a liberal, conservative, socialist—heck, they even have a few *communists* still running around, believe it or not. When it gets down to carving out solutions to problems, most of them are members of a group that's never on the ballot: they're *pragmatists*.

SPEECH TIP: Eaton does a nice spin on conventional categories here. Sometimes the freshest approach to a subject comes from turning old applecarts upside down.

Here, we're still too quick to cubby-hole people. Bring up trade, and you've got two sides: free traders and protectionists. Nothing in between. And you'd better not be unfaithful to whatever ideology you choose first! If you favor NAFTA, for example, but you think the government should get tough with Japan for some of its trading policies, then you're a self-serving hypocrite. You can't have it both ways!

My question is: Why not?

Why not throw ideology out the window (and partisanship, for that matter), and just sit down and figure out what makes sense and what makes intelligent public policy?

That's what I saw in Europe, and it worked.

I was involved in some of the discussions that led up to the EC quota on Japanese cars. There was no ideology involved—or, at least, not enough to get in the way. People from the right and people from the left took a look at what was practical and what was fair and told the Japanese they could have up to 16 percent of the European market. Thank you very much. End of discussion.

But here, any suggestion that we might want to act in our own self-interest for a change is regarded as the surrender of some sacred principles.

Reasonable men and women can agree on the most thorny issues if they check their ideologies at the door. I've seen it happen. It can even happen when it comes to environmental issues. Europe's environmental problems are far worse in some areas than ours because of its size and population density, and the Greens are as militant as you can get on this issue. But somehow, reasonable and practical compromises get made.

Again, in this country, we seem to go to an "either/or" option right off the bat. You can either have jobs *or* a clean environment. Pick one! It takes forever to get to the rational middle position. And sometimes we never do.

The fact is, if you're a businessman looking for a place to locate a new facility, you're not afraid of a state that wants to protect its air, its water, its land and the health of its people. That won't scare you away. It's more likely to *attract* you, in fact. What scares you away is *zealotry*. What sends you to another state is the fear that you're going to be treated as a *target* instead of a potential taxpayer, neighbor, and employer.

And that's why studies like the one done at U of M and the one from Ohio are important. A state's *reputation* as a place to do business is critical. A *potential* employer is going to find out how *existing* employers are being treated.

Deciding where to put a business facility is like buying a new house: *Location! Location! Location!* You ask a lot of questions! And if you don't like the answers, you move on. And sometimes, when you *don't* get answers, you get very suspicious.

Why did GM decide to close its Ypsilanti plant and keep the one in Texas open? Why has the "auto state" not gotten its share of foreign auto plants? Mazda is the only foreign assembly plant in the state, and their Ford partnership probably explains that. All the others are somewhere else. (Like Ohio.)

Now the Germans are coming. (Did you ever think you'd see the day when foreign companies would come to the U.S. chasing lower costs?) But they aren't coming to Michigan. Why do they seem to like the Carolinas so much? Is it just the weather? Have the Germans suddenly become big basketball fans? What's the attraction? I hope we're trying to find out.

SPEECH TIP: Eaton shows that you don't have to know the answers to pose the questions.

"Benchmarking" is big in the business world today. Companies study other companies to find out what those other companies are doing right. I hope the state is doing some "benchmarking" of its own.

Now, a good business development program has two goals: Keeping the jobs you have and attracting new ones. The first one is important because if you can't keep the jobs you have, word will get around, and you won't attract new ones, either.

I don't think anyone could question Chrysler's commitment to jobs in southeast Michigan. Most people know that we spent a billion dollars for Jefferson North in Detroit and another billion dollars for our new technical center in Auburn Hills. But we're making some other heavy investments in Southeastern Michigan as well. They include more than $238 million to tool up our Sterling Heights Assembly Plant for our new JA car next year; $129 million to put our new pickup truck into our Warren truck plant; $110 million to build a new two-liter engine in Trenton; and $100 million over the past few years to upgrade our McGraw Glass plant in Detroit.

We've even done something that's practically been unheard of in our industry for a long time now: We've actually been *hiring people!* We've added between two hundred and three hundred new jobs at Jefferson recently when we started building our Grand Cherokees on two shifts.

There's a difference, of course, between Chrysler and other potential investors in the area: We already live there. We've been in the neighborhood since 1925. Our roots are deep. That doesn't mean that we're soft-hearted sentimentalists, though. We'd move investment and jobs to another state if it made compelling sense to do it. It just means Michigan has a little home-state advantage with companies like ours.

Companies like ours may be the *foundation* of the state's economy, but we want to be able to provide the economic growth that the state needs. The state must attract companies with no prior commitment to the area, no history, no roots, and no reason to come to Michigan except that it's a great place to do business. That's the big challenge ahead.

Now, I was going to stand here and tell all of you in great detail exactly how to meet that challenge. But I notice that my hour and a half is up!

Seriously, I don't underestimate for a minute the difficulty involved. And I truly am optimistic that the state is beginning to step up to that challenge.

I hope the conference goes well this weekend. I want to thank you for asking me to come up. And this is not bad duty if you absolutely have to give a speech on a Friday night!

Thanks again.

Energy, the Environment, and the New World Economy: Reformulating the Regulatory Process

H. L. FULLER
Chairman of the Board, Amoco Corporation

The Raymond G. Thorpe Lecture, Cornell University, Ithaca, New York, October 22, 1992

SUMMARY: Amoco chairman H. L. Fuller reviews the history of U.S. environmental regulation and proposes that goal-oriented, cost-effective policies will best meet the economic and environmental challenges emerging globally today.

Thank you for inviting me to be with you today. Among the things I'd like to discuss with you during this session—to name just a few—are business risk, science, politics, economics, citizenship, and emotion. As to the latter, I feel a great deal of it today. It is always a special feeling to come home and to reencounter some of the same ideas and emotions you remember from three decades ago. Since the days when I sat approximately where you are sitting, I have often imagined an experience just like this. My hope in those days was to hear something that I hadn't heard before or to find myself challenged in a way I hadn't expected—some new way of looking at things, perhaps, or some way of rearranging what we already knew into new patterns, new combinations, new systems.

That didn't always happen, of course. Notwithstanding the old cliché, you don't always learn something new every day. But sometimes you do, and sometimes certain pieces that may seem totally unconnected fall into place, and sometimes your understanding of the world around you is broadened just a bit. That may not happen today. But I'll try. And for those of you who are required to attend the talk for credit, please don't hold it against me.

We are meeting here today at a time of nearly unprecedented historical change in the world, and we are also meeting on the anniversary of what could have been the greatest defining event in history. About a century and a half ago, a resident of upstate New York named William Miller predicted that the world would end on October 22, 1843.

It didn't.

But the Millerite spirit lingers on. (Incidentally, two years after I graduated from Cornell, another upstate New Yorker named William Miller was named Barry Goldwater's vice-presidential running mate. The results were equally disappointing. But the world didn't end in 1964, either.) In honor of William Miller and his descendants, October 22 has officially been declared "End of the World Day," and over the past several years, it has frequently seemed that the end is indeed nigh.

As we all know, change is the only unchanging process in life, but in terms of far-reaching and systemic change and upheaval, these times are unique. Since most of you enrolled at Cornell, we have been passing through one of those great periods in world history when nearly everything we have come to take for granted is in the process of being permanently altered. The world as we have come to know it is changing in ways yet to be determined, and at this moment in history, whatever the outcome, things may never be the same again.

This is true for governments, businesses, and all our basic institutions, and that includes universities. We find ourselves present at the creation of an emerging new world, caught up in one of those rare historic moments when the opportunities are limitless. For business, for government, for all our institutions, there has never been more opportunity or a more open playing field. One American historian recently put it this way: "We are at one of those rare points of leverage in history when familiar constraints have dropped away; what we do now could establish the framework within which events will play themselves out for decades to come."

With the collapse of communism throughout the world—with the total discrediting of Marxism as a "science"—there is no clear challenger to the tradition of democratic capitalism. Opportunities lie before us in unprecedented abundance. The challenge now is to seize them.

The problem, however, is this: Although there are unlimited opportunities, there are limited capital resources available to exploit them. In short, just when the world had opened totally for us, the economic situation has never been tighter. We see this at all levels of international activity. Earlier this year, as I'm sure you'll all remember, one of the big events was the "Earth Summit" in Rio. The ostensible topic was the environment, but the only real question was who would finance the great variety of social and cultural agendas being advanced.

In Europe and in the United States, there are pledges to support the emerging states of the old Soviet Union, but little in the way of meaningful financial assistance. And among the nations of the European Community, plans for constructing a new economic order are running into unexpectedly heavy seas. One reason is the revolt against the mechanistic and deterministic principles that structured the totalitarian ideologies of this century. These concepts were discredited as systemic social principles when Marxism breathed its last.

They were also discredited as economic principles. To many, the proposed economic structure of the European union hearkens back to the rigid command-and-control central economic planning past. But such planning also went the way of the commissars, and when it is resurrected, even in its most benevolent form, it causes deep uneasiness. That was a basic reason for the narrow negative vote in Denmark and the slim affirmative vote in France on European union. In one important sense, these were votes *for* free trade but votes *against* central planning—votes for maximum economic freedom in a time of limited economic resources.

And, of course, in our own country, throughout this protracted presidential campaign year, economic issues have emerged as the primary issues. That is true for all of us as individual American citizens, and it is also true for each of the enterprises with which we are associated.

As enterprises of all sorts rush to establish positions in the emerging post-Cold War world, the search for resources and capital has never been more intense—or more competitive. That is true for all business today, and it is especially true for my industry, which faces sluggish product demand, low oil and gas prices, and fierce and unprecedented worldwide competition. For the petroleum industry, the problem is intensified by being singled out for what often feels like special treatment. In part for political reasons, and in part because we are still perceived as being highly profitable, the petroleum industry has been almost uniquely targeted by both revenuers and regulators.

The whole subject of regulation and its costs occupies a central place in the economic debate this year. As the chief economist of the U.S. Chamber of Commerce recently put it, "The rapid growth of government regulations may very well be the single most important obstacle to U.S. competitiveness here and abroad." This is especially true of environmental regulation. The Environmental Protection Agency itself expects the cost of environmental regulation to increase from about $99 billion in 1990 to nearly $200 billion a year by the end of the decade, and these estimates do not include the full costs of the Clean Air Act, which could add another $30 billion.

For the petroleum industry alone, environmental expenditures will rise from about $8 billion per year to $20 billion during the 1990s. According to one estimate, before the end of the decade, total U.S. environmental expenditures will be roughly equal to the defense budget.

These are huge sums of money, and the problem is that in these days of capital constraints, our industry is having difficulty making the investments required by environmental regulations while meeting the challenge of global competitiveness. This is our challenge. And although we have positive solutions to propose—and I will explore one of them in some depth later in this talk—it sometimes seems we are not being heard. We are trying to talk over the noise of a growing social, cultural, and political movement that, with the help of a trendy media, is in the process of validating environmentalism as the world's newest ideology. And true believers seldom listen to opposing points of view.

How did we get here? Before we discuss the economics of the situation further, it might be helpful to begin with a bit of U.S. environmental history.

In 1962, a year after I graduated from Cornell, a woman named Rachel Carson published a book entitled *Silent Spring*. This was a fictional account of a world where the cumulative effects of environmental neglect manifest themselves through cataclysmic impacts on ecosystems and, ultimately of course, on humans. The result was to heighten the general public's awareness of environmental issues and encourage them to perceive these issues as potential personal threats demanding attention. A year later, in 1963, the first Clean Air Act was passed, followed in 1965 by the Solid Waste Disposal Act, the Water Quality Act, the Motor Vehicle Air Pollution Control Act, and the Air Quality Act in 1967.

Having a first round of what we call media-specific legislation in place—that is, applying separately to air, water or land—statutes with somewhat broader purpose followed. In 1970, the National Environmental Policy Act and the Occupational Safety and Health Act were passed. The Environmental Protection Agency (EPA) was created and the first Earth Day demonstrations were held. (Incidentally, if I can be allowed a brief commercial message, Amoco became the first company in that year to offer regular unleaded gasoline in all of its marketing areas.) But back to lawmaking: In 1972, the Clean Water Act was passed, followed in 1973 by the Endangered Species Act.

The Safe Drinking Water Act came along in 1974, followed by the Toxic Substances Control Act and the Resource Conservation and Recovery Act in 1976. In 1978, Congress passed the Endangered American Wilderness Act. 1980 saw the enactment of the Comprehensive Environmental Response, Compensation and Liability Act, also known as "Superfund." This law essentially reflected the political reaction to the Times Beach, Missouri, dioxin affair and the mediagenic Love Canal buried chemical drums story.

Superfund was then amended in 1986 and expanded to provide for public reporting of releases under the Emergency Planning and Community Right-to-Know title, and, along with the twentieth anniversary of Earth Day in 1990, Congress celebrated by passing amendments to the Clean Air Act—considered the most expensive piece of environmental legislation that has ever been conceived.

SPEECH TIP: One by one, Fuller has listed the inaugurations of specific acts of environmental legislation, and inch by inch, he has moved to establish his point. Sometimes an exhaustive—even self-evidently exhausting—enumeration is the most effective approach.

With all this law out there—and these are only the highlights—we should be assured that we are about as protected as possible, and there is no doubt that over the last twenty years in the United States, substantial, measurable progress has been made. The air is cleaner, more water is fishable, swimmable, drinkable, and a tremendous amount of potentially hazardous materials has been reduced and rigorously managed.

But over time, our national environmental objectives have changed. The debate has been shifted by advancements that we did not foresee, and in part by the successes that have been achieved. Much of what was done in the past was based on gross assumptions, available technical data, existing technology, and immediate political priorities. The cost to the American public since 1970 of addressing environmental concerns in this way has been about $1.4 trillion in taxes and higher prices for products and services.

But what's driving these high costs? Well, for one thing our ability to measure incredibly small quantities of chemicals seems also to be demanding that we regulate to those same infinitesimally low levels. During the 1980s, we measured and reported emissions at the parts-per-million level. That's like being able to pick out one minute over a two-year period. Today, we routinely measure and report emissions at the parts-per-billion level. Now that's like picking out one second in thirty-two years. For the past couple of years, we have been seriously discussing, at the policy level, controlling emissions of some chemicals at the parts-per-quadrillion level.

SPEECH TIP: When dealing with hard-to-fathom numbers, whether tiny or huge, speakers can benefit by converting their data into more understandable terms. The quantity may be changed from one physical medium to another, or it may be converted from a physical medium to a measurement of time, as Fuller has done here. One caveat: Make sure the quantities do, in fact, agree. (There's a math whiz in every crowd.)

Meanwhile, the conservative approaches we have applied to the identification of chemical hazards still depend upon extreme assumptions—for instance, that one molecule of an agent will cause cancer in humans if it causes cancer in rats. And that's even though this rat is force-fed huge quantities of this substance until it dies.

Today, the public's understanding of risk is no better—and may, in fact, be worse—than it was in 1970. For example, the annual fatality rate from car accidents is 50,000 people. A comparable fatality rate due to airline disasters is about 500. Now, while both of those seem like a lot, statistically, we are safer in an airplane. Yet, most people consider air travel more dangerous than travel by car.

The media, and those who use the media, frequently "hype" or exaggerate and do not present the full story regarding possible or actual environmental risks. Villains and victims make good stories. Good news is seldom considered newsworthy. Walter Cronkite once observed that "a cat in the alley is not news, but a cat in a tree is." Or, as the late Warren Brookes of the *Detroit News* put it, "we cover crashes, we don't cover landings."

SPEECH TIP: Fuller's criticism of media hype could not be better supported than it is by these two quotes—from journalists in the field.

Moreover, the American public has been so inundated with reports about the environmental threat of the week—whether alar, asbestos, or dioxin—that they are often understandably unable to distinguish between real and imagined risks.

Such factors as advances in analytical technology, conservative assumptions about risk, poor risk-communication with the public by industry and government, the influence of media on public perception of risk all contribute to EPA projections of costs associated with environmental protection. These costs will escalate some 30 to 40 percent by the year 2000 from the current annual spending levels of $130 billion.

It is important to keep these costs in perspective and accept something very basic: Resources—time, people, technology, money—are all limited.

Consider that, in 1991, Amoco Oil Company spent about half of its $664 million capital budget on environmental expenditures. Consider also that the findings of a joint U.S. EPA/Amoco voluntary pollution-prevention study at our Yorktown, Virginia, refinery demonstrate that equivalent levels of environmental protection of air could be achieved for about 20 to 25 percent of the cost mandated by regulation, if we were allowed to invest in cost-effective alternatives. That is what Amoco set out to accomplish in the first stage of an unprecedented cooperative study of refinery emissions management and reduction methods at our refinery in Yorktown, Virginia. Amoco's Yorktown Refinery is located on 1,400 acres along the York River, near Chesapeake Bay. It is capable of processing 53,000 barrels of oil per day into gasoline, heating oil, and other products. The Yorktown pollution-prevention study was the first joint study of its kind ever carried out at an operating refinery. The project provided for an overall—instead of piecemeal—examination of pollution prevention. In place of individual examinations of water, air, or land emissions, investigators would conduct an integrated review to discover what interaction takes place between these media. The study was aimed at identifying the sources of pollution at the refinery, measuring levels of emissions, and determining the most cost-effective ways to reduce or eliminate those emissions. Finally, each method was analyzed for its feasibility.

To ensure the soundness of the study, a group of scientific, technical, and policy experts were hired by the EPA to review the project's approach, data analysis, findings, and conclusions. The study lasted two years and involved more than two hundred people from thirty-five organizations, including the EPA, the state of Virginia, and a variety of academic and consulting interests. An independent peer review committee, chosen by the EPA, provided oversight. These twelve experts represented many disciplines and were associated with government agencies, private consulting firms, and universities. The peer reviewers were asked to analyze the project approach, methods, and findings, and provide independent, informed opinions on the validity of each step in the project.

The project team divided the study into two phases. Phase one, which was completed at the end of 1990, featured an extensive testing program. About one thousand air, water, ground-water, and soil samples were taken. Most of these were air samples, as airborne releases account for nearly 90 percent of the refinery's emissions. Each sample was tested for fifteen to twenty chemicals. Besides analyzing the make-up of these samples, the project team attempted to associate each sample with a source in the refinery. Phase two was reserved for reviewing data, developing pollution-prevention options, and setting priorities among these options.

Rather than looking at the refinery's operations in segments, the study focused on the plant as a whole, involving the EPA's regulatory groups for land, air, and water. Though these areas overlap in an industrial setting, they are treated separately by the EPA, with little coordination among the agency groups that oversee them. This compartmentalized approach involves multiple sets of regulations that sometimes contradict each other and complicate refinery personnel's efforts to comply.

The results of the study were eye-opening. Among the findings, to single out just one: Amoco will spend about $54 million over the next four years to reduce hydrocarbon emissions from the refinery, as required by existing regulations. But the study found that Amoco could reduce emissions by the same amount for only $10 million if it were allowed to implement scientifically sound alternatives.

From this and a number of other related findings, we can draw several conclusions. One is that improved results at refineries can be achieved at lower cost by using site-specific approaches rather than the current "one size fits all" rules that cover all refineries.

Another conclusion is that government and industry should jointly explore additional opportunities to produce better environmental results more cost effectively.

And it is here that the Yorktown study may have produced the most important results of all—namely, in setting a precedent for our industry and government to work together to achieve mutually understood scientific objectives, with costs sharply in mind. This is viewed in many quarters as consorting with the enemy, but I believe it must be tried in the interest of our economy and the environment.

> *SPEECH TIP:* As Fuller's remarks indicate, controversial issues such as environmental regulation too often breed sharply distinct enemy camps, so speakers who only "preach to the converted" are bound to leave part of their audiences fuming. Fuller's account of actual government-industry cooperation is a creative solution for balancing a presentation, as well as for reducing environmental pollution.

If we are successful in applying the lessons of Yorktown, we may help to moderate the trend in regulation that is imposing increasingly destructive costs on the U.S. petroleum industry in particular, and all industry in general. And in the process, we may well be positioning ourselves to bring our expertise to the world as a leader in confronting those environmental issues that are of growing international concern.

In this regard, incidentally, I find it most significant that Amoco has already been asked to discuss the Yorktown results with the British and Mexican governments. For American business in general, and especially for the American petroleum industry, our environmental and technological expertise can open doors of opportunity throughout the world. Professor Michael Porter, author of *The Competitive Advantage of Nations*, has put it this way: "The resurgence of concern for the environment should be viewed not with alarm but as an important step in regaining America's preeminence in environmental technology." That is the way we all should view it, and I sincerely believe that the global resurgence Professor Porter refers to can be led by American industry.

In the petroleum industry, the current regulatory climate is hostile to domestic exploration and production and plays no small part in the all-out drive toward globalization. But the other side of the coin is that, while this process of globalization may be expedited by adverse domestic external considerations, it is also being encouraged by unprecedented opportunities throughout the emerging new world.

By exploiting the environmental and technological expertise U.S. industry has gained over the years, we can open those doors to world trade even wider. Opportunities throughout the world have never been more abundant. This is true in Russia and in its former satellite nations in ways undreamed of just three years ago.

Nor are the opportunities afforded by the great upheavals of the past three years in any way limited to the former Soviet Union or Eastern Europe. Great international shifts, especially when they involve human aspirations and values, are synergistic, with expanding expectations and opportunities in one part of the world giving rise to similar expectations and opportunities in other parts. And, throughout the world, the natural economic response is to seize those opportunities and satisfy those expectations.

This is true in Asia, and especially in China. It is also true of the countries of the Pacific Rim, of parts of Africa, and of Mexico, Venezuela, and much of Latin America. In the latter case, the possibilities are unlimited, with the promise of exciting new possibilities in this hemisphere that have never been fully explored. And my industry, I sincerely believe, will play a major role in developing these possibilities.

It is important here to look at the process as a whole. The first step in the process has been completed with the initialing of the North American Free Trade Agreement (NAFTA), which will establish a free-trade zone among the United States, Canada, and Mexico. When completed, this free-trade area will bind more than 350 million people together into a $6 trillion economy, more than 25 percent larger than the European Community.

As you know, President Bush has sent copies of the agreement to Congress, and since this is a political year, the debate has already been joined. But despite the often harsh campaign rhetoric, the debate has no immediate consequences. Although the agreement won't escape without some reconsideration, NAFTA won't be voted on until next year, when the political fires will be burning lower.

In the area of energy, NAFTA falls short in many respects, but the involvement of our industry represents only one part of the bigger picture. What is important is the ultimate goal—beyond the NAFTA agreement—a hemispheric free-trade zone stretching, as President Bush has put it, "from Alaska to Yucatan."

In the area of energy, political and constitutional considerations will require resolution. But, in fact, a viable energy trade relationship already exists in the Western Hemisphere. The United States buys most of the oil exported by Canada, Mexico, and Venezuela. Canada supplies natural gas and electricity to U.S. consumers, while Brazil and Venezuela sell gasoline to the United States and we sell gasoline, LPG, and natural gas to Mexico. Earlier this year, Energy Secretary James Watkins summed it up in this way: "Our feeling is that we need to build a new hemispheric strategy with Venezuela, Mexico, Canada, all combined. We have a lot of work to do. But I think here is part of the new world order emerging. And here is the time to take advantage of it."

The vision of hemispheric free trade is the vision of a win-win situation, based on reciprocal obligations and cooperative action and structured by trade, which benefits all parties. And within this vision, there is ample room for the development of a new hemispheric energy alliance. From the point of view of our industry, and as concerned Americans, I believe we can welcome the development of a new hemispheric energy alliance within the Enterprise Initiative envisioned and articulated by the administration.

For the past two decades, our over-dependence on the Middle East for energy supplies has been a central national economic security concern. With each new administration in Washington, our industry has worked for an effective energy policy that would reduce our demand for imports and help stabilize the world petroleum industry. At times, when tensions reach the breaking point and someone like Saddam Hussein threatens to seize control of significant supplies, our resolve to act is strengthened, and we seem about to institute a coherent national energy plan. But then the crisis passes, the political spotlight shifts, and we are once again back at the same old stand.

As you may know, Congress earlier this month passed an omnibus energy bill that its proponents claim would lessen our dependence on imported oil. But, in fact, it relies almost totally on conservation and does little to redress the supply-demand imbalance in our nation's energy equation. Nevertheless, we must keep on trying. And that is what our industry is in the process of doing today, responding both to economic disincentives in this country and opportunities abroad, continuing to search for abundant and secure energy supplies. Daniel Yergin, the Pulitzer-prize winning author of *The Prize*, has put it this way: "We are seeing a fundamental contraction on the domestic side along with one of the greatest migrations in the history of the oil industry." The new energy legislation does nothing to alleviate that situation.

To the degree that we can diversify petroleum supplies, the strategic importance of Middle Eastern oil reserves will be diminished, and the establishment of a coherent energy alliance within our own hemisphere would diminish that reliance further, so that no one part of the world could hold us hostage.

As matters now stand, American business in general and the companies in my industry in particular are doing a great deal—and doing it successfully—to get their houses in shape. In Washington, many politicians may be planning to undo it, but we are making progress domestically, and we must intensify our efforts to maximize our opportunities throughout the world. As President Bush put it when initialing NAFTA: "The Cold War is over. The principal challenge now facing the United States is to compete in a rapidly expanding global marketplace."

And what of excessive regulation?

Perhaps free trade, which is the antithesis of the regulatory imperative, will expose the process to enough economic sunlight to prevent continued distortion of economic incentives. Or perhaps the regulatory process will no longer be able to count on a political free ride, and perhaps a new generation of Congressmen will accept our message of goal-oriented regulations as a way to allow our industry to meet its global investment needs, while at the same time helping our country—and our trading partners—to achieve our common environmental objectives.

Finally, let me close with a few words to my fellow engineers. According to one recent poll, only 5 percent of American adults say that they understand basic scientific ideas. That means that we carry an especially heavy duty. Our society, this great American civilization, has prospered as no other nation on earth because of our leadership in science and technology. Show us a need or a problem, and we can meet or solve it, and we can do so through science and technology. That is true of all the environmental problems we have touched on here tonight. It is also true of each of the problem areas inherent in our technological society.

This is not to minimize the nature or magnitude of the technical problems that lie ahead, especially in areas like the environment, where physical science, political science, business, economics, and culture all intersect. Nor is it just an American intersection any longer. As our concerns grow more global, as economic considerations become increasingly central, and as expectations continue to rise throughout the world, engineers are going to have to work more effectively than ever in the political, social, cultural, and public health arenas than they have in the past.

This will mean taking a broader view of our engineering work—and there is a message here for universities, engineering educators, and curricula designers as well. It will mean working tirelessly to communicate technically sound decisions to a broad audience, knowing that that audience may not be scientifically literate, and it means improving our understanding of the complex relationships among people, our society, and technology.

As the scientifically literate 5 percent, as trained scientists and engineers, we are uniquely qualified to apply our knowledge to human problems—and to apply it honestly and ethically—to the benefit of all our fellow citizens. Above all, we are trained to understand distinctions and to make decisions. And in times of great economic stress and historic opportunity, that ability has never been more important.

Let me conclude by wishing all of you the very best wherever your professional careers take you. Thank you for your attention, and thank you for asking me back. It's good to be home again.

Politics, Technology, and Economic Growth:
The Freedom to Innovate

RICHARD J. MAHONEY
Chairman and Chief Executive Officer
Monsanto Company

Delivered to the Council on Foreign Relations—Corporate Section, New York, May 26, 1993

SUMMARY: What happens when a government creates regulatory and economic policies that threaten a people's "freedom to innovate"?

SPEECH TIP: Before opening his speech, Mahoney takes a moment to cite the accomplishments and expertise of his predecessor at the podium. A guest speaker needn't be too shy to compliment a host, especially if the host's special status or merits have so far gone unmentioned—perhaps foregone in favor of a flattering introduction to the speaker himself!

Thanks, Stan [Turner]. Admiral Turner has been a member of Monsanto's Board of Directors for the past twelve years and brings a keen international perspective to our deliberations. Two years ago, writing in *Foreign Affairs*, Stan pointed out the need for redefining national security to include economic strength and linked it, as he does in our Board discussions, to technology.

Because of the businesses Monsanto is in, technology and R & D *are* the company. We have high-tech R & D efforts in agriculture, food, and pharmaceuticals, and a wide range of industrial products. For the past few years, we have been focusing considerable technical resources on the environment—cleaning up waste and, more to the point, trying to not make it in the first place—by redesigning our processes.

Some years ago, Monsanto placed a significant bet on the new sciences of biotechnology. We are just now beginning to see more than glimmers of real products—and none too soon for our shareowners—who've been extremely patient with our biotech R & D program.

I've watched technology and R & D develop at my company, at other American-based companies, and at other companies around the world. And because of research agreements we have had with universities here in the United States and in Europe, I've also had the opportunity to observe how technology develops in an academic setting. Over the years, I've developed what I call my three rules of R & D.

Mahoney's First Rule of R&D is: If you cite an R & D project in the chairman's letter in the annual report, the project will enjoy perpetual funding whether or not it ever sees the light of day in the marketplace.

> **SPEECH TIP:** Mahoney's first rule may be a little tongue-in-cheek, but his second and third lead directly to the main premise of his speech.

Mahoney's Second Rule of R & D is that you must keep reminding your research staff in companies like Monsanto that you're in business to sell products. We are all gratified by advancing the frontiers of scientific knowledge, but the only thing that ever gets invoiced is a product.

My Third Rule of R & D is what I would like to discuss with you today: When it comes to technology, there is a profound difference between managing the climate and managing the weather. When we forget what that difference is, as our various national governments so often tend to do, then we place the freedom to innovate in great jeopardy. My focus will be on U.S. policy—because we're a nation in the middle of that debate right now—but the symptoms and remedies are common to many parts of the industrialized world.

As a country, we have been living off of our national capital, when we should be living off of our national income. Instead of creating a national climate in which business and industry can flourish, and a national climate in which we foster innovation and new technology, we are increasingly allowing others to manage the climate of the global marketplace, while we attempt to micro-manage the weather.

Peter Drucker, in his new book *Post-Capitalist Society*, notes that the economic performance of both Japan and Germany in the past forty years teach the same lesson. For most of that time, both countries focused on the economic climate, emphasizing long-term growth, the ability to adapt quickly to change, and competitiveness. Only when they attempted to control the economic weather did they lose momentum.

In the past year or so, we have heard that, to address the problem of America's momentum, we need to undertake what's been called the "third rail" of American politics: a national industrial policy. Even *Business Week* got into the act by calling for what amounted to an industrial policy, but recognizing it needed to be called something else—like a national "growth" or competitiveness policy.

Some define industrial policy as a complete makeover of American business into something resembling the Japanese *keiretsu* —the groupings of companies that dominate the Japanese economy. This American version of Japan, Inc. would require both closer cooperation between competitors—allowed and encouraged by law—and closer cooperation between government and business. Such a policy would have to overcome both American history and tradition, not to mention antitrust law.

It assumes that America could achieve the cohesiveness of Japanese society—not a likely possibility. It assumes that Republicans, Democrats, and Perotistas could lay aside fundamental political differences and create a bias toward solutions as opposed to political ideology—also an unlikely possibility. And it assumes an increased role for government in long-term business direction and strategy—when our history is checkered with examples of what happens when government tries to pick economic winners and losers, and technological winners and losers. American politicians appear incapable of resisting the temptation to prop up failing or mismanaged industries. As Daniel Burstein recently wrote in his book *Turning The Tables*: "If given a blank check to select the critical new industries of the future, today's governmental institutions are unfortunately more likely to opt for the interests of pork barreling than national competitiveness."

I'd like to propose a different "industrial" policy: the freedom to innovate.

Some years ago, when I worked in Monsanto's agricultural division, I made a sales call to the Minister of Agriculture in Argentina to tell him about a wonderful new product called Roundup herbicide. I had only one sales brochure in Spanish, and I couldn't leave it with him because I had several more sales calls to make. He was not impressed.

> *SPEECH TIP:* The speaker's dryly rendered account of his own folly in a sales call years before is an effective anecdote in itself, but it also provides Mahoney with a useful metaphor, which he goes on to exploit.

We cannot compete in the global marketplace with the national technological equivalent of one sales brochure. But that's what we've been trying to do. While there has been no hidden agenda, no conspiracy, no secret program to do so, our American society has indeed placed the freedom to innovate in great jeopardy.

I define that freedom broadly. The freedom to innovate is as old as this nation, and it is—perhaps—the idea of America.

It is not explicitly found in the Declaration of Independence, the Constitution, or the Bill of Rights, but it is certainly implied in all of these great national documents. The freedom to innovate is the freedom to dare, the freedom to risk, the freedom to succeed—and, indeed, the freedom to fail.

> *SPEECH TIP:* Americans are justifiably proud of their nation's founding political documents, and of all the ideals that those writings express, none is more fiercely cherished than freedom. When the topic is appropriate, linking one's message to constitutional principles has nothing in common with flag-waving or jingoism; it's a relevant reminder about the radical origins of an ongoing experiment.

This freedom—this freedom to innovate—is being squeezed by our national policies, and has been for some years.

I'm fond of reminding people at Monsanto that policy is what you do, not what you say. That's true for companies, and for nations. If you do something often enough, year after year, then it must be your policy, despite what you *say* your policy is.

Our freedom to innovate is being starved by tax and investment policies that eat our seed corn, rather than save it for planting. If we do it year after year, it must be our policy.

Our freedom to innovate is being extinguished by a product liability system that has become a national lottery where the producer—the innovator—pays all.

It must be our policy, then, to fuel an out-of-control tort liability system— unique in the world—institutionalizing a professional class of ambulance chasers who have attached themselves to virtually every productive and innovative industry in this nation. If we permit it year after year, it must be our policy.

Since our tax policies don't encourage rewarding risk—capital gains—it must be our policy to encourage foreign competitors to buy basic American R & D on the cheap. Foreign companies get all kinds of newspaper ink when they buy Rockefeller Center or Columbia pictures, but their openly announced and openly accomplished moves to buy American biotech companies and research agreements are ignored—yawned at. It happens because American companies often can't find risk capital—in part because of our policy on capital gains—and so they go to get it where they can.

It must be our policy to grow the national deficit, which limits badly needed funds for investment and R & D and forfeits the future of our grandchildren.

And it must be our policy to make a shambles—and a sham—of educating our young people, mortgaging our future intellectual and knowledge capital.

The future of our freedom to innovate is being compromised by an educational system that graduates students who don't know that proper nouns should be capitalized, much less have any notion of what science is and should be about. And, as adults, they become confused and frightened about the science scare of the month, because they can't differentiate junk science from real science. It must be our policy to make our citizens "scientific invalids."

We need to encourage the public not to run from technology and innovation. Junk science and scare stories have crippled the public's perspective. Technology is neither the fifth horseman of the Apocalypse nor a master to be worshipped. It is a tool we use to create jobs—good-paying jobs—to raise living standards—to compete in the marketplace.

And to help interpret science, its benefits and its risks, we need to encourage the regulators to focus on one thing: building public trust. We need to give them the funding they need and the protection from political interference they must have. My company, indeed, every company involved in pharmaceuticals, agriculture, and manufacturing generally, desperately needs an FDA and an EPA that have the wherewithal to get the job done. Good, strong, independent regulation builds public trust. We need an informed public, but we don't need 240 million regulators; that guarantees the failure of innovation.

From so many of these things we do, it must be our policy to discourage investment in innovative technologies that will frame and, indeed, create the global growth markets of the twenty-first century.

Thus: It must be our policy to strangle the American freedom to innovate.

It's time to change the policy.

As we attempt to create the climate that will protect and enhance our freedom to innovate, what are the specific actions that will lead me as a CEO—and other CEOs—to decide to stick our corporate necks out? To invest in R & D, in our physical plants, in the education and training of our workers? To hire? To expand? And—to add one important point—to do all these things in an environmentally sustainable way? Can we rev the engine of technology and growth?

I believe we must. And we can. As Winston Churchill once pointed out, "Americans can always be relied upon to do the right thing—after they have exhausted all the other remedies." Ladies and gentlemen, all the other remedies are exhausted, and it's time to do the right thing.

What's to be done? What should be our policy in reality—not just in words? Each industry has specifics. But cutting across them are these.

Encourage investment. This means more than international trading credits and R & D tax breaks; it means creating an economic climate we can trust—not a social policy masquerading as economic policy. Let's leave the weather alone and focus on the climate.

Encourage savings. Savings create the wealth needed for investment.

> *SPEECH TIP:* Mahoney's use of sentence fragments performs the same function as an outline-style list: it gives emphasis and breathing space to individual ideas.

Reduce the deficit, with emphasis on spending reductions. Challenge major regulations on a cost/benefit basis, starting with dozens of regulations that are of little apparent benefit. Accomplish product liability and general tort reform; the present system is strangling innovation in a number of industries by making the "new idea" a liability.

Encourage knowledge and education. To paraphrase Peter Drucker, we now live in a post-capitalist global marketplace, where the only competitive edge is *knowledge*. Knowledge is our most basic natural resource, our most basic tool for competing. When only 5 percent of our high school seniors understand geometry and algebra, we are throwing this basic tool for competing on the trash heap.

We need a climate where government recognizes and acts upon what are still unique American strengths in the global marketplace, strengths like our leadership in many new technologies, like having the largest domestic market, like our strong position in export industries, like our superb research universities.

We need neither our de facto "de-industrial" policy nor the American version of Japan, Inc. What we need is not an industrial policy at all, but, instead, a climate that capitalizes upon the great diversity that is this country and encourages our freedom to innovate. It is a climate that accommodates the engines of growth, which primarily means new technologies.

It is a climate in which the government permits positive things to happen to the American economy and the American worker, rather than impeding those things with obsolete rules, red tape, unneeded regulations, and partisan politics. Government should follow the rule imposed on all new doctors. First do no harm. Help if you can. But do no harm.

Historian Richard Hofstadter once observed that it has been America's fate as a nation not to have ideologies, but to be one. We are the Great American Experiment, always changing, always moving toward something else, with the hope that the "something else" is something better—for all of us and our children.

That restlessness for something better—that's the freedom to innovate, the freedom we must protect, the freedom we must exercise, the freedom we must make our *policy*, and then make our policy our actions.

Is the Business of America Still Business?

JAMES R. PAUL
President and CEO
The Coastal Corporation

Delivered to the American Association of Professional Landmen, Houston, Texas, June 11, 1993

SUMMARY: An energy company CEO explains the perils of over-regulation, unlimited government spending, and punitive tax policies.

It's a pleasure to join you for this important landmen's conference. I particularly like this year's theme: "We're Fighting Back."

There's no question that the energy industry has gone through some ups and downs. Recently, however, the downs have far outweighed the ups. It was so bad at one company that the devil approached the chief executive with this proposal:

"I'll give you gas prices of $10 an m.c.f.; oil prices of $40 a barrel, and I'll double the price you get for coal. In exchange, you have to give me your immortal soul and the souls of your wife and kids."

There was a long pause while the executive thought it over. And then he said, "What's the catch?"

> **SPEECH TIP:** Paul's intentionally "wicked" joke breaks the ice, indeed, and creates an opening for the speaker to plunge into his topic.

Although we don't have the devil *per se* to contend with, it seems that our opponents are just as dangerous. Government and special interest groups at all levels are seeking to place burden after burden on the energy industry. And there's no question that we've got to fight back if we expect to save not only the energy industry, but all U.S. business.

That's why the question I would like to consider this morning is this: Is the business of America still business?

Most Americans would agree that the number-one problem facing the country is the economy. And with the economy just limping along, the problem is how do we achieve the kind of dynamic economic growth that will sustain the quality of life we're accustomed to?

Now, everyone in this room knows that only U.S. business can make that happen. That means you and I and the work we do, along with the thousands upon thousands of our fellow employees. Why is it, then, that in America today business so often seems to be the enemy—to politicians, to special interest groups, to intellectuals, to Hollywood, and even to much of the public at large?

They don't seem to realize that only a strong, healthy industrial sector can sustain, and expand a $6 trillion U.S. economy. Special interest groups don't create wealth. The only way they can promote their pet projects is through money generated in the private sector. The same holds true for education, academic research, and social services. When business suffers, everybody suffers.

Business is nothing other than the production of goods and services to meet the demands of everyday life, goods and services that raise the standard of living for all Americans.

> **SPEECH TIP:** As the speaker shows here, the best definitions are the simplest.

It's that simple. Yet, somehow, Americans seem to have forgotten what made this country great in the first place. People flocked to this country from all over the earth because they knew that here, in America, they could transform individual initiative, ingenuity, and hard work into a profitable and productive life. Here they did not face the kind of economic and social limitations that they did in their homelands.

What they did face was the risk of real reward and real failure that was inherent in the American way of life. In the process, they made America into the greatest business machine in the history of the world. And now we're on the verge of getting off our historical track, if we haven't done so already. We need to fight back to restore this American heritage.

And the first step in that fight is to remind our fellow Americans that they enjoy the quality of life that they do today precisely because of the fact that the business of America always has been . . . business.

When it comes down to it, there are three broad areas where Americans need a fundamental change of attitude. All three have to do with limits. First, there is a limit to what government can impose on businesses, and individuals, by way of taxes and regulations. Whether it's a one-person operation or a hundred-thousand-person operation, the fundamental principles are the same. And both are being taxed and regulated out of existence.

The tax burden Americans have to bear is bad enough, but it's not nearly enough to meet federal commitments. So Washington has to borrow money from the private sector to cover its deficits. In the past twelve years, that's diverted trillions of dollars away from far more productive uses in private enterprise.

And that's my second limit. There's a limit to our ability to finance an endless stream of deficit spending. It affects this country's investment capabilities both now and into the foreseeable future.

Third, there is a limit to our ability to conform the world to American ideals. And too often, our attempts to do so cost Americans a great deal of money, and actually lessen our influence around the world.

I would like to cover these three limits one by one. First, consider current attitudes toward business. It seems as though Americans today think of business as a vast reservoir that can be continually tapped for money without consequence. I don't think there's much difference in this respect between politicians and the people who elect them to office. They share a similar perspective.

There seems to be no limit to the kinds and amounts of taxes that politicians dream up to impose on business, not to mention individuals. And if they choose not to use tax revenue to fund their programs, then the politicians will impose regulation after regulation to force business to fund their programs for them.

The expectations of the American people don't seem much different. We see this, for example, in the unjust and excessive insurance settlements that juries often impose on businesses.

Too many of us think that someone else, government or business, owes us a living, or at least a certain standard of living. Of course, that takes money. And we seem to have forgotten that that money is created when the machinery of American business churns out the goods and services we all enjoy.

When business prospers, and only when it prospers, is there money available to provide additional wages, health insurance, on-the-job training, vacation, and all the rest. When business falters, the source of money falters, and our standard of living declines. Where there's no productivity, there's no profit, and the business eventually shuts down. No one wins. We all learned that in school. And I just hope they're still teaching that in school today.

Jobs, wages, and benefits are not the right of workers to receive and the obligation of employers to give. A business has to survive first in order to meet its payroll. It's in the employer's self-interest to provide sufficient benefits to retain productive workers. And it's in the employee's self-interest to accept a level of benefits that don't cripple the profitability and, therefore, the survivability, of the enterprise that employs him.

While you and I may understand this fundamental principle, I'm not sure the public, or the politicians they put in office, do understand. It certainly isn't the way the government does business. Apparently, the politicians have no sense of limit. They pass out the benefits without any sense of a bottom line. That's because, in a way, they don't have one. They can, and do, just keep extending their own "credit limit" in the form of deficits. The trouble is, they're doing it at our expense. The federal deficit is absorbing nine-tenths of the net savings of all individuals and businesses in America.

There's no reason the government can't cut down on its spending. After all, it's forced the rest of us to cut down on ours. If we ran our businesses the way the government conducts its business, we'd have to file for bankruptcy. And if we didn't get our act together, we'd go out of business, or go to jail. That's because we are accountable to our stockholders. And the government should be accountable to the people. It's about time the people start fighting back and demanding accountability from their elected officials.

About the only glimmer of hope that I see on the horizon is that more and more Americans seem to want less government. In 1984, a major national poll found that 50 percent chose a smaller government with fewer services over a bigger government with more services. Well, this year, the same poll showed that 67 percent now favor smaller government and fewer services.

Apparently, the voters still haven't gotten mad enough to start throwing the politicians out of office in large enough numbers to make a difference. And so far, there's no sign the politicians have gotten the message. But then, I happen to believe that most politicians have the ability to screw up the working parts of a brick. If they don't start getting the message soon, then I am going to support term limits. Perhaps two terms: one in office . . . and one in jail.

SPEECH TIP: A truly snappy put-down is an ace in the hole for a speaker with a no-nonsense message to convey.

And if the politicians are really serious about the deficit, they're going to have to do a lot more than stop the pork and slash the waste. They're going to have to muster the courage to cut the entitlement programs.

These programs include Social Security, Medicare for the elderly, Medicaid for the poor, food stamps, veterans' disability benefits, farm subsidies, and deposit insurance. They're called "entitlements" because beneficiaries are supposedly "entitled" to them.

Who dreamed up this name, anyway? You, me, or somebody else has to work to pay for these benefits. People are *entitled* to get only what they've worked for. Or, what other workers, like you and me, decide to give them.

About half of today's entitlement funding comes from borrowed money. It's easy to see why entitlements are the real culprits in Washington's runaway spending. So-called entitlement spending accounts for about 52 percent of our $1.5 trillion federal budget. Thirty years ago, it was 28 percent.

Frankly, it's understandable that politicians are reluctant to do what the electorate doesn't want. Americans are too eager to accept these giveaway programs. And they don't want to pay the bill. So we're going to have to *wise* up to the fact that entitlement spending is our real problem. And we're going to have to *toughen* up by demanding that politicians start swinging more axes instead of imposing new taxes.

One of those new taxes was supposed to be a B.T.U. tax on energy. It has provided a textbook case of how Washington works.

At first, there were only two exemptions to the B.T.U. tax rates. When that number reached thirteen, we were still told that there were all kinds of opportunities to negotiate elements of the proposal. In the same breath, we were told the tax would raise as much revenue with thirteen exemptions as it would with the original two. Now, you figure that out. Washington's got a special arithmetic all its own.

It got to the point where the *New York Times* said the tax was "so convoluted that diesel would be taxed at least five separate rates and dyed in enough distinguishing colors to make Crayola green with envy." It's no wonder the tax was finally dropped. It turned out to be a bureaucrat's dream and a taxpayer's nightmare.

By the way, after all we've seen over the past few months, is there anyone in this room who really believes that the current administration is serious about reducing the deficit? If so, could you please raise your hand? I've got some oceanfront property in Oklahoma I want to sell you.

The fact is, the administration's original budget proposed virtually no net spending cuts during its four-year term. And it proposed about $158 billion in tax increases.

If some kind of energy tax is finally enacted, it will be the latest in a long series of taxes that weigh down the economy. Of course, the country, and the industry, will survive yet another energy tax. But there is a limit. Sooner or later, something's got to give. Let me give you a perfect example of a straw that broke the camel's back.

In 1990, our government leaders came up with a bipartisan budget agreement that was supposed to solve our deficit problem once and for all. Well, by fiscal 1992, the deficit had soared to $290 billion. One of the reasons was a grand idea called the luxury tax. The politicians thought they could pick up several million dollars a year in revenue by going after those who buy big boats. So they slapped an extra 10 percent charge onto the existing sales tax for boats built here in the United States.

What happened? Well, since 1991, sales for large boats have plummeted by 55 percent.

What was the human toll? 125,000 workers linked to the industry lost their jobs. That's a real tragedy. Practically all of the manufacturers and retailers hurt by the tax were family-owned businesses of five hundred people or less. Many have been forced into bankruptcy.

I'm sure the politicians thought they were sticking it to the rich. Instead, they gouged the skilled worker. Some of them have literally been forced to drive cabs to make ends meet. Meanwhile, imagine that poor yacht owner who has to sail around an extra year or two in that old, worn-out 55-foot boat!

SPEECH TIP: Paul's example is as advertised: perfect for his point. Furthermore, it's documented with appropriate figures and facts and served up with a final, lemony twist of sarcasm.

Now, boat manufacturing was a successful U.S. industry. Before the luxury tax, the industry had a $600 million trade surplus for this country. And it employed 600,000 Americans in 1989. By comparison, the steel industry employed 300,000 at the same time.

The terrible irony of all this is that not only did the government clobber a thriving industry, but it failed to get its cherished tax revenue. Taking into account unemployment costs, bankruptcy costs, lost individual and corporate taxes, and lost sales taxes, the government has actually lost much more money than it has taken in.

As Chief Justice John Marshall warned back in the early days of our country, "the power to tax involves the power to destroy." And our government proves that day-in and day-out.

I would like to comment on a third area where public policy, and the public opinion behind it, seriously hinder U.S. economic success. And that's our understanding of America's role in the world. Americans want to make the world better. That's not only understandable; that's good. But it's a nasty world out there, and the rules of the game are often different from those we're used to here at home.

Americans have to realize that if they want to make the world a better place in which to live, then they're going to have to get in the game, and stay in the game, even under conditions that are not tolerated in this country. That means that sometimes we'll have to do business with some less-than-desirable characters in some less-than-desirable regimes. And sometimes these countries will do things to humiliate the United States. And then we get emotional and want to strike back. But we have to be very careful here, because when we respond by imposing unilateral trade sanctions, we almost always hurt the United States more than we do the other country. It's usually a classic case of cutting off our nose to spite our face.

There are exceptions, of course. It's obvious that we must prohibit trade with countries that are at war with us, or that are blatantly hostile to us. But we've got to get out of the habit of slapping sanctions on every country we have a disagreement with while the rest of the world continues to do business as usual. The same is true about revoking Most Favored Nation status every time another country fails to live up to American standards of civil liberties.

Today, Americans are restricted or inhibited from trading with more than a dozen countries around the world. And I am not including Iraq or Yugoslavia, which are subject to United Nations sanctions. Those who advocate sanctions, or lessening trade status, always couch their arguments in "moral" terms. It's always a simple case of right versus wrong. Little thought is given to the consequences such actions have on one's own fellow citizens. They don't seem to care if the guy next door loses his job, and how this will affect his family.

The trouble is, I don't know of a single instance where it can be demonstrated that U.S. sanctions have improved social conditions in another country. In fact, they sometimes make the economic burden of the people much worse. And they certainly make things worse in *this* country.

Unilateral sanctions take only U.S. business out of the action, and allow foreign business to fill the vacuum. The result is lost jobs for Americans and lost influence for American values. Now, I ask, what's "moral" about that?

A case in point is Vietnam. While we discuss whether we should do the inevitable—that is, remove U.S. sanctions—other countries are rushing to do business with the Vietnamese. I suppose sanctions make some of us feel good. You know, "Boy, are we teaching 'em a lesson." We sure are. We're forcing them to buy from our competitors, like the French, the British, and the Germans! And that's a shame, because American workers are losing out. And lost jobs, now and in the future, are the consequence.

Another example is China. It has the world's fastest growing economy, at 14 percent a year. U.S. exports to China provide 150,000 Americans with a job. It's no wonder that President Clinton extended Most Favored Nation status to China last week. Otherwise, billions of dollars and thousands of U.S. jobs would have been lost. There would have been nothing "moral" about that course of action.

It's a shame to think what opportunities and influence were lost four years ago when we revoked China's Most Favored Nation status. Self-interest, of course, finally forced us back into business. In the meantime, the Chinese government made no appreciable change in its internal policies. We could have had more influence from within than from without.

We should not try to unilaterally impose American principles on the rest of the world through the use of economic retaliation. We think it's a bullwhip. In reality, it's a feather duster. It never works. It's both arrogant and self-destructive. That's why our allies love it. And that's why we should seek to influence by example, not by manipulation. If our vital national interests are at stake, we should not hesitate to use military force when we know that economic pressure will not do the job.

> *SPEECH TIP:* Most good metaphors—like the tactile images here—appeal to at least one of the human senses.

So, whether it is a misguided approach to foreign affairs, or runaway taxation and regulation, or runaway spending, the common denominator is that we have lost a sense of limits. And history teaches us that there are, indeed, limits.

We can look back either to ancient times or to recent times to learn that lesson. The Roman Empire collapsed from within when it couldn't support the burdens of its far-flung empire. Within the past few years, the Soviet empire collapsed under its own weight, not militarily, but economically. Both empires, and countless others in between, reached a "breaking point" where internal and external obligations surpassed the domestic economy's ability to meet them.

It would be a grave mistake to think that the United States cannot reach such a breaking point. America may be unique in world history and we may be the greatest country on earth. But that doesn't make us invincible. And it certainly doesn't make us immune to economic realities. We are as subject to those realities as the Roman and the Soviet empires. Just because we have survived and prospered for two centuries, does not mean we'll be here even ten years from now.

Something is drastically wrong when we reach the point in this country, as we did last year, when government employs more workers than manufacturing. And we're still stuck with inferior public services. And all of this is taking place while taxes from all sectors of government are siphoning off 30 percent of the gross domestic product.

The failure to recognize limits goes hand in hand with the failure to establish priorities. We all learned early in life that if we had, say, ten dollars, then we couldn't have every five-dollar item in the store. Government is no different. Yet it doesn't act that way.

The whole problem boils down to accountability. The American people have got to expect, and demand, the same degree of accountability from government officials that they are subject to in their own personal and professional lives.

What all this means is that we can't allow politics to be simply a spectator sport. I know it's tempting to want to just sit back and watch the spectacles from Washington. They range from the serious to the humorous, from Watergate to, most recently, "hairgate." But we can't afford to sit on the sidelines.

We don't have Calvin Coolidge around anymore to remind the American people that the business of America is business. The task is up to us. The government's not going to police itself. Hollywood's not going to do it for us. The special interests are not going to do it.

Your theme for this year's conference is right on the mark. We've got to fight back. Whatever means are at our disposal, we've got to get out the word that business is not the enemy. To the contrary, no one has a job apart from a business. Even government jobs are funded by tax revenue that comes from business and from workers who have jobs in business.

The problem is not with business. The problem is with a government that is bent on squeezing everybody, including business, beyond their tolerable limits. And behind that is an electorate that is willing to let government function without constraint. Too many of us are not making our voices heard. We not only have the right, we have the duty, to petition our government. Call and write to your elected officials. Express your views. Tell the politicians pointblank that you're going to work to throw them out if they don't do what you're asking them.

It's either that or sit on the sidelines. And there's nothing worse than some spectator, who didn't even try to make the team, later griping about players who lost the game. I don't know about you, but I would rather get in the game and play ball.

Health Care Reform: Supporting America's Vision

P. ROY VAGELOS, M.D.
Chairman and Chief Executive Officer
Merck & Co., Inc.

Delivered to the Economic Club of Detroit, September 30, 1992

SUMMARY: Pharmaceutical executive P. Roy Vagelos urges a cautious approach to governmental reform of the nation's health care system. He stresses the importance of formulating a plan that will safeguard America's world leadership in medical research and innovation.

Thank you, Dick. I appreciate your good words. I was delighted to receive your invitation to address the Economic Club, and I want to use the opportunity to speak on one of America's most pressing challenges: the need to reform health care in our country.

Before I get into it, let me tell you that last week, Merck received a last-minute call from the Clinton campaign; they said that Bill Clinton wanted to come to Merck to deliver a speech on health care. We don't endorse either candidate, and we'd like Mr. Bush to visit Merck as well. But Bill Clinton did come to Rahway last Thursday, he did speak about health care, and, as I said, that's what I want to talk to you about today.

Detroit knows about the health care issue better than most. You've been on its cutting edge since the 1950s and '60s when The Big Three started full coverage for employees and set the pace for the rest of corporate America. For the past ten years, as health care costs have skyrocketed, the earliest voices were raised in Detroit, that corporations—and the American economy—could not digest these soaring costs without incurring losses in global competitiveness.

Merck is struggling with the same challenge, and like your companies, we're revamping our health care plans so that we can keep our commitments to our people and still keep strong for the future.

The issue is incredibly complex, and neither I, nor Merck (nor anyone at this point) has all the answers, but Merck does business in one hundred different countries with a hundred different health care systems, so I think we can add perspective to the problem.

I did not intend to talk about the election today, but since health care is such a major political issue this year, I'm going to break that resolution and touch briefly on a few points. I think most of you will agree that underneath all the rhetoric, the overriding issue of this election is how to prepare the nation to meet the challenges of the twenty-first century:

- How to ensure that our industries are strong and competitive, and will remain so for our children;

- How to ensure America's continued leadership in technology and innovation;

- And how to ensure that average Americans prosper and enjoy a high quality of life into the next millennium.

I think you'll also agree that we can't achieve any of these larger goals unless Americans are strong and healthy. Nor can we achieve them unless our health care system delivers quality care to all segments of society without sapping our global competitiveness. This is why I say that, as we consider dozens of reform proposals, we have to hold each one up against a backdrop of our nation's history, our culture, and our goals, and see if it supports our long-term vision for America.

To borrow a term from chemistry, we should apply a *litmus test* to every reform proposal and for each one ask ourselves:

- First of all, will this proposal help us deliver quality health care effectively and affordably?

- But we must also ask: Will this proposal help America remain the world leader in medical innovation, education, and biomedical research? Because America *does* start in this position.

> *SPEECH TIP:* At the outset of his speech, Vagelos establishes absolute criteria for the acceptance or rejection of the ideas and proposals he will subsequently consider. By controlling the very grounds for a topic's inclusion in the discussion, the speaker secures control overall.

If this litmus test is negative for any proposal, we should simply reject it as inappropriate for America. So, with this litmus test in mind, I'd like to explore three broad areas today:

First, I want to suggest that we must broaden the debate beyond the issue of expanding access to the uninsured and beyond the issue of controlling costs. These objectives must surely be achieved. But, beyond them, we must be assured that America's leadership in medical science and medical innovation will continue.

Second, I want to raise a red flag. I want to warn against taking precipitous actions without understanding the consequences or without consensus. Such actions risk irreparable damage to our system and to the economic and social well-being of our nation.

Third, I want to share with you several principles and reform recommendations that we've developed at Merck to guide us in this important national debate.

Let's turn first to medical innovation, *and to an apparent dilemma* because, although we have noble goals for health care in our country, these goals seem to be in basic conflict with each other.

The former Surgeon General, C. Everett Koop, put it this way: "Americans want three things from their health care system: immediate access, low cost, and high-tech medicine. While it's easy to deliver any TWO of these things, it may be impossible to have all THREE." End quote.

Dr. Koop put it well, but we simply can't settle for two out of three. That's why the defining challenge of health care reform is to simultaneously expand access to our health care system, to control costs, and to maintain America's world leadership in medical innovation.

I become gravely concerned when the debate centers on cost and access *and doesn't even mention* fighting disease through medical innovation and biomedical research. Make no mistake about it: investing in biomedical research is every bit as crucial to achieving our health care goals as the investments that manufacturers make in research and development to increase their quality and productivity to stay competitive. And for the same reasons. Biomedical investments have a direct impact, not only on the health of the American people, but also on our ability to manage health care costs and to compete in the global marketplace. They are investments in a strong and certain future.

America's research-based pharmaceutical industry is clear proof that these investments pay real dividends, and I ask you to consider the record:

SPEECH TIP: When aiming to broaden the discussion of an already sweeping and complex subject, a speaker may need to persuade the audience to accept the additional conceptual burden. To overcome any lingering resistance to his topic—the importance of biomedical research issues in the national debate on health care—Vagelos outlines the contributions of pharmaceutical innovation.

- In our lifetime a number of diseases have been conquered or controlled through the development of new drugs and vaccines, and our investments have helped hundreds of millions of people to live better lives.

- As our products save lives, they also help people avoid hospitals, surgery, and nursing homes—the most expensive parts of our health care system.

- In terms of competitiveness, almost half of all prescription drugs sold worldwide were discovered by American companies; and the U.S. pharmaceutical industry is number one in the global marketplace.

- Our business success is creating jobs; and our substantial exports are helping our nation's balance of trade.

This year Merck will spend over $1 billion in research, and, while we've seen a discouraging decrease in R&D by government and much of the private sector, Merck has increased its research spending by 14 percent per year over the last decade.

SPEECH TIP: Moving from the general to the specific, Vagelos now details his own company's contributions to the field.

During those years, Merck laboratories introduced twenty new drugs, including vaccines and treatments for bacterial infections, heart failure, high blood pressure, high cholesterol, ulcers, and more. We're giving away free to millions of people one of our drugs, *Mextizan*, which prevents "river blindness"—a disease endemic among tribal peoples in Africa and Latin America.

We're transferring technology to the People's Republic of China for our vaccine that prevents infection by the Hepatitis B virus—a virus that causes liver cancer, a leading cause of death in China.

Now, another great contribution of Merck research has recently hit the U.S. market—a breakthrough drug to control the pernicious age-related growth of the prostate gland, a condition that's present in many men over fifty, causing urinary symptoms, and leading to 400,000 surgeries per year at a cost of $3 billion. The new drug is Proscar, and it not only stops progression of this disease by stopping further growth of the prostate gland, it actually causes the prostate to shrink in most patients. We think Proscar will make medical history by changing the course of this disease, reducing its associated costs, and changing the course of the aging experience for men.

Our approach in discovering Proscar was to stop a single enzyme that's critical to the enlargement of the prostate gland, a strategy that we've used to discover several important drugs in the last fifteen years. We're using the same approach to attack HIV-1, the virus that causes AIDS. This virus has already infected 12 million people in the world. AIDS will cost the United States over $10 billion this year, and these costs will rise until we find effective treatments.

The pharmaceutical industry is targeting several enzymes that are required for the growth of the AIDS virus. Although we've not yet achieved our goal, I'm confident that, in due time, *drugs will be developed* that will safely slow the progression of AIDS. Ultimately, we must develop a vaccine to prevent HIV infection, but that goal is much more elusive, and success will require additional basic research before we know precisely how to accomplish that. My point is that we will conquer AIDS and other diseases, saving millions of lives, and hundreds of billions of dollars, and our victories will be won through biomedical research with weapons forged through cooperation of industry, government, and our nation's research universities.

This is why—in all health care reform—nothing is more critical than preserving our leadership in medical research and innovation. We must never trade away the future contributions of research in order to solve the financial problems of today.

This leads to my second point—my red flag—which is a warning against taking precipitous actions that may look attractive up front but will ultimately leave us with even worse problems. We must be careful for several reasons because, first, despite all its faults, our health care system *does* deliver the world's best medical care to the vast majority of our people. We must also be careful because our system has the delicate internal balance of a living organism. Hasty changes, however well-meaning, could kill it or leave it permanently handicapped.

Congress saw this in 1988 when it passed the Medicare Catastrophic Coverage Act—a well-intentioned law, but one that had to be repealed quickly in the face of outrage by the elderly, the very people it was intended to help. Let's not repeat that mistake, and before rushing ahead, let's be sure that our solutions have core support and consensus, so that all Americans can live with them.

One certain mistake would be establishing a centralized system in which the government sets the rules and pays the bills, like the systems in many European countries or in Canada. These systems may be appealing at first glance because they address two parts of Dr. Koop's equation. They would immediately provide access for the uninsured *and* establish a ceiling on costs. But if something sounds too good to be true, it usually is.

These systems won't work for us medically or politically because they would raise taxes and at the same time smother innovation. They would also require dismantling our private insurance industry, which is the backbone of our payment system for most Americans.

They won't work socially, because Americans don't want rationing or waiting lines for health care. But we have to be especially careful here, because, while it's widely agreed that moving directly to a centralized system is wrong for America, we must be cautious of plans that masquerade as free enterprise but, when stripped down to their essence, would lead to government control. That's the big danger of "play or pay," which would mandate employers either to offer insurance to workers or to pay additional taxes to fund insurance provided by government. We have to be careful because "play or pay" may turn out to be a *de facto decision* that quickly leads to a government-controlled system.

And here's the trap: the initial tax increase to fund such a system would be about 9 percent of payroll, and companies that now spend more than that for insurance would be economically motivated to move to the public system. The Labor Department estimates that about one-half of the U.S. population would quickly end up in the public plan, and with that critical mass, we'd quickly slide into a centralized system. That's not the way to go for America.

In Merck's experience, the big reason not to go this route is to avoid the sclerotic effect that government systems have on investments in medical innovation. The people who manage these bureaucracies are usually far removed from patients. Too often, they see only the cost of medical care but are blind to the promise of medical research and innovation.

So, where do we go from here? How do we tackle the problems of American health care without destroying the very strengths we've worked so hard to build? This brings me to my third area of discussion: the ideas and recommendations we've developed at Merck.

> *SPEECH TIP:* Vagelos clearly marks this division between the proposals he finds wanting and the proposals his company has developed. When an argument shifts from one strong position to another, the speaker's "thumb"—up or down—should be visible to all.

As I said, we don't have all the answers, but we've taken a hard look at our own system and the issues. We've developed a set of principles that pass the litmus test I mentioned before, and that we believe should be the basis for careful debate.

We start first with *the issue of access* because, if it's left unaddressed, it's a national disgrace and a political time bomb. We believe that all Americans, rich and poor, should have access to quality health care.

Starting with the unemployed poor who don't have health insurance, we think Medicaid eligibility should be expanded to cover all of the unemployed who fall below the federal poverty line. This change alone would reach one-third of the uninsured.

The other two-thirds of the uninsured are working people and their families; and we believe that these people, and all *employed Americans*, should have access to health insurance through their employers. To accomplish this without driving small companies out of business, we believe that the insurance industry should be allowed to create new policies of basic coverage, policies that are affordable to small employers and the self-employed.

Insurance companies should also expand their risk-pools to spread their liabilities across larger populations so that small businesses can buy insurance in groups and get the same premium breaks as large companies, and we believe that health insurance should be portable from job to job.

But increasing access to our system requires many other measures, such as incentives for doctors to practice in underserved areas. We have too many high-priced specialists in the suburbs, and too few family doctors in rural areas and the inner cities. During their training, we should send medical students where they're needed most, and we should encourage them to stay there after graduation by expanding student loan repayment programs and loan forgiveness programs.

Turning from the issues of access to cost control, we have a number of ideas, and let's start with two that have potential for huge savings. Defensive medicine costs America at least $25 billion per year through unnecessary tests and procedures and the costs associated with legal liability. We need to change our legal system so that doctors and patients can trust each other once again and stop looking at each other as legal adversaries. Some states have already modified their malpractice laws, with resulting steep declines in malpractice insurance rates. All states should do the same thing.

It's also high time that we streamline our health care system and bring it into the computer age. Estimates vary, but if we cut administration costs by 25 percent, we'll save $20 billion to $40 billion per year. And it seems so simple to do so through standardized claim forms, electronic billing systems, and health care data banks.

As we get serious about rational cost containment, let's also decide to minimize the use of legislated actions and use instead a combination of voluntary self-restraint by all providers; an increase in cost-sharing and risk-bearing by individuals, employers, providers, and insurers; and an extension of market competition further and faster through the proper use of incentives.

Voluntary price restraints do work, and we're proving it at Merck. Years ago we recognized the need to help manage costs and to expand access to our products, especially for the poor, and we've introduced several programs to achieve these goals. To help Medicaid patients, we launched a program to give state agencies our lowest discounted prices in exchange for *their* giving needy patients access to our products. Our concept was subsequently written into federal law, which now does essentially the same thing.

Merck was also the first pharmaceutical company to pledge voluntarily to keep our price increases within the rate of inflation. Six other companies are now doing the same thing. (And, by the way, our prices must keep up with inflation so that we can sustain our enormous efforts in research and development.)

In terms of cost-sharing and risk-bearing, we believe that everyone should have more responsibility for the cost of their own health care, for making better choices in the care they receive, and for how they live their lives to prevent avoidable disease. This seems obvious, but it's absolutely critical. The days of no-deductibles and no co-payments in insurance plans are gone forever, and with good reason. They're not only unaffordable, they result in wasteful consumption of health care. If insurance pays the whole freight, health care is perceived as a free service, and there is simply no incentive to shop for value. It's like a having a credit card with no requirement ever to pay the bills.

On the other hand, if patients share in the cost of their health care, they do shop for value, and the market responds with innovation and competition. This is happening already as managed care is growing, and competition is emerging across the country.

Increasing personal responsibility is even more important for another reason, because all attempts at reform are doomed if we don't get people to concentrate on prevention. Controlling costs simply can't be done if Americans don't take better care of themselves. Think of it: If we had better control of fewer than ten risk factors we could prevent two-thirds of all premature deaths. These factors include: inadequate prenatal care, smoking, the use of illegal drugs and alcohol, and unused seat belts.

It's a human tragedy that 5,000 low birth-weight babies are born every week due to the lack of prenatal care. Keeping one of these infants alive can cost as much as $1 million. We think that prenatal care and pediatric vaccines should be part of every insurance plan, and they should be fundamental requirements in all public health care programs.

And what about smoking? Cigarette smoking causes more death and illness than drugs, alcohol, automobile accidents and AIDS combined. Smoking adds at least $65 billion per year to our nation's health care bill. We should have a *smokeless society*, and the way to do it is not to outlaw cigarettes (although we've done that at Merck). We should go into our schools with graphic education programs that demonstrate the devastating effects of smoking.

Just as an aside, I ask you: Isn't it odd that many people are willing to consider raising taxes to pay for health care, but increased taxes on cigarettes, alcohol, guns, and other causes of health care problems are strongly resisted? It's something to think about.

As we look for ways to pay for reforms, again I say: let's avoid hasty actions and carefully evaluate our current position. Let's remember that we're spending over $800 billion per year on health care, 14 percent of our Gross National Product! Remember, too, that many reform ideas that I've discussed will save and free up substantial dollars. It is therefore clear that we should not rush ahead and decide that we must pump additional money into the system. There are plenty of opportunities to save before we do that. Perhaps some time in the future—but only after we've wrung out the waste from our system, and only after we've made essential reforms—we should consider pursuing some of the politically unpopular alternatives, such as an increase in taxes. But—no matter what we do—we should *not raise the federal budget deficit.* This is a peacetime economy, and we should reexamine and reallocate spending to meet our needs.

Reforming health care won't be easy, and it won't be quick. It will take perhaps a decade, but each year should bring us closer to our goals. It will call for the best from leaders in every segment of our society, and we'll need to stay with it for the duration. Yes, there will be a price to pay. And, yes, we'll need to compromise. Everyone who comes to the table should be ready to leave something on the table. But we must not leave those things that make us competitive, and not those things that stimulate investment and give us hope for victory over disease.

We shouldn't be afraid of the challenge, because this is not a zero-sum game, in which those who win do so at the expense of others. It's a game in which our entire nation will be the winner.

So, as we consider all the ideas that are before us, and all those that will come before us in the months and years ahead, let us apply the litmus test. Let us measure every proposal against our dreams and visions for the twenty-first century.

And what are those dreams and visions?

- Let's dream of strong and healthy Americans, living in a land that offers quality health care to the rich and the poor, the young and the old, and everyone in between.

- It should be a land where people are educated about their own health care needs and dedicated to taking care of themselves.

- Where children are nurtured and protected from disease, even before they're born, so they have a fighting chance.

- And let it be a land that continues to lead the global marketplace in biomedical research and discovery.

Right now, this country *is* the world leader in medical innovation, the world leader in medical technology, the world leader in medical education and drug discovery. And, as we dream of health and prosperity for the American people and strength for the nation's economy, let's be sure to envision the United States as the continuing world champion of medical innovation! This global leadership is one thing that we should never compromise or trade away!

I say this is *a possible dream*, and if we all work together, I firmly believe that we will achieve it.

CHAPTER 8

Ethics and Values

Folks outside of the business community, and even the more cynical individuals within it, are always surprised to learn that the subject of ethics and values is much in demand from speakers. The fact is that the business community is greatly interested in these issues.

Now, many speakers fear that ethics and values are like apple pie and the flag—impossible, really, to argue against, but difficult to say anything truly interesting about. This attitude is born of a superficial view of the subject. Today's business world presents many complex ethical challenges and continually demands that we choose among often apparently contradictory sets of values—and all of this takes place in a very tough, highly competitive economic climate.

The speaker addressing ethics and values enjoys one of the advantages of a writer of gripping drama or fiction. He or she can exploit the very complexity of today's business ethics to offer the audience moral puzzles to solve, presenting a situation to the listeners and asking them: What would *you* do? The fact that there may be no easy, ready answer is, as far as creating a stimulating speech goes, a definite plus.

It is, in fact, important that you avoid easy answers. Begin by refusing to assume that audience opinion is a hundred percent on one side or the other. If you are aware of a majority opinion, think

about making your speech a deliberation of the minority alternatives. This said, however, avoid being provocative for the sake of
provocation. Quite rightly, an audience resents being played with in
this manner.

Without doubt, as our speakers demonstrate, the most effective
way to avoid bland consensus or preachy sentiment on the one
hand and gratuitous provocation on the other is to base your discussion on reality—personal, firsthand reality: a program you have
been involved in, a negotiation fraught with potential moral land
mines, or a risky transaction your company managed to transform
into a win-win proposition.

Commencement Address

PETER EIO
President
LEGO Systems, Inc.

*Delivered at the commencement ceremony at Western New England College,
Springfield, Massachusetts, May 20, 1993*

*SUMMARY: The president of LEGO Systems describes the goals and values estab-
lished by LEGO's Depression-era founder, Ole Kirk Christiansen, and relates how
principles such as fiscal prudence, social responsibility, teamwork, and commitment to continuous improvement and education are still fostered by the corporation today. Affirming the long-term benefits of such values, Eio encourages new
graduates to pursue their dreams with self-confidence and determination.*

President Miller, it is a pleasure and an honor to be here. I want to thank you, your
distinguished faculty, honored graduates, and your parents and guests, for allowing
me to participate in this very special day of celebration.

When Dr. Miller invited me to speak some months ago, I wondered what
comments a toy maker could give to such a large and varied group of young people who are about to embark on professional careers in many different fields. My
first thoughts were to consider what I would tell my own children, one of whom
graduates from university in England next month and two of whom graduate from
high school here in New England next week.

SPEECH TIP: By mentioning his own children's imminent graduations, Eio confides personal information that is emotionally relevant to the occasion at hand. By sharing this information with his audience, he sheds the role of outsider and becomes linked with his listeners in a larger circle of all graduating students, their families, and friends.

In many ways, the '70s and '80s, the period in which they and presumably most of you grew up, were decades of immense change. Technology, and in particular information technology, has changed forever the way we live and communicate with each other. In the 1950s, when I went to school in England, very few people had television sets, and we made telephone calls via an operator—even local calls! When TV did become more widely available, it was on a nine-inch black-and-white screen, and we had one program—the BBC—for two hours a day. Today, we have multichannel TV, and events from around the world are brought into our homes by CNN as they occur. Today, a single fiber-optic cable can carry thousands of telephone calls simultaneously, and the average automobile packs as much computing power as the first Apollo moon module.

But it's not only in technology that the rate of change is accelerating. The geopolitical scene changed in the 1980s far beyond anything we could have dreamt of in the 1970s, when the Cold War and the global nuclear threat were an accepted part of our everyday lives. The passing of world communism almost seventy years after its advent was a historical landmark, an event that will be judged by future generations in the light of how successful the former Soviet empire is in establishing new market economies. The tragic political chaos in former Yugoslavia, the declining manufacturing output in virtually all of the old Soviet bloc—these are issues that should be of grave concern to us. And when you think about it, no communist country has ever yet successfully accomplished the transition from a centrally planned economy to a market economy. Only China has so far attempted to begin this process.

I think it was Henry Kissinger who used the analogy that moving from capitalism to communism was like making fish soup out of an aquarium! The problem, he went on to say, is trying to convert fish soup back into an aquarium. . . .

Whether this turns out to be true or not, one thing is for sure: over the next ten to twenty years or more, the West and the United States in particular will need to assist in the training and education of entire nations in building a new economic foundation. Imagine the immense problems faced by countries that have virtually no accounting or banking systems and where for two generations virtually no one has been taught how to run even a basic business on economic lines. The transition process will be slow and painful, but unless we provide the support necessary, we risk looking forward to an era of destabilization that will be equally, if not more, dangerous than the Cold War itself.

In rejoicing over the demise of communism, we sometimes tend to overlook the flaws in our own system. The 1980s, for example, epitomized what British Prime

Minister Edward Heath once called "the unacceptable face of capitalism." The '80s were a period when rapid growth, in many instances, led to corporate and individual greed on a huge scale. Self-interest was rampant, and the richest part of the population grew richer while a fifth of the American population languished in poverty.

Fortunately, the pendulum is beginning to swing back the other way. Corporate America is starting to recognize that future success depends on an entirely new paradigm; simply put, we have to recognize that greed and self-interest invariably lead to disaster in the long run. Responsibility toward employees and society as a whole is paramount for any organization that wishes to grow and thrive in the 1990s. We must educate and train our employees better. We must provide a working environment and facilities they can be proud of. We must take a real interest in their health and welfare, and we must *empower* employees to take more interest and responsibility for how our corporations and institutions develop. In Japan, the concept of *"kaizen"* focuses on this continual process of improvement. The Japanese recognize that there is no such thing as maintaining the status quo. Either you improve or you decline; it's as simple as that.

> *SPEECH TIP:* Eio's opening remarks on the events and trends of recent decades were no less effective for their wide-ranging scope, but now the speaker—like a historical novelist—zeroes in on the story of a single individual and the company he founded.

The idea that people respond if you treat them well is hardly a new one. Throughout history, there are many examples, and I'd like to tell you about one person in particular. His name was Ole Kirk Christiansen, and he lived in Denmark in the small country town of Billund in the 1930s. Ole was a carpenter and, during the depression of the early '30s, he eked out a living making wooden toys, which he bartered for food with local farmers. Times were tough, but Ole managed to support his wife and children, and he put his heart and soul into crafting fine toys. On his carpenter's shop wall was a carved wooden sign that said, when it comes to our children, "Only The Best Is Good Enough." Sixty years later, "Only The Best Is Good Enough" remains the motto of the company he founded—the LEGO toy company.

Ole and his son, Godtfred, who until last month remained Chairman of the LEGO group, were religious people. They grew up in a rural community with strict Lutheran values: caring, humility, single-mindedness, and frugality. You worked hard, you didn't spend money until you had earned it, and, above all, you had respect for other people, regardless of their origin or social standing.

Now, these standards may seem a little old-fashioned and outmoded in the fast-paced world of the 1990s. Is there really a place for such ideas in today's corporate boardroom or university campus for that matter? Well, it may surprise you to know that Ole Kirk Christiansen's vision and values are still very much alive in a global company with almost eight thousand employees around the world manufacturing and marketing the most well-known toy brand in history. The success of the LEGO building system is based as much on *people* as it is on quality and technology. And don't forget it's *people* who develop the technology and *people* who count in producing a quality product. Our employees in Enfield, Connecticut, take great pride in the quality of LEGO products. In the molding of LEGO elements, for example, you might think that if we achieved a rate of 99.9 percent perfect quality, then we'd have a fine record. However, when you consider that we mold 1.5 billion elements a year, at 99.9 percent perfect quality there would still be 1.5 million defects a year! In actual fact, our molding teams have reduced the defects to less than twenty for every million units produced. That's a quality level of 99.998 percent, and now they're pushing for the ultimate goal: zero defects.

> *SPEECH TIP:* Having asserted that Christiansen's values remain vibrant at LEGO today, Eio wastes no time in offering evidence supportive of this claim, even handing his listeners the tools to further test the proof.

I don't know if we can ever reach zero defects. To me it's not so important as the motivation and attitude of mind that drives people to strive for perfection—to go for that little bit extra—to really believe in the maxim, "Only The Best Is Good Enough." What makes people want to achieve more? What makes them want continually to push out the boundaries of excellence?

We read and hear a great deal in the media these days about American competitiveness—how the American work force is losing in the productivity race against other nations. We hear how American management is less innovative than German or Japanese management. Of course, one can find examples to support such claims, but, as a person who has lived and worked in many different countries, let me tell you that those corporations who have realized the power of a well-motivated work force, a work force that shares a company's goals and values, have discovered that U.S. workers are *more hard-working, more team-oriented,* and *more productive* than their counterparts anywhere else in the world.

Successful companies in the '70s and '80s focused on satisfying consumer needs. The consumer was king. In the mid '80s and early '90s, the focus had moved to logistics, to ensuring that we got the right goods, in the right quantities, to the retailers at the right time. As we move toward the year 2000, consumer needs and retailers' needs will remain important, but the *outstanding* organizations will be those who recognize the needs of their *own* people, who listen to what employees are saying, and who develop a strong people-oriented culture in their own organizations.

> *SPEECH TIP:* Again, Eio first quotes the "talk"—in the company's motto or mission statement—then demonstrates the "walk."

Our corporate mission statement in the LEGO group starts with the words, "Children are our vital concern." Our interest doesn't just stop at their playthings; LEGO employees understand that Ole and Godtfred Christiansen saw in children the future of the world. In play, education, music, and arts, in fact in every endeavor, children are our vital concern. For example, as a company, we strongly believe we have a role to play in education. We are endeavoring, in a modest way, to introduce new educational concepts that shift the focus in early math and science from teaching to *learning*. Learning by hands-on experience in the classroom, by problem-solving—simply making learning more fun. Last year, over twenty thousand K through 12 teachers attended workshops around the country to gain experience in using LEGO Dacta educational materials in the classroom.

Obviously we have a business interest in this area of education because we make products that are sold to schools. But our interest goes beyond this. Education in our schools and universities should be top-of-mind for all Americans. Our educational system should be constantly changing to meet the demands of a changing world. We must, however, also avoid the risk of just turning out technocrats. If we are to have a more caring society, it is essential that we educate all young people in the arts, in literature, and in understanding cultural diversity.

Among the values held by our founder was the belief in fiscal prudence. In today's credit-driven society, use of credit cards facilitates our financial planning, but also all too often gets us into debt. In our personal lives and in our businesses, we have ready access to credit, albeit not quite as easily as in the 1980s. Ole Kirk Christiansen believed that, following a long period of deprivation in the Great Depression of the 1930s, borrowing should always be kept to an absolute minimum. Even this element of fiscal prudence is still there in our corporate strategy. The LEGO group is probably one of the very few global companies that remains private and totally self-financing. Through financial independence comes freedom to maneuver and develop our business without having to submit to pressures for short-term results, which so often lead to long-term problems in many industries today.

So, what has any of this got to do with a group of well-educated and energetic students from the class of 1993 at Western New England College? Well, I believe it has *everything* to do with your future and my future and the future of America. Because success in life—no matter which profession you choose—will ultimately depend on how much you care for other people: for your family, for your friends, for your colleagues at work, and for the underprivileged in society. When you leave here, many of you will find it difficult to find the sort of employment you want. By contrast, when I left school in the early '60s in Britain, there was little unemployment, and everyone with an education was pretty much guaranteed a job. Admittedly, the number of students graduating from high school, let alone college, was fairly small, compared to today's high percentage of college graduates in the United States.

So, even if it's tough out there, hang in, create your own vision or dream, and pursue it *singlemindedly*. It doesn't matter what you do. Just do it well, and stick at it. If you persevere, people will notice and respect your efforts, and, maybe when you least expect them, new opportunities will occur. If you have a hobby or sport or interest you enjoy, develop it, go for it, excel at it because you will automatically cultivate a sense of enthusiasm and positive thinking that will stand you in good stead throughout your life. Most important of all, develop a genuine interest in the people around you. By reaching out to people, talking to them and listening to what they have to say, you will discover that almost everyone responds positively. It can be a lonely world out there, and friendship is the greatest gift you can give or receive.

One of the great things we have learned as a corporation is the value of people working together in teams. American culture has often focused on the individual, whether it be in history or corporate life, but Lee Iacocca didn't turn around Chrysler on his own any more than Michael Eisner single-handedly revived the Walt Disney Corporation. But what they and others like them have done is to motivate their people to work together in teams, where people recognize each other's skills and contribution.

In LEGO, we used to focus on the technical skills of our people. Today, we focus as much on their *people* skills: learning to work *together* in groups leads to far greater success than promoting individualism. The output of a well-coordinated team is infinitely greater than that of a loose group of individuals working on the same task.

Finally, I would stress the need for *self-confidence*. Confidence that you can work with others and make a real contribution to whatever you do. America's future is the "can do" mentality, and you can achieve anything if you really set your mind to it. In 1933, when the Depression was at its worst, Ole Kirk Christiansen had a vision that he would be successful—against all odds. He had the confidence and willpower to succeed, and so have each of you. But, remember also the principle of *kaizen*: education doesn't stop when you leave here. Learning is a continuous process throughout life and, believe me, as you get older and can study the things that interest you most, learning becomes increasingly more fun, until finally it becomes a wonderful and enriching pastime.

To all of you who are graduating today, I wish you success in your chosen career, I wish you good health, I wish you enthusiasm for whatever you do, and I hope that you will have happy memories of Western New England College, its faculty, and the friends you have made here.

SPEECH TIP: Throughout this commencement address, Eio has combined his insights on the values and experiences of the LEGO company with more personal words of wisdom and encouragement. The speaker's warm wishes at closing, however, are a pure and simple benediction for the stars of the day.

Reforming the Civil Justice System

STEPHEN B. MIDDLEBROOK
Senior Vice President and Executive Counsel
Aetna Life & Casualty

*Delivered to The Old Guard (an association of retired business executives),
Hartford, Connecticut, April 28, 1992*

*SUMMARY: Insurance executive and counsel Stephen B. Middlebrook proposes
legal changes and out-of-court conflict resolution alternatives as useful measures
to counteract some of the problems, abuses, and expenses of our current civil justice system.*

> *SPEECH TIP:* Middlebrook's plainspoken introduction gives his speech a rolling start.

Thank you. Today I want to talk about something that's broken—namely, our civil
justice system—and about some ways to fix it.

Voltaire once said of the Holy Roman Empire that it was neither holy, nor
Roman, nor an empire. The same might also be said of the civil justice system in
the United States: that it is neither civil, nor just, nor a system. After all, can it rightly be called "civil," when enormous costs and interminable delays deter citizens
from using it? Is "justice" the right word to describe it, when 80 percent of physicians who are sued for malpractice are not negligent, and 40 percent of those pay
damages anyway? And can we accurately call it a "system," when it has so few standards? For example, so-called "expert" witnesses helped convince a jury to award
$1 million to a Philadelphia soothsayer who claimed that a CAT scan robbed her of
her psychic powers. Even though that verdict was eventually overturned, the point
remains valid: Expert witnesses don't have to be experts; juries are unpredictable;
and the aggregate costs of trying the suit, I suspect, ran well over $100,000.

My talk today will not be an exercise in lawyer-bashing. I am, after all, a
lawyer myself, and see the problems going far beyond lawyers' involvement in the
process.

> *SPEECH TIP:* Once again, the tracing of an idea's origins helps inform the discussion to
> follow.

Let me share with you a bit of history. About forty-five years ago, the seeds
of a legal revolution were sown. Not by the Congress. Not by the U.S. Supreme
Court. Rather, a new idea about liability was put forward by a small group of aca-

demics and jurists, including Justice Roger Traynor of California. The premise for their idea was quite simple: If the legislatures couldn't or wouldn't effect individual justice through social change, then the courts would have to do so.

The idea itself was that victims of accidents should be compensated for their misfortune, not on the basis of who was at fault, but rather, on the theory that the costs of injury should be assigned to those who could best afford to pay, namely, the providers of goods and services—auto manufacturers, doctors, drug companies, and so on. And why could they "best afford to pay"? Because *they* in turn could recover *their* costs by raising the price a bit on their products and services.

In other words, compensate those who suffer enormous misfortune by exacting a small price increase spread widely and thinly among all Americans—similar to the way the insurance and tax systems work.

This redistribution scheme seemed straightforward. For a few accident victims, there would be millions in compensation; for millions of Americans, just a few extra pennies in the marketplace. Gradually, the idea caught on and, over the past thirty years, became an integral part of the civil justice system.

Was the idea a success?

The answer is yes, if you define "success" by the fact that it caught on in the courts. And yes, if you define success by the massive amounts of money that have changed hands as a result. As to whether the system has achieved valuable social change, that's a debate that could last for several hours. But we'll save it for another day.

My purpose *today* is to examine the system itself and ask: Is it efficient? Are people happy with it?

Most experts, business people, and the general citizenry would say no—not when 55 percent of the system's dollars never reach the injured parties. These dollars go to middlemen—expert witnesses, employees of the court, and, most of all, to lawyers who represent plaintiffs and defendants.

The system has been likened to a charity that gives more than half the money it collects to those for whom the money is not intended. That, by anyone's definition, is inefficiency.

The system has other major problems. For one, it is *too slow.* Cases take months, sometimes years. That's not surprising when one considers the sheer weight of numbers. In 1989 alone, two and a half million new liability suits were filed in state and federal courts. That's in addition to the millions already on the docket that absorb the labor of thousands of people and that routinely drag on for months, even years.

The system is also *enormously expensive.* Individuals, businesses, and governments spend upward of $115 billion a year on direct litigation costs. Those costs amount to more than a simple transfer of money. Like nuclear missiles scattered about the Great Plains, the threat of lawsuit amounts to an effective system of deterrence: not against foreign enemies, but rather, against American business.

Consider what this legally induced business deterrence has accomplished:

- 47 percent of U.S. manufacturers have withdrawn products from the market.
- 25 percent of them have stopped some form of product research.
- 15 percent have laid off workers in direct response to product deterrence.
- And, for all American companies, insurance rates are twenty to fifty times higher than those of their foreign competitors.

Which explains why the cause of civil justice reform has been taken up by the President's Council on Competitiveness, under the leadership of Vice President Quayle.

In the area of product liability, the threat of lawsuit is frequently all that is needed to get a lucrative settlement. For example, a few years ago, arsonists burned down the Dupont Plaza Hotel in San Juan, Puerto Rico. Lawyers for the victims sued not only the hotel and the company that built the hotel, but every company that made anything flammable in the hotel—from mattresses, to bar stools, to wallpaper, to wax on the floors, to dice in the casino, and yes, even to wooden doors.

> **SPEECH TIP:** Middlebrook's illustrations are well chosen—and well positioned in his presentation—to get across the points he wishes to make.

This sue-them-all technique has the same effect on small companies that gunboat diplomacy has on small countries: instant capitulation. Rather than go through the time and expense of defending themselves, many of these companies paid $50,000, $100,000, and even more, just to get out of the litigation.

Fear of lawsuits affects not just businesses, but our everyday lives. The fear of medical malpractice suits has deprived thousands of patients of medical care, particularly pregnant women and small children in rural America and in our inner cities. Many obstetricians fear the damage that a malpractice suit—even an unproven one—can cause both financially and in terms of their professional reputation. It is a fear based on experience. Seven out of every ten obstetricians in the United States have been sued for malpractice. For that reason, public clinics in places like Washington, D.C., turn patients away. There are no doctors to treat them—not because doctors are unwilling to donate their time, but because they are not willing to risk being sued, if you can call it a risk. Many would call it a certainty, given the fact that in Washington, D.C., all practicing neurosurgeons—all of them, 100 percent—have had malpractice suits filed against them.

> **SPEECH TIP:** Middlebrook's use of a dramatic Washington, D.C., percentage perfectly demonstrates the value to speakers of city-specific or regional statistics. Localized figures escape the homogenizing effect of nationwide averaging, and they frequently tell a more compelling story—about *specific* places and people.

Well, I could go on with further anecdotes, but the point is clear: the civil justice system has problems that need reform—reform that would benefit all of us.

Now, some people would add, "benefit all of us, except lawyers." I disagree with that.

It is, in my opinion, unfair to claim that the current system is the trial lawyer's version of Rosemary's Baby. It was not created by evil men intent on self-enrichment and self-aggrandizement. It was created by people trying to do some good: Justice Traynor's notion of "valuable social change." It is a case of a good idea—or, at least, a well-intended idea—gone wrong, partly because its creators failed to anticipate how the clock would work when the pendulum changed, and partly because some other folks saw unlimited opportunity for financial reward under the guise of social change.

REFORM AGENDA

The most promising *reforms* fall into three broad categories:

> *SPEECH TIP:* This outline of a reform agenda is as clear and constructive as any could be. Even better, the remainder of Middlebrook's presentation lives up to the outline's promise; it provides creative ideas, exemplary illustrations, and best of all, many concrete and detailed suggestions that the audience could put into use right away.

1. Making trials more efficient and less costly.
2. Improving the lawyer-client relationship.
3. Avoiding trials through alternative dispute resolution.

Here are some examples of each.

Let's start with the legal process known as "discovery." More than 80 percent of the time and cost of a typical lawsuit involves the pretrial examination of facts—the time when each of the parties involved in the suit seeks maximum information about the other party's state of knowledge. Probably everyone in this room has been exposed at one time or another to this process, requesting or providing documents, asking or answering written questions, and giving pretrial testimony to the other side's lawyers through the deposition process. The original purpose of discovery was to allow lawyers to prepare their cases efficiently before trial. In practice, however, current rules of discovery are virtually limitless, permitting parties to roam unfettered through their opponents' affairs, taking depositions that can last days or weeks, and perhaps most onerous of all, creating a crushing demand for documents.

Under these rules, litigants can force their opponents to open a staggering number of their files to inspection. Like a medieval king's demand that his knight ride out and find the Holy Grail, it's a task that's easy to request and hard to fulfill.

The responding party's costs can be staggering—producing the materials, hiring attorneys to review them, copying vast reams of paper, and recording depositions. Almost always—win or lose—these costs must be absorbed by the responding party and can't be transferred to the requesting party.

Discovery can be used—and often is—as an economic weapon against opponents. In a 1988 survey, more than three-quarters of litigators admitted that they used discovery as an economic weapon.

So an absolutely critical reform is to control discovery. The way to do that is *to focus on what is important*: the critical elements of the dispute. This requires the judge to meet with both sides early on: first, to identify the key elements, and second, to use that knowledge as a guide in determining what further information is needed in the discovery process.

This will not only eliminate much of the time and expense of needless "discovery," but also can encourage earlier settlement. Remember that the overwhelming majority of cases are settled without a full trial. Unfortunately, under current rules, this often occurs after most of the time and expense has been expended making cases "trial ready." By focusing discovery on the key issues early on, settlements can be reached before all that time and money has vanished.

A second major area ripe for reform is *the use of expert witnesses*. An "expert" is anyone who has credentialled experience and stature in a given field. Because of this knowledge, experts are presumed to have a special value at trial. There are, of course, rules as to who can qualify as an expert witness and how these witnesses can be used, but the rules are much too loose. They allow for the uncontrolled use of expert witnesses, causing longer trials, more extensive litigation, and in many cases, a dilution in the quality of testimony.

Too often in the courtroom, junk science passes for real science. That soothsayer in Philadelphia who lost her psychic powers to a brain scan was helped by "expert" testimony from a doctor and from officials in the police department. The system will not suffer from the absence of such "experts."

A number of steps are needed in this area:

- Require that expert testimony be based on widely accepted theories, supported by a number of other experts in the field. Does that mean there is no place in the courtroom for novel thinking? No, but let's not call it an expert's view if the experts don't buy into it.

- Forbid contingency fees for expert witnesses. An expert witness should have no financial interest in the outcome of a trial at which he or she testifies.

- Require additional disclosure on experts—their academic credentials, publications, and how they are being compensated for testifying.

Another critical step in the drive for greater efficiency has to do with *time*, which is to say, making better use of it. Some suggestions:

▧ *Early trial dates.* A date should be set immediately after initial pleadings, and, once established, delayed only for a compelling reason. Sticking to the schedule would reduce unnecessary discovery, gamesmanship, and laziness. It would have the same effect on the pace of trials as the twenty-four-second clock has on the pace of pro basketball. Former Supreme Court Justice Lewis Powell calls tougher scheduling "the greatest single step forward" in reforming the system.

▧ *Next, summary judgments.* This means that when the facts of a case are not in serious dispute, judges should be willing to decide the case on the underlying law and not seek a long jury trial.

Our second category of reform, *improving the lawyer-client relationship*, requires two things: subjecting the lawyer to greater control by the client, and giving the client the capability of realistically exercising that control. That's another way of saying: Be an intelligent consumer. This is clearly harder for lay individuals than for large businesses that have attorneys in-house to do their watching and monitoring. Individuals and businesses have only themselves. So it's harder for them, but not impossible. Some guidelines:

▧ Find an attorney who is recommended by someone else whose judgment you trust. Conduct an interview, get references, do your homework.

▧ Get an estimate of costs, fees, type of service provided, number of attorneys required, anticipated motions and depositions, an estimate of billable hours, and a retainer agreement that binds the law firm to anticipated costs.

▧ And, also, discuss legal strategy. Too often clients fail to do this, and six months into the process, find themselves owing thousands of dollars, without the case being resolved, and, by virtue of those two facts, having no choice but to continue the case.

Some of you may have read about the Senoret Chemical Company, a small family-owned business in the Midwest. The Environmental Protection Agency had threatened to take Senoret's insecticide product off the market because the agency deemed it a threat to children, even though there had never been an incident of harm to children in the long history of the product's use.

In fear of a fatal blockage in its modest cash flow, Senoret hired a law firm to stop the EPA from recalling the product. The firm failed to do so, yet ran up $450,000 in fees, leaving Senoret with two problems instead of one: the EPA and its own law firm. The law firm subsequently sued Senoret for non-payment—and won.

One wonders if this tragic case could have been avoided if Senoret had insisted on a discussion of long-term strategy before events spun out of control. Such a discussion should include a realistic assessment of how much the process will cost and the chance of success.

There are many unexpectedly high costs to litigation. For example, a fifteen-minute phone call can cost $50; organizing and indexing a file, $3,000; drafting and filing a complaint, $10,000; and discovery, tens of thousands. Clients should not be timid about going into embarrassing details; for example, does the client get charged when he explains the problem to the senior partner? Yes, that is a reasonable charge. But how about when:

- The senior partner explains it to the associate?

- The associate calls the client for clarification?

- The senior partner reviews the associate's work?

- The senior partner explains the work to the client?

- The senior partner and the associate get together to figure out how much to charge the client?

Finally, on any list of key reforms is the adoption of steps that can avoid the trial process altogether.

Not all, maybe not even most, cases need go through the time and expense of the judicial process—even a perfect one. That's because, as I mentioned earlier, more than 90 percent of all civil lawsuits are settled prior to trial.

Many potential litigants still consider only two avenues for resolving disputes: informal negotiation and litigation. There are others, and they should be more widely used. For example:

- Neutral evaluation, where the opponents meet with an attorney, usually a volunteer with expertise in the disputed subject matter. The neutral attorney sizes up the case, gives an opinion, then asks whether the parties want to work out a deal. An early study of neutral evaluation found that up to 40 percent of cases were resolved on the spot.

- Another method is mediation. Nothing new here. An experienced mediator is chosen by both sides. Even though without any authority to impose a decision, a mediator is often able to settle a dispute. When ITT Rayonier was involved in a court battle with the Green Crow Partnership, a judge endorsed an agreement to select a mediator. The companies chose former Attorney General Griffin Bell to act as mediator and set a three-day limit. Bell, who calls himself a poor man's Henry Kissinger, produced a settlement within forty-eight hours.

■ Minitrials: Here lawyers are instructed to focus on the central issues of a dispute and to keep their arguments short and to the point. Instead of a judge and jury, arguments are presented to executives of the two disputing companies. This method was successfully used to settle a dispute over a sales agreement between Atlantic Richfield and Standard Oil. The executives met in a hotel in Dallas, heard three hours of arguments before lunch, and after lunch met alone. By dinnertime they had an agreement. A survey by the American Bar Association indicates that minitrials have a success rate of 85 percent. Why? Because the settlements are worked out by businessmen negotiating with businessmen, something they're used to doing every day of their lives.

■ Multiparty cooperation, another innovative technique, is designed to cut costs in cases that involve hundreds of individual lawsuits. The defendants agree not to file cross claims against other defendants, which is a common method to divert liability. This technique was used successfully to contain legal expenses in the case of the hotel fire that I mentioned earlier.

There is a notion floating about these days, popular among declinists, that the three branches of American government—the Congress, the Presidency, and the Judiciary—no longer need to provide checks and balances against one another. The reason is that no single one of them is working well enough to remotely threaten the other two!

That may or may not be hyperbole.

At any rate, there is no doubt that the civil justice system needs reform. We can do that without impugning the motives of the legal profession or calling into question the future viability of Western Civilization.

Sam Rayburn had it right when he said, "Any jackass can kick down a barn, but it takes a real carpenter to build one."

We don't have to build a new barn; we just have to repair the old one. The civil justice system is basically sound. The problem is to fix the system, so that its incentives are positive. We have to draw a line between "working the system" and making the system work. Using discovery to punish your opponent "works the system." Establishing rules to control discovery makes the system work.

As you know, the Holy Roman Empire never did become Holy or Roman or an Empire. It just fell apart, and nobody cared.

The civil justice system is different. There are a good many people who care about it and are working to make it what it should be: an efficient system of justice for all our citizens.

Thank you very much.

Agenda for Tomorrow's Agriculture

DALE A. MILLER
Chairman-elect
National Future Farmers of America Sponsors Board,
and President & CEO, Sandoz Agro Inc.

*Delivered at the Annual meeting of the National Association of County
Agricultural Agents, Little Rock, Arkansas, August 10, 1992*

*SUMMARY: An agricultural industrialist discusses the role of candor and honesty
in agribusiness and in its relations with the government and the public.*

I came to Little Rock today seeking political strength from people of power and
influence: not Governor Clinton, but you. By the nature of your work and position
in your communities, you, as county agents, are an influential voice in American
agriculture and control a great deal of power. I am here to ask you to use that
power and influence to make the future brighter for kids who are members of organizations like the FFA, and for technological agriculture.

How many of you wore a blue corduroy jacket when you were in high
school—were members of the FFA? Being a city kid, I was never a member of FFA,
which is a leadership organization for rural, ag-oriented high school kids, but I can
assure you that one of the prides of my business career is my association with that
fine organization. I am really looking forward to this fall, when I take over as chairman of the FFA Sponsors' Board.

I have now been to enough FFA conventions that I am no longer surprised at
the emotion—the pride and the confidence—that engulfs me when I stand on the
floor of the Kansas City Convention Center and look around at the sea of blue jackets and enthusiastic faces. Those 20,000 high school kids are excited about agriculture and their part in it; they radiate an optimism that we could never put there from
the outside; and they simply glow with pride to be part of the team that will keep
us fed and clothed in the twenty-first century.

SPEECH TIP: Opening a speech with expressions of pride, admiration, or other warm
emotions is more than appropriate when the feelings are heartfelt. Such expressions create a shared understanding, between speaker and audience, that the full range of human
communications will be brought into play.

I wish there were a way for all Americans to attend an FFA convention. I
would love it if some of my city and suburban friends could meet one or two of
those spirited, energetic young people. I am certain it would renew their faith in

America's youth. I am here today on behalf of those FFA kids, and their futures in agriculture. No, I'm not going to ask you for money (although if you want to slip me a check after the session, I'd be happy to take it!). Their enthusiasm, as I already said, is contagious. When I am with them, I can share their optimism. But when I return to the real world, I become very troubled. I am afraid that we have done them a great disservice.

For too long, the agricultural establishment—that's you, as County Extension Agents, and me, as a representative of the agricultural chemical industry—has based our talking and writing and teaching and lobbying on an ideal picture of modern agriculture, but not often on a very realistic one. This is a good way to generate enthusiasm among young people, perhaps, but it does not necessarily work as well with the rest of society.

Today, I want to enlist you, as leaders in our industry, to step up, speak out, and take responsibility for what people in American agriculture have done: the bad as well as the good. What I am asking from you is conceptually simple. What I want you to do as teachers, as counselors, as writers of newspaper columns, is to tell the truth.

SPEECH TIP: Miller openly announces his wish to stir the audience to larger action, but as his subsequent words make clear, his actual demands will boil down to a single essence. In stating this clearly, he serves up that essence himself.

Oh, I don't mean to imply that we in agriculture don't tell the truth. But I do believe that we have worked very hard at painting a too-rosy picture, often at the expense of our public credibility.

In the next few minutes, I will describe situations where failure to speak up has limited our ability to set a course for the future. Then I will talk about our additional responsibility to talk about the right things we are doing, even if they happen to be unpopular. Finally, I will explain why this action I am recommending is our best hope of restoring some credibility to the agriculture establishment and returning control over America's twenty-first century food supply to the people who work the land.

In a way, I feel like the story that Kentucky Democratic Congressman Bill Natcher tells on himself: During one of his many reelection campaigns, Congressman Natcher stopped a man in the street, told him he was a candidate for reelection, and held out his hand to shake. The man asked Natcher what party he belonged to, and when Natcher said he was a Democrat, the man frowned. He held out his hand very reluctantly and said, "Well, all right, but just press it light."

I am afraid that many in our society are equally unwilling constituents of American agriculture. A lot of people do recognize that our business is one of the wonders of the modern world. They understand that science and technology enable fewer than two million men and women to feed the other 226 million Americans, and still more millions around the world. A few even know that the land grant system, USDA, and the extension service provide vital links between growers and scientific and technological advancement. But, by and large, when they shake our hands today, they want us to just press light.

Groundwater, farmworker safety, food safety, container disposal, endangered species, soil conservation—agriculture did not endear itself to the American public during the environmental decade.

We have all spent too much time analyzing the decline in popularity of agriculture in America. We point out that most people don't have any idea what farming is all about. We point to the dwindling number of congressmen and state legislators who live in agricultural districts. We whine about the environmental extremists who have organized effectively to discredit some of the very good things we do. And we talk endlessly about the press—a press that, by and large, neither understands nor chooses to hear our side of the story.

We have spent time talking about the decline in understanding and popularity, all of which is true. At the same time, I believe we have contributed to that decline. We've been acting a lot like the establishment politicians, and we should have been acting more like Ross Perot. Now, especially here in Little Rock, I would never claim to have been a Ross Perot supporter. I wasn't. But I do believe that Mr. Perot's short-lived noncandidacy was extremely good for this year's election process. Ross Perot asked hard questions, even if he didn't have many answers. He brought up subjects that the regular party politicians didn't want to discuss—but they were subjects that an awful lot of American people are concerned about today. We will probably never know whether Mr. Perot could have been an effective president, but I believe that we are all better off because he caused Mr. Clinton and Mr. Bush to talk about things they would not have addressed before.

Likewise, I believe that the mainstream ag industry needs to bring up some uncomfortable subjects and talk about them ourselves. By doing that, I believe we will regain some of the credibility we have lost in recent years, and we will gain a platform to talk about legitimate concerns and problems that we have.

My own part of the industry—the pesticide manufacturers—has a reputation with members of Congress for being against almost anything Congress proposes that has anything to do with agriculture. True, some of Congress's proposals are unrealistic or not well thought out. Some are totally ridiculous. But some of them are workable, reflect the mood of the public, and are things we should have done long ago. Yet today we have trouble getting a hearing when we oppose unrealistic bills because we have gone on record so many times against proposals that eventually became law—and that we were able to live with from the start.

Let me now talk for a few minutes about how this situation/idea applies to people who work with pesticides, since that is the business that I am in. I believe absolutely that, when used according to label directions, registered chemical pesticides are safe to the grower and the applicator who uses the chemical, and also to the person who ultimately consumes the farm product.

I believe something else, too: I believe that not everyone uses chemical pesticides the way that they are supposed to be used.

A reporter for a leading farm magazine recently told one of my employees that every time he goes out on a story where there will be photographs taken, he makes sure to take along goggles and gloves. Not because he needs them, but because he can be fairly certain that the subject of his article won't be using the proper protective equipment—even when they know the ag journalists are coming.

SPEECH TIP: One of the most interesting elements you can bring to an out-of-house presentation is the first-hand reports you have gathered, along the way, from people in your particular field. Rather than taking your workday contacts or experiences for granted, remember how radically different people's workdays can be.

This magazine, and most of the other ag publications, take scrupulous care to show only people who are using proper equipment for the job to be done, proper protection, and proper use and disposal methods. Their aim: to reflect the proper ways—the ideal farmers. However, is this reflection of only the "good stuff" actually doing a disservice to the agricultural industry? What about growers who misapply chemicals? What about improper waste disposal? What about companies that allow misuse of their products? What about sales people who knowingly sell or recommend products for off-label uses?

All these things are not just bad practices, but are actually against the law. Yet, for all the general public hears, no one is very concerned. How much harm would it do my industry or your profession or our ag journalists to condemn lawbreaking?

It would sure surprise a lot of people.

Why do we allow these misuses to go on? We look the other way because the dealers and growers I'm talking about are our customers and constituents, and the salespeople are our own employees—and we do not want to rock the boat.

We look the other way at violations because they represent only a small part of the ag community. Ninety-nine point nine nine percent of the people who sell and use pesticides do so with care and in accordance with the law. However, that infinitesimally small group of scofflaws is in the process of ruining the game for all of us. If you believe, as I do, that chemical pesticides are a valuable tool for modern agriculture, then speak out against misuse. We do not need to ask for more laws and regulations. The rules are there. We *do* need to call for enforcement of those laws and regulations. Fines are rarely levied against any but the most flagrant offenders. If we believe in the system of which we are all a part, then it is in our best interest for the system to work correctly.

Let me suggest something to you. We are all fighting, in one way or another, the growing concern about pesticide residues in food. Pesticides are beneficial products, but they are complex chemicals that must be used carefully and prudently to have the desired effect. Examples do exist of situations where misuse has caused damage to crops or illegal residues on food, and mishandling has caused health problems to improperly trained or outfitted applicators or farmworkers.

Can you imagine that a person who doesn't know much about chemical pesticides might think that if a product could harm a farmworker, it could also be dangerous if it were later detected—at any level—in food or food products? I can!

Science and experience, of course, tell us otherwise. We know from the more than a hundred and twenty tests conducted for each chemical pesticide that safety and environmental soundness are the first criteria for registration by EPA. We know from other tests conducted on each labeled crop that the application rates are designed to make the chemical effective during the growing season and assure that any residues remaining after harvest are safe. We know from actual measurement that fewer than 1 percent of U.S. farm products tested show any illegal residues.

The problem is, we preach endlessly about the upfront tests that a chemical pesticide must undergo for registration, and about food safety, but we are reticent to the point of looking the other way when a report surfaces about worker health or product misuse.

In fact, there are almost no federal regulations to protect farm workers. At EPA, Linda Fisher, assistant administrator for prevention, pesticides and toxic substances, is making farm worker safety one of her priorities and apparently is seeking minimum protection standards, medical care, and field reentry limits. These proposed regulations will not be issued until year's end, but already farm groups are wailing that the regulations will bankrupt farmers and the environmentalists are howling that not enough safeguards will be required. I suspect the agricultural chemical industry will also have legitimate problems with at least part of the government proposals.

Rather than automatically react negatively, however, what if we in agriculture went on record with concerns about the potential dangers some farmworkers and applicators face from pesticides when not properly trained and equipped? Every true story about a pesticide poisoning is a step backward for modern agriculture. I am convinced also—although there is absolutely no evidence to support my theory—that every story about a farmworker poisoning raises concerns about pesticide residues in food.

Every time we do not speak out or act out against the few bad actors in agriculture, we are responsible for the creation of more restrictive laws and regulations. Every well-meaning, but inappropriate regulation makes it more difficult for agriculture, and less likely that those FFA kids will have a fair chance for successful farming careers.

Eleanor Roosevelt, wife of our thirty-second president, said once that "a democratic form of government, a democratic way of life, presupposes . . . an education for personal responsibility that too often is neglected." I believe Mrs. Roosevelt's words speak to us today. We do have a personal responsibility, or at least a collective responsibility, to speak out when we see wrong happening, as well as when we do right. Granted, what I am talking about is "just business," but how much different is it, really, than watching a woman be attacked in Central Park, or looking out the window of an apartment while someone else is robbed and beaten, or watching thugs harass an old person on a bus? Most of us know the difference between right and wrong. How many of us are willing to go on record? How many of us would automatically do *something* to help the person being victimized—but stop short of taking action where pesticides are concerned?

Let me ask you a different question. How many of us are willing to go on record and risk misunderstanding when we're doing the right thing about something unpopular?

Here's what I mean: When pesticides were first detected in groundwater several years ago, the pesticide industry was quick to point out that the level of residues in these detections, by and large, did not pose a health problem. That was true, even though that information came too late, and from the wrong source, to calm things down very much.

Besides offering the technical data, which was a good thing to do, the agriculture establishment was also out in force doing damage to our credibility. The manufacturers stormed Washington to resist any new groundwater legislation or regulation. At the same time, hundreds of farmers turned out to testify at government hearings across the Midwest in order to preserve their right to use certain pesticides that had been detected in the groundwater.

Yet, that is not all that the agriculture industry was doing about the groundwater situation. At home, we were all working hard to find new products that were likely to break down more quickly in the soil, and to develop our own management plans for products that had been detected in the groundwater at unacceptable levels. Organizations like the Well Water Association, the commodity groups, and you Extension Agents began providing advice and operating tips on ways to protect the groundwater. Growers all over the country began to be far more careful in their loading and mixing operations, especially around wells. We saw Monsanto introduce a microtech version of Lasso. DuPont introduced the sulfonylureas; companies like mine introduced combination products that use very low rates of atrazine. Yet—publicly—we howled.

Let's face it, I'd prefer that nobody could detect any of my company's products in the groundwater. I'd actually prefer that we find new generations of chemicals that do their job and simply go away. I suspect you agree with me. So why hasn't somebody stood up and said that?

SPEECH TIP: Demonstrating the principle that form follows function, Miller's message and his mode of delivery join together at several points in his speech. Here he states the obvious—in order to question why the obvious too often goes unsaid.

Parenthetically, many people in my industry are opposing a new Safer Pesticide Policy recently proposed by EPA to encourage development of just that sort of product—chemicals that upfront are less likely to find their way into groundwater or cause health risks than others already on the market. This seems to be the kind of program the public has demanded and that our farmer customers would applaud. The truth is, it's a good idea, and the industry should support its philosophical goals and contribute to finding ways to make it technologically and economically feasible.

Daniel Yankelovich, one of the men who raised opinion research in America to an art form, has just written a somewhat disturbing book. In it, he says that although we know a lot about how to measure—and manipulate—public opinion, we know very little about how to help the public arrive at sound judgments, and we rarely differentiate between opinions and judgments.

I believe that is what I am talking about today. We all—you and I and the general public—share the same opinion: We do not want chemical pesticides in the groundwater. Realistically, given the speed at which scientific measurement is progressing, I doubt we will ever achieve zero detects, but I do believe that should be our goal. Our judgment, on the other hand, tells us that what has been detected so far is not a threat. Perhaps, if we give them a chance, our fellow Americans would share our judgment, as we share their opinions. But they won't agree, if we don't give them a chance.

By being unable—or afraid—to admit that we share the concerns of the American public, we are doing those kids in the blue jackets a disservice. By having been unable to say, "we are concerned, too, but—guess what?—we have the ability to make things better," we did ourselves a disservice.

In the past twenty years, the American public has heard so much from everyone in the ag industry about the acknowledged benefits that we provide, and so little about problems and issues with which they are concerned, that they are skeptical of anything we say anymore. They have no idea that any of us share their concerns or that we would do anything proactive to better things, if it were not mandated by Congress or EPA. Of course, they come by that belief honestly. Look at how the agriculture establishment reacted to the concept of soil conservation.

More than a generation ago, when concern about soil erosion turned into serious criticism, the farm community responded vigorously. Cultivating the soil with a moldboard plow was the best way, growers said, that they could get the yield they needed from their land. Their reaction was loud and unequivocal, even though their reluctance had less to do with the plow than their own concerns about the cost of converting equipment, concerns about weed control, and, psychologically, their long-standing attitudes that clean-tilled fields were the mark of a progressive grower.

Yet last year, only 6,300 moldboard plows were sold in the U.S.—down from 60,000 in 1970. A cultural revolution has occurred called no-till, ridge-till, mulch-till, and reduced-till. The U.S. Soil Conservation Service reported recently in *Time* magazine that a quarter of the 281 million acres of all U.S. cropland is now under some kind of residue management program. Perhaps more impressive than numbers is the comment by one of my younger employees that the snow in Iowa isn't black anymore. But it took public and governmental pressure, and finally tying conservation tillage to price supports to accomplish this.

Responsibility, credibility, honesty. Why are we so afraid?

Last April, when New Hampshire Senator Warren Rudman announced that he was retiring, he lashed out at Congress for failing to deal with the budget deficit: "You have got to take some political risks," said Rudman. "It's time to tell the truth. And if you get defeated while doing it, well, it will be worth doing it. At least you do something good for the country."

I share Rudman's sentiments—unequivocally for Congress, and also for the agricultural community, although I do not believe we will be defeated. Quite the opposite. If we take some political risks and tell the truth about the bad as well as the good, it will make the agricultural community stronger, and give us our voice back here in Little Rock and in Washington. If people in agriculture become known as thoughtful and responsible rather than predictable naysayers, I believe we will regain the respect and the power that we have lost in the political and public policy arenas.

As I mentioned when I began my speech, I am very worried about the future of agriculture. I believe that growers and the industries who serve them are being regulated within inches of economic disaster. If something does not change, agriculture as we know it may cease to exist in the United States.

I believe that our defeat, as a strong segment of the American economy, will come from failing to tell the truth and failing to take responsibility as fully for our errors as for our successes—errors, by and large, that we are all working hard to correct when they happen. If we tell the truth, I believe the people will listen. They're as tired of the spotted owl doomsayers as they are of the agriculture industry deniers. They are not, however, tired of wanting to maintain a safe environment and a safe food supply.

I am appealing to you in particular to speak out and own up, because I know of no group that is a more influential link between the growers and the general public. You live in both worlds; you see both sides. Those kids in the FFA deserve a chance to bring American agriculture into the twenty-first century with a flourish, not a whimper—nor an apology. And to do that, the shortage they face is not in technology; know-how we have in abundance. The shortage is of people in responsible positions who are willing to take unpopular stands on important issues.

The press—and our politicians—have commented a lot lately about the way the times have changed: The sixties was the decade of protest, the seventies was the decade of self-interest, and the eighties was the decade of greed. Today, the nineties, is the decade of family values, of back to the basics. Please join me in bringing two old American values back to the agriculture community: responsibility and honesty.

If we can do that, I have no doubt but that everything else will fall into place.

Envy, Honesty, and the Scientific Method

RICHARD W. RAHN
President and Chief Executive Officer
Novecon

Delivered at the Commencement Ceremony, Pepperdine University, Malibu, California, July 31, 1993

SUMMARY: Faulting many opinion leaders for their misrepresentation of economic facts, Novecon executive Richard W. Rahn stresses the long-term value of scientific principles and ethical conduct in business and public policy.

Chancellor Runnels, Provost Lemley, Regent Kemp, Dr. and Mrs. Krieble, distinguished guests, ladies and gentlemen, and members of the graduating class, I am deeply grateful to be here with you today, and I most appreciate the high honor the Regents of Pepperdine University have bestowed on me. I am also honored by the opportunity to deliver the commencement address, and, in part, I will repay the honor by giving a relatively brief talk, which of course is a most difficult task for an economist.

> *SPEECH TIP:* Rahn makes good on this promise. And woe to the speakers who don't! Self-advertising a time frame you do *not* in fact deliver is a magical formula for transforming a perfectly happy audience into a perfectly testy crowd.

Despite my promise of brevity, I realize that some of you may still prefer to nod off; thus I will begin with a one-sentence summary of my talk—a run-on sentence, however. Economic growth and the furtherance of civilization depend upon both the acquisition of knowledge, most often through the scientific methods, and the willingness of leaders to accept and act on that knowledge, even when it is not in their short-run self-interest, and business leaders have the responsibility for vigorously supporting sound policies and practices and for opposing the unsound.

You, the most recent graduates of this distinguished university, will be the leaders or will determine the leaders of tomorrow. Business people can and should have a major influence on the development of a society. A society without involved, courageous, and honest businesspeople will not be a fully developing society. In part, America's ills are a result of too few businesspeople having sufficient interest to get involved with the political process, and having too many of those who do have such interest lose sight of the common good in order to gain some short-sighted advantage. As the next generation, it is your responsibility to clean up the mess of the last.

A new world's record: The leaders of the G-7 countries, also known as the self-defined industrial elite, met in Tokyo last month, and all of them had negative approval ratings. The low approval ratings were blamed on sluggish economies, which are failing to produce jobs. How odd. Here we are, less than seven years from the twenty-first century, having produced and experienced all of the scientific miracles of this century, yet we don't seem to know how to create a job.

The facts are, however, we do know how to create a vibrant economy, and we do know how to create more and better-paying jobs. Our economic problems stem not from a lack of knowledge, but from a denial of knowledge. Economic facts and findings are not always convenient for those who wish to gain power by controlling others.

Witness the communists, who tried through appeals to envy and endless lies, plus torture and murder, to repeal the basic laws of economics. They ultimately were no more successful than those who try to deny the basic laws of physics. Those who continue to try to practice forms of economic management that are dependent upon appeals to envy and dishonesty in the presentation of reality shall not ultimately succeed. But, like the communists who created a culture of envy, they can cause much unnecessary human misery even after they are discredited.

The majority of those, in this country and others, who espouse and advocate economic nonsense, do so not out of malice but because of misunderstanding. The same is true, of course, about some who discuss matters bearing on the physical sciences. Many are untutored in the scientific method, and many who do understand and practice the scientific method in their own fields of expertise fail to use the same discipline when discussing fields with which they are less familiar. Even so, the amount of ignorance concerning public policy matters has probably declined over the past two centuries. What has appeared to increase is the misuse of the English language by public officials often bent on deliberately misleading.

A few examples should suffice. Politicians of both parties regularly claim they are "cutting" government spending. In fact, government spending has not been "cut." It has been growing erratically in both nominal and real terms for several decades and is now a record high percentage of Gross Domestic Product (or GDP). The "cuts" are only from hypothetical spending increases. Increases in "user fees" and some tax increases for social security recipients are falsely labeled "spending cuts." Some of the proposed increases in "investment spending" are actually increases in transfer payments.

SPEECH TIP: Because his theme is largely abstract, Rahn's examples are well-timed.

Tax rate changes are equated with tax revenue changes by many who should know better, including some of those responsible for preparing official government forecasts. As any good economist or businessperson knows, a tax-rate increase may result in more government revenue, in the same way that a price increase for a product can lead to more or less revenue. To use static revenue forecasts for tax-rate changes is fundamentally dishonest. In practice, this leads to tax rates well above the revenue maximizing rate, as in the case of the capital gains tax rate.

Perhaps the most outrageous falsehood perpetrated on the public by many opinion leaders is that increases in government spending will solve most of society's ills and create jobs. For instance, if you knew that since 1960 the percentage of illegitimate births has increased fivefold, the percentage of children on welfare and the teen suicide rate have increased threefold, the rate of violent crime has increased almost fivefold, SAT scores have consistently fallen, the average unemployment rate has risen each decade, total government spending in the U.S. has been growing considerably faster than population growth, inflation, and real economic growth combined, and that in the G-7 countries government spending and economic growth have been inversely related, would you conclude that government is the solution or the problem?

Anyone familiar with the scientific method, which would include most of America's opinion leaders, ought to be severely questioning the hypothesis that government spending is a solution. Additional evidence was provided by the American experiment, which was implemented in 1983 and lasted through 1989, whereby marginal tax rates were sharply reduced, regulatory growth was restrained, and the growth in government spending was kept slightly below economic growth. The result was a slight reduction in government tax revenues as a percentage of GDP, but a big increase in the proportion of taxes paid by upper income groups, a substantial increase in real incomes by all income groups, a record increase in peacetime economic growth, and a reduction of more than 50 percent in the real deficit from its 1983 peak.

The factual statements I have just made are often ignored, denied, or misrepresented by opinion leaders, who nevertheless know better. They include not just politicians and members of the media, but also economists and businesspeople who seek short-term personal gain, applause, or power at the expense of the many.

Fortunately, there are many other opinion leaders who are knowledgeable and principled, and thus are appropriate role models for you, such as Dr. Robert Krieble, whom you are honoring here today. I expect you honor him, in part, because he is a distinguished chemist, who did not forget that the scientific method has equal applicability to the political and economic sciences. He has been a successful entrepreneur and investor because he understood it is better to place your assets in those countries that are pursuing relatively pro-growth economic policies as opposed to anti-growth policies, and are moving toward freedom rather than away from it.

At times, Bob Krieble has been the subject of ridicule by some in the Washington establishment because he has been principled, honest, and has an empirical view of reality. Some laughed when Bob, well beyond the age when most men have retired, single-handedly undertook to provide material and moral support for the dissident groups in Eastern Europe and the former Soviet Union. But he understood that the communist system was in the last stages of a terminal illness, and he did his unselfish best to bring it to a quicker demise. The result is that there is no American businessman who has garnered more affection and respect from both the people and leaders of the newly freed states.

Here at home, some in the business establishment have criticized Bob Krieble for being too uncompromising with politicians, including some in his own party who advocate destructive policies. Yet he has been consistently right in his predictions of what the consequences of misguided policy would be. Again, by being principled and honest, and understanding the difference between nonsense and reality, his prestige and influence in Washington have steadily risen, while those who only coveted an invitation to the White House, or sold their soul for a tax break for their company are increasingly recognized for what they are.

Again, some of you graduating today will be the business and opinion leaders of tomorrow. The empirical evidence is overwhelming, that if business leaders do not have the courage to speak and act with honesty and knowledge, then progress will be slowed. The empirical evidence also indicates, that those leaders who are principled, honest, knowledgeable, and do not resort to appeals to envy, are far more likely to be treated well by their fellow man over the long run and by history. The temptation is always to say and do the things which bring you the immediate applause, but it does not last, as many of the G-7 leaders are learning. If you care about your reputation—over the long run—and the betterment of your fellow man, it is practical to have principles, the courage to speak the truth even when it is unpopular, and to have an understanding of the consequences of actions. Our problems as a nation are not caused by some in power who know little of what they speak. Our problems are caused by those in power who know the truth, yet speak and act as though reality does not exist.

Finally, perhaps the most important thing we can learn from Bob Krieble and others like him, is while there is a certain quiet pleasure in having lived long enough to see one's theories proved and one's predictions come true, these are only a foundation for future vigorous action. Thus, I wish you all a long, prosperous, principled, and happy life.

Values: Key to Moving Beyond

DONALD J. SCHUENKE
Chairman and Chief Executive Officer
Northwestern Mutual Life Insurance

*Delivered to the Northwestern Mutual Annual Meeting of Agents, Milwaukee,
Wisconsin, July 20, 1992*

*SUMMARY: Addressing the annual meeting of Northwestern Mutual Life Insurance
agents, Donald J. Schuenke reviews six small-town American ideals that have
served as "cornerstone values" throughout the history of the company: family, independence, integrity, self-determination, loyalty, and compassion.*

Thank you, Tom. Good morning—and on behalf of everyone at the Home Office,
a warm welcome to the 112th Annual Meeting of Agents. I hope you enjoyed your
visit to the Town of Beyond—I certainly did! And I felt right at home because at
Northwestern Mutual, I'm accustomed to being surrounded by people who have
gone beyond normal expectations. It's simply the way we do business.

I always look forward to the annual meeting. It's an opportunity to touch base
with the fundamentals of our business in terms of people, policies, and practices.
When we talk of fundamentals, there's nothing more basic than values. Particularly
in this election year, values have become a pivotal issue.

Much of the campaign rests on the personal values of the various candidates—what they believe in (or appear to believe in). Voters are looking at candidates' values as much as the solutions they propose. Ross Perot's popularity
stemmed not from his solutions—because he proposed few—but from the values
he espoused. In addition to the presidential candidates, a number of legislators
have found that their values have come home to roost. Congressmen involved in
the House bad-check scandal are leaving in droves. It's not the first time, of course.
Remember Richard Milhouse Nixon? A lot of people thought he ran the country
pretty well. But he was forced out because of real or perceived flaws in his value
system.

The elections this year show every sign of hinging on the issue of America's
value system as reflected in the candidates.

Small-town America—something akin to the Town of Beyond, without the
robots—is what many people still think of in terms of America and its values. Our
country is far more diverse than that. Today we have a balance among small towns,
medium-sized cities, and large metropolitan areas. But most of the small-town
American values that we treasure flourish in each of us—and certainly endure in
America.

Those same lasting values that built this nation built Northwestern Mutual as well.

What are some of those values? Well, there's a long list of possibilities—and everyone probably has their own favorites—but this morning I will concentrate on six that I see as cornerstones.

> **SPEECH TIP:** The six values that Schuenke highlights create the basic six-part structure of his speech. One of the advantages of naming the number of the elements to be discussed is that the audience can attend to each topic and consider its unique contribution to—as well as its order of sequence in—the known total.

The first of these six cornerstone values is the value of the family.

Families today come in many shapes and sizes, but the value of the family relationship for shaping and nurturing the citizens of tomorrow remains. It is within the family that children learn values as diverse as love, responsibility, communication, respect for authority and faith in God. They learn about living up to one's potential, leaving the world a better place, doing the right thing, and doing things right.

I have always seen Northwestern Mutual as a family working together for *each individual* and for the greater good. All of us gathered here today are members of a family brought together by common goals, shared beliefs, and concern for one another. Whether we are single or married, young or old, agents or field staff, employees, family members, policyowners or trustees, we are all members of the greater Northwestern Mutual family. We have generations of policyowners and generations of agents: the Gilbergs, the Steeles, the Hahses, the McTigues, the Hiltons, the Qualys, the Gardners, the Stones, to name just a few.

> **SPEECH TIP:** By calling out specific names, Schuenke strengthens his discussion of the value of familiar bonds at Northwest. In fact, this naming in itself proves his claim for the family's priority; since every audience member cannot be mentioned individually, this shows extra-special appreciation for actual families with multigenerational ties to the firm.

We establish relationships with one another. There are Northwestern study groups whose members have been helping each other for many, many years. I know of one that has been in existence since 1958. This year, a Career School class is having a reunion after twenty years. (It's a pretty high-powered reunion—that Career School turned out to include seven future GAs and many very successful agents.)

Further, our company exists to protect the *family*. If people didn't place value on the family, we wouldn't sell very much life insurance.

The second cornerstone value I will discuss today is the value of independence. Our country is built on the principles of freedom and independence. As a nation, we have never gone along with the herd. From the days of the Boston Tea Party, Americans have stubbornly thought for themselves.

The same is true of the Northwestern Mutual. Our company has always followed what it thought was the best path, rather than the path of expediency, of least resistance, or simply what others were doing. We haven't jumped on many bandwagons. That dates back to our founder, General Johnston, who was seventy-five when he founded a life insurance company on the frontier. Our name tells how old we are. At the birth of the Northwestern Mutual 135 years ago, this *was* the Northwest.

We've steadfastly refused to broker our products. In recent years we've avoided the so-called financial supermarket, turned away from other people's books of business, and said no thanks to GICS.

In the short run, these decisions didn't always make everyone happy—here I'm thinking of our refusal to offer universal life, for example. But in the long run—and this company is structured for the long run—it has been best for everyone.

Our independence of thought and action is recognized even outside the United States. Let me read to you a few quotes from the most recent issue of the *Canadian Journal of Life Insurance*, a penetrating publication that acts as the conscience of the insurance industry in Canada:

> Northwestern Mutual Life , the company that has for many years set a laudable example by taking seriously both mutuality and the operation of a quality career agency system, is sitting pretty. It didn't issue universal life (aka cannibal life) and stayed with whole life. It has no junk bonds. What it does have is a solid reputation, a superior distribution system and assets well in excess of $20 billion.

(It's $37 billion, actually.) The columnist goes on to say:

> Northwestern embodies something too rare these days but still dear to my heart: the intelligence to resist trendy but unwise change and the ability to recognize that not all change is progress.

That was R. A. Rickard, an editor and observer of the insurance scene in both Canada and the U.S.

The third cornerstone value that has shaped both our nation and our company is the value of *integrity*. Fairness and honesty are part of the fabric of our country.

Equally so, the Northwestern strives to be scrupulously fair and honest in all of our dealings—with policyowners, with employees, and certainly with members of the field force.

Integrity shapes our products. Every Northwestern product stands on its own. There are no loss leaders. Integrity shapes our underwriting. We evaluate each and every policyowner rather than saying, "Let's take in lots more business and let the well ones pay for the sick ones." And integrity shapes the people of our company—field and home office.

We keep the actuaries busy determining dividends that reflect the contribution each policy has made to the company, and we strive to pay our policyowners every benefit due them. This, too, is a practice that dates from our earliest days. Many of you have heard more recent stories of benefits paid in unusual cases when another company might have denied the claim.

But you probably haven't heard of James Douglass, who applied for life insurance with the Northwestern in 1888 and sent his premium with the application. The company had questions about his family medical history—things really haven't changed much, have they? But when the agent went to get the answers, he found Mr. Douglass on his deathbed. The agent also determined that his client's illness was unrelated to his family history, and he sent that information in along with news of Mr. Douglass's death.

The company promptly issued a policy and paid the loss. That was in 1888—and we would do the same today. Our values have been consistent for a long, long time.

> **SPEECH TIP:** This remarkable anecdote shows that company history needn't be recent to be relevant—and needn't be boring at all. In-house speakers can benefit from a little investigation into the interesting stories that reside in even the most ancient office files.

The fourth cornerstone value that I want to touch on is the value of self-determination. Each person in our nation is held to be not only of equal importance, but to have the right to determine his or her own destiny.

No one embodies the value of self-determination better than Northwestern Mutual agents. Self-determination is often linked with great personal courage. One example that comes to mind is that of Luther Hahs of Cape Girardeau, Missouri, an emeritus agent who has stood on this very stage. In the prime of his career, Luther suffered a massive stroke that left him unable to walk or talk. He fought long and hard not only to recover but to go on to serve as an inspiration to others.

Each of *you* is in the perfect position to set your own path and make the most of your powers. Your own ability and hard work determine your output and your success. No one can afford to be complacent, and maybe there is a touch of complacency out there.

To be candid about it, we have a larger total agency force selling fewer total life insurance policies. The average number of life insurance sales per agent is less than it was last year or the year before. Granted, there's more premium, but it's the fewer policies that are bothersome. It's something we have to be careful about.

Nothing lasts forever. I believe it's dangerous to plan your future on fewer policies with higher premiums. We must never lose sight of the fundamentals. We must continue building for the future, and a high activity level is your surest safeguard.

Your participation in this Annual Meeting of Agents is but one indication of your commitment to your future. Your high level of formal education before you embark on your careers, and your continuing education through such means as Career School and Chartered Life Underwriter once you join the company, are additional indications. Northwestern Mutual agents are known for achieving and maintaining their sterling qualifications.

In addition, there's no ceiling on success in our company. Just look at the Top 20. There are always lots of new faces—seven this year. There's always room to excel. My congratulations to new—and old—agents among the Top 20. Particularly to Dan Brunette, who leads in both lives and volume, and to those new on the list. My compliments and congratulations also go to each and every Northwestern agent, your office staffs, and your families. Together, you've done a tremendous job this year. This company truly is *everybody*—and I suggest you give yourselves a round of applause.

Next, let me turn to the fifth cornerstone value—the value of loyalty. We believe in our country and what it stands for even in difficult times.

At Northwestern Mutual we believe in and are loyal to our policyowners. The home office believes in and is loyal to the field force. We stand firm in our faith that an exclusive general agency system is absolutely the best way to sell life insurance.

Quite honestly, we expect the same loyalty in return. Here I am speaking of outside business contrary to your contract. I believe it has diminished in recent years, but frankly it has no place within the Northwestern Mutual system.

Our loyalty to and belief in our company empowers us to fight for what we believe in. We are constantly at work with both the federal and state governments to ensure legislation that preserves our policyowners' interests. This includes legislation not only on tax and regulatory matters, but on such issues as AIDS and genetic testing as well.

I salute your intervention with Congress—the many letters you wrote and calls you made—on the recent annuities issue. And I am confident that when the call goes out again—as it surely will—you will answer it.

The sixth cornerstone value that I believe supports both our nation and our company is the value of compassion.

Americans have always been noted for lending a helping hand and for looking out for the less fortunate. These traditions are engraved on the base of the Statue of Liberty: "Give me your tired, your poor. . . ." They are embodied in events as diverse as barn raisings on the Western Plains and the Marshall Plan in Europe.

So too, the business of life insurance is—in essence—based on compassion, caring about our fellow human beings. One of my favorite expressions about our line of work is that we can "do well by doing good." The Northwestern Mutual is noted for its genuine caring for its policyowners, for its aim to rank first in benefits to policyowners.

We also care about our communities, as evidenced by your incredible range of community activities—from church work, to charity fund drives, to the Boy

Scouts, and everything in between. I think of agent Bob Muzikowski, who started Little League teams in the urban war zone of Chicago's Cabrini Green housing project. This company is filled with Bob Muzikowskis.

SPEECH TIP: Once again, Schuenke puts his money (in speakers' currency—special mention) where his mouth is, singling out the exemplary contributions of a specific individual.

Here I should note that home office employees are also active on the volunteer front. Just one example is giving their time and energies (and sweat) to rehabbing houses for Habitat for Humanity. And the company has an extensive Matching Gifts program for education. Last year, more than 1,500 agents donated over $440,000 through Matching Gifts.

You make a difference—a very large difference.

I believe that the Northwestern Mutual is a value-based company in every sense of the word. Our company is constructed upon the values of the family, independence, integrity, self-determination, loyalty, and compassion. It is our mission to preserve those values. Not only do the values have great intrinsic worth—values and reputation are closely linked.

One of the greatest things we have going is our unparalleled reputation. We have been the "most admired company" in the insurance industry category in *Fortune*'s survey for ten straight years. (Incidentally, that's as long as they have run the survey.) And today I have more good news about rankings.

Many of you know that *Sales and Marketing Management* magazine is in the process of redoing its survey asking, "What is the best sales force in the industry?" It's been three years since they examined the insurance industry. The results will appear in the September issue.

This morning I am proud to tell you that we've just received advance word from Richard Kern, editor-in-chief, that the results have been compiled. And the good news is that—for the third consecutive time in these three surveys—the Northwestern Mutual field force has again been named top in the industry!

Each of you has the right to be immensely proud of this designation. You know you're the best, we know you're the best, and now the world knows you're the best. You are responsible in large part for the Northwestern's reputation. That reputation is made up of each and every action of each and every one of us.

Images become real, living, fragile things. Society can be very unforgiving in its view of a person or a company.

Just look at how quickly the Sears image changed in light of that California auto repair uproar. Generations of Americans had counted on Sears. My own view of Sears centered around a bicycle I once bought for my son. After some hard riding, the bicycle frame broke. I had it welded, but eventually it broke again. By that point the bicycle was over a year old and pretty beat up—but on the advice of a neighbor, we took it back to Sears. And to my surprise, they replaced it! Countless Americans had similar experiences with Sears backing its products.

But what do people think of today when Sears is mentioned? Will they think of all the times Sears backed its products? Or will they think of Sears salespeople pushing auto repairs to increase their commissions?

We must keep in mind that every employee, every agent, every field staff person represents our company. We're at risk in that we, too, sell our product on a commission basis. Any product sold on commission is subject to higher scrutiny. So we need to remain alert to possible dangers.

And we need to cherish the six cornerstone values—the value of family, the values of independence, integrity, self-determination, loyalty, and compassion.

Rooted in those values, the Northwestern is ideally situated to move into an even greater dimension—to "move beyond." I have a strong belief in moving beyond. I have never been one of those people who subscribed to the "If-it-ain't-broke, don't-fix-it" school of thought. Everything—no matter how well done—can be done better.

To "move beyond" means remembering the fundamentals of the selling process. These include the value added by a knowledgeable Northwestern agent, building a growing file of clients, and increasing the number of phone calls and personal visits.

As we look into the future, our challenge is to continue to embody the values that have built our company. We must illustrate them in every facet of our own lives. And we must use them as the basis to take the extra steps—to move beyond.

We must remember what we ultimately do: provide peace of mind, fund children's educations, keep families together, and protect businesses. We touch people's lives.

In closing, I propose a personal challenge to each of you. We have all heard stories of policyowners who purchased just in time, and of people who procrastinated too long and left families unprotected. When you get home, take a close look at your clients and would-be clients, your policyowners and potential policyowners. Choose the one or two who are the most under-insured, who are in the most jeopardy without your services. Make the extra effort to serve those people and eliminate their risk.

You can't pursue every potential policyholder to the ends of the earth. But even if you don't make the sale—although I sincerely hope and think you will—you will feel better for making the effort.

And it's something extra, a feel-good effort for yourself. You will have assured your peace of mind and done your best to ensure your policyowner's peace of mind. It will emphasize the vital, meaningful nature of our work.

Approach each piece of business with the values that you hold within.

It is by "moving beyond"—by cherishing the cornerstone values—that we best serve ourselves, our company, our families, and our policyowners.

This is important work that we do—and I thank each of you for doing it so well.

CHAPTER 9

Media and Communication

Of all subjects, media and communication makes perhaps the greatest demand on the speaker—especially in the speaker's own view of the task. After all, to speak about communication is to be a communicator asking others to judge the quality of your communication. This is sticking your neck out.

Fortunately, the field of communication encompasses a broad range of topics, from the highly theoretical, to the highly technical, to the very simple and commonplace. Sooner or later, the jobs we do demand communication, and it is perfectly possible to create a good speech based solely on your area of expertise. For example, David F. D'Alessandro speaks about a specialized niche of media and communications, event marketing, whereas Jean L. Farinelli discusses the more familiar subject of marketing in terms of communication.

For the speaker, the useful thing about the topic of communication is that it provides a new common denominator, an often fresh and refreshing way of exploring an overly familiar subject. The topics almost invent themselves: "Customer Service as Communication," "Effective Sales Begin with Effective Communication," "Doctor's Strongest Medicine: Communication," and so on.

You need not be a communication or media expert to create an effective speech on this topic, but you do need a thorough knowledge of whatever field to which you apply the topic. Of all occasions to avoid abstraction, it is particularly vital to avoid it in a speech on communication. Use plenty of illustrations, examples, and anecdotes to *communicate* your points effectively.

Beyond Giving a Speech: Becoming a Poised, Polished Presenter

PATRICIA WARD BRASH
Director of Communications
Miller Brewing Company

Delivered to Women in Communication, Milwaukee, Wisconsin, August 18, 1992

SUMMARY: Communications director Patricia Ward Brash offers strategic guidelines and helpful hints for making successful business presentations.

Thank you, Suzanne (Kletch). I appreciate this opportunity to share some thoughts with you on the preparation and delivery of presentations. All of us in communications recognize that the farther we advance in our profession, the greater our opportunities and requirements for giving presentations. We also recognize that it's wise to get experience: as *much*, as *soon*, and as *often* as possible. In addition, we can all benefit throughout our careers from taking public speaking courses and studying to improve our presentation skills.

Today I would like to focus on three main areas:

- Preparation, including content
- Delivery, and
- Use of visuals.

SPEECH TIP: Beginning with this clear and straightforward introduction, Brash will herself demonstrate many of the excellent guidelines she espouses.

Let's begin with *preparation*, which includes every aspect of effective presentation skills, such as deciding upon the objective, content development, delivery, and visual support.

It's important to identify our goal before we concentrate on the message, and we should begin by asking ourselves whether our objective is:

- To inform

- To persuade

- To inspire

- To motivate to action, or

- To entertain.

Of course the answer will depend largely upon the composition of the audience. We should tailor every presentation to the *audience*, to the *occasion*, and to the *theme* of the meeting. This involves finding out as much as possible about the knowledge level of the audience and their interests. We should get to know them, talk with them, listen to them, and understand their needs. Only after we have carefully studied the audience are we ready to do research on the topic.

A classic example of someone who tailored his message to the audience and the occasion was Christopher Columbus. Before Columbus met the King and Queen of Spain, navigational experts in both Portugal and Spain had already recommended against backing his rather unusual proposal to reach the Far East by sailing in the opposite direction—westward. But Columbus understood the art of persuasion, of tailoring the message to the audience, and he knew how to put together an effective presentation.

He knew, for example, that the Queen had a fervent desire to win more converts to her religion. So he made frequent references to the teeming masses of the Orient, just waiting to be converted. Columbus learned that the Queen loved falcons and exotic birds, so he searched carefully through the accounts of Marco Polo's travels to the Orient and marked in the margin all references to those kingdoms where there were falcons and exotic birds. He knew the King wanted to expand Spain's commercial power, so he made frequent references to gold, spices, and other fabulous riches of the East. All these points were worked into his presentation, which won the backing that resulted in the discovery of the New World.

While few of us are called on to make presentations where the stakes are quite that high, many of us do make presentations where a critical contract, approval of a major marketing program, or the fate of our own careers can hinge on the outcome.

Regardless of the nature of our presentation, we should begin by developing an introduction that gives the audience a clear understanding of what we are going to talk about and how we plan to proceed. We might want to gain their attention with an unusual remark, story, surprising fact, or question. We might want to tell them about important benefits they will receive, the way Columbus did. The basic purpose of our introduction is to establish rapport with the audience and "tell them what we're going to tell them." Then we can spend the rest of the presentation actually telling them.

As part of tailoring our message to the audience, we should express it in simple English, avoiding acronyms, jargon, or specialized language.

We have a wealth of patterns to choose from when organizing the contents. Choices include chronological, spatial, topical, cause-effect, or problem-solution, as well as several other alternatives. We should use the pattern that best enables us to give the audience a comprehensive picture of what we believe and feel about the subject.

Wherever possible, we should build our presentation around a few key ideas and feelings, not around facts. In today's world of information overload, nine-second sound bites, and short attention spans, audiences demand more than facts. Television has helped to create an impatient society, where audiences expect us to make our point simply and quickly. They are already saturated with facts. What they want is a comprehensive picture. If we can present it with clarity and enthusiasm, it will be more memorable and more likely to persuade them that what we are saying is worth considering.

In order to inject enthusiasm into our presentations, I believe that whenever possible, we should write each presentation with the adrenaline pumping, with a high degree of excitement about the message we are sharing with the audience. The audience should feel that we cared enough to prepare the talk just for them. They must feel that our presentation is like a tailor-made suit, not one taken off the rack.

In addition to clarity and enthusiasm, we should seek opportunities to inject humor. That doesn't mean we have to tell jokes, or try to have people rolling in the aisles with laughter, but if there are any humorous aspects to our subject, we should make reference to them, even if all we are aiming for is a knowing smile or light laughter.

I believe the ideal length for a speech is about *twenty minutes,* and we should know *ten times* more about the subject than we're able to say during that twenty minutes. Having such a mastery of our material gives us credibility, the confidence to ad lib when appropriate, and the ability to answer questions with authority. It should be clear to the audience that we are brimming with information on the subject, that we are enthusiastic about it, and that only the limitations of time are preventing us from sharing even more exciting information and ideas with them.

I would caution that we should always resist the temptation to overstay our time limits in order to go into more detail. After all, it was Voltaire who warned that "The secret of being a bore is to tell *everything.*"

How about rehearsals? I spend as much time as needed to make sure my presentations run smoothly, even if it means working on them at home. If it's a major presentation, I rehearse. Many people find it helpful to videotape themselves during rehearsal. It's one of the best ways to find out how believable you are.

If you decide to have a question-and-answer period, there are two major kinds of questions you may expect. The first kind, a *question of policy or opinion,* is the easiest kind to handle, provided you are well versed in your subject. The second is more likely to be a challenge to you. No matter how much you know about your subject, someone may ask you a *question of fact,* such as: "How many bushels of corn does your company buy each year from Wisconsin farmers?" The worst thing to do is to try to answer the question if you don't know the answer. The best answer is often, "Let me look into this further, and I'll get back to you." Then make sure you actually do get back to them with an answer.

Another suggestion I would make about question-and-answer periods is that instead of ending your speech and following it with questions, you should pause for questions at a suitable point *before* the conclusion of your speech. This enables you to entertain however many questions you desire, and then *conclude your speech using your prepared remarks.* This puts you in control of both the content and tone during those final critical minutes when the audience will be forming their lasting impressions of your presentation. It gives you the chance in your conclusion to drive home those essential points you want the audience to walk away with and leave a positive, upbeat final impression.

Now let's talk about *delivery.*

The importance of an effective delivery is underscored by research showing that only *7 percent* of the speaker's message is communicated by the spoken *words.* Fully 93 percent of the message is dependent on the quality of the delivery. This breaks down to *more than half—55 percent—*of a speaker's message coming across in *body language,* while *38 percent* is communicated through *tone of voice.* What this means is that your words are only a small part of your message. To an overwhelming degree, *you* are your message.

In fact, your speech really begins long before you reach the lectern, because your audience will start forming an opinion, based mostly on body language, as soon as they see you in the room. Research has shown that most people form an initial impression of others within *seven seconds* of meeting or seeing them.

In today's environment, one of the most important factors that will either promote or impede communications is how "likable" you are. This quality is hard to define or teach, but the likable person generally projects an image of:

- Optimism
- Concern for the welfare of other people

- Ability to see the opportunity in every difficulty
- Ability to handle stress
- Ability to laugh easily, especially at oneself
- Ability to perform at one's best in a crisis and to be humble in prosperity.

Knowing that you are being evaluated even before you go to the lectern, the best way to handle this is to smile and feel confident in yourself and your preparation. You might remind yourself from time to time of Queen Victoria's remark when someone asked her about the consequences of a possible military defeat. She replied: "We are not interested in the possibilities of defeat." For her, the possibilities of defeat did not exist. *She understood that negative thinking leads to negative results, and positive thinking helps create positive results.*

You must feel equally confident that your presentation will go well. That very confidence will help ensure that it does go well and that you will be perceived by the audience as both competent and confident. You have every reason to be confident. After all, you are a likable person. You know your material. You've rehearsed as many times as necessary to master the material and feel comfortable with the flow of the words. You're ready, and it shows!

But no matter how much they rehearse, many people still get butterflies when they have to speak in public. What's the solution? Should you try to relax and get rid of the butterflies?

Paradoxically, I believe the answer is "No." The best way to handle the butterflies is *not* to try to relax completely. That would make you seem lifeless, inexpressive, and boring. Instead of getting rid of the butterflies, the best thing is to make them fly in formation.

SPEECH TIP: Brash's creative transformation of the familiar expression "butterflies in the stomach" is so memorable and constructive that it may change her listeners' perception—and handling—of the once-dreaded feeling forever.

This means that instead of worrying about being nervous, you can channel this nervous energy to your advantage for more *enthusiasm*, more *voice inflection*, and more *effective gestures*. As you channel your nervousness—which is a perfectly normal state of mind under the circumstances—it can actually help you come across to your audience as the knowledgeable, enthusiastic, interesting person you really are!

What about *posture?* A natural, easy posture is best. The whole idea is to avoid any mannerisms or actions that distract the listener's attention from what you are saying. It helps to avoid stances and activities such as:

- Arms folded across the chest or clasped behind the back, military-style
- Hands on hip

▦ Arms down in front with hands folded below the waist

▦ Rocking back and forth; and

▦ Jiggling items or crinkling paper in a pocket.

SPEECH TIP: However obvious some of these no-no's may seem, Brash's attention to them is well spent. Such nervous tics are *least* obvious to the speaker who is actually doing them, and conscious mention in this presentation may help foil, in her listeners, the unconscious reflex during speeches to come.

It's not necessary to focus too much on the mechanical aspects of delivery, but most speakers find they do best when energy and arm movements come naturally from their shoulders, not the elbows. You want to appear relaxed in movements, not stiff or wooden. It helps to stand firmly on both feet, without shifting your weight. A very effective way to channel energy is through your voice. Taking five deep breaths before you begin talking forces your body to calm down and opens up your vocal passages so you can speak more effectively.

While you want to control your energy and your voice, you don't want to do it through speaking in a monotone, because monotones give rise to that adjective we all want to avoid—"*monotonous*." Something that is monotonous is tiresome, because it is unvarying. What we want to achieve are changes in inflection, tone, and volume. For example, slow speakers can increase their impact by speeding up before delivering an important statement.

We should avoid non-words or crutch words and phrases that fill in blank spaces and sometimes cause great distraction. They include:

▦ "*Ah,*" by far the worst offender. It's the most misused non-word in the English language. You can choose for yourself which would be the worst punishment: one hundred days of the ancient Chinese water torture, with its slow and endless "drip . . . drip . . . drip," or one hundred days of listening to speeches by someone who uses "ah" every third or fourth word. Personally, I'd be tempted to choose the water every time. We should also avoid:

▦ "*Frankly*" and

▦ "*To be honest.*"

These last two expressions serve no useful purpose, and they may backfire on you by raising the question of how frank or honest you have been in all the rest of your presentation, if, after several minutes of talking with the audience, you say that *now* you are going to be "frank" or "honest" with them.

Another important essential to good delivery is *eye contact*. It's best to maintain eye contact with an individual for three to five seconds or long enough to complete a thought. The speaker benefits from good eye contact. It keeps you as the center of attention and gives you feedback to see if your message is having its intended impact. You can tell if the audience is listening, confused, interested, bored, or disagreeing. If you're not getting the response you want, you can change your communication to get it.

Now let's talk briefly about *visual support.* Slides, overhead transparencies and other visuals can be useful devices to perk up a presentation, as long as they're used responsibly and so long as they add clarity or impact to our ideas. But we shouldn't use visuals just for the sake of using them.

If we do use visuals, we should never deliver our presentation *from* them. The audience can read the slides too, and if we're looking at the screen, we lose eye contact.

We should always make sure the visuals have words large enough to be read from the back of the room. It's best to have no more than six lines per slide or transparency, and to have a "frame" of empty space around the words. It's also best to limit the text to just the key words, and use lists rather than sentences. For greatest visibility, words on slides or flip charts should be in black, brown, dark blue, or dark green. Use red to highlight, underline, circle, box, or otherwise accent a main point.

We should darken the room to show projected visuals, but leave enough light to take notes. Leaving the light turned up slightly also has the added benefit of helping prevent one of the most ego-challenging situations facing a speaker. There are few things that can do more to shake the faith you have in your own charisma than seeing one or two members of the audience with eyes glazed over, valiantly waging an unequal, forlorn struggle against the sandman. If, on occasion, a member of the audience does nod off, don't let it devastate you. It doesn't necessarily mean you're a boring speaker. You have to recognize that in any large audience there is always the possibility that you will have one or two people in whom "the spirit is willing, but the flesh is weak"—or in whom the flesh simply didn't have enough sleep the night before.

Meanwhile—to continue our discussion of visuals—in order to get the most benefit from them, it's always a good idea to rehearse with them. Make sure that all the slides are in the carousel in the proper order and that they show what you want. It's a good idea to number your transparencies in case you drop them and have to reassemble them quickly. Plan your logistics, especially if you're giving a joint presentation. Know in advance the sequence of speakers, where each will stand, and how you will coordinate the slide show.

Manage your timing. Allow enough for the audience to get settled and for questions.

And while I'm on the subject of questions, before I close I'd like to pause now to answer any questions you may have.

SPEECH TIP: Brash follows her own advice here and breaks for questions *before* wrapping up her presentation.

I would summarize my main points by saying that a well-prepared and well-delivered presentation is characterized by:

- A clear goal

- An introduction that gains the attention of the audience and tells the audience what we are talking about

- A simple message tailored to the audience, occasion, and theme

- Humor, where appropriate

- A dynamic delivery based on our mastery of the subject matter, our confidence, and our enthusiasm for sharing our ideas with the audience

- A conclusion that emphasizes our main points and leaves the audience with a positive feeling about themselves and the subject matter we have covered.

I would like to emphasize that the points I have covered are only a few of the many considerations we should keep in mind as we prepare a presentation.

Becoming a poised, polished presenter is a journey of a lifetime, and each time we do a presentation, we should learn something more about ourselves and our subject that will enable us to improve our performance the next time.

I wish each of you the very best of luck as you prepare and deliver your presentations.

Event Marketing:
The Good, the Bad, and the Ugly

DAVID F. D'ALESSANDRO
Senior Executive Vice President
John Hancock Financial Services

International Events Group Annual Event Marketing Conference, Chicago, Illinois, March 22, 1993

SUMMARY: An event marketing expert tells what to do—and what not to do—to make corporate event sponsorship an effective publicity vehicle.

Thanks for having me here today. I'd like to talk about a few things that are relevant to event marketing. First, I want to talk about the people who play the event marketing game today.

Second, I want to look at how they play, and the things they can do to make the game a success. Third, I want to focus on how to measure that success. Fourth, I want to make a few predictions about the future of the game, and the events that will be winners and losers in the years ahead. Otherwise known as the good, the bad and the ugly of event marketing.

All of us make mistakes, and John Hancock has made mistakes, too. The companies I'll be mentioning this morning have done a lot of great work, so I want to apologize in advance for any critical comments I'll make.

> *SPEECH TIP:* By offering compliments and a blank-check apology to the corporations he will name over the course of his speech, D'Alessandro frees himself to spear their follies with great mirth, not mercy.

But I'm going to cite both good and bad examples of event marketing. But before I get too far along, I'd like to make one observation. A couple of weeks ago, there was press coverage about how the TV networks have discovered a new strategy to revive themselves. The article said that some of the best minds in network TV have discovered that if they latch onto big events, they'll draw bigger audiences.

Brilliant.

You can say a lot of things about that discovery, but "new" isn't one of them. The fact is that event marketing has been around for years, and I don't just mean since you and I were born. I mean since the beginning of time.

[*Video is shown*]

I especially like that footage of Michael Jackson.

By the way, how many of you saw Michael Jackson perform during this year's Super Bowl half time activities? Please raise your hands.

Quite a few.

Well, you're not alone. Millions of people who usually skip the half time show stayed tuned this year. The household rating, which was 46.1 during the second quarter of the game, remained an incredibly high 45.5 during the half-time festivities. Last year, before Michael Jackson, the household rating plunged from 42.1 to 32.8. It's the power of celebrity.

But it's also the power of event marketing, and it contains a lesson for all of us in the business.

Here's how the event worked.

Frito-Lay decided to sponsor the half-time broadcast on NBC to launch a new taste test for its potato chips. Last year, you may remember, this same company tried to ambush the half time show and push Doritos by sponsoring counter-programming on Fox TV. It worked so well that sales dropped over 15 percent during the six weeks after the game compared to the year before.

This year, the people at Frito-Lay decided it was smart not to be stupid again. So they decided to buy the Super Bowl half time show, and do it on the cheap.

Michael Jackson, who has a contractual relationship with Frito-Lay's parent company, PepsiCo., would headline the NBC half time show. Frito-Lay and NBC wouldn't have to pay Michael a penny. Instead, the NFL, in exchange for his services, would make a $100,000 contribution to Jackson's "Heal the World" Foundation.

When it was over, everyone was happy. All of us had the pleasure of watching Michael Jackson grab his crotch. Tom Landry got to appear bald and eat potato chips on a nationally televised commercial. NBC finally got something right, and "Heal the World" got a ton of cash and publicity.

> *SPEECH TIP:* D'Alessandro's fast-paced, ascerbic speaking style is no less provocative when describing success. Consistency of voice can be as important for a speaker's critical balance as it is for keeping the entertainment value high.

The rich got richer on that one.

But it's valuable for us, too, because it reflects what event marketing is today: a game with big stakes and egos, but one that, if played right, can make a lot of people, with different marketing and philanthropic needs, very happy.

THE PLAYERS

Now I'd like to talk about the players. In theory, the players in the event marketing game are easy to identify. They are the event organizers, the corporate sponsors, the TV networks, and the public. In real terms, though, the players are a collection of people who really don't like each other. They have little in common and a lot to fight about. But they need each other if they want to play the game.

Let's start with the event organizer.

If you ask an event organizer to describe himself, he'll say he is the visionary who creates the event and the opportunity for which all of us should be grateful. The event is the biggest thing in his life, and he's deluded himself into believing that only he can understand and manage it.

If you ask him about the rest of us, he'll tell you that the only thing we're good for is cash. Once the check is written, he wants the sponsor to go away. But we don't go away so fast. Enter Player Number Two, the corporation in search of an event. The "Sponsor."

We're sometimes at the table because a CEO, who may know nothing about marketing, loves an event and is determined to shove it down his marketing department's throat. Other times, we're there to do someone a favor or because we have no choice.

But, usually, we're looking for a business opportunity, something that differentiates our brand and products, or positions us as a good corporate citizen.

What do we want for our money?

Much the same as the event organizer.

We also want control.

We want tickets and hospitality and PR and recognition and everyone's eternal gratitude. And we want the event organizer to accept the fact that we're going to be involved. That thought doesn't come naturally to all organizers. In fact, the surprising thing to us is just how few understand it. For instance, in 1986, John Hancock stepped forward to invest millions in the Boston Marathon, which at that time was a dying race.

[video is shown]

Despite our having saved the race, the organizers could not understand why we wanted to move the finish line so the race would end in front of the John Hancock Tower instead of its usual place, the Prudential Insurance Company Tower.

> *SPEECH TIP:* With some anecdotes, a moment of "no comment" silence can be the funniest comeback quip of all.

So, to all the event organizers in the room: Come to terms with reality. The corporation's money is on the line, and it needs a lot more than an officially embossed letter of thanks to justify the investment.

Left to their own devices, then, the event organizer and corporate sponsor have a lifetime of things to fight about. The truth is, the only thing they really have in common is a desire to see the event succeed. So they're stuck with each other. But misery also loves company, and it doesn't get much more miserable than our third player.

THE TV NETWORKS.

Now, remember, these are the people who brought America the Amy Fisher story in triplecast. And also the people who insist that programs like "The Flintstones" and "The Jetsons" ought to count as "educational and informational" programming for children, which broadcasters are required to provide by law.

Now, I happen to love "The Jetsons," and I know all of the words to "The Flintstones" theme song. But I hardly think they're educational.

Gary David Goldberg, one of TV's more creative forces, summed it up last month when he described the networks as a group that would televise live executions if they could, except for Fox, which would televise naked executions.

And don't expect things to get better soon. The networks are under siege. They depend on the big event/large audience show, and anything that dilutes or fragments viewership is a threat.

Yet that is exactly what is going on in the marketplace today.

You are going to have more non-network programming available in your home because cable and the Baby Bells and satellite and interactive technology are going to put it there. That's bad news for the networks. But it's good news for event organizers and sponsors.

As our friends at the networks rediscovered this month, a unique event does draw the big audience. That makes people like you and me, organizers and sponsors who produce those kinds of events, very important to the networks. That means we're going to have more leverage.

But let me warn you: The networks haven't figured that out yet, and when it comes to playing the event marketing game, they're as overbearing as ever. They only want two things from us: control and money.

They want what collectively the event's sponsor and organizer wants. They want to dictate the time, content, camera angles, and marketing of our event. They want their own hospitality packages and VIP treatment for advertisers. They care about how the picture looks at home, and not how the organizers and sponsors want it to unfold on the ground. Like us, they have their own agenda.

So far, so good. We've got three players who on many levels deserve each other. But they're not done yet.

Enter the fourth player with a very different perspective: the consumer.

What do they want out of this game?

They want to be entertained, and they're willing to put up with some amount of people like you and me if that's the price of admission.

Here's a number that comes out of research we recently did to assess the public's attitude toward event marketing. Sixty-seven percent of 211 people said that they have observed or attended at least one event in the past twelve months that had a corporate sponsor. That's a pretty good reach.

What kind of event are they looking for?

Finding Number One: Consumers want something that is interesting as well as enjoyable. And, as part of that, people told us that diversity and exposure to new things and cultures is definitely an attraction in the 1990s.

Finding Number Two: More people still love athletic events, but they're followed close behind by audiences looking for family-oriented activities. The one event with the broadest appeal (by far) to consumers, is the Olympics. Eighty-three percent of the national sample we spoke with find the Games appealing, and that appeal cuts across all ages and income levels.

Once you move beyond the Olympics, though, tastes diverge. Generally, men are more interested in sporting events. But more women (51 percent versus 31 percent of men) and younger people (51 percent of adults, age 25-44, versus 31 percent of adults, 45-64) prefer local family-oriented activities like concerts, art festivals, and free days at the zoo .

The good news in our research for corporate sponsors is that consumers like the fact that we participate in different kinds of events. They think there is some kind of public service motivation to our sponsorship, particularly if it involves the Olympic Games or family entertainment.

The study we did also found that consumers are particularly impressed with companies that sponsor local events.

Two-thirds of the consumers in our survey felt more favorably toward corporations that participate in community or grassroots events. That number dropped substantially, closer to 40 percent, when people were asked about corporate sponsorship of national events.

People also have expectations about how corporate sponsors should behave at events: They want us to be seen but not heard.

On-site signage and information about the company and its products are okay. Seventy-six percent said corporate visibility at an event is fine with them. But selling or lead generation is not. Only 22 percent bought the idea that pushing product at an event is very appropriate.

> *SPEECH TIP:* D'Alessandro's speech delivers more than jokes and cautionary tales; this group of market research findings could have hard cash value for his listeners, as could the do's and don'ts he offers.

RULES OF THE GAME (THE DO'S AND DON'TS)

I'd like to move now to some rules of the game.

Let me start by telling you a story about a network.

About a year ago, one network called and asked if I'd be interested in having John Hancock move its bowl game to a New Year's Day slot that was up for grabs. The network executives pointed out that the time-slot attracted better teams and higher ratings than the John Hancock Bowl, which is played on the afternoon of New Year's Eve. They told us that they were also talking with some other corporations, but as the negotiations progressed, the network brass said that they wanted to do business with John Hancock. A date was set to finalize the details, and everyone was operating under the understanding that we had one week to make up our mind.

Two days before that date, without any warning from the network, I picked up the *New York Times* and read that they gave the game to Blockbuster Video.

The network people wondered why we were upset. We're talking about trust here. Events succeed because the players trust each other. Without a trusting relationship, the event will fail.

Establishing that relationship is hard. It has more to do with chemistry and style than some clearly defined protocol. But it can be helped along if the players, especially the organizer and sponsor, follow some do's and don'ts.

Let me take you through a few, starting with ones that apply to corporate sponsors as well as event organizers.

1. Do check your biases about each other at the door. The mating dance between a sponsor and organizer may begin with both sides holding their nose, but it has to end as a genuine partnership, where both sides have confidence in each other. Frankly, you need each other.

2. Do clearly define your respective needs and expectations at the outset of the relationship. It is important to avoid surprises and the anger that is inevitable if either side keeps coming back to the table with new demands.

3. Do recognize the need to check each other out. Sponsors and organizers alike should take the time to do a reference check on any potential partner. Look into their reputation and track record. Examine other events with which they've been involved. Confirm where the sponsor's money is coming from, and how the organizer expects to deliver the athlete or musician or crowd that's been promised.

Example: a few years back, Kodak, a company for which I have a great deal of respect and one with a long track record of event success, sponsored something called the "Kodak Liberty Ride." The organizer's idea was that people in one hundred cities across America were going to pay 23 bucks so they could ride their bike, have a picnic lunch in some arena, and watch a broadcast of Huey Lewis live from New Orleans. The organizers promised Kodak 500,000 people. What Kodak forgot to ask was, how were they going to get them?

It turns out that many of the towns targeted by organizers had no big, organized cycling community. The public relations plan was weak, and radio stations refused to promote an event that had a $23 price tag. The result was a disaster.

Organizers promised 5,000 people in Denver, and they delivered 49. They figured on 5,000 in Baltimore and got 14.

So don't forget to check. When it comes to claims made by either side, the old Russian proverb that Ronald Reagan loved so much, applies: Trust, but verify.

4. Don't take it personally if a player from the other side steals some of your thunder. We all have bosses and boards to impress, and part of the game is to beat your chest, take the credit, and dump on the other guy in front of the home office crowd.

5. Don't depend on the networks or involve them a second before you absolutely have to. A good event with strong organizers and sponsors will always find a broadcast partner who wants in. But you need to strike the deal on your terms, not theirs. The networks need your big event more than you need the complete disruption that comes with their participation. So lead rather than follow the networks around.

If you're an event organizer, I would suggest you keep these do's and don'ts in mind:

1 Don't cop an attitude because you have to share your brainchild with a corporate sponsor. In fact, it may even pay to be gracious. After all, having a partner is better than having no event at all.

2. Don't think just because you have a good idea for an event and understand how to operate the site, you can also manage the bigger event picture. Those are very different things, and the event will suffer if you make the mistake of confusing them.

That's exactly what happened at the most recent America's Cup Race in San Diego.

It bombed.

The organizers knew they had a good idea and could deal with the race course. But they didn't know enough to manage the bigger picture before selling the event to sponsors. What they missed was the fact that they were running an elitist event, which takes place off-shore and out-of-sight of spectators. That makes it a lousy TV property and an event that people are not going to show up for.

No surprises there.

Except to the organizers, who overestimated TV revenues and attendance figures, rang up a multimillion dollar debt, and left a lot of corporate sponsors unhappy.

3. Do be careful not to set yourself up for a fall. Case in point: Have you heard NASA is going into the event marketing business?

It is selling the rights to put your corporate message on the side of its booster rockets. The first company up is going to be Arnold Schwarzenegger. For $500,000, the name of Arnold's new movie will be on a booster rocket that's launching this year.

Brilliant for Arnold.

Not so smart for NASA.

If the rocket blows up, people are going to ask why NASA can't be as successful in running a space program as it is in selling space. But even if it doesn't blow, it's still the agency. NASA has a bad credibility problem in this country today. The American people think the agency is second-rate.

They want to see science and success and heroes come out of the space program again, not gimmicks. NASA may need the cash, but using events that sell its reputation short is the wrong way to raise it.

Let me move to corporate sponsors, and some do's and don'ts for them. If you are a corporate sponsor:

1. Do gravitate toward events that occur more than once and allow you to develop a long-term relationship with the other players. From a marketing perspective, that allows everyone to build on success and get long-term rewards. From

an event management point of view, it says that you're serious, and that helps everyone get along better.

2. Do remember to reserve the legal option of returning as a sponsor in years 2, 3, 4, etc., of the event. If you don't, you may lose your place at the table and put your company at a competitive disadvantage. Example: American Express, a company I greatly respect, is still paying a price for having lost the Olympics to VISA. Before the 1988 Games, 11.5 percent of consumers rated VISA as the best card for international travel. VISA then grabbed the '88 Games, and, as a result of that sponsorship, the number jumped to 27 percent, mostly at AMEX's expense.

There must be AMEX executives still jumping out their Wall Street office windows over that one.

3. Do a reality check before you sign on the dotted line, and ask whether the event fits your company's character. Example: I am often approached by marketing people at public relations agencies who want to reach middle income Americans, especially men, and someone in their marketing department suggested we think about sponsoring race cars. For a lot of consumer companies, it's a good thing. But let's face it, it's stupid for an insurance company to put its logo on cars that go 200 mph and crash. I have this nightmare in my mind. The logo goes on the car, the race begins, the car crashes, and the driver dies.

And the logo is clear as a bell on the instant replays all weekend long.

Not too smart.

4. One final don't: Don't deal with bureaucrats who come to you with special event opportunities. They simply do not understand the realities of life. Another true story: In Boston, there's a cemetery called the Granury Burial Ground, where patriots like John Hancock are buried. A few years back, the city was having trouble coming up with funds to maintain the cemetery, so some bureaucrat called us and asked for $100,000. I said "We're happy to help the homeless, but not the dead. Call us if there's something we can do for people who are alive." But, being good bureaucrats, they didn't give up. They decided it was better to sweeten the deal, and they offered to let us have John Hancock's body if we made the contribution.

They finally gave up when we told them we wouldn't settle for anything less than Hancock plus a patriot to be named later.

MEASURING SUCCESS

I'd like to turn now to the topic of measuring success.

First, let's be honest about the business of event marketing.

Event marketing is a never-ending food chain. Everyone in this room feeds off of each other. Event marketing is a symbiotic relationship, and that means it can perpetuate itself only if it works to everyone's advantage.

So, Rule Number One: In the event marketing game, all the players need to win.

Rule Number Two: Anyone who relies on things like CPM to measure success, is naive.

A corporation trying to measure the success of an event may be interested in how many people they potentially reached, which is all CPM tells us. But it's a passing interest. Besides, most events you're involved with are not broadcast, so CPM is irrelevant. But even if it were relevant, most sponsors have marketing agendas that are much bigger than minimizing cost per thousand.

Let me give you John Hancock's agenda.

We measure an event's success by its ability to do seven things for us.

1. *The event enhances our brand.* Our brand image is that of a company that understands people's needs and can help them to achieve important goals in life. The event must be consistent with that image, and help us to reinforce it. This is the heart of our strategy.

2. *The event elevates awareness and consideration of John Hancock.* Let's be up-front about event marketing; this is all about getting our name out there, and finding ways to predispose consumers to our products. The event has to help in that way, and we'll do pre- and post-event tracking surveys to see if it works.

3. *We can use the event to increase productivity and sales.* For example, we'll be holding one of our most important 1994 sales conventions in Lillehammer, Norway. Sales people who hit ambitious quotas set by the company are to go. The convention will take place while the '94 Winter Olympic Games are under way. Here's what we recently showed to some of our top producing agents.

[*video is shown*]

The response to this has been overwhelming. Agents from all over the country, including people who have never been excited about qualifying for conventions, are calling to get copies of the tape and more details. But, more importantly, the opportunity to attend an event like the Olympics is such a powerful force that we were able to increase the sales quota for our unionized sales force by 20 percent without an argument. That 20 percent could mean an extra $20 million in revenue to John Hancock. Now *that's* success.

4. *The event boosts morale.* Our employees and agents should love the event and get excited about it. Success is if it makes them feel better about their job and the company.

5. *We are good corporate citizens.* That means the event helps us to meet our civic and philanthropic obligations, and demonstrates the value we place on giving something back to the community.

6. *We get hospitality opportunities out of the event.* And that lets us get important customers and prospects into a setting where we can stroke them. They love it, we love it, and we do more business together because of it.

7. *The mix of corporate sponsors is right.* Meaning we get category exclusivity, and only reputable companies from other business sectors, as co-sponsors.

So as you can see, we use lots of tests, as do all corporate sponsors. But I don't want to suggest that an event has to pass all of them before a corporation should sign up as a sponsor.

If you are a corporation, only you can decide which measures are most important to your company at the time you evaluate an organizer's proposal. But approach that decision as a hard-headed business one, and resist the temptation to play to the CEO's taste in events, or your own.

If you are an event organizer, be aware that while the decision to sponsor an event is not yours to make, it is yours to shape. But that means you have to stop kidding yourself into believing that your great idea is going to sell itself. Wake up and sell it based on what's in it for the sponsor.

THE FUTURE OF EVENT MARKETING:
WINNERS AND LOSERS IN THE 1990S

I'd like to talk a bit about the future of event marketing.

Event marketing has a great future in this country. Consumers love events, corporations love consumers, and all of you have figured out that this is a match made in heaven.

But expect some events to be winners and losers in the years ahead.

The biggest loser of all is golf.

Think about it.

Most people don't like golf.

In our survey, maybe one in ten said that golf is of some interest as an event. People tune in and out, maybe watch the last five holes, and the networks are lucky to pull an average adult rating of 1.4. And for the pleasure of that small company, you, as a sponsor, are asked to pay a premium to reach an upscale audience that's available in larger numbers and at much lower costs through other televised sporting events, like NFL or college football. The fact is, golf sponsors for the most part overpay for ratings delivery so their executives can play golf in the PRO-AM.

Meanwhile, back at the PGA, they're having fun at your expense.

They've conceived so many tournaments that consumers can't keep them straight or remember their corporate sponsors.

And they're pushing the purses higher and higher, knowing that all they have to do is pass the bill along to you.

This year the purse is going to be about $60 million, which is $7 million more than last year's purse, and $43 million more than it was ten years ago. Talk about being taken advantage of.

But sponsors have no one to blame but themselves. They got into this mess because the CEO loves to play and can't wait to do the back nine on a PRO-AM date with Fred Couples.

That strategy may work when money is no object. But marketing budgets are tight these days, and in the '90s, companies should take a harder look at what they get out of golf.

Some of them, like companies that are in the sporting goods business, may find that it still makes sense. But most are going to confront the fact that golf does nothing to drive consumers in the door. Just ask the J.C. Penney or K mart or Toyota customer if he's buying because the company spends millions to promote golf.

The answer you'll get is "No," and as marketing departments and even CEOs become more accountable to the bottom line, golf is going to become an expendable high cost/low return item.

The second-biggest losers are something we're involved in, the college bowl games. The whole college bowl system is becoming a joke under the new NCAA coalition rules. The final standings determine the teams under the new NCAA coalition rules.

You've got a bunch of inbred organizing committee members who wear silly blazers and spend every fall running around the country, attending games and parties. And every week, they go home, swap stories, and pretend that this has something to do with deciding which teams are going to play in their bowl. The only things these trips do is run up the bills. And since the networks decided it wasn't in their interest to foot them anymore, the organizing committees are passing them along to corporate sponsors. There are simply too many games now, and the ratings are dropping like a stone as the games cannibalize each other. There will be some questions as to whether John Hancock will be in this business for the long term. It won't work much longer because it's not in our interest to help them live lifestyles of the rich and famous.

It's time to face up to the fact that the organizing committees and the way they run the events are becoming obsolete and should be replaced by a simple, common sense play-off structure by the NCAA as they've done in basketball.

Some other predictions.

Expect a big tick up in local community-based events. People may feel better about our national government these days, but they still expect to exercise more power and make more progress back in their own communities. For corporate America, that's the place to be in the 1990s.

Cause marketing is also going to be a winner in the '90s. Baby boomers are middle-aged and more concerned about issues that affect their lives. And causes that not too long ago were "fringe," like saving the rain forest and recycling house-hold trash, are today part of our kids' curriculum and vocabulary. That's a big change, which will drive the creation of events and decision-making by corporate sponsors.

But if there is one single prediction I'd leave you with today, it is that the Olympic Games are going to be the most valuable event marketing opportunity of the decade for the big players.

No other single event creates as positive a halo effect for its sponsors or as powerful an incentive for their employees and customers, as do the Games. And that impact and benefit to the sponsor is going to grow as the Games move toward their centennial in Atlanta, 1996.

Let me wrap up.

What I've tried to do today is give you my perspective on how the event man-agement game should be played. I think it's pretty simple.

- You have to understand the players and their needs.

- You should live by some rules and be able to trust the other players.

- And you have to think about the future and make sure you pick an event that's going to be viable and right for you in the 1990s.

Thanks for having me here today.

The Media and the Mature Marketplace

HORACE B. DEETS
Executive Director
American Association of Retired Persons

Delivered to the UCLA Television Conference, North Hollywood, California,
September 11, 1993

SUMMARY: *Denouncing age discrimination and the media's negative stereotyping of senior citizens, AARP executive Horace B. Deets urges television industry profes-sionals to present a more subtle and realistic view of the diverse experiences of older Americans.*

My task today is to focus on the fallacies, myths, and stereotypes of aging. After lis-tening to Bob and Dolores Hope, I think I can rest my case. They demonstrated that fallacies about aging are just that—stereotypes with no basis in reality.

But unfortunately, it isn't that easy. We have many converts to make.

In the preface to her new book, *The Fountain of Age*, Betty Friedan says, "When my friends threw a surprise birthday party for me on my sixtieth birthday, I could have killed them all. Their toasts seemed hostile, insisting as they did that I publicly acknowledge reaching sixty, pushing me out of life, as it seemed, out of the race."

Clive Barnes called television "The first truly democratic culture—the first culture available to everybody and governed by what people want." The fact is, television is incredibly influential. I heard John Sculley say that 70 percent of the American people get 100 percent of their information from television. Now I couldn't research that or prove it. Just saying it is frightening.

It's certainly not for me to say that television is the defining element of our culture, or that is the "vast cultural wasteland" that Newton Minnow described in 1964. It's probably somewhere in the middle. It's different things to different people. And we can't stereotype television any more than we can stereotype older Americans. Its potential is practically unlimited. And that's what I'm going to talk to you about today.

Like all of us, I am interested in the relationship between maturity and the media. And my interest lies primarily in seeing older Americans portrayed realistically on television.

As our speakers this morning graphically illustrated, television perpetuates a number of myths, misconceptions, and stereotypes about older Americans. Today's television viewer is led to believe that most older Americans

- are alike
- are institutionalized
- are in poor health and inactive
- are senile, constipated, or incontinent, and
- are either extremely poor or very wealthy.

As you heard from earlier speakers, these myths and stereotypes are plain wrong.

Not only are they wrong, they convey a negative picture of aging that leads many Americans to view growing older with disdain and dismay. If we buy into the role models we see on television, we may begin to behave accordingly and begin to become burdens on society—not useful, productive, vital contributors.

George Burns said that because of the kinds of birthday cards we get when we turn fifty—like "Happy birthday; you're over the hill"—we begin to act that way, and by the time we are sixty we've got our act together. That's the frightening thing about the myths. It's bad enough that they can influence public policy and employment policy. What's more frightening is that we can begin to believe them.

In reality, older Americans are an extremely diverse, heterogeneous group defined more by their lifestyles, values, experiences, and beliefs than by their age.

In fact, age itself is not an effective gauge for communicating with or about an aging population. Age is irrelevant. You heard Lydia Bronte say it this morning—nothing happens biologically on your fiftieth birthday, or on your sixty-fifth birthday. What is relevant are the experiences people share, the values and beliefs they hold dear, and the lives they choose to lead.

To me, one of the great contradictions of life is that many businesses force people out before age sixty-five—and won't hire people for certain jobs after age forty—yet some of these same businesses will pay $1,000 a head per day to send their managers to a lecture by a ninety-two-year-old guy named W. Edwards Deming or an eighty-three-year-old named Peter Drucker. Deming and Drucker are sought after—not because of their age—but because of their ideas, their experiences, and their values. Their ages are irrelevant. Like many of the people Lydia described earlier, Deming claims that his years after age seventy have been his most productive.

A recent interview with violinist Joshua Bell gives us a different perspective. Bell was a "child prodigy" who began performing professionally at the age of eleven. Now twenty-five, he made a very astute observation. He said, "I'm actually glad to be out of that category of young performer or prodigy. Now I'm treated as a musician, and people don't go to my concerts to hear some sort of young prodigy. They're going to hear the music." To Joshua Bell, age is irrelevant. He wants to be known as a musician—not as a young musician, not as a child prodigy—but as the fine violinist that he is.

One of the more popular attractions at movie theaters this summer was a film about the life of Tina Turner entitled *What's Love Got to Do with It?* Now I don't know how many of you have seen Tina Turner perform recently, but I think the question should be, "What's age got to do with it?" Tina Turner is fifty-three years old, but she still performs with the vitality and passion of "the world's oldest living teenager."

If there is any lesson to be learned from the panel discussion this morning, it's that people like Tina Turner—who, by the way, is old enough to join AARP—are the rule, not the exception to the rule. No longer does turning fifty mean you are over the hill. As baby boomers age, they are challenging the old ideas of growing old. They want to maintain their youthful vitality for as long as possible, and many have adopted lifestyles to achieve that goal.

Proper nutrition, a focus on fitness, and a more active lifestyle have greatly extended the vital years—not old age, but active middle age.

It's difficult to imagine, but the normal life span has grown more in the course of this century than it has in the preceding two thousand years. That's amazing and, unfortunately, we were not prepared for it. We don't yet understand its significance. Much of what we have assumed about aging is simply not accurate, and we have to adjust our ideas of what it is to be old. By "we," I mean everyone.

Television is reflecting a life course for older Americans that is at least forty years out of date, if it ever has been in date. The current portrayal of older Americans may be convenient, but it's not accurate.

As an industry, television needs to broaden its image of older Americans. It needs to recognize that middle-aged Americans don't view aging as it is portrayed on television. Life isn't over when you retire. Turning sixty-five doesn't mean moving to a nursing home, or giving up your life to move in with your children so they can take care of you. In fact, only 5 percent of older Americans actually live in nursing homes.

For more and more Americans, fifty and over is the jumping-off place for a new lifetime, not a descent into the dungeon of old age. They are fulfilling plans and adventures that had to be postponed—traveling, going back to school—and taking on activities they didn't have time for earlier in their lives. It may surprise you, for example, that in 1987, one in ten college students was over the age of fifty, and that percentage is growing.

I think rock star Elton John put aging in clear perspective for many aging baby boomers. When asked what growing older meant to him, he replied, "I still want to play music, but I don't want to look like Donald Duck while I'm doing it." Bill Cosby put it another way. He said, "Experts agree that the elderly are usually not losing it, they are just not 'using it' as often." And Andy Rooney observes, "I don't notice too many bad things about getting older except that it hurts more to go barefoot."

SPEECH TIP: Given his subject and his audience, Deets has a top-of-the-line license for incorporating celebrity quotes. He makes effective use of this license by including a wide range of entertainers and by juxtaposing their comments in quirky combinations like these.

What these people are saying is, "Okay, so I'm older, it's not that much different. I still like to do the same things, I still enjoy life. I still have goals to achieve and contributions to make. Aging is a subtle process—not a drastic change."

In fact, if you think about it, aging is synonymous with living. That's something we often ignore.

SPEECH TIP: Here again, a strong speaker points out how much the obvious is overlooked. Stop-and-think moments such as these can work lasting wonders in arguments against prejudice or other forms of blind assumption.

What our society is beginning to realize—and Dr. Birren (who has been a pioneer in this field) and Dr. Bronte both demonstrated the same thing in their research—is that because of increased life spans, people—many of them aged sixty-five and over—are experiencing a second or prolonged middle age. They're not spending more time in "old age," they're spending more time in "middle age."

These people do not live in nursing homes; they do not have Alzheimer's; they are not necessarily sitting around waiting to die. They are active, alert, and full of vitality. They want to contribute to society and enjoy life—and they are doing it.

SPEECH TIP: Preparing to introduce survey results that indict the television industry for age discrimination and stereotyping, Deets confronts the issue—and therefore the audience—in a calm, courteous, even understated way. Demonstrated tip: When your statistics are most telling, let the numbers do the talking.

I don't think it's any secret that the television industry has been slow to recognize and respond to these new attitudes, patterns, and trends in aging.

Age, as portrayed on television today, is simply the loss of youth—and its perceived consequences. It's portrayed as a "problem." Where are the images of older people leading active, productive lives—like the 130 individuals that Dr. Bronte interviewed for her book? Except for a handful of programs, they're virtually nonexistent.

According to the UCLA School of Medicine's survey—the results of which you heard earlier today:

- Half of the members interviewed believed older adults are portrayed unrealistically

- 64 percent said, yes, we did a poor job of characterizing the concerns of older adults, and

- 78 percent said there should be more television programs featuring older characters.

The UCLA study also provided some insight into why the television industry portrays older adults unrealistically: in two words—age discrimination.

- Almost half of those surveyed said they have been discriminated against in the television industry because of their age, 59 percent because they were considered too old.

- One-quarter of the respondents said that, at some point in their careers, someone had suggested that they alter their appearance to look more youthful.

- And slightly more—28 percent—had claimed at some time to be younger than they were, or avoided disclosing their age. Or, in order to get a job or keep one in the television industry, they had to portray themselves as something they weren't.

The UCLA study provides the statistical evidence of systemic age discrimination in the industry, but this morning's documentary, *Power and Fear: The Hollywood Greylist*, really dramatizes the impact on the industry.

It's no wonder television portrays older adults unrealistically—the people who can best relate the experiences older people face aren't around to share them.

If you categorically deny access and jobs to people based upon their age, you are robbing yourselves and your industry of the talent and creative force best suited to appeal to this vast audience. In the long run, the industry is only hurting itself.

Not only is age discrimination wrong. Not only is it illegal. It's plain bad business.

> *SPEECH TIP:* With right and legal might on his side, Deets continues to forgo sermonizing; instead, he stresses age discrimination's economic harm to his audience's own interests.

Assistant Secretary for Health and Human Services, Dr. Fernando Torres-Gil, talked about demographics and social changes this morning, so you know what's happening: your audience is getting older. But more importantly, their lifestyles are changing, and they are experiencing new things, and facing new situations that challenge their attitudes and beliefs.

You also know what this means. One of the primary tenets of marketing—and advertising—is that if your audience can't identify with your product, they won't buy it. If your programs don't start reflecting the lifestyles, attitudes, values, and experiences of the aging population, you risk losing an extremely large and loyal part of the television viewing audience, and that's a risk neither you nor your sponsors can afford to take.

Another finding of the UCLA study—and one of the most often-cited reasons for not having more programs featuring older characters—is the belief that most advertisers are not interested in pitching the over-fifty market. Eighty-five percent of the respondents to the UCLA survey thought advertisers' lack of interest was a major deterrent.

Our experience in publishing *Modern Maturity* magazine indicates just the opposite. And just for perspective, let me point out something: *Modern Maturity* magazine is the number-one circulation magazine in this country, reaching 22 million households. For perspective, that is 7 million more than *Reader's Digest* or *TV Guide*. And our ads are not cheap. One page is $230,000. Our competitor is television. And yet we reject more ads, probably, than any other magazine, because they don't meet our standards.

> *SPEECH TIP:* Deets knows that hard information is the best cure for ignorance.

Advertisers are beginning consciously to move toward the mature market—not only because of the sheer numbers, but because of the advantages that the mature market offers. *Modern Maturity* editor Henry Fenwick will be on the panel this afternoon discussing the maturing marketplace and will relate some of his experiences to you.

In her new book, *The Fountain of Age*, Betty Friedan went on to say:

> It is time we start searching for the fountain of age, time that we stop denying our growing older and look at the actuality of our experience and that of other women and men who have gone beyond denial to a new place in their sixties, seventies, and eighties. It's time to look at age on its own terms and put names on its values and strengths, breaking through the definition of age solely as deterioration or decline from youth.

This is the challenge the television industry must face. And I can tell you from experience, it's not an easy challenge, but it's an exciting one.

SPEECH TIP: Simple inversion can provide the means for resolving a confrontation. Deets begins to outline how the power being abused could be the power that is best used to fight society's myths about aging.

And it's a challenge ideally suited for television. Almost since its invention, television has visualized the images which have helped to shape popular culture. We now have a vast, growing segment of our population looking for images that mirror their new aging experience. And if television doesn't provide them, this audience will look elsewhere.

I will admit that reshaping the image of aging is easier said than done. But I do have some ideas on how the television industry can achieve a more realistic portrayal of older Americans—one more in tune with the lifestyles, attitudes, and experiences of an aging population.

First, put an end to age discrimination in the industry. Seek out—and preserve—the creative talent that knows and understands what the aging population is experiencing.

Second, don't look at aging as a "problem," look at it as an "experience." Age in and of itself is not the problem. By focusing on age as "the problem," we never get beyond it to face the real problems that keep us from leading vital and productive lives.

Third, remember that aging is a subtle process—synonymous with living. It's not a drastic change. Sometimes just little changes in characters, plots, or settings can make all the difference in the world. MTV asked middle-aged Eric Clapton to unplug his guitar and developed a whole new audience for their "Eric Clapton— Unplugged" special.

Finally, don't be preoccupied with age. Recognize that most people—regardless of age—are looking forward, not backward. Older people like to mix with people of all ages. They have spent a lifetime deciding what they like and what they don't. At last they have become the people they are.

Jean Louise Calmet—age 117—is listed in the *Guinness Book of World Records* as the world's oldest living person. When asked her secret to living so long, she said, "I just got old and couldn't help it."

I think that's probably how most people would like to view aging. They don't want to see it as simply the decline of youth, or the beginning of the end. They want to view it as a new stage of life full of new experiences, new adventures, and new anticipation.

People age. It's a fact of life. And most people would like to see aging portrayed as a positive experience. Not one reflecting illness, dependence, and hopelessness.

And if Clive Barnes was right—if television is "the first culture available to everybody and governed by what people want"—then the television industry must begin to recognize the new faces of aging. It must help us to create a new vision of aging. And it must reflect a realistic image of society—one which shows people growing older with independence, dignity, and purpose.

Publishing for the Individual: Alternatives to Traditional Textbooks

JOSEPH L. DIONNE
Chairman and Chief Executive Officer
McGraw-Hill, Inc.

Delivered to the American Association of Publishers (College Division), Washington, D.C., May 13, 1992

SUMMARY: McGraw-Hill chairman Joseph L. Dionne describes his company's PRIMIS system, which electronically generates "customized" textbooks. He calls for other publishers to preserve the industry's heritage—the selection and distribution of knowledge—by embracing new opportunities in information technology before non-publishing competitors overtake the field.

Sometimes complex arguments are best illustrated by a simple anecdote. You may recall the scene from the movie *Dead Poets Society* where Robin Williams insisted that his students rip out the first chapter of their poetry textbooks. This was a dramatic flourish, intended to shock as much as to instruct, but the point was made: Instead of assisting, that chapter was inhibiting the way he wanted to teach poetry.

SPEECH TIP: By calling up this movie scene with the first words of his speech, Dionne borrows some of its shock value to open his own discussion.

We can certainly debate whether the method the character chose was, in the end, the right one. But I think all of us here would defend his right, as a teacher, to present the subject to his students in a way that he felt would most enlighten them. By its very nature, teaching is a process that involves choosing from many different resources and techniques. No instructor teaches in exactly the same manner as another instructor. "Customization" in the classroom is a given.

Since 1989, McGraw-Hill has been investing significant resources in trying to satisfy that need for customization as we see it emerging. We've given this process a name; it's called PRIMIS.

Many of you have been asking, "What in the world is McGraw-Hill doing?" Today, I would like to try to answer that question, share with you some of the process involved in developing PRIMIS, dispel some myths about this new endeavor, and ask a question of my own about where the publishing business is headed.

SPEECH TIP: This introductory statement could be made no more concise.

Let me state at the outset that I am not here to try to convert anyone. One great advantage that we as publishers have is that our business is still one of ladies and gentlemen; we believe in the dispassionate exchange of ideas; we treasure the individuality of our respective companies; we applaud the fact that we each have a somewhat different approach to our profession, even as we endorse the overriding goal of disseminating information and knowledge.

Now, for the record, PRIMIS is an electronic publishing system. It lets college instructors select from a growing database of educational and professional information to create a customized textbook tailored to the specific needs of a particular course and its students. Today, those instructors can choose core chapters from existing textbooks, journals, case studies, and magazine articles; arrange them in any order desired; and add one's own materials or notes.

Eventually, as the technology evolves even further, PRIMIS will allow the utilization of a virtually limitless collection of databases and printing locations. That is important as our industry moves from "print and distribute" to "distribute and print."

The experience we've had so far with PRIMIS is that instructors like it because it allows them to tailor their courses; bookstores like it because they can cut down on inventory; and students like it because it puts a wealth of diverse information in one book at a reasonable cost.

We like it because it changes the economics of publishing: There's no inventory or returns. And it improves the flow of information, resulting in a more timely and better product. The used-book people don't like it, but you can't please everybody.

SPEECH TIP: The sole exception here foreshadows, ever so slightly, a later topic in the speech.

However, some publishers still feel uneasy about PRIMIS. They wonder whether publishers will yield too much control over their books by opening them to PRIMIS. They believe a textbook should be encyclopedic; it should cover every important aspect of a subject and should have a demonstrable "logic path," much as a novel has a beginning, a middle, and an end. They just feel that the best textbooks are those with breadth, depth, and heft.

Equating size with quality is an understandable result of the basically industrial approach we have taken toward book publishing in the last five hundred years. When Gutenberg popularized moveable type, he contributed to the democratization of knowledge. But it's clear to me that at the same time he was also putting in place a process that would inevitably lead to the constraint of the dissemination of knowledge.

Like many businesses that developed during the Industrial Revolution, we publishers have long been locked into an "assembly line" approach. We would select a manuscript that we felt was worth wider distribution. We would tell the printer how many books we wanted to print, the kind of binding desired, the number of colors needed, and so on. Then the printer would educate us on the costs involved.

By the time the type was set, the plates made, the sheets fed and cut, the pages bound, and the books distributed, assembly-line publishing became a fairly expensive proposition.

This was especially true in textbook publishing. As anyone here can attest, creating a textbook for a national market forces every publisher to take advantage of economies of scale. Rather than a book covering a limited range of interests, a publisher includes virtually every aspect of the topic. The more aspects, the greater appeal in the marketplace. Besides, it's a competitive necessity; everybody else is doing it! Which is how a textbook publisher comes up with the sort of hefty tome that typifies today's textbook market.

Please don't misunderstand: I believe there will always be a place for the traditional textbook. It is efficient. It is often economical. It is even convenient in many cases.

But for many courses and many situations, it is the wrong approach. One thing I'm certain of: Very few of today's core-course textbooks are actually read from cover to cover.

So in a sense the printing press has come full circle: from a "freedom fighter" for knowledge in the fifteenth century to an information "tyrant" in the late twentieth century.

This is one of the realities we've had to confront at McGraw-Hill as we've tried to better serve the needs of our customers. In the old days, we would have tried to make a better textbook.

Today, the marketplace—our customers—is forcing us to re-invent the textbook.

Some would dispute this statement. How, exactly, are we being "forced" to re-invent the textbook?

There are two aspects to this question. The first, and broader aspect, is something everyone in this room can understand and identify with: the explosion of the used-textbook market.

Twenty years ago, the used-book market didn't exist—or at least it didn't exist in the size and sophistication we know it today. I came of age in an era when the accumulation of books—and especially textbooks—was a sign of a liberally educated person. For a relatively small sum, one could collect a well-rounded personal library covering topics from philosophy to physiology—and keep that library for life.

> SPEECH TIP: Speaking to an industry-wide audience, Dionne must establish the recent trends in his particular sphere. Specialization is so great and speedy changes are so many within all business areas today that none of us can be expected to keep up with all of our neighbors' news.

But then a subtle change took place in the textbook market. Publishers began to expand the appeal of their textbooks in response to competition. As we tried to become all things to all people, development and production costs rose rapidly—and prices increased accordingly. In some state colleges today, the cost of required textbooks approaches the cost of tuition. Clearly, that is an untenable situation for many students—and many colleges, too.

Partly as a result of these pressures, instructors no longer tried to "teach the textbook." They freely told students to ignore certain portions, which had the effect of diminishing the book's overall credibility. Students came to regard the textbook less as a lifelong reference and more as a temporary guide to the course that would be abandoned as soon as finals are over. Indeed, knowledge was changing at such a pace that any personal library would be outdated before graduation. The textbook edged closer to becoming a commodity. Many students later regret not having a personal library as they learn that basic principles and concepts don't change rapidly.

That change in perception helped create the used-book market. A few entrepreneurs, who shared none of our intellectual values, saw that bucks were to be made by paying exiting students for books they would never use again and selling them to students for the short time they would need them. Operating at first out of the backs of station wagons, dealers eventually developed an elaborate and sophisticated infrastructure, buying and selling hundreds of thousands of books over the course of the academic year. Many publishers spend their lives avoiding technology, but the new technology harnessed for the used-book market ate our lunch.

Meanwhile, we kept telling ourselves that this was a fringe movement, destined to be no more than the "hula hoop" of the campus. But we were wrong. Today, a significant portion of the market could be characterized as "rent-a-book," with the used-book dealers enhancing that portion of the market virtually every year.

Perhaps the worst aspect for traditional publishers is the fact that our "back lists" are the parts of our business most severely impacted. In the old days, a popular new textbook was ensured a long, profitable life. Today, popularity is virtually a guarantee that the used-book dealers will make their own market in the book. Unfortunately, the "publisher's new book" has become the "book of last choice" for many bookstores.

And, as you all know, we're not the only ones who suffer. The authors who write the textbooks are not paid royalties; they watch in enraged silence like the recording artists whose pirated tapes are sold on street corners.

The second impetus McGraw-Hill had in veering away from the traditional textbook was a purely logistical one.

Several years ago we were preparing a new edition of our Meigs accounting text, which was already very popular but becoming a logistical nightmare. Instructors using the text were insisting on more and more supplemental teaching packages; each instructor, it seemed, had a different way of using the text, and if we wanted to sell the book, we had to accommodate those teaching idiosyncrasies.

We finally reached the point where it just made sense to put the Meigs text and all the supplemental materials on a computerized database. Then we could manipulate the database into as many different forms as our customers were demanding, a technology being developed at our corporate R & D center.

It was not with any grand scheme of creating a computerized, customized book that we started this effort. It took us a while to even realize that we were assembling the basis for an entirely new form of publishing. But once we announced that Meigs would be available in virtually any form and any quantity the instructor wanted, the response was overwhelming and we knew this was a market we either had to serve—or slowly walk away from.

This was not "technology in search of a market." Quite the contrary. Because the concept was so new, we were scrambling to create a lot of the necessary technology ourselves. Some industry analysts predicted we would never be able to make the customized book work because the process would, in the end, prove to be too expensive. The printing alone, the theory went, would be too costly to make small book runs economically competitive. This is exactly what I mean by the term "tyranny of the printing press."

Well, a few weeks ago, we announced a new technology that cuts through the theory that customized printing will be too expensive. The new Electrobook Press, using digital technology, is able to print and bind individual books in any quantity, without stopping for set-ups. For example, a 2,000-book run can be followed by a 55-book run, which can then be followed by a 450-book run, and so on, without stopping.

The press is web-fed. It runs at 250 feet per minute, can print both sides of the paper at once, and automatically folds, collects, and delivers complete books.

It's a matter of pride that McGraw-Hill's development efforts have helped make this press available to our industry.

Let me emphasize that PRIMIS is not an experimental process. Today, we are selling PRIMIS customized texts on 300 campuses, and that number grows daily. The technology continues to evolve, but the customers are already buying the product.

Now there are many myths that in the last few years have attached themselves to PRIMIS, and I would like to briefly address them.

Myth number one is that PRIMIS sales are "cannibalizing" other McGraw-Hill sales. This simply is not true. None of the hardback books we have published on PRIMIS have experienced sales declines. I know that's counter intuitive, but in ten instances when we created an electronic version of a print product at McGraw-Hill the print version grew too.

SPEECH TIP: Dionne counters the first myth with actual (and admittedly surprising) fact, then offers—as a luxury—the conceptual argument that follows.

Plus, I would make a distinction between "cannibalized" losses and "carnivorized" losses. One means that a publisher plans on minor setbacks with one book in order to achieve overall greater sales. The other means that an outsider eats your market and you never get it back. If that were the only choice, I'd rapidly develop a taste for cannibalism.

Myth number two is that authors whose works are used in PRIMIS are somehow suffering because people only buy a portion of their work. In the first place, anthologies have been around for many years, and authors usually regard being included in them as a sign of distinction—and, I might add, an additional source of income.

If anything, PRIMIS opens up an exciting new universe for an author's work. Since we handle all copyright questions quickly and authoritatively with your help, an instructor's agonizing decision over whether to illegally reproduce an author's work or just leave it out of the syllabus is eliminated. That should certainly mean that the best of an author's work will be read and appreciated by many more students.

The third myth people have about PRIMIS is that it destroys a publisher's identity. This is an ill-founded belief that is particularly difficult to refute, since identity is often more in the mind of the publisher than in the mind of the customer. I will say that many, many, college instructors today do not perceive the differences in texts that we, as publishers, perceive. Many of them see textbooks as essentially alike.

The last myth is that customized publishing is somehow optional for our profession. This is the greatest myth of all, reminding me of how the once-mighty railroads considered the DC-3 and the two-axle truck as mere irritants, failing to recognize that these upstarts would eventually drain the lifeblood from their business.

It has been observed that the traditional book has dominated written communications for only a brief time in recorded history. There is no "divine right" of publishers. The fact that our future hangs in the balance is not a situation that McGraw-Hill likes or desires but simply accepts. We must recognize this fact if we are to continue to be a vital force in the textbook market.

This subject leads me to the last point I want to make, and I will couch it in the form of a question: Have we as publishers mistaken the book we want to publish for the market we want to serve? Have we fallen in love with our own products and given short shrift to the actual needs of our customers?

Leaving aside how we as publishers see the college textbook market, what are our customers telling us?

They are saying, through the growth of the used-book market, that they find textbooks too expensive in many instances. Through the fact that books are generally only half-read at best, they are telling us that we're giving them more information than they need—or at least more than they can use in a timely manner. And with the increasing popularity of "course packs" and other customized applications, they are telling us that they want to be able to teach courses in ways that meet the individual needs of their students.

We have to recognize and accept that advances in technology are bringing more and more information under the direct control of the end user. This technology is "empowering" the individual to find and use the information he—or she—wants when it is needed. The time-tested image of the editor selecting important data for publication is changing. Now, we're in the paradoxical role of increasing the available information that our customers want direct access to.

Technology is remaking publishing in the image of our original and long-standing customer: the individual. And whatever it takes to serve that individual's needs is what will succeed in tomorrow's marketplace.

For those who say that this is not "real publishing," I would say that history shows that the successful publishers are those who meet the informational needs of the customer and deliver value to that customer. Tomorrow, "value" may mean a CD-ROM that a student picks up for a few dollars at the bookstore, uses all semester in his or her PC, and returns to the bookstore after exams. Or maybe the student will bypass stored data altogether and use on-line access to the college's central library computer.

All that information will have to come from somewhere, and that is still our province as publishers: providing the information our customers need, in the forms they need it, and at prices they can afford.

When we provide that information in a form other than the traditional textbook, we're not diminishing our role as publishers. In fact, we're enhancing it. By empowering our customers, we empower ourselves. Gutenberg did not diminish the publisher's role when he took the distribution of knowledge out of the hands of monks and delivered books into the hands of thousands of readers; he empowered himself and his profession even as he empowered his customers.

There is a great opportunity here for us, like Gutenberg, to meet the information needs of an entirely new generation of customers. I don't limit the term customer to just instructors; I mean the students who read the books, the bookstores that sell them, the parents who see their children learning more, and even the school boards and trustees who share in the satisfaction of greater learning taking place.

The genie of customization is out of the bottle. Whether we like it or not, a market has developed for alternatives to traditional textbooks. I want to make sure that publishers respond to and begin to retake that market. Because if we don't, it's very easy to see how an IBM, or an AT&T, or even a Microsoft could step in and grab that market right from under our noses. They know full well how to electronically serve the needs of individuals; they've been doing that for years.

I don't want to see more publishing customers migrate to non-publishers. After all, this is our heritage, not the heritage of quick-buck artists or technologists who want to deal in books only as commodities. We have the institutional memory. We know how to recognize the true talent of writing for the instruction of young minds. We know how to build a course of study and stock it full of the most provocative and incisive thinkers of our time.

This is our domain—to hold or to lose. What say ye?

SPEECH TIP: The speaker's use of parallel, but gradually more intricate sentences builds to a strong staccato finish.

Passports—Not Provincialism: Marketers and Communicators Need New International Skills

JEAN L. FARINELLI
Chairman and Chief Executive Officer
Creamer Dickson Basford and Eurocom Corporate & PR (U.S.)

Delivered to a joint meeting of the Charlotte World Trade Association and the Carolinas Chapter of the Business/Professional Advertising Association, Charlotte, North Carolina, April 14, 1993

SUMMARY: Corporate and public relations expert Jean Farinelli illustrates the dangers of "thinking locally while acting globally" in today's worldwide market-place. Farinelli shares five guidelines for successful marketing across national—and cultural—borders.

Good evening, everyone. It is a pleasure to be here with you in Charlotte, and I will tell you why.

My public relations firm is a partner in the Eurocom Corporate & PR group, which is the world's fourth-largest public relations network. We counsel U.S. firms on their communications in other countries, and we counsel European firms on their communications in the United States. Day in and day out, we are concerned with international issues.

And so it is a great pleasure to be here, in a region that is a *model* of international business. Many, many years before it became fashionable, you were attracting foreign investment and foreign operations here. I understand that nearly 300 companies from twenty countries have operations within Charlotte and Mecklenburg County.

> **SPEECH TIP:** Farinelli's opening remarks not only compliment and commend the community he is addressing, they also introduce many of the issues he will subsequently discuss.

North Carolina's imports and exports grow year-over-year. Generally your state has run an annual trade surplus. These are claims that few parts of our country can make.

As one of my colleagues here has told me for years, you have the right business infrastructure: A major international airport. The center of the nation's largest consolidated rail system. Good highways. World-class bankers who have an interest in pre-export financing. A similar interest at the local office of the Small Business Administration.

And even further in the background, I can see something that is very close to my own business interests: The right *cultural* infrastructure. Universities, such as North Carolina State, which are interested in doing pioneering studies of international business. Dozens of international clubs. A thriving "sister cities" program. International House, which may be unique in the United States as a "home away from home" for international businesspeople. And I am told that the state may set up an Institute of Language and Culture, with public and private funding.

These are wonderful advantages as you compete for investment and business. I have spoken on international communications and marketing in many American cities. Here in Charlotte, for the first time, I fear I may be preaching to the choir.

I know I do not have to convince *you* that international trade is good business. However, because most of you are marketers or communicators, I do want to zero in on some of the *marketing and communications* challenges of today's international business environment.

When we look at world trade today, we see more volume than sophistication. American companies have expanded their international business to unprecedented levels. No one is more aware of the pace than you are, here in Charlotte.

And yet, it often seems that many of us are making some old, familiar mistakes on the world scene—mistakes that we should have learned to avoid back in "Marketing 101." Here are a few examples from my own travels and associations.

SPEECH TIP: Despite his mention of college business courses, Farinelli's speech will amply demonstrate that many lessons are only learned at the esteemed university of hard knocks—hence their inestimable value here.

Recently a Fortune 500 consumer goods company was planning a major European product introduction. The company's product is a personal care item that is popular here in the United States. As part of its European introduction, the company planned an international satellite news conference, originating in New York. All well and good—except for the *timing*. Because it is the time of the year that we in the United States push our clocks forward by one hour, you would think this company would be especially aware of time zones. But, amazing as it sounds, this giant company forgot about the time difference between the U.S. and Europe. It scheduled the press conference for 11:00 AM in New York—which of course is the end of the business day in Europe.

Needless to say, this timing would prevent many European daily newspapers from covering the new product introduction. And certainly, it would be an insult to most journalists, whether from daily papers or not. This is the 1990s—it is too late to be making mistakes like this! Fortunately, the company's European agency avoided disaster by persuading the company to change the timing.

Another example. Tambrands recently began marketing its brand of tampons in France and Germany. So far, the company has gained a very small market share. The key problem, according to one marketing source, is product design. The product was designed for sale in the United States and the United Kingdom. Generally, it does not appeal to French and German women.

This was simply a failure to do market research—focus groups and so forth. It was not a problem of a "foreign" brand—in fact, 80 percent of the French and German market is owned by *another* U.S. brand, Johnson and Johnson's "O.B."

Even Mickey Mouse is in trouble. I am sure you saw the uniformly positive press coverage about the opening of Euro Disney outside of Paris, one year ago. If you follow the international press, you also noticed more recently that Euro Disney attendance is below expectations, and the operation may lose as much as $185 million in fiscal 1993. Apparently, the big splash was due mostly to novelty, and it is now clear that the appeal of the park is not fully consistent with European culture.

However, I do not want to single out only *American* companies. European companies are fully capable of making the same kinds of mistakes.

For example, a French management-services company acquired operations in the United States a few years ago. During the first two years, this company lost more than one-third of its U.S. sales volume—it was perceived as a "foreign" supplier. The company's sales rebounded when it successfully repositioned itself as a "multi-local" company, which seemed less remote to its customers.

In another case, a leading European maker of medical products was having difficulty reaching its target market—American surgeons. A marketing study revealed that "foreignness" was a major problem. Although the surgeons respected and even admired the quality of the *products*, they complained that the product reference materials sounded *translated*. They also said the European marketing people had a different *thought process* from Americans and that, as a result, they did not *listen* well. The surgeons also wanted American-style local support—including "help" lines, fax numbers, training videos, and additional U.S.-based regional reps.

Here was a company with unquestioned *product* quality—yet this company was having trouble *selling*, simply because it did not meet the American customers on their own cultural terms.

In another case, a German software developer wanted to expand its sales to the United States. The company hired a small, U.S.-based public relations agency that specializes in helping software companies.

Before it hired the agency, the client had planned an American announcement based entirely on the customs of the *German* computer press. Germany is a much smaller country than the U.S. If a local software company issues a press release on a new product, or invites the press to a trade show, reporters almost always pay attention. The U.S. agency startled the software company by predicting that this approach would likely result in *no press coverage at all* in the United States.

The agency persuaded its client to take two important steps to establish credibility *before* the product announcement—opening a U.S. office and building a following among the important computer consultants in the U.S. As a result, the German product received decent press coverage here.

If you think about each of these six examples, you perceive a common denominator in the mistakes. In every case, a company failed to take into account some of the culture and customs of a target market. These exporters—some large and some small—all made the mistake of trying to export their marketing methods along with their products. Or to reverse the familiar slogan, these companies were "thinking locally and acting globally."

What I see happening today is this: World trade is expanding, but marketers and communicators are not keeping up with the pace. We still think of other countries as "foreign." We *know* that we do not know enough about "foreign" countries, so we fall back on what we *do know*—how to market and communicate in our *own* country. We repeat the slogan, "Think globally and act locally," but we do not really mean it. I am not speaking only of the United States—as my examples demonstrate, marketers and communicators from *many* countries lack the international skills they should have in order to be effective.

We have to realize that "international" is not "foreign" anymore. If we marketers and communicators are going to live and prosper in a world of international business, we must become *figurative citizens* of every country in which our companies operate. We need passports—not provincialism.

Companies that pursue international business need marketers and communicators who truly are *internationalists*. They need people who can help reinvent marketing and communications to meet global needs. They need marketers who can participate in the process of explaining global corporate strategies. They need communicators who can persuade senior managers to step outside of their familiar thought processes, in order to meet other cultures on their own terms. They need communicators who can articulate—simply and consistently—the outcomes of very complex global decisions.

And yet, as more American companies go global, they find most of their employees lacking the background, the understanding, even the *interest* necessary to be truly effective. Why is this happening?

The answer lies in our *provincialism*, coupled with an inability to keep up with what is taking place in the rest of the world. Like most Americans, we are primarily focused on what is happening in our own companies and communities. As I mentioned, you often see the same inward focus in other countries, too.

Few businesspeople in our country even speak a second language fluently. A 1991 Dunhill survey found that most American managers not only do not *speak* another language, *they do not even think it is important.* Even our *State Department* recently eliminated language aptitude from its battery of employment tests.

Even here in North Carolina, where international business is thriving, few business schools require international studies. According to the latest edition of *Barron's Guide to Graduate Business Schools*, only three of the fifteen MBA programs in this state require a course in international business.

Most of our counterparts in other countries have had educations that emphasize languages, cultures, and international business issues. Business schools in other parts of the world routinely integrate international studies and languages into *all areas* of their curricula.

By the way, our educational myopia translates directly into lower salaries. The graduates of Europe's two top business schools now command substantially higher starting salaries than do graduates from MBA programs at Harvard and Stanford. The world market for personnel has spoken—European sophistication is now a highly valued commodity.

Only recently have our American business schools reacted to this trend. You probably noticed the article on B-schools in the current issue of *Business Week*. The article mentioned that Wharton now has recruiting offices in Paris and Tokyo and is hosting receptions overseas for admitted students. The same article gave a "four-star" rating to a new promotional video in which MIT's flashy dean Lester Thurow touts his school's international focus.

Corporations are scrambling to catch up, too. Some large companies, such as General Electric, are completely rewriting their management training programs to make them more international. Expensive—but necessary. These employers *used* to provide international training only when the need for an overseas assignment came up. Now, they do the training far in advance. They are afraid our competitors in *other* countries will be better prepared. In most cases, they are right.

So, how can we as businesspeople ensure that our companies—and our employees—can compete against our sophisticated international counterparts? How can we become figurative citizens of all the countries in which we operate?

I do not claim to have *all* the answers, but I do want to mention *five ways* we can gain a competitive edge.

1. *We must remind ourselves not to make assumptions about our target markets.* As I mentioned, the international mistakes we make tend to fall under the category of errors of *omission*—not errors of commission. Time and again I have seen this in my work with clients. It is not that we *misinterpret* the culture of a country—more typically, we do not do any interpretation *at all*. We simply assume that international markets are "pretty much like here, except that people might speak a different language."

In contrast, let me describe a client who is setting an excellent example of learning about international markets. The company, called Transitions Optical, is based in Tampa, Florida. It has a patented process for making prescription lenses that darken automatically in sunlight. The benefit is obvious: Your everyday prescription lenses adjust to sunlight through an infinite gradation of gray shading, as opposed to traditional lenses with a fixed tint.

Transitions is becoming successful in the United States, and it is currently looking to expand its markets by selling in Europe. But Transitions is wisely making *no assumptions* about European markets, even for such a universal product as eyewear. Instead, the company is *learning*.

Through a series of local focus groups and customer interviews now being carried out by my network, the company is gathering very useful information. For example, the U.K. market is slow to adopt innovations—until recently, the optical industry there was government-owned. It will take time for this market to become more entrepreneurial.

A surprising bit of information has to do with the product itself. We learned, for example, that the lenses do not behave the same way in all countries—local differences in sunlight, cloud cover, temperature, and humidity affect the shade and even the *color* of the lenses. These differences are true even for France, which is within the same latitudes as many North American cities. As an extreme case, the low angle of sunlight and high humidity in Norway make the lenses turn a dark *green* instead of gray.

So, in spite of the proverbs about one sun shining down on all of mankind, my client is learning that you cannot even make assumptions about *sunlight*. The moral: Never assume. Instead, find out.

SPEECH TIP: Each of Farinelli's five steps is well presented, from the clarity and positive phrasing of their headings, to the vivid support of their illustrations, to the concision and emphasis of their summations.

2. *Use local agencies, and use them wisely.* Most of us know that it is suicidal to try to do international advertising and public relations by remote control. For example, there are several service companies in the United States who will translate your press releases and distribute them in other countries. But you and I know that sophisticated companies do not rely on these services. Even casual readers of the business press have seen several humorous articles over the years about embarrassing translations.

Most of us are well beyond that stage. We know that, if we want to do business in Italy, we need an Italian advertising agency and an Italian PR firm.

However, many companies still *under-utilize* their agencies, especially in Europe. Very frequently, for example, an American company hires a PR agency in a European country, tells it to keep cranking out news, and then virtually ignores the agency.

This is often a mistake. The local agency people can be a valuable source of intelligence about the country in which they live and work. I mentioned the example of the German software developer. This company *thought* it was hiring a U.S. public relations agency just to write English-language press releases and to make a few press calls. But when the agency immediately started offering unsolicited *strategic* advice, the client was wise enough to *listen*.

In short, the local firm offers you important intelligence, strategy, and feedback on the target country. However, I would suggest taking one *additional* step. Ideally, you also should have a communications firm that can give you sophisticated *global* advice. Many of the larger public relations and advertising agencies and networks—mine included—offer worldwide strategy *and* local tactical support and execution.

We supply this combination of services because multinational clients *demand* it. In most industries today, there is no longer any such thing as just local communications. Each action we take can be—and frequently is—instantly visible around the world. A world in which our audiences are increasingly well-informed. In some industries, such as pharmaceuticals and financial services, it is becoming *impossible* to operate without a truly integrated, worldwide strategy for marketing and communications.

3. *Take a tip from the world's largest companies—start a program to build international skills among your employees.* I mentioned that large American companies such as General Electric are beginning to integrate international skills into their management training. Those of you who run large companies can emulate these practices through *benchmarking* programs—you may be doing so already. For smaller corporations, it can be a challenge. In terms of cost per employee, training can be very expensive. I would like to offer a few suggestions that are effective but not necessarily costly.

Take advantage of the wonderful cultural infrastructure you have here in Charlotte. You can swap information informally with non-competitive companies. You can collaborate with universities and government agencies. Use your corporate buying power—negotiate *group rates* for language instruction. A second language is so basic, and yet so overlooked by most Americans, that it offers an *immediate competitive edge* in the international market.

> *SPEECH TIP:* Practical suggestions that can be taken up immediately—and that apply the very enthusiasm a speech like this will generate—are a real gift from the speaker to the audience. And the lower the cost of the suggestion, the better the gift.

Try some inexpensive creativity and leadership. For example, the offices of my firm sponsor "country nights" every few months. At a "country night," our people spend the evening discussing the business, politics, and demographics of *one country*. Expert guest speakers guide the discussion and widen staff knowledge. This is an easy, inexpensive, and highly effective way to learn. Here in North

Carolina, you certainly would be able to recruit many guest speakers without looking beyond your home state.

Consider establishing an informal international employee *exchange program* within your company. Or, barter with another company. This could be the most mind-broadening thing that ever happened to your employees.

And if you *are* considering an exchange program, I urge you to take a look at the March-April issue of *Harvard Business Review*. In this issue, a business manager from India describes his career selling Vicks Vaporub worldwide. He warns managers who transfer overseas not to move into "golden ghettos," or neighborhoods of people just like themselves. He says that you really need to have daily contact with the people of the country—that "the key to success is a tremendous amount of local passion for the brand and a feeling of local pride and ownership." You cannot tap into this passion and pride if you deal only with people from your home country.

Another approach to training is to look for creative ways to help your employees help *themselves* learn. For example, you might have seen the *Wall Street Journal* article two weeks ago, about PepsiCo's new "concierge." The company wanted to make its managers more efficient by reducing their personal distractions, so it hired an experienced concierge. This man, Andy King, does what traditional secretaries used to do. He finds contractors to fix roofs, takes cars for oil changes, and so on.

SPEECH TIP: Farinelli's intermittent mention of published information is in itself a subliminal lesson: a reminder of the business value to be found in media resources.

What if we took this very creative idea into the realm of international skills development? For example, you could designate one person in your company who would be responsible for helping employees pursue their international training. Your "international concierge" could set up the "country nights" that I mentioned. He or she could obtain foreign-language movies on videotape and perform a host of other useful individual services. The concierge also could maintain your library of international business publications, and your database of information on target countries—demographics, economics, politics, culture—and help employees use these resources.

Best of all, your international concierge could be your company's liaison officer to the cultural infrastructure of this region: international clubs, universities, the sister cities programs, International House. In fact, the concierge is very much in the spirit of your International House.

4. *Hire internationally.* Although that probably goes without saying for most of you, I do want to touch briefly on this subject. As you probably have seen in the business press over the last year or two, the largest U.S. companies are more frequently recruiting senior managers from other countries.

During the past sixteen months, at least five giant U.S. corporations have hired senior managers from France, Italy, The Netherlands, and Spain. This is a key trend in multinational business. Coca-Cola's chairman Roberto C. Goizueta, for one, maintains that you simply cannot run a multinational business without a multinational management team.

In my own firm, I try to practice what I preach. I have recruited internationally for my staff and even for senior management. Without the viewpoints of managers from other countries, we would lack the insight we need to counsel international clients.

Even *governments* are starting to see the light. For example, recently the French Ministry of Commerce wanted to hire a public relations agency to communicate its viewpoints and interests in the United States. In France, the country that gave us the word "chauvinism," the Ministry had the good sense to hire a U.S.-based firm.

5. *We managers must learn to think differently—to approach problems and opportunities more creatively.*

Most North Americans think *linearly.* That is, we approach problems and opportunities in a linear, sequential way. Conversely, many Europeans and Asians think *laterally*—they approach problems and opportunities from several angles *simultaneously.*

In Europe and Asia, lateral thinking has always come more naturally than it has here. But the tendency got a big boost during the last three decades by the British consultant Edward deBono. He has promoted lateral thinking for more than thirty years and has written thirty-six books on the subject. Here is a sample of deBono's thinking:

There are three stages of business. In Stage One, we pay attention to the *product.* We ask, "How can we get it right?"

Stage Two focuses on the product relative to the *competition.* We ask, "How can we do better?"

Stage Three, which deBono calls "sur-petition" or going *beyond competition,* emphasizes "integrating (our product) into the complex values of the customer." This is where linear-thinking companies miss out on colossal worldwide opportunities.

For example, you know that the Swiss watch industry invented the quartz movement, but did not use the invention for fear of killing its existing market. The Swiss wanted to protect their *skill monopoly*—after all, they were the people who had the precision skills to make tiny cog wheels and balance springs.

They were right in their thinking but wrong in their strategy. Watchmakers in Japan and Hong Kong seized on the idea of the quartz movement. In one year, sales of Swiss watches dropped by 25 percent. What *rescued* the Swiss watch industry was a very *un-Swiss* idea—the now-famous brand called "Swatch." Telling time was no longer the important thing in an inexpensive watch. Swatch was not selling *time* so much as *costume jewelry.* Swatch was one of the most dramatic reversals of traditional thinking in the history of international business. And it happened because a company learned to look at its *product* and its *customer* from a completely new angle.

Probably deBono's most famous *individual* student was Peter Ueberroth. As Commissioner of the Olympic Games, Ueberroth transformed the Games from an event that *no* city wanted, to an event for which cities now compete vigorously. He credits lateral thinking for his success in making the Games profitable.

Only during the last few years have North American corporations begun to seek deBono's advice. One local example here is Hoechst Celanese Corp.'s Fibers and Film Group, which recently set up a "laboratory for innovation" and has hired deBono and other consultants.

We have a lot of catching up to do. None of us wants to wake up one morning and find that an international competitor has created the Swatch of our industry.

I will leave you with this thought about our role as international marketers and communicators.

In the world of international diplomacy, there is an old saying: "When *goods* cannot cross borders, *armies will.*" Today, the whole world seems to have taken heed of this warning. Dictatorships are crumbling everywhere, as citizens clamor for personal freedom and for free trade.

Free markets are winning. For the first time in history, politicians and philosophers are seriously discussing the possibility of lasting world peace. As we enter the twenty-first century, world trade and world peace may replace world war.

As marketers and communicators, we have a proud role to play. We are the people who can help promote international understanding through international trade and competition. Together, we could do more good than all the debates in the United Nations General Assembly.

And I ask you: What could be better than making a profit while promoting prosperity all over the world?

CHAPTER 10

Women in Business

The world of business, even at the top, is no longer exclusively a man's world. Nevertheless, and despite strides that have been made, women in business must negotiate obstacles different from any their male counterparts face. There are prejudices spoken and unspoken. There are issues of family versus career. There are the particularly ugly—yet confusing—issues of sexual harassment. Most pervasive of all, there is the issue of inequity in pay. In the United States, equal pay for equal work is mandated by law, yet that law is routinely evaded, flouted, or ignored, apparently without penalty.

As the speech by CNN's Bernard Shaw, included here, demonstrates, discussions of women in business do not necessarily have to come from women themselves. Inevitably, however, most do, and the first thing the speaker will have to determine is the composition of the audience: Will it be predominantly female, mixed, or predominantly male?

Speeches by women to women are probably most profitably centered on sharing experience, giving advice, offering strategies, and even advising of legal rights and/or the employment policies of various firms and institutions. These speeches may be, in effect, public extensions of the kind of informal networking that many women in business have evolved as a creative response to the equally informal, but even more deeply ingrained, "old boy" networks that operate in many companies and even professional and political organizations.

Speeches to mixed groups or to predominantly male audiences are most usefully viewed as essays in consciousness-raising. Few people set out to be deliberately bigoted, and, in North America, despite undeniable evidence to the contrary, political tradition abhors injustice in general and discrimination in particular. A speech that makes the realities and consequences of sexual discrimination—especially at its most subtle and unconscious—*real* to such an audience goes a long way toward at least beginning to change thinking and, ultimately, policy on the subject. Many of the difficulties women face in business result from—or, at least, begin with—a lack of awareness.

Fortunately, these days and in many situations, it is also quite possible to talk about women in business in wholly or predominantly positive terms without sounding naive. This can be a refreshing and constructive approach, as CIBC vice-president Janet Martin demonstrates in her talk. Even framed in positive terms, women's business experience has certain unique features, discussion of which makes for an interesting speech that also heightens awareness and serves the purposes of peer-to-peer networking.

Room at the Top:
Women in Banking

JANET MARTIN
Vice-President
CIBC

*Delivered to the North Toronto Business and Professional Women's Club,
Toronto, Ontario, December 4, 1991*

*SUMMARY: A top executive in a Canadian bank discusses her company's strategy
for offering women greater opportunity and representation in the work place.*

> *SPEECH TIP:* Too many speakers in a business context studiously avoid the "I." This is a mistake. Making a speech, even before a hundred people or more, is an intimate act, and the first person is a powerful vehicle of expression. Don't be afraid to use your experience.

When I tell people I work for a bank, they almost always assume that I am a teller. Unlike other preconceptions, however, this one has some basis. First, it underscores the fact that most bank tellers are women. Second, it suggests that women do not occupy senior positions—in banks or any other organization. And third, it points to the barriers people have erected in their minds concerning women in the work place. The business world is starting to examine why these barriers exist. At CIBC, we are removing and replacing them with an environment that more accurately reflects demographic realities, an environment in which no one is disadvantaged and where every member of the work force can perform to his or her potential. We believe this not only creates a more balanced, bias-free work place, it enriches the organization. Companies that most effectively draw on the talents of both halves of the human race will build the better mousetrap.

This evening, I want to share with you my views on why few women have reached the uppermost level of today's corporations, why CIBC is breaking barriers from the top rather than waiting for them to crack from below, and how we are going about doing it.

> *SPEECH TIP:* After establishing the "I" and announcing that she will speak from *her* experience, Martin skillfully generalizes, setting her individual experience into a national and historical context. Effective speeches often begin with the specific and work outward to the general.

Make no mistake: Canadian women have made solid gains politically, socially, and professionally. Toronto recently elected its first female mayor. Half of the
Ontario government's cabinet are women. And while female representation in the
House of Commons is low—only 13 percent—it's almost three times higher than
legislatures in the United States and Britain.

In 1982, Canadian women won an equality clause in the Charter of Rights,
something that American women have been unable to attain. And significant legislation affecting women has been passed, namely the 1986 Federal Employment
Equity Act and Ontario's Pay Equity Act.

During the past couple of decades, women have made unprecedented
progress in their education. Today, half of undergraduate and graduate students are
female. Women are represented fairly in disciplines such as medicine, law, and
business administration. Even in traditionally male-dominated fields of study such
as engineering, women have increased their numbers. The 1970 undergraduate
class at the University of Toronto's faculty of engineering included thirty-three
women, just slightly over 1 percent of the students. In the 1990 class, there were
465 women, or almost 17 percent.

Women's progress in the business world has been no less remarkable. In the
last five years, an increasing number have started their own companies or have
become self-employed. Anita Roddick, who heads The Body Shop International, is
just one of many successful, enterprising women in the world today.

Women, of course, have always worked, but it wasn't until the second half of
this century that they entered the paid labor force on a permanent basis. Then, during the '60s and '70s, women went out to work in record numbers. Today, women
make up 44 percent—nearly half—of Canada's work force. According to *Statistics
Canada*, two-wage households are now the rule. The government's study, which
was done in 1989, found that in nearly two out of three families with two partners,
both spouses worked. That's almost double the percentage of dual income families
that were reported in 1967.

Within the banking industry, women have a large and visible role. In fact,
banking is one of the top industries for recruiting and promoting women. Women
make up the majority of the industry's work force. Three out of every four bank
employees are female, and almost half, or 48 percent, of middle and upper management positions are occupied by women. This is an improvement over four years
ago, when only 39 percent were managers. These numbers are better than those for
the general labor force, where, according to the 1986 census, only 33 percent of
middle managers in Canada were women.

Despite the progress women have made in the labor force, despite gaining
access to virtually every discipline, and despite our ability and ambition, women's
career advancements have not kept pace. When it comes to capturing the top jobs,
women are so near and yet so far.

> *SPEECH TIP:* Clearly signal the course of your argument. Martin has built a case demonstrating the progress women in business have made. Now she observes that, "despite" this, much has yet to be achieved.

While we're adequately represented in middle and upper management, our careers stall at this level and go no further. Only a small fraction of women move up to the senior ranks of large companies. In both Canada and the United States, 2 percent of senior executives are women.

> *SPEECH TIP:* Don't be afraid of introducing statistics, but be sure to subordinate figures to the point you are making.

Careers are limited by a glass ceiling that enables women to glimpse but not grasp top executive positions. While the barriers are invisible, they are there nonetheless. In a 1990 poll conducted by *Business Week* and Louis Harris Poll, 60 percent of management women in large corporations identified "a male-dominated corporate culture" as an obstacle to women's success.

Why is there a glass ceiling?

> *SPEECH TIP:* Put yourself in the place of your audience and ask yourself the questions they want to ask. Notice the amount of insight the self-asked question generates. It propels this portion of the speech.

Might it exist because male executives tend to support and sponsor people like themselves? That almost automatically excludes women. Organizational studies provide plenty of evidence showing that leaders of various institutions favor subordinates who are similar to them.

Might it exist because men are sometimes reluctant to admit women into their informal office networks, the game of golf or the round of drinks, where friendly but important business banter is exchanged? Women have yet to form comparable networks.

Might it exist because of the double standards we have for men and women in the work place? Women who are excitable and emotional may be dismissed as temperamentally unsuited for management. Yet men who vent their emotions by slamming the door and pounding the desk may be considered "aggressive."

Might it exist because sexual harassment, an ugly form of power politics, has not disappeared? Whatever might be said of the Clarence Thomas/Anita Hill case, it has heightened awareness of sexual harassment as a work place concern. Bias doesn't have to be blatant or insidious in order to diminish women. It can take seemingly innocuous forms. A woman I know attended an awards banquet held by her employer a short while ago. The men who were honored received a handshake. It was presumed that the women would prefer a corsage and a kiss.

Might the glass ceiling exist because the personal trade-offs and sacrifices women must make are greater than those their male counterparts face? John Kenneth Galbraith once told writer Michael Bliss that, "In the modern world, women's liberation consists of submerging a personality to a corporation rather than a husband." Harsh as Galbraith's view may be, he does have a point. Reports published from the *Wall Street Journal* a few years ago revealed that while 94 percent of male executives were married, only 41 percent of their female counterparts were. Ninety-five percent of male executives had children, compared to 39 percent for women. A very small percentage of men were divorced or never married. For women executives, the number was 45 percent.

For average working women with children, the responsibility for family and home rests with them and keeps careers in check. In a study of fifty middle-class, two-career couples, an American sociologist found that the women do 75 percent of household work, even if there are no children involved. This is what's known as working "the second shift." And if you believe Naomi Wolf's thesis in her much-discussed book, *The Beauty Myth*, women also work a "third shift." Her theory is that because women are catching up to men, society has found a new burden with which to rob women of their energy and weaken their confidence. This third shift is the labor for beauty, the obsession with thin bodies and youth.

Not everyone will agree that all the examples I have just outlined are barriers to women's success in the work place. Yet the imbalances that exist at the executive rank prove that there are too many impediments for women to clear on their own. Employers must start widening the path for women, and there are compelling reasons for doing so.

> *SPEECH TIP:* This transition not only admits room for differences of opinion and interpretation, it signals the beginning of the part of the speech that outlines solutions to the problems defined in the first part of the speech.

First, there is the question of fairness to women. Progressive employers, like CIBC, pride themselves on being a performance-oriented culture. This means recognizing and promoting employees based on their potential. By failing to reward the contributions of women in management, organizations compromise their standards for performance.

Second, it makes good business sense. For economic reasons, if nothing else, companies will have to move to establish a fairer representation of women across all levels of the organization. The words "quality," "service" and "excellence" have become a mantra for competitive businesses. Firms recognize that mastery of these concepts depends on the human factor and getting the very best from every employee.

But attracting and keeping good employees is becoming more difficult for a number of reasons. We're seeing trends such as "cashing out." As trend-watcher Faith Popcorn points out, baby boomers are retreating from promotions and opting for life at a slower pace. In the United States, for example, some sixteen million people work from their homes, running their own businesses.

This situation is compounded by a more powerful trend. Canada's labor force has grown at its slowest rate in two decades. The birth rate is low, and the number of young people entering the labor force is declining. At the same time, the country's population is aging. Canada's changing demographics are creating a labor shortage, which makes talented people a scarce resource. This is a reversal of the situation from just a decade ago, when the supply of male baby boomers was an adequate source of management and labor potential. But companies can no longer afford to employ a predominantly white, male work force. Employers must look at the broader population from which to draw their talent. This includes aboriginal people, people with disabilities, and visible minorities, as well as women. Women, in fact, will be the fastest growing segment of the Canadian work force over the next decade. People may very well choose their employer based on the company's record for fairness and diversity.

Similarly, as Canada's population and demographics change, organizational structures must reflect the societies they serve. In the years ahead, a representative and diversified work force will become a source of competitive strength. As more women are becoming professionals or running their own businesses, they want to do business with people like themselves. A company that mirrors the general population is better prepared to understand the needs of its customers and come up with the products and services that meet their demands.

In a more competitive world, organizations will also require the strength that comes from a variety of leadership styles. While men and women may have similar abilities and motives, their management styles are often different. Traditionally, men have structured organizations as hierarchies, with authority reaching down. Women, on the other hand, tend to view their authority from a center reaching out. The president of CIBC's retail bank, a man, has pointed out that some of our female branch managers are more flexible in their management style and better motivators of staff. That's why, he suggests, they often get better sales results than some of their male counterparts.

An interactive leadership style will become vital to organizations. We're already seeing that team effort is more valuable to a company than individual heroics. In the near future, organizations will become flatter, less hierarchical, and more participatory—structures and styles that many female leaders are already comfortable with.

There is also a social reason for advancing more women to the executive level. The glass ceiling that keeps women out, also keeps the men in. According to one academic, men may be trapped in a culture that forces them to concentrate singlemindedly on their careers. Unlike women, men have often been taught to place job and career ahead of their role at home. He suggests that "men and women cannot be equal to one another in the world of work until they are equal at home." Breaking the glass ceiling, then, could lead men to reassess their values and allow them to choose a greater family role.

Fairness to women and sound business sense are the two forces driving CIBC's new women's program. CIBC's policy is to ensure that opportunities for development and advancement are based solely on merit. A bias-free work environment is also a competitive necessity. With the approaching seller's market for job skills, CIBC must attract the best available employees. That's why becoming a leading financial services employer is a primary goal for us.

About a year ago, a senior level committee, of which I am a member, was appointed by the chairman of the bank to review the status of women at CIBC. We found that while women are adequately represented in middle and upper management, women comprise only 11 percent of senior executives. This is substantially higher than the national average, but too low to adequately represent women at the most senior levels of the organization.

Women have been unable to break the glass ceiling from below, so we have to try from the top. CIBC is now proceeding to establish a "critical mass" of women at the senior executive level. We want to increase the representation of women in executive positions to approximately one-third, a level that will more adequately voice the aspirations and values of women.

One of the questions people ask about CIBC's women's initiative is, "Why are you more concerned with women at the top? Surely women at lower levels have more pressing problems." My view is that the concerns of women at any level of the organization are inseparable. Without a sufficient number to champion women's issues in the executive offices, women's concerns will not be given the attention they deserve. And the inroads women make at the top will flow to other levels.

Let me tell you about some of the key aspects of the program. While it emphasizes the importance of promotion of women, it is not a substitute for competence. Women can't skip the experience and activities that help prepare them to run a business. To ensure that women are promoted purely on the basis of merit, we are bolstering our development programs for both men and women at all levels of the organization. Advancement of women, however, will only accomplish so much. An equitable work environment must be supported with additional measures. For many women, the responsibility for home and career creates a heavy burden. So we are trying to lighten the load in some ways. Our human resource policies are being reviewed and have already led to improvements to maternity benefits. We are also exploring flexible work arrangements, such as alternative work hours and daycare.

SPEECH TIP: An effective introduction to—and exposition of—an example.

Another important measure of the women's program is a process to ensure that women make up at least one-third of CIBC's various task forces, steering committees, and project teams.

While this may not sound extraordinary, participation will provide valuable experience for women. More importantly, it will ensure that women's views on a given issue are not overlooked. Getting a seat at the table means that women's concerns will be raised and championed.

The program also includes awareness training for men and women. That's an important component. To change institutions, it's also necessary to change attitudes. Biased behavior is often modified as one becomes more aware of the unconscious ways women's talent, skills, and ability may be undermined or underestimated. Awareness training helps encourage this kind of modification.

The changes CIBC is advocating will not happen overnight, but I'm optimistic. Women now have a better chance of getting to the top than did their predecessors. And there is an increasing number of qualified women within CIBC, and within the work force in general, to draw from. Executive men are becoming more accustomed to having women as their peers. Evidence also suggests that men are giving family life more priority. When my previous boss was offered the job of president of CIBC's retail bank, his concern was how the promotion would affect his family. Just a short time ago, such conflicts would not even have been acknowledged, much less made public.

So I think the doors are opening, women's voices are being heard, and the changes are now irreversible. This leads me to believe that while women still have a long way to go, our women's initiative is a good beginning. We may not get there quickly, but we will get there.

Thank you.

An Uneven Playing Field in America

Bernard Shaw

Principal Washington Anchor
CNN

The Alfred M. Landon Lecture on Public Issues, Kansas State University, Manhattan, Kansas, November 20, 1992

SUMMARY: One of the nation's most highly respected television journalists speaks out on discrimination against women in the work place.

Thank you very much and good morning. To President Wefald and your colleagues of the faculty and to you, Madame President, and to you, ladies and gentlemen who came up from the elementary schools across this state, good morning and I thank you. My wife, Linda, says hello and that she regrets that she could not be here with you this morning because our two young people, our son and daughter, are in school, and one of them is having a test today.

I must tell you, I have not been this pensive since October 22, 1990. That was the afternoon I had been driven around Baghdad for about forty-five minutes because of President Saddam's preoccupation with his personal safety; I wonder why. We were taken to a house along the Tigris River, and it was well guarded. We were convinced that the man was going to show up and, indeed, he was going to do an interview with me and my colleague, Richard Blystone. We stood on a highly polished white marble floor, and all of his lieutenants and sublieutenants were scurrying about in this immaculate mansion. Then we heard the screeching wheels of cars, and I looked through some curtains and saw three or four olive-drab Mercedes Benzes drive up, and he got out and walked up. When he entered the hallway, you could hear the clicking of heels, and as you looked into the eyes of this man's top advisers, you knew that he commanded total respect, and—in some instances, as we know—respect on pain of death. As I say, I have not been that pensive since.

Ladies and gentlemen, I come to you at the invitation of one of the finest universities to grace this land.

I come to you as a fellow-Midwesterner—just two states away—an Illinoisan who is fond of simplicity and directness, two of many characteristics you Kansans appreciate.

I come to you as a fellow American, proud that our nation—once again—has changed presidential leadership without one mortal shot fired in the process and relieved that a numbingly too-long campaign is over!

There were two surprises in this election: Bob Dole was reelected, and Kansas voted Republican!

You know, in capitals around the world, leaders and their advisers are squirming. Most were pulling for our incumbent president. Had you polled them after the euphoric Desert Storm victory in the Gulf War when George Bush was riding an 80 percent-plus popularity wave, those leaders would have said Bush was a reelection certainty. But as our electoral marathon for the White House unfolded and as candidates dwindled, so did the certitude in world capitals about who would be raising his hand to take the oath of office on January 20, 1993.

Overseas observers seem to forget that Americans are utterly serious about choosing a president, that they are capable of surprising holders of the smart money, that Americans are capable of electing a general, a peanut farmer, an actor, a haberdasher, and a governor from Arkansas.

Generally, as a people, we have been blessed to have had solid performances from the forty-one presidents in our nation's history.

> *SPEECH TIP:* One of the greatest challenges a speaker can set for himself is to create a colorful *extended metaphor.* It is to the speechmaker what the triple axel is to the figure skater: a dazzling and memorable move—if you can pull it off.

Democracy is not a smooth sauce.
Democracy is a chili of different currents, changes, and contradictions.
Democracy is the lone dish in constant need of seasoning, stirring, and tasting.
Democracy is never, never done.

The United States of America were not always united. We were not and will never be a nation of one race, one religion, or one tongue. Some think, indeed some say, if only we had the homogeneity of the Japanese, the Chinese, the Germans, the British, we would not be bothered by problems which slow us down. That cannot be because that is not our history.

Our richness is directly because of what we are: many forming one. Our nation's greatness is its potential to become greater. Each of us is an instrument for change.

Most of us want to awaken one morning in our lifetime, to say, for example, our long racial nightmare is over, our fire in the night has been put out. But as we begin streaming by the millions into cinemas to see the movie *Malcolm X*, as we wonder when and where will the next Los Angeles explode in deadly fury, as we struggle to dissolve with reason and understanding racial and ethnic stereotypes, we know the next generation will receive from us the state of the nation as we leave it for them.

If you, an American, fear for your country; if you, an American, agonize over our faults and fissures, remember this: no other nation—no other nation on the face of this earth—is struggling to do what we as a people profess to believe in and have undertaken to make reality. No other nation.

"You ought to believe something in life . . . believe that thing so fervently that you will stand up with it till the end of your days." Dr. Martin Luther King, Jr., said those words.

Alfred M. Landon believed and acted out those words. Landon. King. Two Americans who made their lives instruments for change. What they felt, the many causes they fought, held this nation's and this world's interest and attention. We, all of us, are the beneficiaries of their legacy. It is regrettable that we sometimes take for granted what two of our finest sons did unselfishly to make life better for all.

But, you know, globally, we Americans have been selfless to a fault. Japan's and Europe's ashes of war became our challenge to help rebuild with billions of dollars in massive aid and assistance. Some argue we did the job too well. Today the playing field is not level. Europe is acquiring economic and trading muscle that cannot be ignored, and Japan's proficiency in the international marketplace is legendary.

For decades, we helped the world community while paint was peeling off our walls back home. We have sent lifesaving care and medicines abroad, knowing full well that our own people in urban and rural communities were and are in need.

World events whipsawed our leaders in Washington. First things first: our collective defense of ourselves and our allies had priority.

Communism's demise has been the most expensive death in the political history of mankind. Our federal treasury bears the bruises of this long, worthwhile fight.

Our national debt, our federal budget deficits are the shrapnel of battle. Those world leaders and their advisers worry because, regardless of the language they speak, they understand clearly what the American people said when they voted on November 3rd: instead of fixing the world's problems, fix our problems now.

In those capitals, they do not know what to expect from us now. They do not know what to expect from the new 103rd Congress when it is sworn in. They do not know what to expect from the forty-second President of the United States of America. And because of that, human beings fall tentative in the face of the unknown. And, yes, even some of our international friends lapse into taking us for granted sometimes. And yet, back home, those same Americans, those same voters know their nation's role is too pivotal to tolerate withdrawal symptoms, too crucial to relax vigilance. They know that United States leadership is costly, but they are demanding and expecting action here on the home front.

Ironic, isn't it? Ironic that the relatively peaceful and prosperous corridors we helped carve out around the world are now the very gauntlets along which we must compete for jobs and market share. Ironic.

But we as a people know what is happening. The alarms have long since sounded. We are mobilizing. Our schools must be and are becoming better. Our production lines are leaner and more efficient. Everyone, everyone hearing my voice knows that competition is global.

SPEECH TIP: To make a moral point, say something to make your listeners view their old familiar world in a brand new way.

But, ladies and gentlemen, we in this great country are not putting on the field all our players, nor are all those players being rewarded fairly, and that is what I really have come to speak to you about this morning. We cannot win this fight if we do not change our attitude about women in our nation.

SPEECH TIP: Here is another metaphor. Thoughtful listeners will realize that, if democracy is a "sauce," the one ingredient with which it is incompatible is "poison."

Sexism is a poison we have been drinking far too long. Twenty-two months ago, the United States led twenty-seven other nations in the Gulf War. Erase the hot exchange of words, put aside Saddam Hussein, and you see why that war was fought. The Gulf War was about a resource precious and essential to the industrialized world: black gold, oil. Ponder this, if you will. In the fullness of time, everyone in this auditorium will be dead. Everyone listening to my voice will be dead. Everyone looking at my face will be dead. Now just ponder this.

To learn about us, people will either read or they will watch hours of video images. "They fought a war to protect a valuable resource," some will conclude. But some, some looking more closely at how our society functioned, looking more critically at our society, some will say, "But why, why weren't those Americans as fierce and as passionate about their greatest resource—their people?" Especially why, why did they abuse women in principle and in fact? Why?

In a letter to her husband John, Abigail Adams wrote, "If particular care and attention are not paid to the ladies, we are determined to foment a rebellion and will not hold ourselves bound by any laws in which we have no voice or representation." She wrote that more than one hundred years ago.

In Washington, before election night, November 3rd, Mrs. Quentin Burdick of North Dakota, Barbara Mikulski of Maryland, and Nancy Kassebaum of Kansas were surrounded in one of the most exclusive male-oriented clubs in this country. Now they have company: from Illinois, from Washington State, and from California. Regardless of your opinion of how the all-male members of the Senate Judiciary Committee comported themselves in the confirmation hearings of Supreme Court Justice Clarence Thomas last fall, the manner in which law professor Anita Hill was questioned and treated had a profoundly catalytic and, yes, explosive impact on American politics and American women. This nation will never be the same.

More than one Senate candidate said she was outraged by the tough and rude handling of Professor Hill and what she was insisting happened. Resonating throughout this election campaign was and is one undeniable truth: most American men possess in their psyches a winking double standard for the charge, the complaint of sexual harassment.

Reminder: in the 1988 presidential election, women outvoted men by nearly six million, or by almost 20 percent. Ladies and gentlemen, women now constitute nearly 50 percent of the United States work force. Yet, where they work full-time, women barely earn an average of 75 cents of the dollar taken home by their male coworkers. Why? Ask yourself, why does this exist? Why does this persist?

And then, there is the stench of discrimination in promotions along executive row, described by one of the most odorous euphemisms ever thought up: "the glass ceiling." Promotion. Pay. What do you think of these words from Dr. Fran Conley? She is a neurologist at Stanford University. "I have been told over the years I do not need to be paid as much because I am a woman, because I am married. *They* are married," she said.

Women are fighting this poison in our work place on all fronts, enduring the frustration of proving job discrimination, of proving sexual harassment and abuse, of resisting the dumping ground for female managers, and women in the military have it especially hard because of the military command structure. Talk about barriers to the top.

The Center for Creative Leadership says on an average nine out of ten female managers are pushed into staff jobs such as human resources and public relations—positions that do not lead to the top of corporate America. If people are not given work experiences to broaden themselves, how can they ever get the opportunity to be more responsible?

Presently, fewer than 6 percent of all the top executives in the United States of America are female. This problem, this crisis, this scandal is exacerbated by a natural human tendency: to surround yourself with people like you. [Former] Labor Secretary Lynn Martin says, "If the person at the top is male and white, invariably he picks people around him who are just like him." And as this happens each day in our cities, each day in our counties, and each day in our states, each day we as a nation suffer. And when this great nation suffers, we lose another step in competition because we are failing to use fully our most precious talent and resource—our own people.

Federal, state, and local laws are there. But laws are given life and force by people and companies and universities willfully looking after their best interests, and, fortunately, that is happening. But it is happening too slowly. Some companies and some executives are acting with conscience to change the way the work place and society treat women. Some. Not a majority.

SPEECH TIP: Find a way to make your issue intensely and immediately relevant to your audience. Find a way to bring it home to them.

Folks, we are talking about our very existence, our survival as a competing nation, a nation whose greatness is its ability to become greater. But the hour is late. I have discussed very briefly matters of money, position, and wealth, but what of the essence of life and health?

Did you know that heart disease is the number-one killer of American women? Sixty-one percent of the people dying from strokes are women. According to studies, heart disease many times goes undetected in women until it is virtually too late.

The [former] director of the National Institutes of Health, Dr. Bernadine Healy, says, "As a result, 49 percent of women suffering from heart attacks die within one year, compared with 31 percent of men."

One reason for this gap is that, over the years, billions more research dollars have gone into studying heart disease among men than women, especially women over sixty-five. That is a damned outrage!

Women outlive men, and they have their heart attacks later than men. My point in all this is simple. We must change. We must change now. Our attitudes must change in some most basic of ways, most elementary of ways. For example: My boss is Ted Turner. When we are together, I do not greet him by saying, "Hi, Ted honey" or "darling" or "sweetie." And I do not have a compulsion to get physically close to Ted, so that I can put my arm around his waist. If I do not do that with him or with other males with whom I work, what makes me think I should be able to do that to a person just because she is a woman? We must stop subjecting women to subtle and blatant abuses we men would never, *ever* tolerate.

I will recognize the instant that time arrives especially in the business I know—television news. This point: there are men over age fifty on television reporting news. They are wrinkled. They are gray. And they have this appearance of being very experienced because of their wrinkles and because of their gray.

It is time for television and our nation, in general, to stop this deluding fixation, this silliness, this preoccupation with youth. It is time to respect the right of women, especially in television news, but in other professions. It is time to respect the right of women in television to wrinkle and to gray on the job.

Ladies and gentlemen, we must change so that those who study what we did in this time, in our lifetime, we must change so that those who study what we did correctly conclude that our society matured and our society affirmed that a woman does not have to out-man a man to be respected and respectable.

Those were thoughts I wanted to share with you this morning, and I thank you for inviting me.

CHAPTER 11

Minority Viewpoints

When the Civil Rights movement got into full swing in North America during the 1960s, the theme of ethnic and racial minorities in business was principally focused on injustice and inequity, and even addressing outrage. Today, by no means has all injustice and inequity been eliminated, and, it is true, there is still outrage, but the emphasis, at least in business, has shifted from righting a wrong—repairing a serious flaw in the system—to learning how to capitalize on and celebrate ethnic and racial diversity. Just as the image of personnel in general has shifted from a mass of employees to be controlled to human resources to be cultivated and developed, so the issues associated with ethnic and racial minorities have shifted from topics of legality, mandated quotas, corporate conscience-soothing, and downright appeasement to a corporate realization that an ethnically and racially diverse work force is not only morally *right*—plain and simple—but very good business, even essential to staying *in* business in today's highly diverse marketplaces.

The editors of *The Business Speaker's Almanac* do not advocate sugarcoating and whitewashing. We have read and reviewed enough speeches to conclude that neither the business community nor the community at large will tolerate such an approach.

However, the strident, narrow approach that exclusively hammers away at the injustices and inequities that persist in business is also likely to be met with at least as much resistance and resentment as meaningful attention.

What's wrong with that when you're telling the truth?

We'll answer bluntly: It may be more self-indulgent than genuinely productive.

Business audiences are naturally more receptive to opportunities for positive investment than liabilities to be avoided. Let's face it, the prospect of minority issues sets off alarm bells in the heads of many managers. Why not surprise them with the *good* news: ethnic and racial diversity is good business, *profitable* business that happens also to benefit the community.

Diversity:
The Key to Quality Business

JOHN E. CLEGHORN
President and Chief Operating Officer
Royal Bank of Canada

Delivered to the Alberta Multiculturalism Commission, Calgary, Alberta, November 19, 1992

SUMMARY: A bank president discusses the power and potential of ethnic, racial, cultural, and other diversity in the corporate work place.

When I started thinking about this evening, I was reminded that John Diefenbaker compared Canada to a garden, ". . . a garden into which has been transplanted the hardiest and brightest flowers from many lands, each retaining in its new environment the best of the qualities for which it was loved and prized in its native land." It is this diversity that makes our country unique among the nations of the world. We are more than an extended family—with all the benefits and disadvantages that implies. And, as we have seen in the past few weeks, our many and varied members are struggling to retain their individuality; they are frustrated and angry by the differences; and consequently, we are all wondering whether the ties that bind us together are strong enough to hold.

SPEECH TIP: It is not always a good idea to begin with a quotation, but Cleghorn introduces this one skilfully, and he has chosen it carefully to provide a vivid word picture that enlivens an abstract concept.

We have a gloriously fertile and varied environment: forests, fields, lakes, and mountains. I don't have to remind Albertans what a great gift nature has given us. In every direction you look, it's there.

Our first nation's peoples, who knew this great land for millenniums before we arrived, long respected the strength of its diversity. Their concept of guardianship of nature, rather than ownership, underlines the importance they give to its role in our ongoing evolution.

To this rich terrain of ours have come an equally rich variety of people from all over the world to make their home. Forget our recent difficulties for the moment; Canada has utilized its diversity in both topography and population with remarkable success. Somehow, and not without challenge and adversity, the Canadian model of peace, order, and good government has led to an evolving society in which the best and the brightest from all over the world can flourish. Between us, we have made Canada the most desirable nation to live in, which as you all know, was confirmed by the United Nations in the past year.

SPEECH TIP: Signal the next stage of your argument clearly and unmistakably with the simple "But . . . if " formula.

But we risk losing this enviable position if we cannot continue to capitalize on our diversity; if we do not do a better job of living side by side, accepting, respecting, and valuing our differences so that we use them as building blocks instead of impediments. Right now, the focus is on the difficulties. The "no" vote in the referendum was in part a reflection of the failure to reconcile the split between those who think equality means sameness and those who believe that in diversity there is strength. What was missed, it seems to me, are the positive aspects of our differences. Our future success as a nation depends on us harnessing the richness of diversity within this country of ours to make ourselves truly competitive in the global marketplace.

The ability of our economy to face this challenge depends on several underlying characteristics: our public policies, our educational institutions, our infrastructure—and our work force.

As Harvard's Michael Porter pointed out in his study on Canadian competitiveness last year, Canadians have traditionally enjoyed a relatively insulated environment with protected markets and paternalistic government policies. Many people agree with Professor Porter that these can no longer sustain us in a world of increasing globalization, accelerating technological changes, and rapidly evolving company and country strategies.

These forces demand a changed approach to the new diversity in the population. In most countries, the traditional approach has been assimilation. Newcomers were expected to adapt so that they "fit." If you immigrated to the States, you became hellbent on becoming "American." The same existed in Australia, where until very recently the numerous Greek, Italian, and British immigrants learned quickly that "Australian" was the only way.

Indeed, historically, it might be said that that was the original Canadian approach to our immigrants. But, for whatever reason, immigrants to this country have retained their cultural differences. And, of course, in more recent years our federal policy of multiculturalism has had a strengthening hand.

Multiculturalism has been fostered for primarily societal reasons. Yet it is critical also to business. In the past, within the corporate world as with countries, assimilation was the accepted norm. Companies and their managers insisted that people who were different must themselves bear the brunt of adjusting. It was as if they said, "This is our corporate mold, adapt yourselves to fit." You became an oilman—or even a banker. You wore the particular uniform of hard hat or pin stripe. You lived in the right neighborhood. You drove the right car. You learned the jargon.

It seemed reasonable, sensible, natural. The culture of a company had evolved over the years in response to the realities of business, and employees were expected to conform. Assimilation into the culture is what ensured unity and common purpose; without it, there would be chaos.

Or so they thought.

And employees bought into this idea: to conform meant to succeed. Ethnic and gender identity—and even unique personality—had to be dropped at the company door.

But the homogeneous work force is history. And the days ahead promise even more diversity than we're seeing now.

Demographic shifts are altering our work force in many ways. They're bringing in more women, more partners in two-income families, more employees who are caring for children or elderly parents, more physically disadvantaged workers, and increasingly now, more older workers.

Add to this the growing racial, ethnic, and cultural diversity in our communities, and you begin to view the emerging picture of the Canadian work force. And among all of these people, there is a new consciousness. This is the age of the individual. People are less willing to be assimilated, even if it's only for the working part of their day. As leading U.S. diversity expert Roosevelt Thomas Jr., puts it, prospective employees are saying: "I'm different, and proud of what makes me so. I can help your team, and I would like to join you, but only if I can do so without compromising my uniqueness."

This reluctance to change is true for the new ethnic minority employees who see their predecessors who "fitted in" to have lost some of their identity. It's true for new women employees, it's true for young workers, it's true for highly educated professionals. All of them, in their own way, are saying: "Don't assimilate me. Don't dilute my strengths."

More than twenty-five years ago Marshall McLuhan told us that television had transformed the world into a "global village." If he were alive today, I'm sure he would be astonished to see how Canada has become a global village in microcosm.

That is why this conference is so important. As a percentage of our total population, visible minorities are projected to increase from 10 percent last year to 18 percent in the year 2001. But that 18 percent will have a per capita Gross Domestic Product 8 percent higher than the rest of the population.

Furthermore, current estimates are that by 2001 visible minorities will be half the population of Toronto and 40 percent of the population of Vancouver. From 20 to 25 percent of the populations of Montreal, Winnipeg, Windsor—and yes, Calgary and Edmonton—will be visible minorities.

SPEECH TIP: Give voice to opposing views honestly and straightforwardly. Use logical argument and factual evidence, not name-calling or mockery, to oppose these views.

Some people think multiculturalism is a real problem. To them, multiculturalism is a threat. In fact, it is one of the greatest competitive advantages we could have. Quite simply, multiculturalism is the internal globalization of Canada. And it will be one of the key factors contributing to our ability, to our sense of confidence that we can succeed in the global economy of the future.

Companies that have recognized the benefits of diversity have long ago come to the conclusion that reflecting the new reality in their work force is not simply "the nice thing to do." They've gone way beyond "nice." Diversity is a fact of the marketplace.

It starts with hiring. Smart recruiters today seek people who represent the markets to which they sell. And they're finding some significant and unique talent that in the past was often overlooked. Moreover, companies are learning that it is sound business logic to keep these people.

Hiring and developing new people is expensive. Studies show that organizations spend anywhere from $30,000 to $60,000 to recruit a university graduate. Once hired, they are immediately trained, which can take anywhere from a few days to several months. Add it all up, and within the first year you may have spent up to $100,000 to recruit, train, and compensate a new employee. Losing ten of these people means a million-dollar impact on your bottom line.

To attract and retain quality people requires a quality work place. In a work environment where diversity is not regarded as a benefit, sexual, racial and other forms of harassment fester. Studies estimate that Fortune 500 companies in the States lose five to ten million dollars a year due to harassment.

To market goods and services today requires an understanding of the values inherent in society now.

The challenge for all business is to take a good long look in the mirror and see reflected the image of the society it serves.

> *SPEECH TIP:* Remember, your audience is always asking itself: *How will all this benefit me?* Be sure to give them the answer.

Japanese car producers recognized this. When they started up manufacturing operations in North America, they quickly learned not to impose all their work practices on their employees here. And they began having vehicles designed in California, their leading market on this continent. In fact, they've gone even one step further. Honda station wagons and Toyota convertibles, designed and built in the U.S. by Americans, are exported to Japan.

The Japanese learned to produce better products and services at reduced costs and gave birth to the quality movement in the '50s, which is now regarded as the life raft of North American business. What quality boils down to for a corporation is continued improvement through streamlined processes, teamwork, and individual employee empowerment and motivation combining to meet real-life customer needs better than ever before.

The quality challenge is to do things differently, find new approaches. This happens when employees feel that they have a voice in their company, when they know that their ideas are valued, when they are confident that they are truly part of the team, no matter who they are or what their background.

Without diversity of thought, without employees feeling esteemed and valued for their individuality and uniqueness, companies can spend millions on quality efforts to little or no avail. It is *valuing differences*, increasing *communication in teams*, and *individual empowerment* that help build a quality environment.

The important thing for business to understand is that diversity includes everyone: It is not something that is defined by race or gender. It encompasses age, background, education, and personality. It includes lifestyle, physical challenge, and geographic origin. It even includes, if I may say so, that popular Canadian pejorative phrase, "white men in suits." In my experience, they are as diverse as their colleagues. So a commitment to managing diversity is a commitment to all employees. There's nothing exclusionary about it.

At Royal Bank, our employment equity thrust of the '70s and '80s has expanded to embrace the broader understanding of diversity of the past few years. We've recognized that diversity is the way to do business. It affects the products we develop, the way we serve our customers, the way we advertise, the people we employ and the support we provide the community through donations, sponsorships and employee involvement.

Serving the diverse clients we have across Canada and around the world means having a work force that represents our markets. With the projected labor shortage in the latter part of this decade, and the growing diversity of Canada's population, we can't move quickly enough. This means speaking different languages to our clients, understanding their different values, respecting different traditions.

Only by doing this can our staff reach their potential in fulfilling the objectives of the bank by capitalizing on their differences as well as their similarities.

Our challenge is to develop a financial institution that really respects everybody on an equal basis and offers opportunity on an equal basis. We're aware that we're considered a leader as an employer. We believe we have sound diversity programs in place that should build the increased representation we need, but we still have a long way to go to achieve the kind of diversity we view as ideal.

From what I see as I travel across the country, there's goodwill and good intentions at every level of the bank. But we still have cultural barriers to break through. In the context of employment equity, we're continuing to work with designated groups during this slow economic period, but we're not hiring the numbers of new employees we used to. This doesn't help us quickly increase our numbers of Native employees, or people who are physically challenged, both of which fall short of where we would like them to be. While we are certainly making progress, we need to accelerate our programs to bring women and visible minorities into executive positions.

> **SPEECH TIP:** Your audience is also thinking, *Talk is cheap. Can this guy deliver?* Support your assertions with real-life examples and hard evidence. Demonstrate commitment.

In 1991, we made a commitment to the Canadian Human Rights Commission. We set ourselves a three-year timetable to increase the numbers of our women executives by 50 percent, visible minority executives by almost 100 percent, and to emphasize the hiring and promotion of Native peoples based on their skills and qualifications. We also expect to reach a similar agreement on the status of people with disabilities.

We have accepted this challenge because we believe that the best performers in the long run are those companies with adaptive cultures—cultures that accommodate and encourage constructive change consistent with the changes taking place in the market and in society at large. The adaptive culture can be identified by managers at all levels initiating change whenever necessary to satisfy the legitimate interests not just of customers, or stockholders, or employees, but all three of these key constituencies.

We've made managers accountable for success in diversity. We've done a lot about the raising of awareness. I'd like to be able to say that we've eliminated discrimination and narrow thinking totally. But in an organization as large as ours, unfortunately, we still have some. We've got to work harder to educate our managers.

That it is both important and productive to do so becomes obvious when I visit units like our Toronto Operations Centre. The 250-person staff, 90 percent of whom are women, 45 percent visible minorities, speak forty languages and dialects. That's a very different picture from twenty years ago, and it's one that's paying dividends. Some of our best ideas for change are coming from people from different countries, who have experienced totally different processes.

We have heard a great deal in recent months, specifically in the U.S. presidential election, about family values. North American society is often criticized for the breakdown of the extended family. But, in Native culture, the extended family still exists. If a family member calls for help, if there is a ceremonial or traditional obligation because of birth, death, or illness, traditionally, nothing should stand in the way of that obligation. All other obligations become secondary.

Understanding these different values has helped us in establishing our branch on the Six Nations Reserve near Brantford, Ontario, where our business is increasing significantly as a result of Native clients being served by our predominantly Native staff, enhancing the understanding and trust of the client-banker relationship.

Across the country, our Asian Banking Centres have been set up to respond to a specific market need. There, we have come to a new comprehension that architecture, interior design, and traditional beliefs are just as important as language in providing the quality of service that our customers have a right to expect. When we opened our Asian Banking Centre in Vancouver a few years ago, we had what is known as a *fung shey* specialist help plan the orientation of the premises to ensure they conformed to the Chinese ideals of harmony with the natural elements in nature.

But one thing was overlooked. We made a mistake when we installed the lighting. The lights had a strong blue tinge, a color the Chinese associate with death. It made both customers and staff feel very uncomfortable indeed.

We changed the lights.

Persons with disabilities are constantly battling our assumptions and our stereotypes. Their biggest barrier by far is society's attitudes toward them. All they ask is a chance to be seen as a person with abilities, an individual who can contribute. And when you think about it, that is what we are all looking for.

We seek the help of wheelchair users in making our branches more accessible for staff as well as for customers. We borrow a wheelchair so that we can discover for ourselves what the difficulties can be. This has helped us understand that even little things can be important when hiring a teller who uses an electric wheelchair, such as placing the chair closer to the cash dispensing unit, so that the batteries on it will not wear out by the end of the day from traveling back and forth to the counter.

For people with hearing loss, accessibility has a different meaning. Barriers are removed by interpreters or by co-workers who learn sign language.

There's still a lot to learn, a lot of progress yet to be made. For women, the issue continues to be, "Are they being promoted fast enough to middle and senior management?" For many, the answer is, "No." We are making progress, and, because of our promote-from-within policy, it is just a matter of time before we achieve our goal of true equity.

Our goal is to be representative of the communities we serve—in other words, to represent Canadian society as it is and as it is evolving. And that includes every branch in every province, our regional offices, and our Head Office.

What skills are we looking for in our people to manage diversity? There are certain basic characteristics, which include an openness to other cultures and experiences.

We want our managers to realize there is more than one way to approach a situation. We want them to be flexible, so that they can be open to challenge and to the expression of other viewpoints. They should not feel that their leadership is questioned or threatened by the process. They should understand that there is great value in building on differences, as well as continuing to affirm our similarities.

Sensitivity to other cultures and experiences allows our managers to see and feel what it is like for various members of their team. Respect for others and for their individual differences allows managers to respond constructively and to appreciate and nurture the uniqueness of each one of us.

Ninety years ago, one of our great prime ministers, Sir Wilfrid Laurier, visited a cathedral in England. It was made of granite, oak, and marble. When he returned to Canada, he said, "That is the image of the nation I wish Canada to become. For here, I want the granite to remain granite, the oak to remain the oak, the marble to remain the marble. Out of these elements I would build a nation great among the nations of the world."

We have come a long way to fulfill that image. Our different linguistic, cultural, and regional backgrounds constitute our greatest strength. Our challenge is to harness all the elements of our diversity to maintain and enhance the quality of life that we all cherish so much.

Thank you.

Securing the African-American Future:
A Challenge for Today and Tomorrow

VIRGIS COLBERT
Vice President, Operations
Miller Brewing Company

*Delivered to the Omega Psi Phi Fraternity Anniversary, Milwaukee, Wisconsin,
November 13, 1992*

*SUMMARY: Brewing company executive Virgis Colbert enumerates some of the
major difficulties facing contemporary African-American communities, and he
urges fellow Omega Psi Phi Fraternity members to participate in overcoming
today's dilemmas in order to help secure a better future for Milwaukee residents—
and all African-Americans—tomorrow.*

Good evening, my Omega Brothers, other members of the dais, and ladies and gentlemen. As a "Q" (member of Omega Psi Phi), I am indeed honored to have been
invited to speak at our 81st anniversary dinner.

As I thought about the theme of our celebration—"What We Must Do to
Secure Our Future"—I reflected on the achievements of our founders, Ernest E. Just,
Edgar A. Love, Frank Coleman, and Oscar J. Cooper.

Brother Just, who was the faculty advisor to the group at Howard University
in 1911, was a renowned biologist who practiced his profession as a scientist even
though shackled by racism and stunted opportunity. Irrespective of these handi-
caps, he mentored scientists and black physicians, and he provided the primary
leadership to the founding of this great fraternity—Omega Psi Phi. Brother Just
decided early on that he would work to enhance and secure the future of African-
Americans through service to his profession and to his community.

SPEECH TIP: Having begun with an inspirational example, Colbert announces and focuses the theme of his speech.

I would like to take a few moments to share some personal thoughts on how
we can secure the African-American future. However, success will come only if
each of us rises to the challenges that face us.

African-American communities today are going through an extremely difficult
period of adjustment to a rapidly changing local, national, and global economy. Our
people are regularly assaulted by social and economic factors that make it difficult
to finish school, to build strong families, or to simply survive. These factors are

especially severe in our urban areas, where most African-Americans reside, and are especially acute for many blacks here in Milwaukee.

My perspective on these issues has been formed from observations during my travels across the country, from my volunteer work with community-based organizations, and from my own experience as an African-American male.

> *SPEECH TIP:* It is often useful to establish your authority early in the speech. Do so clearly and unambiguously.

While the black middle class has admittedly doubled over the past quarter century, the social, economic, and occupational opportunities of most blacks have worsened. We not only continue to lag behind whites in these categories, but even more disturbing is the expanding gulf between the have's and the have-not's in our black community.

As an eternal optimist, I believe that organizations like Omega Psi Phi Fraternity, with its coalition of motivated, strong and dedicated African-American males will be key in helping black Americans overcome the social and economic barriers in positive and productive ways. After all, what African-American citizens *need today* are expanding opportunity structures, assistance in making positive life decisions, greater access to successful role models, and social and economic support. Omega Psi Phi's creed: "Scholarship, Perseverance, and Uplift" is indeed what African-Americans *need.*

> *SPEECH TIP:* Nothing rings more hollow than an inspirational speech that fails to face facts. Colbert faces facts, squarely but without hysteria.

Unfortunately, an overwhelming problem being faced by African-Americans today is a deeply held and growing sense of hopelessness. Many believe that they cannot succeed as individuals, as students, or as family members. Many feel they have no chance to make it today or tomorrow. And many believe that they have no control over, or input into, the factors that will determine the outcome of their lives. And unfortunately, even a casual examination of urban black communities anywhere in this nation appears to provide a firm basis for this pervasive lack of hope.

In Milwaukee, we have a socially and geographically distinct black community. It is largely located on the north side of the city. In these neighborhoods, blacks comprise the majority of all residents. The city's highest proportion of black residents under eighteen years of age live in this area—the youth of the city. More than a third of all black families in these neighborhoods are headed by females—the highest concentration in the city. But even more troubling is the fact that many, if not most, of these female-headed households are engulfed by poverty. Unemployment in this area is more than double that found elsewhere in Milwaukee, and for black males, the unemployment rate is dismal.

Even though the U.S. Department of Labor has defined an income of *$20,000* as the amount needed to adequately support an urban family of four, and though the families I am talking about are typically larger than four people, only a modest number of them have a median income above *$11,000* per year.

Finally, adult educational levels, as measured by high school graduation, are among the lowest in the city. And when one examines the educational skills of many of those who have graduated, the picture is even more dismal. Collectively, these stark realities narrow aspiration and opportunities, and reinforce that empty, hollow feeling called "hopelessness."

Meanwhile, at the societal level, we seem to have lost our moral compass. The new lifestyles that have evolved have pushed aside many of the traditional rules of personal conduct. They encourage greater tolerance, permit more sexual freedom, and place less emphasis on those nurturing structures that guided society in the past. And our youth—especially our males—are being pushed, or rather thrown into being adults, often without having been nurtured or allowed to experience the joys of childhood. Society appears to single them out for punishment as early as the fourth grade, when many become alienated from public education. Unfortunately, very few of us in the black community are attentive enough to the social and cultural needs of our young black males.

These societal changes have created huge dislocations in our lives and in the lives of black youth and adults.

- Ralph Bunche and Martin Luther King have been replaced as role models by neighborhood drug dealers. In many instances, our youth do not even know who they were and what they did.

- The Boy Scouts, the Girl Scouts, the YM and YWCAs and other youth agencies have been upstaged by the youth gangs in our community.

- And many black professionals, who previously united to foster programs for black community benefit through institutions such as the Omega Psi Phi Fraternity, now too frequently direct their primary energies toward personal fulfillment and enjoying the good life, at the expense of the urgent needs of their less fortunate brothers and sisters.

Given the larger society's move toward selfishness and greed, many African-Americans have been left to fend for themselves in an environment characterized by unemployment, racism, and loss of hope. This situation has been especially devastating for black males.

Young black men in the nation's inner cities are drifting and receive no help in building constructive lives, in respecting authority or themselves, in being honest, in being fair, or in looking toward the future. Many are without the moral compass provided by an ethical code of personal conduct. For instance:

- Nationwide, blacks comprise approximately *50 percent* of all males in state juvenile and adult correctional institutions.

- In Wisconsin, young black males under age eighteen are entering Wales (a juvenile correctional facility) faster than they are graduating from high school, and

- There are more than four times as many black males over age eighteen in Wisconsin's prisons as there are in the entire University of Wisconsin system.

- The overall homicide rate for black males is 60 per 100,000—higher than that of white males, white females, and black females combined! Moreover, a black male homicide victim is most likely to be killed by another black male.

> *SPEECH TIP:* After defining the problems, Colbert proposes solutions. Note that, as Colbert used a list format to enumerate the problems, he uses a list format to enumerate possible solutions.

The list could go on and on. But clearly, something must be done to secure their future, which is after all, *our* future! As Brother Langston Hughes so eloquently stated:

> Life for (us) ain't been no crystal stair.
> It's had tacks in it, and splinters
> and boards torn up, and places with no
> carpets on the floors . . .
> But all the time
> (we've) been climbin(g) on,
> and turnin(g) corners
> and sometimes going in the dark . . .
> and life for (us) ain't been no
> crystal stair.

We . . . all of us *African-Americans* . . . must take the responsibility for being role models for our children, our next generation. If we do *not*, our very existence in America may be threatened. We must save our youth! If we don't, who will? And black professional organizations, fraternities, and sororities are in a position to take the lead—and we must do so.

Black youth in dysfunctional families need to be exposed to honest, stable, upright and moral black men and women. But our male youth, in particular, must know and have contact with positive black males!

- They need to know black men who do not father children they cannot support.

- They need to know black men who do not exploit or physically abuse women.

- They need to know black men who do not kill other blacks for trivial or no reasons.

- They need to know black men who *cure*, black men who will *share*, and black men who *adhere* to a moral code.

SPEECH TIP: The most successful speakers never fail to remember that *they*—not someone else—were asked to speak; therefore, they present their personal experiences in a way that illuminates the subject at hand.

Growing up in Ohio, I knew such men and women in my neighborhood who worked long hours to support their families. Men and women who nurtured and disciplined their children, as well as their neighbors' children. Men and women who faced racism at every corner, yet had hope and courage to push and pull their children to take advantage of every opportunity, no matter how small, and wait to aggressively take advantage of the next opportunity.

My father, Quillie Colbert, was such a person. He worked all day and many nights throughout my childhood. On Saturdays I rode beside him in his old Chevy truck. We picked up junk and sold it to salvage yards. My dad was my real, live role model. His job didn't stop at work, and it didn't stop with me and my three brothers and four sisters. My dad was also a nurturer and a disciplinarian for my cousins and neighborhood pals. He motivated me as a student, nurtured me as a son, and provided for me and our family. And on Sunday, my mother—the other half of the team—scrubbed and greased us, and we all sat together as a family in church. And on Monday, we went to school—no excuses.

Black men and black women, in partnership, were not all college graduates, but they were the bedrock of our communities because they cared and had hope for a better tomorrow. They set the standards of conduct and aspirations for the next generation.

Blacks in Milwaukee, and across the country, have an awesome responsibility. They must keep their own lives on an even keel, and they must extend themselves to the troubled adults and youth in their midst. They must plug the leaks in the social fabric of the black community because it *is* a black thing—*only blacks can save blacks!*

Now we move to the more difficult part of the problem facing African-Americans—the causes! Many people, both black and sympathetic whites, believe the cuts in the various social programs are a thinly disguised expression of racism. While *overt* as well *as covert* racism *is* a problem, there are others. Five stand out.

1. Poverty, in generation after generation of many black families, has been fueled by a welfare system that fosters dependency—economically, psychologically, and culturally.

2. The economic gap within the black community is widening. The bottom two-fifths of blacks are poorer in 1992 than they were in 1967 in constant dollars.

3. The widening economic gap is causing an increasing lack of unity and mutual concern in the black community.

4. There is a decline in the work ethic among many blacks as a result of an increase in hopelessness; and finally, there is

5. A lack of positive black role models.

These internal community factors must be addressed irrespective of racism. Black people can and must deal with the problems. Many are within our control. We must not charge them solely to racism! The real problem for black people is not just the existence of racism, but how we cope with racism.

> *SPEECH TIP:* Building on the examples cited from his own experience, Colbert proposes an idea some might resist. In doing so, he empowers his audience.

The resolution must start at home. We must critically examine and improve our schools, homes, and personal environments. And we must:

- Teach our youth right from wrong. Teach them to say "no" to drugs and illegal fast rewards.
- Encourage them to delay parenthood.
- Preach that education is the key to economic viability.
- Proactively demand better public education.
- Embrace and pass on our rich Afro-centric heritage.
- Join in pooling resources of black organizations.
- And finally, use an informed and cohesive voting bloc to demand change for the least of us.

At the financial level, we must contribute more: When the top two-fifths of black Americans are earning an increasing share of total black income, we must therefore do more for our less fortunate black brothers and sisters!

At the policy level, we must come to grips with the fact that although the problems of blacks have been historically defined in the "*streets*," the solutions are being framed in the "*suites*"—of corporate institutions, public bureaucracies and voluntary agencies. Therefore, we must make certain that we are active in policy formation *and* implementation. We have to make it a point to be informed and attend those meetings where resources and programs are developed and distributed. We must demand jobs for our people, and we must demand the resources to create jobs for ourselves. Here, the investment is one of time!

To quote Frederick Douglas: "Men may not get all they pay for in this world, but they certainly pay for all that they get." In many instances, the payment must be a commitment of time.

I commend my brothers of Omega Psi Phi Fraternity; you have been engaged in a noble initiative of human development. With your leadership in promoting manhood, scholarship, perseverance, and uplift, black people will expand their horizons and increase their life options, and become stable family members who are employed in a productive manner in our society. Our changing society has presented African-Americans with barriers that have inhibited their advancement, but an organization such as Omega Psi Phi can aid them in overcoming these barriers.

As I reflect upon my youth, I remember a time when the African-American community was stronger. I do not mean to criticize today's black community, but I remember when black people united and regularly overcame adversity. There was a period in our recent history when African-Americans came together to solve problems in their community.

Black people also once put their lives on the line to provide a young black kid from Toledo, Ohio, the opportunity to achieve. These were strong and powerful black people who looked racism right in the eye and defied it. They challenged it through the excellence of their work, the building and nurturing of strong families, the motivation of their children and all black children, the promotion of a strong work and education ethic, and the strength of their character.

Obviously, the road ahead will be difficult. But as California Congresswoman Maxine Waters put it:

> When I look at what is currently happening to the masses of black people, to America's poor in general . . . I am angry and frustrated. But we cannot yield to feelings of helplessness; we must transform anger and frustration into bold and direct action. When other refuse to think of us, it is (all) the more urgent that we think of ourselves. . . .

These are indeed difficult times for the black community here in Milwaukee. But our people have faced difficult times before. We must somehow rekindle that same spirit which allowed us to come out of the many difficult periods of our history with new hope and new determination.

> *SPEECH TIP: **End** the speech. Here Colbert uses a rhetorically rousing here-and-now strategy to galvanize his listeners' resolve to take positive action. Again, he leaves his audience empowered, having taken them from an orderly and thorough statement of a set of dismal problems that create a sense of powerlessness, to the brink of action.*

Milwaukee is the name of the place where we must begin to accept and to embrace our responsibility for the black community. *Today* is the name of *when* we must begin. The *present* is the last name of the *past*, and the first name of the *future*. The *present* is where we are now.

Let us all commit ourselves to both *personal* and *collective* action to enhance the quality of life in our community. Only then will we secure the African-American future!

A Belief in What's Possible

BARRY SULLIVAN
Electronic Data Services Corporation

Delivered at the Vocational Rehabilitation Commencement at El Centro College, Dallas, Texas, August 19, 1993

SUMMARY: In this warm, thoroughly personalized commencement address, Barry Sullivan celebrates the cultural and physical diversity of the graduating class— and of America, the "nation of immigrants," as a whole—and commends individual members for their courage, determination, and success.

Thank you, Stacy [Atkinson].

Good evening, everyone.

I'm honored to be here with you for a couple of very good reasons. The first reason is that I believe in this program. The great things it's achieved. The students it's educated. The jobs it's filled. The lives it's enriched.

> *SPEECH TIP:* This brief paragraph and the one that follows offer an excellent lesson in establishing a bond with your audience.

And, the other reason is that I get to share this special night with all of you, our graduates. I get to hear your stories. Listen to your accomplishments. Shake your hands. I simply couldn't be in better company.

Earlier this year, when Stacy, whom I know from her days at EDS, asked me to speak, I said: "Sure, Stacy, I'd be glad to. But on one condition: I want to know about the graduates. Who are they? Where do they come from? And, what brought them to El Centro College?"

Well, I found out that class valedictorian, Darrell Dillard—whom we've already met—had once owned his own mobile glass service company. I discovered that class salutatorian, Dennis Stewart, had worked as a roughneck in off-shore drilling and was also nominated Phi Theta Kappa. And I learned that Yefim

Shnayderman, who arrived in America from the Ukraine only a few years ago, has taught math in this country and in Russia.

> *SPEECH TIP:* The only subject that commands more attention than a talk about oneself is a talk about your audience. *You* is one of the most powerful words in a speaker's vocabulary.

You're a very interesting group of people. And, you know what really stands out? It's your great *diversity*. It's all the different places you've been, all the kinds of jobs you've had, and all the changes you've experienced. But what impressed me the most are the "journeys in life"—the personal passages—that you've all gone through to arrive here tonight.

> *SPEECH TIP:* Here is a simple and common metaphor: "journeys through life." What elevates it above the banal here is the way Sullivan develops it.

Journeys that, I know, at times must have been long and hard.

Journeys that must have meant great personal sacrifice.

Journeys that must have taken faith, courage, and a desire to succeed, not only on your part, but on the part of your families, your friends, and your teachers.

Now, we all take journeys throughout our lives, and they can take many different forms. As you might guess by my name, Sullivan, I'm Irish. I'm a second-generation American, but I wouldn't be where I am today—standing in this blue suit, white shirt, and tie—if it weren't for the sacrifices that my parents and grandparents made along the way.

When my grandfather came to this country, there were signs in the shop windows that bluntly stated: "*NO IRISH NEED APPLY.*" So, he had to take the hardest and dirtiest jobs there were. He cut stone—by hand, using a saw—in a quarry. It was awful work. The dust from the stone would get into your lungs. And, as a result, the workers would die very young. Throughout his whole life, my grandfather made his living entirely with his hands.

Growing up, I heard the stories around the dinner table about the hardships that my grandparents, as immigrants, had endured because their differences set them apart: The way they talked, the way they looked. They were thought of as second-class citizens, along with the Italians, the Poles, the Czechs, the Germans, and all the others whose foreign accents and Old World ways made them stand out.

Well, I would argue that they weren't second-class citizens at all. They were the very opposite: first-class.

Sure, they struggled, but they also persevered. It was their guts and determination that made them the most courageous, the most self-reliant, and the most successful people that this country could ever hope, or pray, for. These were people who were willing to take on a journey to where they had never been before, trusting only in their *ambition*, their *intelligence*, their *abilities*. And it's paid off.

My father earned a living for the first half of his life with his hands; and the latter half with his mind. And because of what he and my grandfather did, I'm able to make my living with my mind.

To me, the lives of my father and grandfather represent, more than anything else, "a belief in what's possible."

> *SPEECH TIP:* After relating his family's experience, Sullivan drives home the relevance of that experience, using the very title of his speech to do so.

It's that same belief that all of our graduates share with the immigrants who came before them.

At Ellis Island in New York, there are more than 400,000 names recorded on the American Immigrant Wall of Honor. One of those names is Jack Ubaldi. The other day, we talked with Jack. He told us about his journey. It's a journey based on faith, hope and love. The virtues that so many of you possess.

Jack arrived with his family at Ellis Island at the age of seven. It was Christmas Eve in 1918 during World War I. His trip was a dangerous one, but they were so lucky. While the rest of the convoy carrying them to America headed out to sea, the captain of Jack's ship decided to stay close to the coast of Spain and Portugal. The shallow waters gave the ship protection against German U-boats. It was a smart move, because U-boats later sunk the rest of the convoy.

Jack said what saved him and his family was "the hand of God."

The heroes in Jack's life were his parents. They gave their children values to live by: a religious faith, a belief in family, a solid work ethic, and an attitude of acceptance of people who are trying hard to make it.

When people speak out against today's immigrant, Jack says their attitudes are wrong. Here's what he believes, and I quote: "These people have a right to the same opportunity. They deserve the chance to have the dream I achieved."

Jack is living his dream today as the author of *Jack Ubaldi's Meat Book* and as a professor at the New York Culinary Arts Institute. So, if you ever go to Ellis Island, be sure to stop by the Immigrant Wall of Honor, and listen to the oral history that Jack's recorded so others can share his own personal passage.

> *SPEECH TIP:* A great idea for a commencement speech is to *honor the graduates*. Sullivan does so in a most specific and intimate way.

Well, just as Ellis Island has its Wall of Honor, so does El Centro College. On this wall are hung the names and the photographs of the graduates who have gone through this program. Now, it may not be as big, and there are certainly not as many names. But, as a recognition of human achievement, it stands just as tall, and has just as much meaning.

In front of me are seated two very special people whose faces will grace our Wall of Honor. One is Rachel Hock. The other is Jackie McBride. Theirs is a story of friendship, of caring, and of being there for each other. It's a story about the passage of education and the new life it brings.

Rachel has cerebral palsy. She's the youngest graduate and one of the top students in this class. Recently, Rachel wrote down some of her feelings about El Centro and what she's tried to accomplish. Here's part of what she had to say: "I have always wanted to be able to live as independently as possible, even though I have a severe physical challenge. I think I have always felt that I've had to prove that I'm just like anyone else. I think that is the reason that I have been so successful."

Rachel doesn't believe she has a disability. But sometimes, she wrote, she'd be lying if she said she wasn't bothered by some people's attitudes.

Don't worry about Rachel, though.

Because she *believes.* Again, I quote: "People with physical challenges cannot dwell on the way that some people look upon us. We have to lead the most fulfilling lives as possible. And if we happen to affect someone in a positive way, all the better!"

That brings us to Jackie McBride, one of the greatest inspirations in Rachel's life.

Jackie is blind, although she doesn't consider it her biggest problem. She lost her eyesight when she was about sixteen. After that, Jackie decided to pursue a career in medicine because she felt it was her calling. Jackie earned a degree in psychiatry and a doctorate in chiropractic. She practiced her profession very successfully until severe tendonitis restricted the use of her right hand.

Then, she says, the question became: "How do I make a living?"

Well, years before, Jackie had shown a talent for programming. That eventually led her to El Centro, where she met Rachel.

Jackie likes to tell this story to illustrate how well the two of them work together. Once Rachel had a problem with her fax modem in her personal computer. So Jackie offered to help her out. As Rachel read the directions, Jackie took the computer apart, installed a new modem board, and reconnected all the contact points.

Rachel's fax modem now works just fine, and that's very important. Rachel writes that, because of technology, she now has freedom she otherwise wouldn't have. And, as for Jackie, technology enables her to be a *first-class citizen*, just as it has for others who came before her.

Jackie says that a hundred years ago, blind people were often beggars. A man named Louis Braille was one of them. But, he was also the same man who would develop the technology that enabled blind people to "read" with their fingertips. That technology was named after him: the Braille System.

You might be interested to know that before Yefim came to El Centro, he said he had never touched a computer. He found the experience to be almost "magical."

Well, I believe that the *magic* isn't in the *machines.*

Because technology is only a tool, no more, no less. Its value comes from the people who use it well—people like Yefim, Jackie, and Rachel. It's their ambition, their intelligence, and their abilities that give it meaning. To me, their *belief in what's possible* is the real magic.

SPEECH TIP: After honoring the graduates, their experiences are subordinated to the leading theme of the speech.

But, that belief doesn't stop in the *classroom.* You can see it in the *workplace,* where the graduates of this program have made their mark. All you have to do is ask their managers.

Bob Gray, at Lone Star Gas, will tell you that Tim Brozovich is "a self-starter and highly motivated." Bob Haney, at E Systems, will talk about how impressed he is by Rick Larson's courage and desire to succeed. And, when you ask Ken Tomchuck, at Central and Southwest Services, he'll send you a newspaper story about Robert Sorrels, who works for him.

The article states, and I quote: "When Tomchuck talks about Sorrels, there's excitement in his voice as he describes his . . . analytical and verbal skills, as well as his integrity." That's the kind of story we all like to read.

Not long ago, I came across this rather small book called *A Nation of Immigrants.* It was written by John F. Kennedy, the grandson of an Irish immigrant, who went on to become the 35th president of the United States. There's a passage I'd like to read to you. It touches upon the very idea that I've talked about tonight— a belief in what's possible. Here's what Kennedy wrote about what he called "the American faith":

> It gave every old American a standard by which to judge how far he had come, and every new American a realization of how far he might go. It reminded every American, old and new, that change is the essence of life and that American society is a *process,* not a conclusion. . . . More than that, it infused the nation with a commitment to *far* horizons and *new frontiers,* and thereby kept the pioneer spirit of American life, the spirit of *equality* and of *hope, always alive* and *strong.*

Well, the graduation you celebrate tonight is part of your process of change. Part of your own personal passage. You, too, are like the immigrants. Other graduates have gone before you to help show the way, just as sure as others will follow in your path. And, they'll benefit from the sacrifices you've made, and be inspired by the great things you've done. That's the way it's always been—and always will be. Class after class. Generation after generation. That's the way it is for people who truly *believe in what's possible.* That's the way it is for *all of you.*

I wish you Godspeed in the years to come, and congratulations for everything you've done, and everything I know that you will do.

Thanks for listening.

SPEECH TIP: It is traditional and customary—and, at the end of a heartfelt speech, highly moving as well—to conclude a commencement address with a wish for good fortune and success.

CHAPTER 12

Trends and Predictions

If, as one of the speakers in this volume proclaims, ideas are the new wealth of nations, those ideas that concern what H. G. Wells termed "the shape of things to come" represent this wealth raised to an even higher power. In planning a speech, you can be sure of precious few things, but one thing you can count on is that your audience is intensely, personally interested in trends and predictions.

There is only one catch: you have to come to the task armed with some credibility. The more you have, the greater the degree of interest. When John Sculley, who was, when he gave the speech included here, CEO of Apple Computer, proposes to outline the challenges of what he calls the "New Economy," we listen—ever mindful of the cutting-edge track record of his company. But you don't have to be as high-profile an executive officer as Sculley to command an audience—if you pick the appropriate subject and the appropriate audience. Joe Neuberger, CEO of ARA Services, Inc., one of the nation's largest suppliers of "outsourcing" services, speaks to the Los Angeles Rotary Club about the trend toward outsourcing—its benefits as well as its liabilities (and, given his role as CEO of ARA, his discussion of the liabilities is disarmingly candid). Neuberger's position gives him great credibility, not as a universal soothsayer, but certainly as an expert on trends in outsourcing. Moreover, an audience of Rotarians, business people associated with enterprises of widely ranging size, is sure to be intensely interested in all aspects of this trend.

Trends and predictions pack tremendous potential for the speaker, but you cannot depend on the material alone. Before you take on a speech of prognostication, critically examine your own credentials, then carefully define the area and extent of your predictions.

Beyond this, the speaker should also apply two additional yardsticks to his predictions:

1. Are they reasonably specific and detailed?

2. Are they of importance—of *use*—to my audience?

Empty generalizations about the future tend either to annoy, disappoint, or move an audience to unexpected and unwelcome humor. No one needs to be told that the sun is likely to rise tomorrow. But even a very specific prediction concerning trends in the price of soybeans will be of no interest to a gathering of computer chip designers.

Finally, how cautious should you, the speaker, be? Probably less cautious than you think—as long as you *are* careful to ensure that your remarks have an identifiable basis, which you take pains to identify explicitly. Provided that you keep your audience fully informed of the circumstances and conditions that apply, it is also better to make a significant "iffy" statement than to keep silent. The general advice that is given to writers and speakers in any field— *show, don't tell*—particularly applies here. Wherever possible, demonstrate the basis for your predictions. Give real examples. Point out the signposts. In short, let your audience begin to anticipate your conclusions before you actually make them. This not only lends credibility to your forecast, it provides it in a context that will be of maximum value to your listeners.

Blueprint for Boldness

JOHN E. BRYSON
Chairman and CEO
Southern California Edison Company

*Delivered at American Institute of Architects Convention, Chicago, Illinois,
June 18, 1993*

*SUMMARY: The chief executive of a major public utility proposes a partnership
between energy suppliers and architects to create buildings that will contribute to
an environmentally sound and a resource-sustainable future.*

Thank you, Denis [Hayes].

> **SPEECH TIP:** Begin by anticipating your listeners' questions. This focuses the relevance of all you have to say to them.

Maybe you're wondering what a CEO of an electric utility is doing addressing a gathering of architects and designers. On the face of it, it seems unlikely. But in the context of sustainability, perhaps it makes sense.

The world is expecting a lot of us as it embarks on a new century. The pressures facing it will not be solved step by step. They will be solved by bold new thinking and breakthroughs. Breakthroughs of vision, of design, of execution—a bolder blueprint.

> **SPEECH TIP:** One characteristic of an effective speech is that it shows us the familiar in a new light, delineating relationships that might have escaped our attention.

For us, that means energy efficiency and energy services: a new array of opportunities to improve customer productivity and strengthen the economy while conserving the earth's resources. For you, it means new thoughts on how to provide the shelter, comfort, and emotional security that distinguish the human habitat. We supply our product—energy—to your product—structures. When, together, we design and energize an individual building, we weave a portion of the fabric of a neighborhood—of a city—of a nation—of the world.

As we talk about sustainability today, we have the opportunity to flesh out the interplay of environmental protection, productivity, and economic prosperity. Structures are a physical manifestation of the choices we as a society make around those three issues.

In our part of the economic chain, we utilities are confronting a whole new set of realities: global competition and increasingly complex environmental issues, for example. They have forced us to fundamentally rethink what we do and how we do it. We once saw our job as building power plants, delivering kilowatt-hours to a meter. Now we are defining ourselves more broadly—as providers of energy services, economic and environmental problem solvers, and strategists in the shaping of a sound energy policy, nationally and globally.

This change is a response to the new awareness of the cost—economic and environmental—of an outdated mind-set. It's not about sacrifice—about turning down thermostats or wearing sweaters. It's a change that says—with new approaches—we can have it all: comfort, growth, and a healthy environment.

What we know about the world *you* deal with—buildings, landscapes, and so on—suggests that a similar transformation in architecture is taking place. You know more about that than I do, but it seems to me that you're challenging yourselves to re-create your sense of what constitutes beauty, and function, and richness in what you produce.

I was greatly impressed, for example, with the much-praised Holocaust Memorial Museum in Washington, D.C. Its brick and limestone, steel and glass do more than *house* a message of tolerance. The *structure* is, in itself, much of the message. Its paths and pyramids, columns and crossbeams, skylights and stairwells, arches and atria translate through the language of their armature into something palpable that visitors can feel and understand. What a feat—to be able to weld both the horror and hope of human history into the girders of this powerful creation.

Architecture can extend its scope in another direction—the direction of something I'll call "archi-technology."

> *SPEECH TIP:* If a concept becomes memorable through skillful summary, it is most memorable when distilled into a single word. Here Bryson coins a term and then defines it, thereby most effectively labeling his key concept.

What does that mean?

It means smart use of environmentally advantaged, energy productive, and economically savvy technology in the design, building, and operation of structures, old and new. It means jobs today and improved competitiveness tomorrow. It means the fusing of economic growth with environmental protection.

Architects and designers have long been problem solvers: the masons of change, hewing innovation from the stone of necessity, carving public acceptance into the friezes of everyday life:

- Apollodorus of Damascus, for example—the emperor Hadrian's personal architect, who designed the Pantheon and linked parts of the Roman Forum with an aqueduct to ensure a fresh water supply.

▨ And the people of Colorado's Mesa Verde who, one thousand years ago, built the pueblos—the world's first high-density housing—to accommodate their fast-growing population.

Technology will play a major part—a hopeful part—in our joint response to environmental challenges. It will allow us to create a new synthesis that improves the quality of life for individuals and broadens the prospects for future generations.

Energy efficiency—energy productivity—will be the mortar that holds all these things together. Between those of us in the energy business and you who create structures, we can mix this new mortar, which will cement economic progress with environmental protection.

SPEECH TIP: "Energy inefficiency" is an abstraction—until its causes and consequences are made real with examples and a "what-if" scenario.

Energy *in*efficiency hurts productivity in a number of ways. It is costly. It's a major drain on scarce investment capital. And it's the single biggest avoidable source of environmental degradation. For example, we could save $100 billion a year of the $440 billion annual U.S. energy bill by adopting proven energy-efficient technologies: technologies available *right now*, like the ones in the literature that floods your in-basket: compact fluorescent light bulbs, electronic ballasts, occupancy sensors, new kinds of glazing and insulation, heat pumps and CFC-free high-efficiency chillers, electronic adjustable speed drives.

Our world could do a lot with those savings. Spend it on educating our children, for example. Twenty years ago, for every dollar spent on energy, America was spending four dollars on education. Today, for every dollar spent on energy, we're spending just 85 cents on education.

Energy efficiency will help both developing and developed countries become more competitive in a new global marketplace. Energy *in*efficiency is a disadvantage. For example, U.S. products like cars and steel have suffered.

Development of an energy-efficient infrastructure over the next twenty years in the U.S. alone could result in over a million jobs—jobs *created* by freed-up capital investment and an energy-efficiency industry; jobs *retained* when companies increase productivity and are able to comply with environmental requirements. By the year 2010, we could cut carbon-dioxide emissions by 40 percent, nitrogen oxide emissions 50 percent, and sulphur-dioxide emissions more than 60 percent if the full potential of energy efficiency were realized.

So, why isn't all this happening?

The message is not getting through. This is where your business and my business can take the wrecking ball and smash down some of the barriers. We must focus on locking in energy productivity by designing proven technologies into everything we build. We must use technology as a tool to drive behavioral change.

We must implement a broad plan—a comprehensive strategy that involves you and me—from your first pen stroke to the moment a building owner first puts his key in the lock.

A wider scope will offer broader, more integrated solutions —not just a light bulb here and a window there, but a whole context of technology and natural resources that protects quality of life at a reasonable cost. Sunlight, wind, trees, glass, water, rock—it's all there for us to meld with our machines to meet our needs.

Larger-scale efforts will lower manufacturing and distribution costs, make technology more affordable through economies of scale.

We must also make the whole energy-efficiency process easier for our consumer: easier to get, easier to operate, easier to maintain. *You* can be the agent of breakthrough here. Because you're where it starts. You—and your client—at the drawing board. *You* will be the conduit —sharing what you know with the person seeking your expertise. *You* will be the one to show your client that it's more cost-effective to make energy efficiency part of a structure's initial design. And more user-friendly.

> *SPEECH TIP:* This is a speech from one industry to another, a fact reflected in the bold use of "we" and "you."

You will show him or her that, in the long run, it's more expensive to be energy *in*efficient. That initial investment in the right technologies may cost a little more, but that after the payback period—which is only a fraction of the life of the building—the savings (like the Energizer bunny) keep *going* ... and *going* ... and *going.*

We'll support you. We'll share with you every speck of our experience, every ounce of our expertise. And we'll listen to *your* ideas, as you help us understand our customers' needs.

For both of us, it's more than *doing good.* It's *doing good business.* Because when our customers are strong, we are strong. In helping them, we help ourselves.

Many U.S. electric utilities are intensifying their focus on energy efficiency. From Bangor to Bellingham, from Orlando to L.A., we're all playing matchmaker between design and technology. There are similar programs abroad. Edison's efforts include a program that has helped homebuilders provide thousands of more energy-efficient and comfortable new homes to value-conscious buyers. We also have a program that promotes the installation of energy-efficient equipment in nonresidential new construction. We just helped dedicate a new water district headquarters, whose integrated technologies will enable it to heat and air-condition four times the space it used to, for about the same cost.

All of these initiatives are on the right track, but they are not enough in themselves. Sustainability will take a more conscious partnership and a broader vision. Looking at the "big picture," Edison has pledged to reduce CO_2 emissions from our power plants 20 percent by the year 2010. We plan to do this by meeting almost all our new customer needs over the next decade through energy efficiency. You can help us succeed.

We are also responding to the need for affordable housing. Energy efficiency is a big factor in making it affordable. This is part of the bolder blueprint.

In conclusion, I'd like to cite the World Architectural Congress's "Declaration of Interdependence," which embraces the thought of John Donne: "No man is an island." In this declaration, you acknowledge a special responsibility to pursue conceptual and technological change, to innovate, to play an ongoing leadership role in improving the economic, social, cultural, and environmental conditions of the world.

I am struck by how close we are in these goals. I look forward to strengthening and reinforcing our alliance, because, as partners, that bolder blueprint for a sustainable future is within our reach.

The Future of Knowledge

JOSEPH J. ESPOSITO
President
Encyclopaedia Britannica Publishing Group

Delivered at the Smithsonian Institution, Washington, D.C., May 10, 1993

SUMMARY: "Can the blood and guts of creatures whose basic form evolved during the Paleolithic era be accommodated to the new environmental stresses of microprocessors and fiber optics?" Encyclopaedia Britannica president Joseph J. Esposito ponders the future of knowledge in the age of Information Explosion.

> *SPEECH TIP:* One sure way to pique your listeners' interest is to begin with a paradox— a kind of riddle, to which your audience naturally wants the answer.

I was both pleased and perplexed to be invited to participate in this conference. The reason for my perplexity is the title itself: "The Future of Knowledge." It sounds so stout! It promises so much! It implies something more than a symposium on the future of *information,* and it is distinct from a discussion of the future of the distribution of information. Nor is it the same thing as the future of the communications industry or the future of the publishing industry. The future of knowledge is big stuff indeed. When I mentioned this conference to my colleague, Dr.

Frederick Mish, who is the editor-in-chief of Merriam-Webster dictionaries, a Britannica subsidiary, Dr. Mish replied: "The Future of Knowledge! Oh, my! The future is very dim indeed."

It is hard to get one's arms around knowledge as a subject. Part of the reason for this, I believe, is that knowledge implies a *knower*, someone who knows. Unlike the information, which can exist "out there" in the world independently of a human agent, knowledge, to quote Dr. Mish, "applies to facts or ideas acquired by study, investigation, observation, or experience." To talk about knowledge, then, requires us to think as well about the people who *know*: who they are, how intelligent they are, and what resources, including time, they bring to the task.

This subject strikes close to home for EB for the simple reason that since EB was founded 225 years ago, the editors of *Encyclopaedia Britannica* have always had the same goal: to create a summary of the world's knowledge. This was a daunting task in 1768; it is a daunting task in 1993; and when we peer into the future, with its inevitable increase in the amount of information of every kind, we quiver at the challenges before us. To create a summary of the world's knowledge: how to do that in the brave new world of fiber optics, client-server technology, and hand-held microprocessing units?

> *SPEECH TIP:* Essential to a how-it-is-done speech is the definition of a challenge.

We do not come to this challenge totally unprepared. Over the 225 years of EB's history, we believe we have come to know something about the knowledge business. That experience will help us as we go forward. As a matter of fact, in order to ensure that we take advantage of that experience, we still have some of the original staff working for us now. But it is a new world, and the rules of the game have changed. To be successful in the knowledge business in the future will require making some educated guesses as to how things will play out. Businesses and other organizations that guess wrong may find themselves without a constituency.

> *SPEECH TIP:* After presenting a daunting, seemingly overwhelming challenge, Esposito fascinates his listeners by actually defining—even quantifying—an approach to the great task.

In our strategic assessment of the future of knowledge, we have identified three broad categories of issues and trends. These categories are the political area, the implications for business, and what I term the intellectual category, where the subject is the nature of knowledge itself. In my remarks I want to focus primarily on the last category, but allow me to touch briefly on the first two, as they are all related and will inevitably work together.

The political question is, What will the role of government be in developing knowledge infrastructure? In my opinion, the question is not should the government play a role; the only question is what form it will take. For example, since knowledge implies a Knower, the infrastructure for the future of knowledge necessarily involves education; and no plan for the privatization of education has been put forth that would take from the government its leading role in educating the vast majority of Americans. Another fact of life is that the government is the largest institution in American life today, and it will remain the largest institution even if we had twenty successive conservative administrations in Washington. Such a large institution will operate in the marketplace for knowledge as a major buyer and seller. The future of knowledge is governmental business, like it or not. We may not be a well-governed people, but we are a highly governed people, and the future of knowledge will be a highly governed future.

In the business category, the question that seems to be on everyone's lips is: How will electronics affect the distribution of knowledge? Then there is the matter of business strategy: What businesses stand to benefit from the electronic distribution of knowledge? Is it Time- Warner, Ameritech, or someone else? A related question about strategy is what new business niches will be opening up, allowing entrepreneurs without the resources of an AT&T to make money nonetheless? This last point is often overlooked, but I like to bear in mind what Stewart Brand said about the California Gold Rush: the people who made money were not the ones who struck gold but the ones who sold eggs to the prospectors for $10 apiece.

The last category is the *intellectual* dimension. How will electronics affect knowledge itself, both in terms of quantity and form? This point is a bit subtle but it may be the most important of all. It is quite possible that what we mean by knowledge is rooted in print technology. Electronics may alter the very form of knowledge; indeed, it may change the nature of consciousness itself.

The final point, also in the intellectual category, is the human response to the increased access to information. It is a cliché, but it is true nonetheless, that we are in the midst of an information explosion. We can't take it all in. There is a small but growing group of people who have stopped subscribing to electronic mail and who have disconnected their car phones. The amount of information is overwhelming; we can't convert it into knowledge because we don't have time. The basic question is, Can the blood and guts of creatures whose basic form evolved during the Paleolithic era be accommodated to the new environmental stresses of microprocessors and fiber optics? What we need are filters to take the demands of the Information Age and simplify them for the Stone Age users—in other words, ourselves.

SPEECH TIP: What better way to present a speech about the future than as a series of questions and answers?

At this point, let's take a step back and ask, what's so special about knowledge? Won't new information technologies affect every aspect of life, and not just knowledge? The answer, of course, is yes. Digital technology will change—in fact, it is already changing—the way foods are grown, how they are packed and shipped to supermarkets, how they are merchandised, and ultimately how they are consumed. The supermarkets of the future, if we have supermarkets in the future, will be temples of data processing technology. Cereal boxes will sing to us and tell us to buy; every selection will be carefully monitored to improve inventory management; the computerized check-out will automatically deduct the appropriate sum from our bank accounts. In this world, where we have made a god out of the microprocessor, aren't the issues concerning knowledge the same as for everything else?

The answer is "no" for the simple reason that, unlike corn, tomatoes, shirts, and ties, knowledge can be transported digitally, without the use of trucks or trains, without the need for a physical object. In the supermarket business, knowledge is a tool; in the knowledge business, knowledge is the product.

Let's look at how this works right now. We can sit at a computer, access Internet, and then dial into literally thousands of databases. We can request to view the contents of the French literature database that resides on the University of Chicago campus network. On the screen we have the works of Voltaire, Rousseau, and Diderot. If we want to, we can print out hard copy.

The situation is different with physical objects. Let's say we wanted to buy a golf shirt online. We could dial up an online catalog, make a selection, and pay with a credit card. But the shirt still has to be transported. We can imagine a further stage in technology, which would permit us to customize a shirt online. The manufacturer would then make up a unique product for us, but it would still have to be transported. The only way to get around the transportation problem is to do the manufacturing in our homes or offices. So our online services would send instructions to our computer, which, instead of outputting through a printer, would connect to a sewing machine. I do not expect to see this new kind of computer peripheral anytime soon.

So the truly radical dimension of electronics with regard to knowledge is that the cost of distribution of information will surely plummet. This is very significant. In every business I have personally been involved in, the cost of distribution is by far the biggest component, averaging about 60 percent of the retail price. By comparison, the cost of product development is usually around 10 percent to 15 percent, and the cost of manufacturing is about the same.

In the future, then, knowledge—or at least information, knowledge's raw material—will be cheaper; and if it is cheaper, there will be more of it—much, much more. We are already in an information explosion; what will we call this explosion of explosions? How do we cope?

One of the curious things about the developments in information technology is that Encyclopaedia Britannica, which heretofore had been viewed as a staid, even stuffy academic reference publisher, is now getting a lot of unfamiliar attention. The entrepreneurs of Silicon Valley have come a-courting. The moguls of the media conglomerates now return our phone calls. Perhaps most surprising of all is the fact that we are regularly mentioned in articles about a national data highway. The general idea is that if we build a national data highway, we should then put *Encyclopaedia Britannica* on it so that every American could have access to it. To the best of my knowledge, no one has yet suggested how we would be compensated, or even if we would be compensated, for making *Encyclopaedia Britannica* available online. Another reason that *Encyclopaedia Britannica* has been appearing in the news more and more is that reporters have picked up on a remark of Vice President Gore's, that a fiber-optic superhighway could transmit the entire contents of *Encyclopaedia Britannica* in one second. Suddenly, *Encyclopaedia Britannica* has become a unit of measure like pounds, meters, newtons, or square feet. An *Encyclopaedia Britannica* represents a huge amount of information, an almost inconceivable amount of information, which for the first time in history is available literally at the speed of light.

Now, some of the more precise among you will point out that I am cheating, that the Vice President was referring not to *Encyclopaedia Britannica* but to the capacity of fiber optics. And of course, that is true, but I will ask you to indulge me, as this metaphor is useful in assessing the human side of the future of knowledge, because, at least for me, the limiting factor is not technological but biological.

A set of *Encyclopaedia Britannica* contains 44 million words and 23,000 illustrations. It comes bound in 32 volumes. The first edition, which was published in 1768, had 3 volumes. We can conclude that knowledge has grown in 225 years because the goal of *Encyclopaedia Britannica*'s editors has not changed, and that goal has been to provide a summary of the world's knowledge. In computer terms, *Encyclopaedia Britannica* is 300 megabytes of text and 600 to 700 megabytes for the illustrations, for a total of about 1 gigabyte. The actual capacity of fiber optical cable can be more than that, three gigabytes per second, or three *EB*'s, but as a workable unit "one *EB*" gives you a pretty good idea about a substantial amount of knowledge.

The fact is that everything about the size of *EB* is a direct outgrowth of the technology of printing and binding, and this has been true since 1768. *Encyclopaedia Britannica* is 32 volumes long because that's how many volumes we can sell to an individual customer at one time. In other words, in setting out to create a summary of the world's knowledge, the limiting factor for the editors was not, "*How much knowledge is there in the world?*" but "*How many volumes can we print and bind and how much will people be willing to pay?*" So knowledge is not a transcendental idea but a historical one, which is defined by such pedestrian things as the nature of a printing press and the amount of discretionary income available to a consumer. Potentially all of this could change with electronics, which could handle much more than one gigabyte; and our editors would be relieved to work in a totally electronic environment because they want to put in much more information than we permit them to. I say "potentially" because the vision of unlimited fields of knowledge presumes unlimited capacity on the part of users, whose ancestors only a few generations back were swinging from trees.

As a unit of measure, one *EB* is sometimes simply too big. There is a small number of individuals who have read the entire *Encyclopaedia Britannica.* We know some of them. They correspond with us, offering comments and criticism, but they are a tiny, elite group, and they know it. I venture to say that probably no one in this room has read all of *Encyclopaedia Britannica*; the editor-in-chief hasn't read all of it; and anyone who would even attempt to do it strikes us as being unusual or exceptional. The plain truth is that one EB is already too much knowledge. It is good to know that it is out there and that it is reliably crafted, but for any one person it is simply impossible to *know* it.

You will protest at this point that even though the general range of knowledge in *EB* is more than one can handle, all of us have specialized knowledge, and huge amounts of it, in our respective fields. Yogi Berra had the equivalent of one *EB* in the area of baseball; a surgeon has an *EB*'s worth of knowledge about human anatomy; a Wall Street financier has one *EB* of knowledge about stocks and bonds. We can say this, but I just don't think it is so. We are talking about knowledge, not information, and actually to know one gigabyte seems beyond even the brightest of us. The fact is that the knowledge explosion is already history; we have been swamped by what we could know, if only we had the time, for decades if not longer.

> *SPEECH TIP:* The phrase "information explosion" has become a cliché. Espositio revitalizes it by setting it into historical context.

There is documentary evidence that the editors of *Encyclopaedia Britannica* have been acutely aware of this at least since 1910, when the famous eleventh edition was published. The problem for encyclopedia editors has not so much been the gathering of information as it has been selection and organization. The question of, *What do we put in?* is perhaps better expressed as, *What do we leave out?* And how do we assemble all that knowledge in a way that seems, well, knowledgeable? Where do you expect to find something on Lincoln's cabinet, in an article on Lincoln or in an article on the structure of government? Where do we discuss Mideast terrorism? under Israel? Palestine? or in a general article on terrorism? Do we provide a separate biographical article on Madonna, or do we discuss her in an essay on sexual iconography in mass culture? The art of being in the knowledge business is the art of selection and classification; it is the art of imposing form on the huge and ultimately unembraceable world of information. The single most important volume of an encyclopedia is the Index.

Let's return now to Vice President Gore's comment about fiber optics. He said it had the capacity to transmit the equivalent of one *EB* in one second. Transmit, not communicate. To communicate implies reception; it implies thoughtful, intelligent people with the time and interest to listen. Most of the information of the Information Age is simply wasted; it's just noise. The Information Explosion is aptly termed; the explosion blocks out our ability to actually hear much of anything. If we can't hear, we can't know.

Lest anyone jump to the conclusion that I am something of an information reactionary opposed to the creation of global networks, let me hasten to say that the kind of networks currently being contemplated were something of a boyhood dream for me. To get access: that is a very powerful idea. Once we get access, though, the question is, *Access to what?* How do we eliminate the empty noise? How do we get to know what we want to know? After all, the index of discretionary income is no longer very important because information is comparatively cheap. What is more important is our discretionary time and perhaps what we could call our discretionary attention and intelligence.

What is essential for the future of knowledge is filters and classifiers, information tools that cut out the noise and give us pieces of the universe in knowable units. A good classifier could make even our Paleolithic ancestors comfortable with five hundred cable TV channels or fifteen hundred newspapers or scores of databases. A number of organizations, including Encyclopaedia Britannica, are at work on classifier technology. At EB, we are attempting to create software that replicates the principles of organization of *Encyclopaedia Britannica* itself. We call this product Mortimer, after Mortimer Adler, the Chairman of our Board of Editors, who conceived of this classification scheme over thirty years ago. Other classifiers will be coming to market as well. I doubt that any of them, including EB's, will speak with such absolute authority to be adopted as a standard, but they will enable users to get to what they have the time and inclination to know about.

SPEECH TIP: Summing it up: Don't leave your listeners hanging, waiting for a conclusion that never comes. Esposito distills his conclusion into a difference between two concepts defined by closely related words: *knowledge* and *knowledgeable.*

What we envision for the future of knowledge, then, is a world that is long on information, but not necessarily more knowledgeable, because knowledge depends on the thoughtful interaction of people and information, and there is little evidence that people can be much improved. To work through this huge amount of information will require a whole new class of software tools, which we call classifiers, to enable people to connect information into knowledge. We see the government as being the principal agent in influencing the shape that the future of knowledge takes. The businesses that will benefit will be the two or three that dominate the distribution of information and the many small ones that develop classifier technology for market niches. If the future of knowledge is not going to be dim indeed, then these various institutions will have to work together to ensure that the human or "knowing" component is given as much emphasis as the information itself.

The Changing Consumer:
Predicting the Marketplace of the Future

WENDY LIEBMANN
President
WSL Marketing

*Delivered to the Drug Store of the Future Symposium, Tarpon Springs, Florida,
January 14, 1992*

*SUMMARY: A marketing specialist predicts retailing trends for the twenty-first cen-
tury that emphasize best value over cheapest price and are customized to serve ethnically diverse and age-specific markets.*

> *SPEECH TIP:* This is a stylish speech, made deliberately contemporary and hip through
> the use of a stacatto, telegraphic style that uses short sentences and even sentence frag-
> ments. A speech like this requires skillful delivery, but, given the cutting-edge topic, the
> style is well chosen.

Picture it. Twentieth-century America. It began as an age of immigration.
People flocking to these shores from Poland and Russia, from Ireland and England,
from Italy and Germany. Sometimes by choice. Often by necessity. Often through
no free will of their own. Arriving in their millions, they landed in New York,
Galveston, New Orleans, and made their way throughout the country.

They came looking for the American dream. A chance to work for a living, to
earn enough to feed their families, to practice their own religion, hold their own
political views —with no fear of persecution. They came to be Americans.

And they were. They assimilated as fast as they could learn the language. The
immigrant children cast off their foreign ways. They wanted to dress like Americans,
look like Americans, eat like Americans, speak like Americans, live like Americans.

And so was born the dominant face of twentieth-century America. And so was
born an opportunity—to sell the American dream to *the* American consumer. One
idea to one group of people.

It began with a man named Henry Ford, and a revolutionary concept: mass-
producing an affordable product—an automobile—for a universal consumer.

As the century evolved, mass marketing became the way of business.
Returning from a war that crystallized the American ethos, young, aggressive men
and women, eager to succeed, demanded their "chicken in every pot, car in every
garage"—and a television in every living room. As a result, brands like Coca-Cola,

Levi's, Ivory, Revlon, Ford, Gillette, and McDonald's came to define America and Americans—both in this country and throughout the world.

With mass-market brands came mass media to spread the word, and mass-market retailers to sell the product. In the '50s and '60s it was Sears, Roebuck & Company, Montgomery Ward, J. C. Penney, E. J. Korvette, K mart, Kroger, A&P, Publix, Winn-Dixie, and Safeway. In the '70s, '80s, and '90s it was Eckerd, Wal-Mart, Walgreens, Drug Emporium, Food Lion, Sam's, The Gap, Price Club.

Brand name products in their hundreds and thousands came to be purchased in just about any mass retail store—from the drug store to the discount store, from the deep-discount drug store to the warehouse club. The over-extended distribution of branded merchandise contributed to the blurring of retail channels, and by the 1980s the "massification" of American business was complete.

Unfortunately, however, it was complete just in time to confront the *"demassification"* of the American consumer.

> **SPEECH TIP:** After a build-up that explains one style of marketing, Liebmann pulls the rug out with a one-sentence paragraph. Again, skillful delivery is required to make sure that such fast rhetorical footwork doesn't get by your listeners.

Like the old South of a century ago, the homogeneous America of the twentieth century is now gone with the wind. The mass market is dead. The consumer of the twenty-first century is not one, but many: a kaleidoscope of demographic and psychographic segments each with distinct, and often mutually exclusive, needs and desires. While twentieth century America was a melting pot, twenty-first century America will be a mosaic.

> **SPEECH TIP:** The speaker had begun by asking us to "picture it"—twentieth-century America. Now she uses the same imperative to contrast that picture to another snapshot—this one of twenty-first century America.

Picture it. Twenty-first century America. It will begin as an age of immigration. People will flock to these shores from Haiti and Cuba, from Mexico and China, from Hong Kong and Uzbekistan. Sometimes by choice. Often by necessity. Often through no free will of their own.

Arriving in their millions, they will land in Los Angeles, Seattle, Miami, and stay just where they land, in a ghetto-like community reminiscent of their homeland. Like their twentieth-century counterparts, they will come looking for the American dream. A chance to work for a living, to earn enough to feed their families, to practice their own religion, and hold their own political views—with no fear of persecution. They will come to be Americans, but different Americans, diverse Americans, maintaining a strong sense of their own heritage and the character of the land from which they came.

They will *not* assimilate as fast as they can learn the language. In fact, English will never be their primary language. They will be proud of their national tongue.

They will not cast off their foreign ways. They will not dress like Americans, eat like Americans, speak like Americans, live like Americans, as those of the twentieth century did. Instead they will retain the essence of their own distinctive culture.

And so will be born a new face for twenty-first century America. And so will be born an opportunity—a necessity—to sell a new American dream to many diverse American consumers. The specialization of American business will arrive to meet the diversification of American consumers.

America in the twenty-first century will be characterized by its differences, not its similarities. America in the twenty-first century will be a mosaic of different ethnic groups and cultures that no longer view assimilation as their American dream.

> *SPEECH TIP:* A staccato style and highly charged rhetoric have propelled this speech into realms of speculation. Liebmann now anchors her remarks with some carefully chosen statistics. Don't shy away from informed flights of fancy, but do lay a firm foundation under them.

By the year 2000, nearly one-third of the U.S. population will be non-white or Hispanic. By the year 2056, the "average" American will be African, Asian, Hispanic, or Arabic. In parts of California, Florida, and Texas, Spanish—not English—will be the predominant language.

America in the twenty-first century will be characterized not *only* by its ethnic diversity, but also by the aging of its population.

Picture it. Twenty-first century America. An aging nation. No longer a nation of youth. By the year 2000, nearly 30 percent of the population will be over fifty. No longer young, aggressive men and women eager to succeed, demanding their "chicken in every pot," car in every garage, and television in every living room. Instead, they will be older men and women, who are determined to, who must—through necessity—stay fit and healthy to live their longer lives.

Wellness will be of great concern. As much because of the fear of the high cost of health care, and how to afford it, as for its psychological rewards. These will be cautious men and women, who understand the value of money and the need to save it. Men and women who know that price alone is not the issue, but that value for their money is paramount. Men and women who will not pay more for anything than they believe it is worth. To whom worth and value have a new meaning. No longer confined to the old "price + quality" equation, but expanded to include service, convenience, selection, and the overall purchase experience. Intelligent, experienced—oftentimes cynical—men and women who will demand quality information upon which to base their choice of stores and products.

They will be men and women who will choose a store based on its brand image—its ability to deliver on a unique promise, a promise confirmed by the products and service it offers. Men and women who will not accept the promise of health care from a store that sells liquor and tobacco; will not accept the promise of everyday low prices from a store that offers weekly sales. Loyal men and women who know when to value a brand and a store—and when to reject it—when it does not address their specific needs.

And so will be born a mature face of twenty-first century America. And so will be born an opportunity—to sell a realistic, real, caring American dream to older and more experienced American consumers.

America in the twenty-first century will be characterized *not* only by its ethnic diversity and the aging of its population, but also by a diminishing level of aspirations. What began in twentieth century America as an age of immigration, of hope, of new beginnings and boundless aspirations, of streets paved with gold, will be no more.

Picture it. Twenty-first century America. An age of diminished expectations. A realization that doing better than your parents is no longer guaranteed. That having a job for your entire working life, owning your own home, sending your children to college and retiring to a warm climate at age sixty-five are no longer assured—even if you are willing to work hard all your life.

An age of adult children living at home. Of two-, three-, and four-income families—grandparents, parents, and children helping to make ends meet. The necessity of multiple generations living together, to share the burden of daily life.

And so will be born a concerned face of twenty-first century America. And so will be born an opportunity—to sell the American dream to a consumer who does *not* believe he or she can afford it.

So, how will we market to, and satisfy this consumer of the twenty-first century, this ethnically diverse, aging consumer with significantly diminished expectations?

Certainly for the one-size-fits-all mass marketer of the twentieth century, it is an all but impossible task. *The mass market is dead.*

And so *must* be born a new face for retailing in twenty-first century America. The mass market is dead; *long live specialty marketing.*

> **SPEECH TIP:** Note how much meaning hangs on the auxiliary verb *must*, which is used here to contrast with the verb *will* repeatedly employed earlier in phrases parallel to this one.

Picture it. Twenty-first century America. The retailer will be part of, and reflect, the community. The store's environment, the products it sells, the employees and the message it evokes will be tailored to the specific nature and needs of the community it serves.

If the store is in a Hispanic community, the employees will be Hispanic. The merchandise will be tailored to the color preferences and taste preferences of Hispanic consumers. The signage and advertising will be in Spanish. The promotions will support traditional Spanish holidays and festivals. And manufacturers' sales representatives will come from or be part of that community.

If the store is in an older community, the employees will be older. The merchandise and service levels will be tailored to the needs and preferences of older consumers. The store will be designed to make for a comfortable, relaxed shopping trip. A coffee shop (a meeting place), motorized shopping carts, a personal shopper, numbered parking spaces, store-to-car delivery, home delivery twenty-four hours of the day.

In all, a store's image and credibility will come from its roots within the community—its commitment to that community. Not merely from its success as a well-known "national brand" retailer.

Even today, there exist examples of successful retailers who have begun to practice this twenty-first century philosophy. Von's Tianguis in California and England's The Body Shop are two examples of specialized, community-oriented retailers.

Tianguis with its tortilleria, instead of a bakery. Stores loaded with chili peppers, cilantro, beans, salsa, Mexican cheeses, over 600 items of produce tailored to its predominantly Mexican customers.

The Body Shop is an environmentally and socially conscious bath and body store, where store personnel are required to spend several hours per week working for a local charity or social program.

In twenty-first century America, *value* will be the key to all successful retailing. Picture it. A retailer who emphasizes value of purchase *and* shopping experience above all else. Whether that retailer sells apparel, health and beauty aids, prescription drugs, electronics, toys, sporting goods, stationery, or food. Not necessarily the lowest prices in town—but the best value in town. The customers will know—before entering the store—that they will find exactly what they want and pay no more for it than it is worth—*every day of the week.* In fact, when they leave the store they will believe they got more than they paid for. Sale-driven retailing of the twentieth century will be no more.

> *SPEECH TIP:* Good predictions are essentially imaginative extrapolations from present reality. Liebmann is careful to ground her trend predictions in present-day cutting-edge examples.

Twentieth-century examples of value-based retailers include Wal-Mart, Toys 'R' Us, warehouse clubs, deep-discounters. They are the first signs of twenty-first century value-based retailers.

Picture it. A twenty-first century retailer where *service* is a given regardless of the price of the merchandise. Customers will know—before entering the store—that if they need help, they need only ask. Someone will show them where the appropriate merchandise is, answer their questions, offer suggestions, and give recommendations—but only if the customer wants it.

Customers will know that if they don't have time to go to the store they have only to call their personal shopper who will take their order, charge it to a credit card, and deliver it—free of charge—within forty-eight hours.

If they want to return or exchange an item today, tomorrow—or six months from now, they need only return to the store to get their money back. No receipt necessary. No questions asked. If too busy, they have only to call the store to arrange a door-to-store pick-up to return the merchandise—free of charge.

Sound familiar? Perhaps a twenty-first century Wal-Mart store?

Picture it. A twenty-first century retailer where *selection* of merchandise defines the image, credibility, and essence of the store. No longer the same merchandise replicated store after store after store as in the twentieth century. Instead, a tightly tailored mix defined by the nature of the store and the community in which it operates.

Picture it. An apparel store designed to attract value-conscious, style-conscious consumers. A narrow mix of quality fashion basics in multiple colors and fabrications. No sales. Just everyday great values.

A quick and easy store to shop. A mistake-proof selection. Mix anything with everything for faultless fashion. A constantly changing mix of merchandise to pique the shopper's interest. Need help, just ask and it's there. A different size, a different color, a different fabric. Not in that store. Not in another store. "We'll special-order it from our factory." And it will be delivered to your door, within days, free of charge.

Sound familiar? Perhaps a twenty-first century Gap store?

Picture it. A twenty-first century retailer where the store is a brand unto itself. A "Good Health Store." Every imaginable product for fitness, beauty, and health: vitamins, food supplements, medications, beauty products, weekly health and beauty lectures, a health-food bar. Next store a fitness club. "Good health" advisors. Beauty advisors. No cigarettes, no liquor, no soda, and no chips!

Sound familiar? Perhaps an Eckerd store of the twenty-first century?

The twenty-first century consumer will not be satisfied with me-too stores and copycat products, with empty promises of service and selection, with poor quality and snake-oil mentality: "Come and get it, come and get it. Today only. . . ."

Consumers will shun me-too stores and me-too products and instead expect—demand—credible, innovative products with realistic benefits, tailored to their specific needs.

In the twenty-first century consumers will reject new products that are merely knock-offs of existing items. Another brand of two-in-one shampoo and conditioner will not be tolerated. Product innovations that make life easier, more comfortable, are more economical and efficient, that consciously reflect the needs of specific customers will succeed. Quality will be paramount.

> *SPEECH TIP:* Talk is cheap. Good words are valuable. Liebmann repeats the key words that describe the value trends she had predicted for the future of marketing.

Innovation, quality, service, and value will be the price of entry to the twenty-first century. Distinctive, credible messages from a retailer and a manufacturer to its community. Not department stores selling service and selection when they offer none. Not drug stores selling promises of health care and cigarettes at the same time. Not manufacturers promising an innovative new product—the tenth of its kind on the market. Instead, marketers who will be accountable for their message, who will guarantee their performance, who will provide affordable quality, who will listen to and respect their customers.

Picture it. Twenty-first century America. An age when the specialization of American business will arrive to meet the diversification of American consumers. An opportunity—a necessity—to sell a new American dream, an affordable American dream, a credible American dream to the mosaic that will be America.

Design for the Environment: The Challenge for Year 2000 and Beyond

DR. JOSEPH T. LING
Vice President, Environmental Engineering
and Pollution Control (Retired)
3M

Delivered to the National Industrial Waste Minimization Conference, Taipei, Taiwan, June 2, 1993

SUMMARY: With five decades of experience in environmental engineering, a 3M executive outlines past, present, and future approaches to pollution prevention and waste control.

Rachel Carson's book *A Silent Spring* helped trigger the world's environmental consciousness. Then the energy crisis of the early 1970s made us aware of the need to conserve natural resources. These two events created a firestorm of environmental awareness around the world. Carson's book and the oil shortage had the same impact as the musketfire at Bunker Hill in Boston that began the American Revolution. They, too, were "shots heard round the world."

While these environmental shots were fired in the right direction . . . it has taken time and effort to hit the bull's eye on a regular basis.

For example, the idea of resource conservation was often presented very simplistically at first:

- Stop making things, and you won't pollute.

- Only by reducing consumption can we conserve resources.

Many people began looking at the environment in terms of polar extremes. You could have the environment, or you could have production, but you couldn't have both of them. A Broadway show provided an anthem for those who find production incompatible with the environment. It was called "Stop the World, I Want to Get Off."

> **SPEECH TIP:** Contrary to what many believe, a figure of speech is not just a convenient way to add color to your speech. A good metaphor vividly translates the abstract or unfamiliar into terms that are concrete and familiar. This and the next paragraph do just that.

This "Stop the World" approach is best suited for abstract contemplation from an ivory tower. That's because—thanks to the laws of motion and gravity—we can neither stop the world nor get off. Mother Nature herself requires that we keep our feet on the ground, even when our heads are in the clouds. In addition, the ivory tower is a precarious perch. It can be too high to see the real needs of ordinary men and women, and too far away to hear their aspirations for a better life.

But, while keeping human needs in view, we also must not lose sight of the environment. We need to sustain the environment, because the environment sustains us. Together, environmental protection and production are in harmony and contribute to what we are coming to know as a *conserver society*. This is based on development that means total human and social development in which the key factors are not primarily economic, but are human and social needs. These include:

- Job creation, enrichment and satisfaction

- Safe water to drink

- Clean air to breathe

- Fertile land on which to grow food

- Basic health service and shelter from the elements

In a broad sense, a conserver society covers not only production but product use, energy, raw materials, and waste disposal. It is what the International Labor Organization has called "a technology which is appropriate to meeting all these needs within the constraints of a sustainable resource base and one which is compatible with one's culture."

SPEECH TIP: Ling defines a "conserver society," thereby giving a name to an important concept.

The nature of a conserver society was spelled out at a U.N. environmental conference in 1976. The U.N. said this society is based on "the practical application of knowledge, methods and means" to plan and manage human activities "to provide the most rational use of natural resources and energy and to protect the environment."

The conserver society sustains the environment and natural resources while permitting the progress that allows developed nations to maintain a high standard of living and less-developed nations to improve their lifestyles. As a native Chinese who has worked for many years in the Western world, I view this situation from both perspectives—sustaining and achieving a good lifestyle—and find them to be equally valid. There is no dark side to the conserver society, the essence of which is to use a minimum of resources to produce maximum human benefit—for our generation and for all the generations to follow.

The paradigm is—as best we can—to employ renewable resources and produce no waste, and to strive for 100 percent usage of all raw materials. Ideally, absolutely everything that goes into the north side of a factory should come out the south side as a product or useful byproduct. The scrap from one manufacturing process becomes raw material for another. One example is the creation of nylon from the waste byproducts of petroleum some years ago. A few months ago, my company introduced a product that cleans like steel wool, but without rusting or splintering. And it's made from recycled plastic bottles.

I use this formula:

Pollutants + technology = potential resources.

I have come to believe in and count on perfecting a conserver society. In my mind, a conserver society is the key to what I want to talk about today: that is, how to meet "The Environmental Challenge of Year 2000 and Beyond." I think the world is off to a promising start toward achieving this conserver society. But to get there from here requires change in exponentially greater quantity. In our quest, change is just like "death and taxes." Change is also *unavoidable.* Change will occur whether or not we participate. Thus, managing change is the key to achieving a conserver society.

President Harry Truman once observed that "The only thing new is the history you don't know." In that context, I will look backward to see forward.

My perspective is obtained from a half-century of environmental engineering in academia, government, consulting, and industry. I've worked on both sides of the Pacific Ocean.

Looking at the past two decades alone, the change is mind-boggling. Over the past twenty-five years, we have progressed

- from looking at air, water, and land as separate and unrelated issues . . . to considering total environmental impact.

- from spotlighting only industrial pollution sources . . . to highlighting all sources, including agriculture, transportation, and energy production.

- from a narrow focus on factory emissions . . . to a broader view including product use, consumption, and disposal.

- from confrontation . . . to cooperation among industry, government, and the general public.

- from seeing the environment as a local concern . . . to addressing a national issue, and now, seeking a truly global solution.

The whole environmental movement can be defined as a series of changes that have occurred over time. In the 1950s, the environment was a minor issue or a non-issue. In the 1960s we had confrontation and accusation. In the 1970s there was legislation and regulation. In the 1980s government applied command and control solutions to "end of the pipe" treatment, which means "conventional" pollution controls.

Now—and this is important—the 1990s are focusing on prevention and minimization. From the year 2000 and beyond, the issue will be *sustainable development*, which involves designing national policies—as well as products and processes—to eliminate or reduce impact on the environment. I refer to this as "Design for the Environment." It's a phrase that I believe will gain as much notice in the decade ahead as "pollution prevention" has in the past ten years.

I've described some steps that are history, and others that are occurring. Still more remain to be developed as we move toward the twenty-first century. Time forces me to concentrate on the last two steps: prevention and minimization, and sustainable development.

Prevention and Minimization

SPEECH TIP: Having established a philosophical, theoretical, and historical context, Ling details an actual environmental policy and program. Note the use of a list format.

My perspective is from a company that began working on prevention and minimization in the early 1970s. In 1975, for example, 3M introduced a company-wide environmental management program called Pollution Prevention Pays—or "3P" for short. The 3P Program has two objectives that remain as valid today as they were in the 1970s. They are:

- First, to eliminate pollution at the source, before clean-up problems occur. This lowers environmental costs and also reduces the amount of energy and other raw materials required for production.

- Second, to consider pollutants as unused raw materials that just happen to be passing through the production cycle. For example, one 3M plant uses recycled scrap from medical masks to make an absorbent material for cleaning up oil chemical spills.

Over the past seventeen years our Pollution Prevention Pays Program has made a considerable contribution to the environment—and to 3M's profitability. During these years, our scientists, engineers and technicians have come up with more than three thousand individual 3P projects. Each and every year they eliminate

- Over 170,000 tons of air pollutants;

- More than 18,000 tons of water pollutants;

- In excess of 2.7 billion gallons of wastewater;

- And 480,000 tons of solid wastes.

Let's look at several examples:

- A tape plant in Canada sells waste plastic to a maker of coat hangers and flower pots. It also sells scrap steel, solvents, and other waste materials. As a result, the plant needs 96 percent less landfill space today than it did five years ago.

- A manufacturing plant in the Netherlands reduced use of solvents by 90 percent.

- And a U.S. facility is recovering for reuse 2.8 million pounds of cleaning solvents that formerly were incinerated.

Efforts like these have saved the company more than a half billion dollars in first-year accumulative savings over the past seventeen years. That's a major contribution to profitability, even to a relatively large company like 3M. Last year, we had net income of $1.2 billion on sales of $13.9 billion. On its 1992 list of the 500 largest U.S. manufacturing companies, *Fortune* magazine ranked 3M twenty-eighth in sales—and eleventh in profitability. Our pollution-prevention activities, over time, contribute to this top ranking for profitability.

While the 3P Program has tracked the amount of pollution prevented, we really did not know until recently the relationship between total plant output and the amount of waste generated. We corrected that in 1990 with a comprehensive measurement system. It showed very good results. In 1991, the company reduced the rate of waste generation by 8.3 percent . . . and by another 8 percent in 1992. The ultimate goal is to keep reducing the rate of waste generation until it gets as close to zero waste as technologically possible.

Zero waste may not be obtainable today for each and every process, but it's a motivating goal for employees. By implementing a measurement system, employees can see the results of their efforts. In normal 3M tradition, we recognize those in operating units who produce the best results. To encourage further waste minimization, 3M has published a list of best practices, as illustrated on this chart. This fits with management concepts calling for total quality, or zero defects. After all, what is waste but a defect in the manufacturing process?

Pollution prevention now is an integral part of 3M's business decisions and also has been adopted by many other companies in the United States and other countries. In 1976, the United Nations Environment Program gave early recognition to 3M's efforts. This came at a conference on no-waste technologies held in Paris, France. Since then, many countries have scheduled similar conferences to promote the non-waste concept in ways that suit their needs.

In the 1980s, the subject of hazardous waste further strengthened the prevention approach. That's because the problem was great, and effective control technology was lacking. So the U.S. government turned to prevention as the most effective way to minimize production of hazardous waste:

- Congress passed the Solid Waste Disposal Act, which mandates a prevention approach to deal with hazardous wastes.
- In 1989, the U.S. Environmental Protection Agency issued its National Policy Statement on Pollution Prevention.
- Congress added a Pollution Prevention Act in 1990.
- And the President's Commission on Environmental Quality issued a report in January 1993 recommending a strong push aimed at pollution prevention.

It appears that the prevention approach will continue at the forefront for some years to come. When Carol Browner was confirmed as the new U.S. E.P.A. administrator, she said that "While regulatory schemes obviously will be part of environmental protection . . . I hope we can really focus the great part of our energies and resources on pollution prevention." Her environmental priorities included: "Take limited resources and apply them to pollution prevention." Then comes source reduction, recycling, and disposal. She urged development of an awards program for companies that prevent pollution and engage in recycling.

SUSTAINABLE DEVELOPMENT

Now let's look at how the term "sustainable development" has been introduced.

In the 1970s, when the 3P approach was planted and taking root, pollster Daniel Yankelovich predicted that the world would become a global village. He said that satellite communications and fast jetliners would compress time and space to make all of us neighbors.

We're there now.

When I pick up the telephone at home, I can place a call to almost anywhere in the world as easily as I can call my daughter who lives only a few miles away. It took me less than one day to fly halfway around the world to attend this meeting. My children may someday make the trip in a few hours, on a hypersonic jetliner. Products from any given country are sold and used almost everywhere: Japanese-made video cameras and VCRs are a global phenomenon. So are those famous U.S. exports, Coca-Cola and Pepsi-Cola. And "Made in China" or "Made in Korea" are found on myriad products in many markets.

We are also aware that environmental problems are not local problems we can ignore because they are not in our own backyard. In the global village, everywhere is our backyard. So-called "local" pollution problems become transnational problems:

- Air pollution crosses borders with the impunity of the wind.
- Water pollution flows easily from one country to another.
- And worn-out products become discarded waste in countries far from where they originated.

Again, there is an historical perspective to the issue. The United Nations held a conference in Stockholm in 1972 that was devoted to sustainable development, and that same year, it founded the U.N. Environment Program. UNEP enthusiastically supported sustainable development but ran into strong resistance because of economic difficulties in the 1970s and 1980s. Realizing the important relationship between well-being and environmental commitment, the U.N. General Assembly created a World Commission on the Environment.

Prime Minister Brundtland of Norway chaired the commission, which, in 1987, issued a final report called "Our Common Future." It promoted sustainable development as the only realistic way to meet the needs of the present without compromising the ability of future generations to meet their own needs. It called for transnational cooperation on the issue.

These events were stepping stones to the so-called Environmental Summit in Rio de Janeiro that was held in 1992. More than 170 countries took part, with 118 heads of state attending the meeting. Thousands more represented industries and other non-governmental organizations. (Ironically, Maurice Strong of Canada was chairman of both the Environmental Summit in Rio and the 1972 environmental conference in Stockholm that I mentioned a few moments ago.) The Rio summit adopted "Agenda 21," which calls for establishment of an "equitable global partnership" to deal with a wide range of concerns, including the environment, the economy, and various related social and political issues. The Earth Summit also came up with twenty-six principles, ranging from efficient resource development and international trade policies to liability and compensation for victims of environmental pollution and damage.

DESIGN FOR THE ENVIRONMENT

All of this sets the stage for achieving our environmental goals in the year 2000 and beyond. This is to meet the challenge of "Design for the Environment."

> *SPEECH TIP:* Another valuable signpost, which points the way toward the dramatic and intellectual climax of the speech.

What do I mean by "Design for the Environment?"

In my view, "Design for the Environment" is a process for development. It means including environmental concerns right at the beginning of development. The idea is to reduce the environmental impact as the design objective. In other words, "Design for the Environment" is a method to develop environmentally compatible products and processes while maintaining desirable product pricing, performance, and quality characteristics.

For example, 3M now applies adhesive to many tape products using water instead of hydrocarbon solvents. We designed another product so scrap can be trimmed before the curing process. This means the uncured raw material can be recycled for reuse, whereas the cured scrap could not be used at all.

Obviously, all sectors of society must cooperate to achieve global sustainable development through "Design for the Environment." That includes industry, government, and the general public.

■ The public must demand, and be willing to support, appropriate government and private-sector actions to encourage environmentally friendly development. Also, the public should be open to the idea of modifying lifestyle to reduce their own impact on the environment.

▦ Government must consider environmental concerns and build them into existing or new policies and regulations for not only industrial processes but also for economic development, transportation, and agriculture.

▦ Industry must design environmentally compatible products and market them effectively to meet public demand. Industry took the initiative in pollution prevention; now it must become a leader again, working for sustainable development. This includes achieving the cooperation of suppliers and customers to implement their own "Design for the Environment" programs.

New and innovative technologies are vital to the practice of "Design for the Environment." Government and industry—together—should support and fund research in academic institutions to develop appropriate technologies and accelerate transfer of this technology to industrial and other applications.

As for industry, we have incentives to take the leadership toward "Design for the Environment." The best incentive is to improve our competitive situation. The U.S. National Research Council estimates that early design work determines more than 70 percent of the cost of product development, manufacturing and consumption. It is very costly and troublesome to deal with pollution problems. It is less so to eliminate or reduce pollution potential early in the design stage. That's when it's effective to consider material substitution, packaging, transportation, storage and product disposal issues.

Thus, pricing advantages accrue to those who can eliminate or reduce pollution-control and waste-disposal costs that would otherwise appear downstream in the product life cycle. There's an old American phrase, "Get the lead out." It means get yourself going right away. It's also good advice to "get the lead out" early in the product design stage.

Here is an example of why: Pollution elimination helped 3M gain competitive strength in printing plates and color proofing materials. These products now can be processed using aqueous solutions instead of conventional chemical developers. Customers like this because they don't have to deal with the problem of handling and disposing of processing chemicals.

Sixteen years ago, I addressed a National Association of Manufacturers conference in Washington, D.C. At the time I said this:

> Pollution is waste . . . and waste today leads to shortages tomorrow. "Waste not, want not" is a motto as true now as it was before the affluent/effluent society. The sustainability of the desired standard of living for the future will depend upon re-establishing a conservation-oriented society, a conservation-oriented economy, and a conservation-oriented technology. This technology, by necessity, is based on a total concept of resource conservation that involves raw material supply, production, consumption and disposal.

It appears that the concept of sustainable development is quite similar to the conservation-oriented economy and value system. It also seems that the concept of

"Design for the Environment" is similar to conservation-oriented technology. While progress has been made, we need a continuing flow of new technologies to correct environmental problems of the present and solve those of the future. By working together, industry, government and academia can make this happen.

With much experience, we know that conservation and production are not separate. Rather, they are inseparable. "Design for the Environment" will be the link that makes this happen.

Keeping conservation and production inseparable is "The Environmental Challenge for Year 2000 and Beyond."

Sticking to Your Knitting:
The Increasing Trend Toward Outsourcing

JOE NEUBAUER
Chairman and CEO
ARA Services, Inc.

Delivered to the Rotary Club of Los Angeles, June 4, 1993

SUMMARY: The leader of a leading support service provider discusses the potential and pitfalls of corporate downsizing, focus of resources, and outsourcing to attain and retain competitiveness in today's increasingly challenging marketplace.

Thank you for that very gracious introduction. On behalf of the 12,000 Californians who also happen to work for ARA, thank you for the opportunity to be with you today.

> **SPEECH TIP:** In a single paragraph, Neubauer clearly and in detail sets out the three-fold subject of his talk.

Good afternoon. Today I would like to talk with you about choices: choices we as the leaders of the American private sector must make if we are to keep our global competitive edge. We can play defense or we can play offense. In the balance hang the essentials of corporate survival: from cost containment to productivity to effective human resource management. While the choices we make are driven by many of today's business trends, let me today focus on just three: the move away from diversification and back to "sticking to your knitting"; second, the restructuring of corporate management; and third, the increasing trend toward out-sourcing.

Along the way I may explode a few myths and shatter a few misconceptions, but if anyone can handle a little broken china, I do believe it's Californians.

> **SPEECH TIP:** The classic teaser well handled. The promise to "explode" myths and "shatter" misconceptions is hard to resist and commands attention.

Since the turn of the century, market share and internal hierarchies were the twin pillars of corporate doctrine. The conventional wisdom driving decision-making could be summed up by two words: control and dominance. For most of the last hundred years, the giants of American industry have used those words as a mantra—creating a corporate culture in the process.

Integration was the name of the game. From the steelworks of my home state of Pennsylvania, to colossal computer corporations, to the four-wheeled legacy of Henry Ford, extending the scope of the enterprise—making it broader and deeper in its range of activities—was the defining corporate mission.

> **SPEECH TIP:** If you propose to predict future trends, it is always a good idea to trace the history of past trends and where they led.

So what was the "company"? In the early days, the company was everything. Some companies fed you, others clothed you, some even housed you. "I owe my soul to the company store" was more than the melancholy refrain of Tennessee Ernie Ford's classic, "Sixteen Tons." It was a way of thinking throughout many of America's basic industries. For many years the culture of the corporation was the culture of the community. Life wound tight around the work place. Whether its soul was a textile mill or an oil rig, a silver mine or an assembly line, dotting the landscape of twentieth-century America was the company town. And ironically, blue collar, white collar—it made no difference—both were the colors of the company man.

Later, the fifties revealed the man in the gray flannel suit. Identification with the company was different, but definite. The thousands of college grads who joined IBM each year typified the appeal of a career moving up the ranks. The uniform was different, but the white shirt and short haircut were a uniform nonetheless.

Total commitment had its parallel in the strategic bearing of the company: bigger was better: market dominance and management control. The more stages of production under the corporation's control, the more the corporation could crowd out the competition. What does this mean? In the case of an automobile manufacturer, it meant owning as much upstream and downstream as it possibly could. That didn't just mean the battery plant, the headlight plant, and the upholstery plant.

Theoretically it also meant the steel plant, the glassmaker, and even the iron mine. It meant not just a nationwide sales and distribution network, but also a service contract company, a financing company, and a leasing company.

Hidden were the multiplying layers of decision-making—the growing and bulky management pyramid within the overall corporate structure. But the theory of dominance and control dictated that the company expand to command and contain as many inputs to the cost of business as possible, regardless of the distance between those particular functions and the basic, or core, function of the original company. Integration was a powerful and accepted business strategy—extraordinarily successful at creating gigantic global market-dominating corporations. For many years General Motors, IBM, U.S. Steel, and a host of other U.S. giants ruled the world marketplace, using precisely this paradigm.

Many companies took this a step further: diversify—acquire new lines of business unrelated to the core product or service. Protect profits by broadening the base; if one market declines, another market expands. As a defense against the vagaries of the marketplace, the theory held that wise diversification would average out the bad times, amplify the good times, and thereby guarantee greater security for shareholders. The corporation diversified the portfolio for the shareholders.

Diversification brought with it new tiers of management. The corporation's headquarters became the family authority figure, increasingly called upon to answer the question, "What does corporate think?" Not surprisingly, at the headquarters, the same question was asked, only with a different intonation, "What *does* corporate think?" To effect a reply, added to layers of decision-makers, usually bright MBAs, were layers of information gatherers. The pyramid swelled, the slab of middle management becoming more massive than ever.

As the saying goes, a funny thing happened on the way to the twenty-first century. The world got smaller. Global competition got fiercer. Wherever we wanted to go, whatever we wanted to do, technology and information got us there faster. First, in Europe and Japan, later, in Korea and Brazil and Thailand and a host of other countries, the post-World War II boom evolved into a new era of global competition.

For decades we grew and we prospered, but, slowly, our competitors began to get a foothold in our traditional markets, not only abroad, but right here at home as well. For years we dismissed the challenge. We rationalized it. By the 1970s we were behaving like the proverbial patient; we denied the problem. Then we reacted angrily, as if it were wrong that our competitors actually read our management textbooks or sent their students to our universities and graduate schools. The facts spoke for themselves: We'd lost 30 percent of the U.S. automobile market to the Japanese; the steel industry was reeling; from consumer electronics to shipbuilding, whole industries were struggling to stay afloat. We began to talk as if we were a nation in decline. Some actually believed it.

Well, I didn't believe it then, and I don't believe it now. Let me tell you why: We've changed. We've changed rapidly and radically. Now, the hallmark of competitive industries is defined by an exciting new culture with a new cluster of words and beliefs. Service and speed have replaced dominance and control. Hierarchies are giving way to decentralization, flexibility, and greater autonomy. Modular organizational structures, innovative business networks, and cross-corporate alliances—unheard of fifteen to twenty years ago—allow companies to better focus precious capital and human resources. That's longhand for being smart with a buck and good to your people.

In 1946 the mentor of modern management, Peter Drucker, redefined employees as a resource, not a cost. During these last forty-seven years, we've been to the moon and back; the Beatles, the hula-hoop, and Johnnie Carson have all come and gone; and the Berlin Wall is a pile of rubble—symbolic of a world turned upside-down. About the only certainty left is the Chicago Cubs' fall fade. They're a client of ours, so I hope that will change, too!

It took a long time, but we have finally begun to accept Drucker's premise about the inherent value of workers. Today, he writes that the "Post-Capitalist Executive" must build new organizations by replacing power with responsibility. Let's hope it doesn't take forty-seven years this time to give Drucker his due.

The old way of diversification crumbled because diversified companies had difficulty being "best-in-the-world" at all of the things they attempted. The company was diversified, but power and responsibility were concentrated. The additional layers of management didn't add value to what the company sold. They added overhead. They didn't speed things up, they slowed things down. On the other hand, specialized companies leveraged more talent, more time, and more resources to more singular goals. More than just saving overhead costs, they brought focus to the corporate mission.

That's why diversification must be grounded by a wholly different perspective: strengthen the corporate basics—not the corporate bureaucracy. Stick to your knitting. Only engage in activities that directly relate to the core business. Greater autonomy goes to the successful units. Sum it up in three words: focus, focus, focus. At my company we try to practice what we preach. Over time, ARA divested those units that were simply too far afield of our core business. We used to be in the trucking business, the construction management business, retirement homes, even school buses. No more. We've added heft to our core businesses, so today we are bigger but more focused.

Some diversified firms actually moved out headquarters staff to the operating units to achieve independence within those units. By taking away the hand-holders at headquarters, these companies forced people in the units to rely on themselves—develop initiative, take risks, assume responsibility—exactly what it takes to compete today.

For example, at an ARA-managed cafeteria, we guarantee our service. That is perhaps not unusual. What *is* unusual is that we train our line employees to handle customer complaints on the spot, and we empower them to resolve them without turning the problem over to management. In short, flattening the management pyramid means our people take on more responsibility for themselves, solve customer problems faster and better, and that's good for our business.

> *SPEECH TIP:* Another refreshing element: buzzwords that combine the conventional with the informal, the unexpected. We expect a business person to talk about "customer relations" and "flexibility," but it is this sports-inspired thing called "hustle" that most intrigues us—and keeps us listening closely.

Customer relations, flexibility, hustle—these are now the paradigms of the twenty-first century business world. I am fortunate to lead a company that is a direct beneficiary of this changing corporate philosophy. Ours is a service company, with face-to-face customer contact happening literally ten million times a day. The strength of our success begins and ends with doing those ten million things right each and every single time.

A growing number of enterprises—businesses, educational institutions, even churches—are turning to specialized firms like ARA to provide or manage a service they previously handled in-house. Why should a university, for example, spend $500,000 less on scholarships for needy students because it spends $500,000 more on its own cafeteria operation than it needs to? From child-care centers to hospital emergency room care to food service and uniform rentals, we develop partnerships with our clients that assure them better service at lower cost than if they provided the service themselves. Though sometimes controversial, the outsourcing or privatization of government functions is gaining acceptance as a way of improving service and cutting costs. Outsourcing is certainly not new, but the range of outsourcing possibilities is now immense and still growing.

Using a large company like General Motors as an example, at any of its facilities it would be easy to find the following employees: data processors, accountants, mail clerks, lawyers, janitors, cafeteria workers, artists, security guards, copywriters, nurses, painters. Their closest encounter with the car business is the drive home. How many actually make cars? Virtually none of them. Yet, the company invests tremendous resources in those employees in the form of salaries, benefits, training, work space, and capital equipment. Outsourcing these kinds of functions would free up decision-makers. They could focus more of their expertise on the core activities of the business—what it is they know how to do—and how to beat the competition.

But line functions are also becoming candidates for outsourcing. This presents a different kind of challenge for managers. The starting point is generally a discussion about something called the "value chain." At different stages of the enterprise there are differing amounts of value added to the product or service. The question becomes, where is that core competency of the company, the genius around which the rest of the company must revolve? James Brian Quinn, in his book, *Intelligent Enterprise*, would insist that it is the competency for which the company is "the best in the world." Understanding that helps define which links in the chain are critical to retain and which are the ones to outsource.

> *SPEECH TIP:* Learn how to strengthen your argument by fully exploiting the *downside* as well as the upside, the *negatives* as well as the *positives.* Leave your listeners with the belief that they are hearing all sides and being presented with evidence to judge for themselves.

Make no mistake, outsourcing fundamentally challenges a central tenet of the old corporate culture: control. With outsourcing come risks—from the loss of critical skills to loss of leverage over large suppliers. Morale may suffer, as employees wonder if theirs will be the next function to be outsourced. Too narrow an outlook may leave a company too insulated, disengaged from the reality of the marketplace. Finally, there is the concern that we will outsource our way to the hollow corporation.

There is the example of the toy company that receives designs for new toys from outside entrepreneurs. It sends the designs to contract manufacturers for production. It hires outside ad firms to promote the new products. Its data processing, billing, sales, and marketing are entirely outsourced. The Lewis Galoob toy company's sales are about $170 million dollars, and it employs 250 people. Another toy company, California's Mattel Toys, has almost ten times the sales, but *forty* times the work force: $1.3 billion/10,000 workers.

Where are the jobs created, and where are they lost? One can certainly argue that because the functions don't actually disappear, the jobs don't disappear; they just relocate. While the toy company doesn't employ data processors, somebody does employ data processors that do the toy company's data processing—better and more efficiently than it can. Is there a problem here?

There are actually two problems. The first problem is in the numbers. When my company takes over an operation that previously was handled in-house, we are able to provide a better service for a lower cost. We are more efficient, our systems are more sophisticated, our training is more advanced. In other words, it's all we think about twenty-four hours a day. We are *supposed* to do it better. Not surprisingly, though, we usually do it with fewer people.

The second problem is in the strategy. Companies that try to compete simply by cutting costs and overhead may be in for some surprises. Outsourcing is no panacea. It's often called the "make or buy" decision. Well, let me tell you, it can quickly become the make or break decision. It can make or break your human resource management, wreak havoc on your productivity, and ultimately hurt your profitability. There are plenty of examples of chopping overhead or "farming out" a function to save money and finding out that expenses go up rather than down.

Still, many industries are tempted by the lure of outsourcing to reduce costs. Coming from a company that can only benefit from such a decision, it may surprise you when I say this: Think about it; think about it long and hard. Outsourcing just to beat costs is a mistake. Outsourcing as a defensive strategy is a loser. If you are going to consider outsourcing, remember: It should be a positive strategic decision, measured by long-term strategic criteria. Judging it by short-term cost-cutting criteria is short-sighted and often counter-productive. And don't give away important learning opportunities that link you with customer preferences, supplier capabilities, or new technologies.

California, particularly Southern California, has had a rough time. The recession was deeper and longer here than in many other parts of the country. I say "was" with the full knowledge that many believe the recession is still here, with no end in sight for the short term. Add to that an already downsized defense industry that's going to take more cuts in the coming years.

For California's workers—both blue and white collar—more efforts toward greater competitiveness are threatening: Think about it! If their company "gets competitive," they may be out of a job; if their company doesn't "get competitive," they may surely be out of a job. Ultimately, their jobs become at risk either way. They are left with little but Yogi Berra's line about hard choices: "When you're at a fork in the road, take it."

However, there are some bright spots for the employee. I mentioned earlier that by restructuring management, employees are given more responsibility. That's good for the business, **and** good for employees who want to excel. There's an equally interesting human resource dimension to outsourcing as well. Let me ask you a question. Does a GM data processor have any chance at being the president of General Motors? Will the maintenance supervisor at IBM ever be tapped to head up IBM's R & D operation? Any chance we will see that individual rise to the ranks of top management? You know the answer. No. They are effectively off the career track. The career ceiling for them isn't glass—it's concrete.

Outsourcing brings people into those enterprises that are geared to advance them. At ARA we invest in our people; we spend millions on training and skill development. Let me tell you why: Any employee, whether a concession worker at Mile-High Stadium in the Rockies, a teacher in a Children's World Learning Center, or a cook in an ARA cafeteria—any one of them can advance to top management at ARA. And you know what? They already have.

Is it because we are so enlightened at ARA? I'd like to think that's part of the reason. But the major reason is that both the ARA guy on the line and the ARA guy at headquarters are focused on doing those ten million things right every day. That's what we believe we do "best in the world."

Here in California, the competitive pressures from both home and abroad aren't going to let up. Whether we're talking about diversification, restructuring management, or outsourcing, the new realities of the world market demand greatness. The great managers are the ones who can conceptually break their company into its parts, determine which parts house the essentials, and which house the extraneous. The great strategists are the ones who can put it all back together again.

Many can see what it will take to compete. Many understand that we must make tough choices. But while all may aim for the greatest good for the greatest number, the truly great business leaders recognize the costs as well. The fact of the matter is that we are using far fewer people to produce more products, deliver more services—something that is good for productivity numbers, bad for laid-off workers. We are thinning the ranks of America's middle management, with no immediate place for them to go. We are closing inefficient facilities, and in the process hobbling whole communities. As a nation we have not yet found the way to ease the pain along the road to a healthy future. That cannot be a license to stop trying. It is a major policy challenge.

I began by talking about three of the trends in today's business culture: sticking to your knitting, shortening the distance between the customer and CEO, and strategic outsourcing. I am confident that California businesses will build strength upon strength, leverage a very talented work force to a higher level of achievement, and focus their energies on a brighter future. In the end California will do what it does best: from technological innovation to state-of-the-art design, from product development to enlightened management of human beings, I believe California will continue to lead the nation.

Thank you.

Components of Success: Quality Control, Investment in Human Resources, and Applied Technology

RICHARD M. ROSENBERG
Chairman and Chief Executive Officer
BankAmerica Corporation

Delivered to the Executive Club of Chicago, May 21, 1993

SUMMARY: Bank of America chairman and CEO Richard M. Rosenberg examines three fundamental principles of good business that he believes will grow ever more essential to corporate survival, achievement, and prosperity in the marketplace of the future.

SPEECH TIP: It is always a good idea to begin by saying something positive about your audience.

Good afternoon. Thank you for your invitation. I am delighted to be here in this uniquely American city, and I am honored to appear before such a distinguished group.

I am here today to share some thoughts on the future of banking and, in a larger sense, the future of business in a competitive environment, where the pace of change seems to accelerate every day. I say this with a caveat uttered by the physicist Niels Bohr more than three decades ago: "Prediction is very difficult," he said. "Especially about the future." But I believe all of us here today share the feeling that if we do not contemplate what our future will look like—next month, next year, or in the next century—and if we do not *prepare* for that future, we may wake up one morning without a business to plan for anymore.

SPEECH TIP: A highly refreshing quotation. Rosenberg's listeners are saying to themselves, *Niels Bohr? Sounds more like Yogi Berra to me.*

Another great physicist, Albert Einstein, once remarked that "I never think of the future—it comes soon enough." Einstein may have been one of the three pivotal figures of the twentieth century, as the *Wall Street Journal* recently noted, but with that sort of philosophy, it is probably a good thing that he did not go into business.

> *SPEECH TIP:* Your audience can't fault you for failing to perform something you never promised. Note how the speaker carefully qualifies the goals and scope of his speech.

I will not pretend to predict the future today, but I will talk about what I believe are the key components for success in the future—especially in a future that is simultaneously becoming more global *and* more local; more demanding of quality, yet more conscious of cost; more driven by technology, yet in even greater need of well-trained, well-educated human resources.

It always helps when contemplating the future to look briefly back at the past.

> *SPEECH TIP:* A lesson in the technique of the then-and-now illustration, carried out on a grand scale.

Does anybody here remember what they were doing on October 4, 1957? That was roughly thirty-five years ago, well within many of our working lifetimes. It was the day that the Soviet Union launched Sputnik, which many historians say was the symbolic transition from the Industrial Age to the Information Age—a time when the value of the human mind began to eclipse the value of natural resources. On October 4, 1957, the top ten businesses in Chicago were Swift, Standard Oil, Armour, International Harvester, Inland Steel, Wilson, Sears, Montgomery Ward, Prudential Insurance, and the First National Bank of Chicago. Thirty-five years later, the list of Chicago's top businesses, ranked by sales, is a little different. It still includes Sears and First National, but it also includes CNA Financial, Amoco, Continental Bank, Diner's Club, and Commonwealth Edison.

But, ranked by market capitalization—which many would agree is a more meaningful measure—Chicago's biggest companies include Ameritech, Abbott Labs, McDonald's, Motorola, Waste Management, and Baxter.

These lists dramatically illustrate the evolution that American business has gone through over the past thirty-five years—an evolution characterized by a move away from commodities and commodity-type manufacturing to services, health care, and technology in many different formats.

The lists also lead to the next question: Which companies will be among the top ten in the next thirty-five years?

The more appropriate question may be not *who* will be on the list, but how a company—any company—can get there.

Change may be constant, but I believe successful companies in the twenty-first century—which, for all intents and purposes is already here—will operate against three fundamental components of success:

> *SPEECH TIP:* An unspoken covenant between a speaker and his audience is the promise to give the listeners something valuable in return for their attention. What is given here? Nothing less than a *list* of three keys to success.

1. A strict adherence to quality control

2. Strategic investment in human resources

3. Efficient and productive application of technology.

Of these three components, quality control may be the most visible and carry the potential for the greatest returns, but only because it may be the by-product of strategic investment in human resources and the efficient and productive application of technology.

John Young, recently retired CEO of Hewlett-Packard, pointed out a startling statistic: Studies have shown that one-quarter to one-third of the time and resources at large companies today are spent *fixing* problems, that is, remedying situations that never should have occurred in the first place. This represents time and resources spent undoing things that could otherwise have been focused on customer service, product innovation, or employee development. It represents—simply—waste.

> **SPEECH TIP:** A "startling statistic" indeed! And *startling statistics* are absolutely the best ones to use in any speech.

Obviously, a fundamental goal of successful companies should be to drive out that type of waste, which is why quality control—preventing the problem in the first place—is the key component for successful companies.

At Bank of America, we have targeted three primary areas of our business in which high quality is one of the fundamental goals:

1. Operations

2. Our loan portfolio, and

3. Customer service

Let me briefly explain our focus in these three areas.

Quality of operations, we believe, is a key to profitability, especially at a time when revenues face so many challenges from competitors in an industry marked by over-capacity, similar to so many other industries in the nation today. To give you an idea of the scale of operations at Bank of America, we process approximately seventeen million checks each day—on some nights, we process almost 8 percent of all the checks written in the country. Our peak night was twenty-six million checks following a holiday weekend. Is 99 percent accuracy satisfactory performance? If we achieve 99 percent accuracy, we make 170,000 mistakes every day, and I think you would agree that that is not satisfactory performance.

Our Teleservice unit provides customers with twenty-four-hour access to information about their accounts. In any given month, we accommodate approximately fifteen million telephone customer account inquiries.

Our network of more than 4,600 ATMs makes us the largest proprietary provider of ATM services in the world, and we handle over thirty million ATM transactions monthly in California alone.

Thus, when we talk about quality in these types of operations, we must have in mind, and we must set standards for, transactions that are absolutely error-free and develop efficiencies that yield the best service at the lowest costs.

Control of expenses and delivering high-quality service were once thought to be mutually exclusive endeavors. Obviously, we absolutely do not believe that, but every element in the organization must be examined in order to reduce expenses while still delivering high-quality service. And, of course, there must be an absolute commitment to quality in order to achieve such results.

A second major focus of quality control, of course, is our loan portfolio. The paper-thin margins that are usually present in lending demand uncompromising quality in our loan portfolios, while still meeting the needs of the consumers and businesses that we serve. Because one bad loan can eat up the profit from many good loans, we need to be right when we make a loan about 99 1/4 percent of the time to achieve satisfactory earnings. Therefore, it is critical that the risk/reward ratio be an inherent part of the quality process. At Bank of America, our credit culture is one that attempts to balance risk with the potential rewards from that risk. BankAmerica's credit culture uses a systematic procedure to build quality into our assets. For example:

- We have guidelines to foster portfolio diversification.

- We set credit limits by country, by industry, and by product.

- We use market intelligence creatively and aggressively.

- And we use an approval system that relies on teamwork between relationship officers and credit specialists with specific areas of expertise.

But, in the final analysis, the key to quality control in the services industry is how the customer is handled at the "moment of truth," when customer contact is made by telephone, written communication, or in person. An idea we communicate very strongly to employees at Bank of America is the belief that customers represent a long-term relationship, not just a transaction, and that relationship is becoming more and more complex.

It was not always so. In the not-too-distant past, customer service at a bank was defined primarily by transactional standards: You came in, made a deposit or withdrawal, and expected the bank's records to be accurate.

The banking world is different today. When you take the time to see a personal banker or bank officer, you expect to be exposed to the best rates on a wide variety of CDs, and the discussion may include municipal bonds, mutual funds, or other types of investments. This is even more true on the business level, where the customer relationship is usually defined as fewer customers with more services as contrasted to the consumer area, where there are more consumers but with fewer services per customer.

We can expect the level of service to both businesses and consumers to become even more sophisticated in the 1990s as banks offer a wider variety of products and services, from more exotic derivative products to businesses, to more exotic savings plans for consumers. This sophistication factor leads us to the second component of success: a commitment to recruiting and developing the highest level of human resources.

Successful management is committed to staying ahead of the quality-of-service curve by training employees, giving them the support and tools they need, and rewarding them for outstanding performance. But, more than that, successful companies have to become strategic about where and how they develop managerial talent and how they allocate resources to that development. For instance, does a company need to concentrate on market share, and thus ramp up its marketing resources? If so, there should be a strategic decision to recruit marketing talent, whether it be newly graduated MBAs, established marketers at peer firms, or those with great potential for that need within the company.

Recruiting is the first step, both internal and external. The next is development. If these managers are being considered as strategic resources, they should be treated as such and not be allowed to be swallowed up by an indifferent corporate process.

What makes this commitment to development of human resources especially challenging is the simultaneous demand we all face to become as efficient as possible, which often means downsizing, rightsizing, re-engineering, or whatever term is being used at the moment. "Rightsizing," in fact, is more often than not a competitive necessity. This is especially true as many companies move toward a structure based on a relatively small, permanent core of managers surrounded by a more flexible work force made up of part-time, temporary, or contracted employees.

Successful management realizes that a stable core of talented, dedicated employees is crucial if the company is going to prosper in this period of extraordinary change.

> *SPEECH TIP:* Anecdotes used in speeches should have at least two qualities. The anecdote should be on-target relevant to the speaker's point and purpose. And the anecdote should make your listeners wonder in amazement: *Where did he get that one?* It also helps if the anecdote is genuinely funny.

The third component of success is technology—not technology of itself, but how efficiently that technology is used. The story of the traveler and the Arkansas chicken is a good illustration of this point. According to the story, a motorist was clipping along at about 65 mph through the Arkansas back country when he was passed by a three-legged chicken running along the shoulder of the road.

The amazed driver followed the chicken as it turned onto a dirt road that led up to a run-down poultry farm. As the chicken ran behind the barn, the man pulled up and asked a farmer standing nearby if he had seen the amazing sight.

"Yup," the farmer said. "Those are three-legged chickens I breed. My wife and boy and I all like drumsticks, and we grew three-leggers so we can all have a drumstick from one chicken."

"That's amazing," the traveler said. "How do they taste?"

"I do not know," the farmer replied. "I haven't caught one yet."

Such is the peril with new technology. It may be inexpensive and remarkably fast, but if it is not harnessed to achieve specific business objectives, chances are it will not be of much use. Worse, it may be a serious drain on capital and resources.

In fact, technology itself is increasingly becoming a simple commodity. It is the *application* of technology that adds value to a business and poses the real challenge to management. I say this with some certainty, because in the banking industry, technology has yet to realize its full potential in spite of the fact that without the application of technology in the early '50s at Bank of America, we believe the financial system, as we know it today, could not exist.

In the 1950s, Bank of America and Stanford Research Institute pioneered the development of the industry's first computer system to process checks by reading the magnetic ink on the check. That system was called the Electronic Recording Method of Accounting—or ERMA—and it revolutionized check-processing in our industry. Today the first ERMA machine is housed in the Smithsonian Institution.

There has not really been an equivalent leap of applied technology in the banking industry since then, although technology continues to increase the volume of business and consumer transactions that banks can process at ever increasing speed. But technology has yet to be used to the maximum to truly gather and analyze information, to process more simply and fundamentally to assist businesses and consumers to manage their financial requirements in an optimum fashion. Some major developments have taken place—from corporate treasurers' workstations to scores of failed attempts at home banking—but another big breakthrough like ERMA has yet to take place, and maybe never will.

Banks are in the process of capturing and analyzing information contained in the customer transaction stream in the same way that bar code scanners capture and track information on purchases at grocery stores. Safeway and Lucky stores in California, and Jewel and Dominic's here in Chicago, already can tell market researchers precisely what goods are most popular in any zip code, how much people are willing to pay for them, the incentive effect of discount coupons, and other purchasing trends. There is a constant feedback loop to manufacturers, buyers, distributors, the kid who stocks the shelves, and the consumers who want to see their favorite products on those shelves. In fact, as we know, some manufacturers have their computers directly linked to retailers in order to provide automatic restocking of inventory. The latter is a trend that is creating a major change in the distribution industry.

If banks effectively captured the information from their customers' debits and credits, that information could be used in many ways to provide better service and reduce costs. To some extent, this is being achieved as banks try to identify more customers who can benefit from an additional service based on their current banking patterns. Just as artificial intelligence is being developed to make better loan decisions, artificial intelligence, combined with real-time and accurate data, can lead a banker to more intelligently offer the appropriate service to a consumer. This may be the next major technology breakthrough in the industry.

Externally, the information surely would be useful to those economists, both in government and non-government, whose statistics today are often suspect and thus lead both private and government economic plans down the wrong road in developing business plans and public policy.

> *SPEECH TIP:* A good rhetorical question spurs thought—and, moreover, it spurs thought in the direction desired by the speaker.

Is there any government statistic on consumer purchases as good as data captured in VISA or Mastercard processing nationwide? I doubt it. Today, most major retailers aggregate and segregate some of this data, to balance and speed inventories, but banks are just dipping into this information stream on a limited, customer-permission basis.

It is certainly within the realm of possibility in the immediate future, for instance, that banks will track the frequency of customers' use of bank services, correlate that use with their deposit balances, and provide an incentive for a desired service level. Retail customers pay less for their car insurance while building a no-claims bonus, and get extra miles by frequently flying with one airline. Why not build new incentives into consumer bank accounts, as has been achieved with corporate relationships?

Banks can also broaden the uses of their ATMs. What if ATMs, which are on virtually every street corner in the country, were more useful as a distribution system? In fact, they could be the new interim alternative distribution system of the nation. They could access airline and auto reservations, stock quotes and share trading, electronic mail and fax, real estate offerings—just about any product or service that can be transmitted electronically, and that covers almost everything. But note that I said interim, because cable and telephone will ultimately change the nature and usefulness of ATMs.

Again, these sorts of opportunities, in some cases, are already realized by companies that seize the initiative to apply technology creatively and efficiently.

More must follow to remain competitive. It is a fundamental irony that, in the age of technology, the machines that were supposed to make life easier for us are making us work harder than ever before! But that effort also offers returns that we never before dreamed were possible.

The benefits that flow from practicing these three components of success—quality control, human resource development, and the efficient use of technology—are manifold.

One of the most obvious is their impact on earnings. When you control for quality and expenses and deliver the best customer service you can, you can be sure it will positively impact earnings. Strong earnings, of course, enhance shareholder value, and any publicly owned company today that does not hold increased shareholder value as one of its primary objectives simply is not relevant.

But one of the key benefits may also be one of the most overlooked: how effective management can affect the cost of capital, which will be one of the most critical elements of long-term growth in the 1990s.

Conventional wisdom says that the high cost of U.S. capital stifles investment and drives many businesses offshore, and that U.S. companies are at a competitive disadvantage with Japanese companies, due to their access to inexpensive capital. While there may have been some truth to that in the past, there is also growing evidence that external factors play an increasingly limited role in the cost of capital, and internal management plays a much larger role than we may think.

Carl Kester and Timothy Luehrman, writing in the *Harvard Business Review* last year, contend that in the new global economy, all companies increasingly compete for the same capital. In this global marketplace, they argue, companies that obtain capital at favorable costs will be those that are the most efficiently managed and organized.

So, the benefits of these components of success are many, and they are real. Quality control, investment in human resources, and applied technology are not just management buzz words. When practiced right, with commitment and discipline, these techniques are the keys to competitiveness in the twenty-first century. They are beacons by which we can guide our direction while moving rapidly to effect the changes that are necessary to compete and, in most cases, survive.

All it takes is our commitment—and one more old-fashioned, time-honored component of success known to everyone in this area: hard work.

Thank you very much for allowing me to share these thoughts with you. I will be pleased now to take your questions.

Remarks by John Sculley

Chairman and CEO,
Apple Computer, Inc.

Delivered at President-elect Bill Clinton's Economic Conference, Little Rock, Arkansas, December 15, 1992

SUMMARY: John Sculley, at the time CEO of Apple Computer, defines the "New Economy" and outlines the challenges and opportunities it presents.

SPEECH TIP: Don't be afraid of Big Themes. Just make sure you introduce them—as here—in a way that alerts your audience to their magnitude.

We are at a major turning point in the world economy. This is a change as significant as the transformation of our nineteenth-century agricultural economy into the twentieth-century industrial economy, which took place a century ago.

The hallmark of this twentieth-century industrial economy has been mass production and mass consumption. The mass production/mass consumption model of business was pioneered in this country by early twentieth-century leaders like Henry Ford and the industrial engineer Frederick Taylor. This model assumed that all important decisions were centralized around a small managerial elite. "Thinking" was purposely separated from "doing." Work was broken down into repetitive tasks, and management consciously eliminated as much decision-making as possible for the workers. Quality was defined around rigid standardization. There was little flexibility in the work process.

Perhaps the biggest change in this decade will be the reorganization of work—that is, re-engineering the ways in which work gets done productively.

But here's a major problem: Most Americans don't know what the New Economy is, yet it will dramatically impact their lives in the years ahead. Today we measure economic health on internal comparisons like GDP (Gross Domestic Product) growth and unemployment rates. In the New Economy, the key indicator is standard of living, as measured externally by comparative productivity versus that of other industrialized trading regions. Our high standard of living already requires higher productivity than the rest of the world. Fortunately, we are still ahead. But we are losing ground. Real income is down. Only the best-educated, higher-income families are holding their own.

In the New Economy, that old industrial model is being replaced by a rapid move toward customization of goods and services and the decentralization of work. Today, new products can be developed in a fraction of the time it took in the old industrial economy, services and products are being custom built to order, quality is dramatically improving, and costs are being driven down through the use of new technologies such as computer systems, robotics, and measurement systems.

In the New Economy, workers are on the front line interacting with customers, and workers on the factory floor are empowered to make decisions. This is the only way customized goods and services can be created quickly, with the highest quality, at the lowest cost, and with maximum flexibility.

In the old economy, America had a real advantage because we were rich with natural resources, and our large domestic market formed the basis for economies of scale.

In the New Economy, strategic resources no longer just come out of the ground—as did oil, coal, iron, and wheat. The strategic resources are ideas and information that come out of our minds. The result is, as a nation, we have gone from being resource-rich in the old economy to resource-poor in the New Economy almost overnight! Our public education system has not successfully made the shift from teaching the memorization of facts to achieving the learning of critical thinking skills. We are still trapped in a K-12 public education system, which is preparing our youth for jobs that no longer exist.

The New Economy is global. We are no longer alone at the top. In fact, the United States is underprepared to compete with many other major industrialized trading regions in the world. Students in other industrialized countries are learning math, sciences, and critical-judgment skills that are more relevant to the New Economy. Other industrialized countries have an alternative path for the non-college-bound, including vocational study and a school-to-work transition that is tightly linked with apprenticeships and worker training in industry. We have few alternatives for non-college-bound students, so they can participate productively in the highly skilled work of the New Economy.

The greatest certainty about the New Economy is the pace of change. Young people in school today can reasonably expect to have four or five careers. Skill needs will constantly change, as well. Education, therefore, must become a lifelong pursuit, not just an institutional experience early in one's life. Education, training, and retraining must become as much an ongoing experience in our lives as exercise and vacations.

Most Americans see our largest corporations going through massive restructurings, layoffs, and downsizing. People know something has changed, and they are scared because they don't fully understand it and they see people they know losing their jobs. They also see their neighbors buying high-quality, lower-priced products from abroad, and they ask why we can't build these same products or better ones here at home.

SPEECH TIP: Provide an unmistakable pivot upon which you can turn your speech.

The answer is, we can. But only if we have a public education system that will turn out a world-class product. We need an education system that will educate all our students, not just the top 15 to 20 percent.

A highly skilled work force must begin with a world-class public education system. Eventually, the New Economy will touch every industry in our nation. There will be no place to hide!

In the New Economy, low-skilled manual work will be paid less. The United States cannot afford to have the high-skilled work being done somewhere else in the world and end up with the low-wage work. This is not an issue about protectionism. It is an issue about an educational system aligned with the New Economy and a broad educational opportunity for everyone.

The reorganization of work into decentralized, higher-skilled jobs is the systemic key to a vital American economy in the future. We are talking about the standard of living that we, and our children, and their children will have well into the twenty-first century.

It's America's choice: high skills or low wages.

Strategic Alliances Old and New:
A Caltex Perspective

PATRICK J. WARD
Chairman, President, and Chief Executive Officer
Caltex Petroleum Corporation

Delivered to the International General Meeting of the Pacific Basin Economic Council, Seoul, Korea, May 26, 1993

SUMMARY: The head of Caltex Petroleum believes that strategic business alliances can offer companies many advantages in competing worldwide. Citing examples from a variety of industries—and drawing from his own experiences with a long-standing joint venture—Ward presents some management advice for successful corporate collaboration.

SPEECH TIP: The tone of this speech is serious and informational. Don't be afraid to let your audience know that they are about to learn something valuable.

The concept of a strategic alliance is as old as history. Since ancient times, two or more kingdoms or nations have joined forces to achieve common objectives. Often, those objectives have been military in nature, and alliances against common enemies were as common in the days of chariots as they are in our era of "smart bombs" and tactical missiles. Strategic alliances have not, however, always been formed for military purposes. As multilateral organizations have proliferated, we have seen nations come together for many peaceful purposes, such as trade. ASEAN, NAFTA and the EC are examples.

As we read history, we can see that strategic alliances in some cases have been short-term. Cooperation between the United States and the Soviet Union during World War II did not survive the new realities that emerged with the Cold War. Only now, a generation later, with the Cold War ended, are the two former adversaries renewing cordial relations.

Other strategic alliances stand the test of time. The United States went "Over There" to fight beside the British and other Allies in World War I, was closely allied with Britain in World War II, and has enjoyed an enduring "special relationship" ever since. In terms of military operations, the United States and Britain were on the same side in Operation Desert Storm.

The use of strategic alliances in business is nearly as old as military or political alliances and has become extremely important to corporations as we enter the twenty-first century. Business alliances can be of short-term duration, with two or more corporations coming together in joint ventures that are disbanded as soon as objectives have been reached. However, business alliances can also be more or less permanent. Across all industries, products, and services, no one corporation alone is likely to be able to perform all of its operational tasks, satisfy the growing needs of different customers, and stay innovative all by itself.

Alliances have become a vital modality for helping firms to compete and learn new skills and technologies to revitalize their operations. Witness the widespread popularity of alliances, joint ventures, and consortia to share research and development in everything from computers to communications and biotechnology.

The virtues of the strategic alliance for business have been recently popularized in books like *The Virtual Corporation* and before world business groups by leading management consultants such as Cyrus Friedheim of Booz-Allen, Hamilton. He predicts that today's global firms will be replaced by "relationship enterprises," which will embody strategic alliances between very large firms from different industries, geographic regions, and technology levels to achieve certain common goals. Achieving these objectives means that the members of the alliance will act almost like a single firm.

> *SPEECH TIP:* An opening sentence like the one in the following paragraph would appear at the beginning of many speeches. Here, the speaker uses it as a transition from a general, historical introduction to the concept of strategic alliances to his company's experience with such alliances.

Today, I would like to share with you some of our experiences and views regarding both the creation and the operation of strategic alliances and joint ventures. I will begin with a brief sketch of how Caltex has evolved through a series of strategic alliances. Caltex itself embodies the essence of a long-term relationship enterprise, both among our many partners and in our spirit of laying foundations for growth. Then I would like to explore some of the practical aspects of what makes strategic alliances work. Finally, I would like to outline a few principles for the future.

In the best of worlds, a strategic alliance is more than a mechanism to achieve narrowly defined objectives; it is the basis for building and solidifying a human relationship that transcends immediate differences to forge a new vision and new ways of mutual understanding. The formation of Caltex was a strategic alliance between the Standard Oil Company of California (now Chevron) and the Texas Company (now Texaco). In the early '30s Chevron had taken a bold gamble and had explored and discovered oil in Bahrain and Saudi Arabia, which was well beyond its requirements as a regional oil marketing company in the western United States.

Also in the early 1930s, Texaco had marketing assets throughout Asia supplied from Port Arthur in the United States—a very long voyage. Forming Caltex in 1936 was thus a natural combination. The Caltex venture, centered in Bahrain, afforded Texaco a closer source of supply for its Eastern Hemisphere and African markets, while providing Chevron with an outlet for the oil. Each partner took 50 percent interest in California Texas Oil Company, now Caltex.

In addition to being important commercially, the Caltex venture also became important to the Allies during World War II. Wartime disruption in the normal flow of petroleum made Bahrain a key supply point for the Allies in the Middle East and the Eastern Front in the USSR. It was a critical supply line that facilitated U.S. lend-lease aid to Russia and helped to lubricate the workings of the Allied war machine.

In a management sense, Caltex looked like a traditional U.S.-based company, but in reality was quite different. Caltex was avant-garde in the sense that this formal joint venture between two competitive companies enjoyed considerable autonomy and latitude to undertake its own strategies in new markets across the world.

In 1936 the U.S. headquarters housed senior management, but operational decisions were made halfway around the globe. A tradition of local executive decision-making started—indeed, was required—from the very first days of the joint venture. In a very small way, Caltex began to develop its own corporate culture and management style.

The new Caltex joint venture planted the seeds of a uniquely blended corporate culture, which embodied the best operating characteristics and procedures of the two parent companies. The pre-existence of a common business and social culture in our parent companies helped get this early stage of Caltex off the ground. The hurdles would have been greater if our venture had been attempted across contrasting corporate cultures.

The war and its aftermath created a tremendous vacuum in the oil industry. Caltex formed new subsidiary companies in Asia and assumed Texaco's marketing and distribution facilities in Europe and North Africa. To meet fuel requirements, Caltex built and took interest in twenty-four refineries in a twenty-year period from 1946 to 1966.

Originally, the chairman was drawn from one shareholder and the president from the other. But Caltex also hired aggressively on its own and trained, developed, and managed its own employee and officer corps. I've always thought that Chevron and Texaco showed great wisdom in allowing Caltex to mature as a separate organization.

Many in Asia will remember Jim Voss, the first Caltex chairman to be elected from Caltex-developed executives. Jim formed our first strategic alliance in 1950, in Japan. Caltex entered the Japanese market with the purchase of 50 percent of Koa Oil Company, a major refining company. In 1951, Caltex entered into an alliance with Nippon Oil Company and used the familiar form of a 50-50 joint venture to establish Nippon Petroleum Refining Corporation. Subsequently, Koa and NPRC established Tokyo Tanker Company and the Nippon Oil Staging Terminal Company, which are among the largest tanker and oil holding facilities in the world.

> *SPEECH TIP:* Refining the definition by defining one kind of strategic alliance: the joint venture.

The joint-venture form of strategic alliance met the requirements of the restoration of postwar Japan—something which the governments of Japan and the U.S. greatly desired. Equally important in a commercial sense, we were able through our partner to become an insider in the Japanese market, something that is highly touted as management advice today.

Caltex's second strategic alliance was in Korea in the 1960s, when Lucky Ltd. and Caltex joined together to develop the nation's refinery. Caltex and Lucky signed a 50-50 joint venture agreement in 1966, which established Honam Oil Refinery Co. Ltd. This culminated in the building of the Yocheon Refinery, which was completed in 1969.

In the interim, our Korean partner has grown considerably and has become the Lucky Goldstar Group, a major *chaebol*, which produces consumer electronics, cement, textiles, and other goods. Lucky Goldstar is a leading global competitor across many industries.

Caltex contributed oil, capital, technology, construction, and management expertise to the Japan and Korean joint ventures, while Nippon Oil and Lucky contributed extensive local knowledge and considerable business wisdom.

Like the joint venture with Nippon Oil Company, the strategic alliance between Lucky Ltd. and Caltex culminated in a long-term, friendly relationship that helps and sustains both partners in the Far East.

I might mention here that our distinguished international president of PBEC, Mr. P. H. Koo, has been associated with Honam Oil since its founding and has been instrumental in its great success, first as a vice president of Honam from 1967 to 1974 and then as president from 1974 to 1987.

P. H. will remember that, in the early days, Caltex participated in the day-to-day management through a system of joint directorships. In 1986, the joint venture evolved further when local management assumed full responsibility for day-to-day management operations. Caltex continues to play a significant role in Honam's strategic direction, through its representation on the board of directors of the company.

> *SPEECH TIP:* Step back to put everything in perspective. What does a good strategic alliance add up to? A "win-win scenario."

Helping our partners to help themselves is important to helping everyone grow and prosper together.

> *SPEECH TIP:* Transitions are as vital to an effective speech as road signs are to a highway. There is no mystery to writing a good transition. Just tell your audience where you are taking them.

Now I would like to turn to the more practical aspects of strategic alliances. Caltex has prospered in Asia because its management recognized the needs and opportunities that would come with the cessation of World War II and put Caltex in position to grow across Asia, mainly through wholly owned subsidiaries. On the other hand, the strategy in Japan and Korea was to develop through strategic alliances with the best Japanese and Korean partners.

According to Jim Voss, most internationals at that time were insisting on management control, either through ownership over 50 percent or special codicils. Caltex realized that percentages and codicils do not offer security in joint ventures. If your local partner is unhappy, owning 51 percent does not guarantee success.

As a result, Caltex took advantage of being in the right place at the right time by structuring our strategic alliances in Japan and Korea on terms acceptable to our partners and the host governments. This approach quickly led to major positions in these important markets.

Our experience shows that the seeds planted early in alliances can become the trees and pillars of strength that allow partners to take on new challenges by investing in new technologies, markets, industries, and, of course, the managerial/technical talent to make it all happen.

The most important key is people. To set the pace of future endeavors, it is important to build a management team that focuses on the strategic alliance as an evolution. We find models of cooperation in such enduring and successful joint ventures as Dow-Corning (USA), Fuji-Xerox (Japan), GE-SNECMA (France), and Dupont-Toray (Japan), which span a host of industries.

Positive working relationships are critical to any company that needs a management team capable of dealing with multiple issues and projects at the same time.

A career as an executive with an international strategic alliance is rich in multicultural experience. Many of the executives of the more successful ventures have spent most of their working lives away from their home countries. Companies such as BASF, IBM, Whirlpool, BP, CIBA-GEIGY, and Unilever encourage their managers to adopt a global perspective early in their careers. In Caltex, we are proud that an increasing number of our executives are natives of the countries in which we operate. Diverse both in origin and in the way they view the world, their broad experiences enable them to participate in the development and exercise of Caltex's strategic decision-making process.

Just as Caltex has expanded its vision and horizons to accommodate the changing needs and technologies of its partners, so have many other companies that are involved in joint ventures.

For example, Corning Glass has more than twenty different relationships with other companies such as Samsung of Korea, Iwaki and Asahi of Japan, Vitro Kristal of Mexico, and Siemens of Germany. Corning gives its managers ample autonomy to build close ties with its partners.

The Japanese like to say that binding roots is as important as binding technologies; we agree. High levels of independence with room for personal involvement help to bridge relationships and to deal with problems on an ongoing basis without having them mushroom into a loss-of-face situation.

The roots of the company are the employees who represent the technical, intellectual, and managerial strength of the company.

> *SPEECH TIP:* Another crystal-clear transition.

Let's shift our focus from the people to the organization and begin to examine the concepts of the "virtual corporation" or "relationship enterprise."

I'm struck with the similarity in the development of the oil industry. All of the large oil companies started either with production or refining and added the other phases to become fully integrated companies by the 1960s.

The 1970s, with the rise of OPEC and heightened nationalism on the part of some producing countries, began a trend of delinking the upstream from downstream, which lasted into the 1990s. We are now seeing the national oil companies of both oil exporting and importing nations beginning to form new strategic alliances in order to regain some of the advantages of integrated relationships, which were part of the industry before 1970.

Striking similarities to these transitions are now occurring in the telecommunications, computer, and communications industries. For example, the breakup of

AT&T in the early '80s parallels the streamlining of the oil industry. Now AT&T faces a rapidly changing environment, in which computers, video technology, consumer electronics, and communications are converging. To meet the dual challenge of entering new markets and building new companies, AT&T is forging a series of new and complex relationships in the upstream aspect of its business. The personal computer, fax machine, flat-screen television, and cellular telephone are roots of a new technology that promises to transform relationships as well.

We might ask what can be done to anticipate and keep up, or preferably, keep ahead of change in the economic and business environment in which we operate. That is particularly important when we see long-established industry leaders suddenly finding themselves behind the industry tide and threatened with the loss of their business. This trend is particularly significant as we witness such highly vertically integrated leaders as GM in autos, IBM in computers, Sears in retailing, and NBC in broadcasting come under siege by more agile and nimble smaller companies—many of whom have formed partnerships and alliances with firms from other industries to seize the initiative away from established market leaders.

One U.S. firm that has done much to revitalize its operations through internal efforts and close working relationships with its joint venture partners is Motorola. A leader in cellular telephones, specialized computers, microprocessors, and memory chips, Motorola works with a host of partners to enter new markets and to exchange skills and technologies to foster continual learning. With Toshiba, Motorola learned how to improve its manufacturing skills in making memory chips. Later, the close alliance with Toshiba grew to include even more advanced products such as high-density TV chips. In the U.S., Motorola has become a networked company that teams up with Apple, IBM, Northern Telecom, Amtech, and other companies to develop budding new technologies that promise to transform many of today's products. Behind the technologies, however, is a steadfast effort to form lasting relationships where mutual respect and understanding make for powerful, industry-changing alliances.

It's good to see Motorola joining with our partner Lucky Goldstar. Good luck to them.

As we enter the era of virtual corporations and relationship enterprises, history can provide some guidance for what will be an exciting future in alliance formation.

> ***SPEECH TIP:*** Sometimes the simplest organizing structures are the most effective. Literally enumerate your key points: "First . . . Second . . . Third."

First, it is important to consider relationship building as a long-term endeavor. Building successful alliances is more like growing rice and wheat. You have to know your partners and work closely with them in laying the roots for long-term sustenance. Binding personal roots takes precedence over binding technologies:

you want to lay the groundwork for the long term before harvesting the short term. A close rapport is much akin to planting and nurturing so that the plants can thrive and grow. The more they are nurtured, the richer the crop yield. Simultaneously, it's important to know when the seasons or technologies change. These changes provide the catalyst for working with both existing and new partners to cooperate on those projects that no one can handle by themselves.

Second, relationships depend on a series of small ventures, which culminate in gradual successes, which foster mutual respect and trust. Respect and trust are necessary if the partners are to explore and pursue new opportunities.

Third, networks of alliances are a dynamic process. Keeping up the momentum to prevent a relationship from decaying into stagnation requires not only a give-and-take attitude, but also new insights as executives from both sides try out innovative strategies and procedures that may not have been spelled out in the original agreement. Autonomy and operating latitude are key to dealing with contingencies that always surface in any kind of relationship. A networked environment is a negotiated environment.

Fourth, developing people in the joint venture as well as those who represent the owners of the joint venture is key to success. The human assets of any organization are the most important in its success and contribution to society. Recall that people are the primary source of competitive advantage. And we must remember the globalized company of tomorrow will need the talents and leadership of people from many nations.

Looking for the next strategic alliance is also very important. Will it be in some new geographic area, which has not been available or attractive in the past? Will it be in some new areas of business in which the virtual corporation is not a customary feature? Will it be in the form of a relationship enterprise with someone in a totally different line of business?

The prospect is very exciting and, indeed, can provide new incentives and blood for an ongoing strategic alliance that is reaching middle age.

A final note. The global or strategic alliances we have been talking about require economic cooperation, open regionalism, and open trade. Here in Asia, the true meaning of "open regionalism," "open trade," and "economic cooperation" could very well serve as a model for the rest of the world. These are higher-level variations of the virtual corporate concept applied to the nation-state entity. The oil industry operating in this area provides an excellent example of how capital and trade can move freely, without barriers, to spur economic growth and prosperity.

We are hopeful that the Asia-Pacific nations and their economic and trading partners in other parts of the world will continue on the high road of harmony and cooperation, and will avoid the mistakes of restrictive trade and investment policies that could be spawned by short-sighted regional or national interests. We must remember that, just as a rising tide floats all boats, a falling tide grounds them.

The continued progress of the region requires that the public and private sectors of all nations recognize the key drivers that have been responsible for their past successes and build on them for the future.

Thank you very, very much. It has been my pleasure to be with you today.

Clintonomics:
The Information Revolution
and the New Global Market Economy

WALTER B. WRISTON
Citicorp

Delivered to The Independent Institute, San Francisco, California, January 25, 1993

SUMMARY: Walter B. Wriston of Citicorp explores how today's electronic communications technology has indeed created an "information revolution" that dissolves national borders and profoundly alters crucial aspects of conventional political sovereignty. From military security to currency control, from human rights awareness to concepts of international trade, the global communications network is causing power to change hands.

When we think about the world and the never-ending stream of events that capture our attention, we tend to break the passage of time into neat segments delineated by years and months, but world events move at their own pace, paying little attention to man-made metrics. The new Clinton administration, which has just taken office, will find a new world waiting for it that has been years in the making. During the campaign we all heard a great deal about change, each candidate vying to excel as agent of change to move the country forward. If one listens to the rhetoric and even to the music at the inaugural galas, it is clear that much of the change being suggested is merely an attempt to return to yesterday. The problem is that that world no longer exists. Instead, we find ourselves in the midst of a great transition that is working fundamental changes in the structure of our society.

> *SPEECH TIP:* Laying to rest myths and misconceptions is an effective way to open a speech.

Despite the campaign verbiage about the decline of American manufacturing, the percentage of our GDP contributed by manufacturing has not changed in any significant way in the last ten years. What has changed is that the number of people employed in that sector has been steadily declining as productivity has gone up. Indeed, the American worker is the most productive in the world, but those manufacturing jobs that were a mainstay of our society for so many years are never going to come back, any more than we will ever see again American farms employing the twenty million people who worked on them at the turn of the century. These massive historical transitions are not only disruptive, and often painful, but also upset long-held beliefs and require us to think anew—itself a painful process. The industrial age in which we all grew up is slowly fading into the information society, and as much as some may wish to do so, we can't go back again. As the journalist Mike O'Neill put it: "Today's world cannot be remodeled with yesterday's memories: there are no U-turns on the road to the future." This is the new reality that the Clinton administration will have to deal with. Old solutions will not yield answers to new problems. Examples abound.

The information revolution has often been announced by futurists, but many of the innovations that have been predicted have never arrived. No one has yet seen the paperless society, nor a helicopter in every back yard. What we have seen instead is that information technology has demolished time and distance, but instead of increasing the power of government and thus validating Orwell's vision of Big Brother watching our every move, the proposition has been stood on its head, and we have all wound up watching Big Brother. No one who has lived through the last few years and watched on live television as the Berlin Wall came down, or as the first protesters in Prague in 1988 chanted at the riot police, "The world sees you," can fail to understand that information technology is changing the way we think about the power of government, about the way the world works, the way we work, and, indeed, the nature of work itself.

The massive upheaval in the former Soviet Union is a case in point. While governments maintain elaborate intelligence-gathering facilities, when a crisis arises, eyes in all countries turn to the CNN monitor, which is standard furniture in all government crisis management offices. The foreign minister of the former Soviet Union, Eduard A. Shevardnadze, during the Yeltsin coup put it this way: "Praise be information technology! Praise be CNN. . . . Anyone who owned a parabolic antenna able to see this network's transmissions had a complete picture of what was happening." And this from a senior officer of what used to be a closed and secretive society. The only ones in Moscow who did not know what was going on were those at the American Embassy, which did not have CNN.

SPEECH TIP: A speech about the future must first tell us clearly where we are at the present. If this comes as a momentous revelation—as here—so much the better.

While historians rarely identify these sea changes when they are living through them, I would argue that the signs are unmistakable that we are now in the midst of a new revolution at least as drastic and far reaching as that which occurred in what the great historian Paul Johnson describes as the birth of the modern world society at the beginning of the nineteenth century. Different people see different talismans; each constructs his or her own scenario, as we are all the product of the velocity of our own experience. Social analysts observe political and social change, while scientists tend to emphasize their own specialties.

The start of this revolution may perhaps be dated in this country from the passage of the G.I. Bill, which made it possible for so many returning servicemen and women to get a college education and begin to build the base of knowledge workers. The importance of intellectual capital to the future of the world is not lost on the people of what used to be called the Third World. Today, more than half of all the college graduates in the world are from the Third World, and indeed, Mexico has more graduate engineers than France, and India more than all of Europe. By the year 2000 it is estimated that students from the developing nations will make up three-fifths of all university students. The idea has gotten through to large segments of the world that economic progress is largely a process of increasing the relative contribution of knowledge in the creation of wealth. Knowledge, which at one time was a kind of ornament for the rich and powerful to display at conferences, is now combined with management skills to produce wealth. The vast increase in knowledge in the last decade has brought with it a huge increase in our ability to manipulate matter, increasing its value by the power of the mind, generating new substances and products unhinted at in nature and undreamed of a few years ago.

The world is changing, not because computer operators have replaced clerk typists, but because the human struggle to survive and prosper now depends on a new source of wealth: it is information applied to work to create value. Information technology has created an entirely new economy, an information economy, as different from the industrial economy as the industrial was from the agricultural economy. And when the source of the wealth of nations changes, the politics of nations change as well.

SPEECH TIP: A good speaker stretches and sets ambitious goals. Here the topic is a redefinition of wealth. It is, we are told, not to be measured in dollars and cents and things, but in information.

There are many in the new administration who long for the increased regulation of all phases of our economy. Sometimes the concept is expressed as an industrial policy, and sometimes in more primitive terms. Whatever way it is phrased, it is designed to increase the power of government. In an economy whose products consist largely of information, this power erodes rapidly. As George Gilder has written:

A steel mill, the exemplary industry of the industrial age, lends itself to control by governments. Its massive output is easily measured and regulated at every point by government. By contrast, the typical means of production in the new epoch is a man at a computer work station, designing microchips comparable in complexity to the entire steel facility, to be manufactured from software programs comprising a coded sequence of electronic pulses that can elude every export control and run a production line anywhere in the world.

SPEECH TIP: Once you have defined a new way of seeing the world, make sure you maintain the new focus. If information is wealth, then it is appropriate to speak in terms of "intellectual capital."

Intellectual capital is the most mobile in the world, and it will go where it is wanted, and it will stay where it is well treated. It will flee from manipulation or onerous regulation of its value or use, and no government can restrain it for long. The president in his inaugural address acknowledged that "investment is mobile," but gave no hint as to whether his administration will try to create the conditions to attract it.

The pursuit of wealth is now largely the pursuit of information. The competition for the best information is very different from the competition for the best bottom land. Today, the proliferation of information technology ranging from the telephone and fax machine to fiber optic cables has flooded the world with data and information moving at near the speed of light to all corners of the world. This does not just mean more of the same, as it is a well-established principle that a change of degree—if carried far enough—may eventually become a difference in kind. In biology this is how new species are created and old ones die out. Speed is what transforms a harmless lump of lead into a deadly rifle bullet. This explosion of information and the speed at which it can be transmitted have created a situation that is different in kind and not just in degree from any former time. This change affects not only the creation of wealth, but also military power, the political structure of the world, and thus international relations.

For thousands of years, news could travel only as fast as a horse could run or a ship could sail. Military power was similarly impeded. Indeed, Napoleon's armies could move no faster than those of Julius Caesar. Great national leaders were almost anonymous to all but those who had seen them in person. Today, the minicam is omnipresent, but in the late eighteenth century there were no photographs of Washington or Jefferson, and the tsar of Russia traveled unrecognized throughout Europe. The ability of the sovereign to keep information secret, and thus maintain a tight grip on power, began to erode with the invention of the paved road, the optical telegraph, and the newspaper. Richard Brown has observed that, when "the diffusion of public information moved from face-to-face to the newspaper page, public life and the society in which politics operated shifted from a communal dis-cipline to a market-oriented competitive regimen in which the foundation of influ-ence changed."

> *SPEECH TIP:* Nothing speaks louder than reality—actual events. Move your speech from abstraction to example as quickly as possible. It is better to show than to tell.

Government viewed all of these developments with a wary eye. In 1835, Emperor Francis I of Austria turned down a request for permission to build a steam railroad, lest it carry revolution to his throne. He was more right than he knew. Years later, with the advent of the telephone, another sovereign saw danger in a new technology. Leon Trotsky reportedly proposed to Stalin that a modern tele-phone system be built in the new Soviet state. Stalin brushed off the idea, saying, "I can imagine no greater instrument of counter-revolution in our time." What would he have thought if he had lived to see the Yeltsin coup, which utilized an independent computer network called Relcom, which links Moscow with eighty other Soviet cities and can and was plugged into similar networks in Europe and the United States to spread the news of the coup. Even more ironic was that, after the KGB blocked many trunk lines, Yeltsin communicated with his greatest ally, Mayor Sobchack in Saint Petersburg, via the government's own telephone network. This is in sharp contrast to the fact that it took four to six weeks for the news of Tsar Nicholas's abdication to reach the people.

In America, each new administration comes into office with an agenda, and the seven a.m. staff meetings in the Roosevelt Room are full of optimism. After a month or two, the meeting opens with, "Did you see what the *Post* said this morn-ing? Or what Brokaw said last night? And what is our response?" As Jack Kennedy once remarked, "The Ship of State is the only one that leaks from the top." While one can argue—and should argue—whether this is good or bad for public policy, in the late twentieth century, it is reality.

There are other realities President Clinton will face in this new world. Fernand Braudel in his great historical work has written that the sovereign's first task has always been to "secure obedience, to gain for itself the monopoly of the use of force in a given society, neutralizing all the possible challenges inside it and replac-ing them with what Max Weber called 'legitimate violence.'" In the Middle Ages, the central government took over the private armies of the feudal lords and the city states to create that monopoly of power. Today, the new administration will find that we are once again facing new private armies, not loyal to feudal lords, but ter-rorists controlled by small countries or factions within countries. No one under-stands information technology and its uses better than the modern terrorist. The ter-rorists who stormed the American Embassy in Teheran on November 4th, 1979, were equipped with their own television cameras and their own microwave links to Iranian TV. U.S. television networks outdid themselves to cover the event.

Indeed, ABC's "Nightline," now a fixture of late-night television, was originally created just to cover the hostage crisis every day. They gave the terrorists, in Margaret Thatcher's words, "the oxygen of publicity." Whatever your views of the matter, few would doubt that it presents difficult dilemmas for the sovereign. There are just some problems that are too big for any one country to handle, and terrorism is one of them. Many years ago, sovereigns in many different countries came to the same conclusion about piracy and banded together to outlaw the practice. Slavery is another case in point. The first significant international agreement was reached in 1885 at the Berlin Conference, which was followed in 1890 by the Brussels Act signed by eighteen countries. The security of our modern states may require similar joint treaties to outlaw terrorism.

All of these events are being played out against a background of massive shifts in the political structure of the world. There are fewer and fewer dictatorships and more and more democratic regimes. At the same time that freedom is sweeping the world, old tribal values are being reasserted, and more, not fewer, nations are being formed. This is good news for the people of the world, but makes the practice of diplomacy and the formation of national security policy more difficult. Dealings between superpowers was a high-stakes game, but at least one knew all the players. Today, new players are being created, and, doubtless, more are on the way.

The president referred to the fact that his inauguration was seen in real time by virtually the whole world. He might have added, and surely understands, that since the whole world is now tied together by an electronic infrastructure, we now have what amounts to a continuous global conversation. The implications of the global conversation are about the same as the implications of a village conversation, which is to say enormous. In a village there is a rough sorting out of ideas, customs, and practices over time. A village will quickly share news of any advantageous innovation. If anyone gets a raise or a favorable adjustment of his or her rights, everyone else will soon be pressing for the same treatment. The global conversation prompts people to ask the same questions on a global scale. To deny people human rights or democratic freedoms is no longer to deny them an abstraction articulated by the educated elite, but rather customs they have seen on their TV monitors. Once people are convinced that these things are possible in the village, an enormous burden of proof falls on those who would deny them.

Today, village and, indeed, national borders have ceased to be boundaries. Data of all kinds move over and through them as if they did not exist. Arthur C. Clarke, who first postulated the viability of a geosynchronous satellite, put it this way: "Radio waves have never respected frontiers, and from an altitude of 36,000 kilometers, national boundaries are singularly inconspicuous." Satellites now peer down into every corner of a nation-state, data and news are received by people within national borders on every device ranging from a hand-held transistor radio to personal computers at home and work tied into huge data networks. In short, the sovereign has totally lost control of what people can see and hear and can no longer maintain the fiction that there are no alternate types of political structures.

Not only does the information revolution make the assertion of territorial control impossible with regard to what people can see and hear, but also less relevant in other ways. The physical control of territory has always been one of the most important elements of sovereignty, but this control in many important respects is fading away. Not long ago, armies fought and men died for the control of the iron and steel in the Ruhr basin, because the ownership of these assets conferred real economic and political power. The same was true of the rubber in Malaysia. Today, these once fought-over assets may be a liability. To the extent that new technology replaces once-essential commodities with plastics or other synthetic materials, the relative importance of these areas to the vital interest of nations is bound to change. Even control of the so-called geographic "choke points" have less significance than they once had. A few years ago, the conventional wisdom told us that all the lights would go out all over the world if the Suez Canal were ever closed. The power of a sovereign state, in this case Egypt, to block the flow of oil from the Middle East was believed to be absolute. The conventional wisdom did not take into account the technology that would allow the building of supertankers that could carry oil around the Cape of Good Hope economically. This velocity of change is shifting the tectonic plates of national sovereignty and power in ways that are still unfolding and only partially understood.

Whatever facet of sovereignty people discuss, in the end, the central concept is that the actions of the sovereign are not subject to contradiction by any other power. The development of sovereignty as a political theory has a long history dating back at least to Roman law, moving through the absolutism of Bodin in the seventeenth and eighteenth centuries, to Hobbes, and then John Locke and Rousseau. While the ruler, in whatever era, could always find a political philosopher to validate his or her assertion of power, the information revolution has now given history a new reverse twist, which stands conventional wisdom on its head. So great is the desire of some nations for the approval of the world, that they call in outsiders to validate their own national elections. This is an extraordinary development far removed from the assertion of absolute power in conducting a nation's internal affairs.

Consider the Council of Freely Elected Heads of State, whom Noriega called to Panama to observe the election. Former President Jimmy Carter and some European counterparts told the world in no uncertain terms that the Panama election in 1989 was dishonest and, in a sense, paved the way for the American military action, which followed. The same group was asked to witness the Nicaraguan elections in 1990 and gave their seal of approval, which started that country along the road toward a fragile democratic government.

World opinion, focused and illuminated by the global television set, achieved what few if any armies could ever achieve. The same pressure is felt in the whole field of human rights, which is rapidly becoming a world concern transcending national sovereignty. Today, as the chanters in Prague told the police, the world sees what is going on. The cold print in the newspaper now has a human face in living color and in real time. It makes all the difference. The Kurds, for example, have suffered from subjugation by others on and off since the Arabs conquered them in the seventh century, but it was the images of horror on CNN last year that awoke the world to their plight in Iraq. Indeed, the history of the last few years has seen the growing popular support for the rights of individuals in all nations against the prerogatives of sovereigns, wherever located.

Since the beginning of time, intelligence gathering has played a big part in national security. Whatever new team the president appoints to take over the various facets of our intelligence agencies, they will find that while the agent in place still plays a vital role, information technology has made us both more secure and more vulnerable at the same time. Weapons of war are no longer the exclusive product of the armorer's art.

> *SPEECH TIP:* A well-chosen statistic can make your point very powerfully. However, be careful not to drown your listeners in numbers.

It is generally estimated that computer software is about 80 percent of United States weapons systems now in development. From the point of view of our enemies, attacking the software that controls or operates these weapons may be the most effective and cheapest way to cripple our defenses. Extensive work on this possibility has been done by Scott Boorman of Yale and Paul Levitt of Boston. Software attacks, they have written, can "strike key civilian targets, such as electronic funds transfer systems . . . air traffic control systems, and even vote-tallying machinery at the heart of the democratic process. . . . The so-called 'logic bomb,' which was planted in the computer software of the Los Angeles Department of Water and Power in the spring of 1985 made it impossible for that utility to access its own files for a week."

In today's world, wars can be won or lost in a week. If nothing happens when the president presses the button, if our communication networks froze and our radar failed to function, our defense posture would be changed dramatically. With the story of the John Walker family fresh in our minds, it does not take much imagination to imagine that some software programmer might sell out to our adversaries and plant a few logic bombs to disrupt our military response. This would be a very cheap way to attack and is open even to very small countries. Lest this sound like science fiction, we should remember that in 1985 a hacker, who turned out to be in Germany, broke into the computer files in the Lawrence Berkeley Lab, to say nothing of dozens of military bases in the United States. A man called Clifford Stoll tracked the hacker to Germany, where it was discovered he was selling information to the KGB. Stoll summed up the problem from the point of national security this way: "I might train an agent to speak a foreign language, fly her to a distant country, supply her with bribe money, and worry that she might be caught . . . or I could hire a dishonest computer programmer. Such a spy need never leave his home country. . . . And the information returned is fresh—straight from the target's word processing system." The impact of these facts on the way we think about our national security is significant: physical security can be bypassed, and we have to devise other ways to insure military effectiveness.

Another traditional aspect of sovereignty that is fading away is the power to issue currency and control its value. From the earliest times, governments have wished to monopolize this powerful medium and control its value in the world markets. Until recently, governments retained substantial power to manipulate the value of their currencies, but as the information revolution has rendered borders porous to huge volumes of high-speed information, the task has become difficult if not impossible. The control of currency has always given the sovereign great leverage over the most crucial material endeavors of his citizens. The regulation of money markets is the regulation of a society's resources in their most convenient and fungible form. The new Clinton administration is already firing warning shots across the bow of the Federal Reserve.

> *SPEECH TIP:* Wriston had begun by redefining information as "intellectual capital." Now he addresses the transformation of money itself into a kind of abstract intellectual concept.

Until recently, what we call money, be it a piece of paper, a bookkeeping entry, or a physical object, has been linked to a physical commodity that put some limit on a sovereign's ability to inflate the currency. The nature of the commodity varied with the interests of the people using it. American colonists used tobacco money. American Indians favored the cowrie shells, or wampum, and, of course, the more familiar copper, gold, and silver still circulate in the world. The link between commodities and money became slowly attenuated over time. On March 6, 1933, President Franklin D. Roosevelt issued a proclamation prohibiting American citizens from holding gold. The Congress followed on June 5 that year by passing a joint resolution repudiating the gold clause in all private and public contracts. While various other actions were taken to weaken the tie to gold, the final blow was administered on August 15, 1971, when President Nixon terminated the convertibility of the dollar into gold, and the era of floating exchange rates began.

In today's world, the value of a currency is determined by the price that the market will pay for it in exchange for some other currency. Indeed, the market is no longer a geographic location; instead, it is more than 200,000 computer screens in hundreds of trading rooms all over the world, all linked together by an electronic infrastructure. The latest political joke, the newly released GDP figures, or the statement of some world leader appears instantly on all screens, and the traders vote by buying and selling currency. The market is a harsh disciplinarian. When Francois Mitterand became president of France in 1981, he was elected as a committed Socialist, and almost immediately money began to flow out of the country, foreign exchange reserves were rapidly depleted, and within six months Mitterand had to reverse course and become pro-capitalist. This is not to say that governments can no longer influence the value of their currencies. They can and do, but their ability and those of their central banks readily to manipulate that value in world markets is declining. Increasingly, currency values will be experienced less as a power and privilege of sovereignty than as a discipline on the economic policies of imprudent sovereigns.

This new discipline is being administered by a completely new system of international finance. Unlike all prior arrangements, the new system was not built by politicians, economists, central bankers, or finance ministers. No high-level international conference produced a master plan. The new system was built by technology. The system is partly the accidental by-product of communication satellites and engineers learning how to use the electromagnetic spectrum up to 500 gigahertz.

The convergence of computers and telecommunications has created a new international monetary system and even a new monetary standard by which the value of currencies is determined. The Information Standard has replaced the Gold Standard. We sit at home and watch a live broadcast of riots in a country on the other side of the earth, and a currency falls—in minutes. We hear by satellite that a leadership crisis has been resolved, and a currency rises. Ten minutes after the news of the disaster at Chernobyl was received, market data showed that stocks of agricultural companies began to move up in all world markets. For the first time in history, countless investors, merchants, and ordinary citizens can know almost instantly of breaking events all over the earth. And depending on how they interpret these events, their desire to hold more or less of a given currency will be inescapably translated into a rise or fall of the exchange value.

SPEECH TIP: Nothing falls flatter than a revelation that turns out to be old news. Note how Wriston anticipates this response here, then goes on to prove that the phenomena and trends he has identified really are new.

The natural first response to this claim is: It has ever been so. The pressure of events has always been a major factor in determining the value of currencies. But the speed and volume of this new global market make it something different in kind and not just in degree. Cherished political, regulatory, and economic levers routinely used by sovereigns in the past are losing some of their power because the new Information Standard is not subject to effective political tinkering. It used to be that political and economic follies played to a local audience, and their results could be in part contained. A relatively small club of central bankers and politicians representing their sovereign governments believed it could control the value of a given currency. This is no longer true; the global market makes and publishes judgments about each currency in the world every minute and every hour of the day. The forces are so powerful that government intervention can only result in expensive failure over time.

Governments do not welcome this Information Standard any more than absolute monarchs embraced universal suffrage. Politicians who wish to evade responsibility for imprudent fiscal and monetary policies correctly perceive that the Information Standard will punish them. Moreover, in contrast to former international monetary systems, there is noway for a sovereign to resign from the Information Standard. Like many administrations before it, the Clinton team displays a wide spectrum of economic philosophy. The new secretary of the treasury has been a strong supporter of supply-side economics, while the designated chairperson of the Council of Economic Advisors believes that "there is no relationship between the taxes a nation pays and its economic performance." To complete the confusion, the new head of OMB—a former congressman—is distressed to learn the deficit was bigger than had previously been thought. It was a performance reminiscent of that of Inspector Louis Renault in *Casablanca*, who was shocked to learn there was gambling in the back room of Rick's Saloon. It will be interesting to see how the market sorts this out. Whatever political leaders do or say, the screens will continue to light up, traders will trade, and currency values will continue to be set not by sovereign governments, but by global plebiscite on the soundness of their fiscal and monetary policies.

The new global market is not limited to trade in financial instruments. Indeed, the world can no longer be understood as a collection of national economies. The electronic infrastructure that now ties the world together, as well as great advances in the efficiency of conventional transportation, are creating a single global economy.

The new administration will learn, despite the wails of the special interest groups, that the very phrase "international trade" has begun to sound obsolete. It can be argued that the very concept of a trade balance is an artifact of the past. As long as capital—both human and money—can move toward opportunity, trade will not balance; indeed, one will have as little reason to desire such accounting symmetry between nations as between California and New York. Commerce and production are increasingly transnational. More and more products have value added in several different countries. The dress a customer purchases at a smart store in San Francisco may have originated with cloth woven in Korea, finished in Taiwan, and cut and sewn in India according to an American design. Of course, a brief stop in Milan to pick up a "Made in Italy" label and leave off a substantial licensing fee, is de rigueur before the final journey to New York. Former Secretary of State George Schultz recently remarked in a speech: "A few months ago I saw a snapshot of a shipping label for some integrated circuits produced by an American firm. It said,

'Made in one or more of the following countries: Korea, Hong Kong, Malaysia, Singapore, Taiwan, Mauritius, Thailand, Indonesia, Mexico, Philippines. The exact country of origin is unknown.' That label says a lot about where current trends are taking us."

Whatever the correct word for these phenomena, "trade" certainly seems an inadequate description. How does one account in the monthly trade figures for products whose "exact country of origin is unknown"? How are national governments to regulate the complexities of transnational production with anything like the firmness with which they once regulated international trade? How are politicians to whip up nationalist fervor against foreign goods when American car companies build cars in Mexico for export to Africa and pay the profits to pensioners in Chicago, and the Japanese build cars in Tennessee for export to Europe and use the income to refinance real estate in Texas? Nevertheless, if the new interventionists get their way, it could cripple the global economy.

The new president will find that many of the terms we use today to describe the economy no longer reflect reality. Everyone knows, for example, that all the lights would go out, all the airplanes would stop flying, and all the financial institutions and many of the factories would shut down if the computer software that runs their systems suddenly disappeared. Yet these crucial intellectual assets do not appear in any substantial way on the balance sheets of the world. Those balance sheets, however, are chock full of what in the industrial age were called tangible assets—buildings and machinery—things that can be seen and touched.

How does a national government measure capital formation, when much new capital is intellectual? How does it measure the productivity of knowledge workers, whose product cannot be counted on our fingers? If it cannot do that, how can it track productivity growth? How does it track or control the money supply when the financial markets create new financial instruments faster than the regulators can keep track of them? And if it cannot do any of these things with the relative precision of simpler times, what becomes of the great mission of modern governments: controlling and manipulating the national economy? Even if some of these measurement problems are solved, as some surely will be, the phenomena they measure will be far more complex and difficult to manipulate than industrial economies of old.

> *SPEECH TIP:* Too often, we think of the future in terms of things—new inventions, new scientific wonders, what Wriston calls "gadgets." This paragraph, which, to use a term from classical rhetoric, begins the speaker's peroration, carefully sets all of the preceding remarks into perspective. We've talked about a lot of things, Wriston says, but what we're really talking about is the balance of power.

These remarks today have not dwelt on the wonders of the gee-whiz technology emerging from your Silicon Valley, not because they are not wondrous—

they are—but because revolutions are not made by gadgets, but by a shift in the balance of power. The technology is the enabling factor, not the cause. When a system of national currencies run by central banks is transformed into a global electronic marketplace driven by private currency traders, power changes hands. When a system of national economies linked by government-regulated trade is replaced—at least in part—by an increasingly integrated global economy beyond the reach of much national regulation, power changes hands. When an international telecommunications system, incorporating technologies from mobile phones to communications satellites, deprives governments of the ability to keep secrets from the world, or from their own people, power changes hands. When a microchip the size of a fingernail can turn a relatively simple and inexpensive weapon into a "Stinger" missile, enabling an illiterate tribesman to destroy a multimillion-dollar armored helicopter and its highly trained crew, power changes hands. When the president picks up the phone to talk to another head of state rather than have an ambassador deliver a meticulously drafted note to the foreign ministry, power changes hands.

This is not to say that sovereign power will disappear—it will not—but what it does mean is that no government, over time, can act alone not subject to contradiction. The protesters in Prague were right: The world is watching, and the power of world opinion is transmitted and focused and reported by the telcon network. The world looks and reacts and brings pressure on everything from the destruction of the rain forest, the allegations of global warming, the disposal of toxic waste, to the violation of human rights anywhere on the planet.

All of this is good news for freedom. Ronald Reagan's powerful speech on May 31, 1988, delivered at Moscow State University, was literally heard around the world. He spoke of the power of freedom in a land that had seen little of it; he spoke of economic freedom to release the innovations of entrepreneurs; he spoke of the information revolution "quietly sweeping the globe, without bloodshed or conflict." Few realized at the time how this message, carried on the global electronic network, was working on the hearts and minds of people. Our new president in his inaugural address recognized that "profound and powerful forces are shaking and remaking our world."

All of these forces profoundly affect the way the new administration has to go about its business, because they affect the very foundation of modern society and international relations. The president said the "urgent question of our age is whether we can make change our friend and not our enemy." Americans handle change better than most of the world's people. We know that new circumstances will require new solutions, but diplomats and politicians, like old soldiers, often concentrate on fighting the last war, not the new one. Whatever the new policies, the screens will light up all over the world and judgments will be instantly reflected in the cross rate of our currency. There no longer is any place to hide.

Choice Openers, Quotations, Anecdotes, and Closings: A Miniature Anthology

CHOICE OPENERS

Sometimes complex arguments are best illustrated by a simple anecdote. You may recall the scene from the movie *Dead Poets Society*, where Robin Williams insisted that his students rip out the first chapter of their poetry textbooks. This was a dramatic flourish, intended to shock as much as to instruct, but the point was made: Instead of assisting, that chapter was inhibiting the way he wanted to teach poetry.

We can certainly debate whether the method the character chose was, in the end, the right one. But I think all of us here would defend his right, as a teacher, to present the subject to his students in a way that he felt would most enlighten them. By its very nature, teaching is a process that involves choosing from many different resources and techniques. No instructor teaches in exactly the same manner as another instructor. "Customization" in the classroom is a given.

—*from "Publishing for the Individual: Alternatives to Traditional Textbooks," by Joseph L. Dionne, Chairman and CEO, McGraw-Hill, Inc.*

It's great to be on Mackinac Island again. I was a little worried when I saw the agenda, though. I don't want to sound ungrateful for the opportunity to speak to this august gathering, so don't get me wrong. But this is a Friday night. The bar's been open for hours. We just had a great meal. And the coffee is going right to your kidneys. Now, would you like to try to hold a crowd like this with a speech entitled "Corporate Strategies in a Global Economy?"

Then somebody reminded me that the ferries have stopped running, and there's only one TV set in the hotel . . . About that speech title, by the way: that's what you get when you call the office seven months ahead of time and insist on knowing what the speaker will talk about. Obviously, I didn't have the foggiest idea what I was going to say way back last fall, so we sent in one of our generic speech titles—something that sounds kind of high-toned and cerebral but is actually so broad that it'll cover almost anything.

We have one, for example, called "Looking Back and Looking Ahead." That works just about anywhere.

—*from "Corporate Strategies in a Global Economy," by Robert J. Eaton, Chairman and Chief Executive Officer, Chrysler Corporation*

This past summer, there was a story going around Moscow that the most popular item at flea markets was a used light bulb. Yes, a *used* light bulb. Here's why: You buy a used light bulb for a few kopecks and take it to work. You then unscrew the good light bulb from your office lamp and replace it with the blown-out bulb. You tell your boss you need a new light bulb because yours is out—and you take the original good bulb home. If you are lucky, you can also take the dead bulb home after it has been replaced, sell it at a flea market—and start the cycle all over again.

—from "Perestroika from Pleasantville: Lessons Learned Launching Reader's Digest in the Soviet Union and Hungary," by Carole M. Howard, Vice President, Public Relations and Communications Policy, The Reader's Digest Association, Inc.

It's a pleasure to join you for this important landmen's conference. I particularly like this year's theme: "We're Fighting Back."

There's no question that the energy industry has gone through some ups and downs. Recently, however, the downs have far outweighed the ups. It was so bad at one company that the devil approached the chief executive with this proposal:

"I'll give you gas prices of $10 an m.c.f.; oil prices of $40 a barrel, and I'll double the price you get for coal. In exchange, you have to give me your immortal soul and the souls of your wife and kids."

There was a long pause while the executive thought it over. And then he said, "What's the catch?"

—from "Is the Business of America Still Business?" by James R. Paul, President and CEO, The Coastal Corporation

CHOICE QUOTATIONS AND ANECDOTES

So, our relationship with MMC [Mitsubishi Motors Corporation] continues to be "win-win." But we're no Ozzie and Harriet. We have our share of difficulties and misunderstandings. (Just like a *real* marriage.) Now and again, we've encountered some unique, and even humorous, situations in our cross-cultural business relationships with MMC.

One of my favorite stories is one that Lino Piedra, the former Chairman of the Board of Diamond-Star Motors, likes to tell. According to Lino, the American managers thought it would be a good idea for the Japanese managers at Diamond-Star to use "anglicized" first names. So, the public relations manager suggested to Osamu Itoh, the assistant general manager of human relations, that he might like to be known as Sam. "No," Itoh replied, "I think I would like a different name."

"What would you like to be called?" the P.R. manager asked.

"Awesome. I think Awesome Itoh is a very good choice," was the response.

They had a similar problem with Mr. Watanabe of MMC International Corporation. He choose the name "Handsome," remarking that he had always wanted to *be* handsome. In the end, our Japanese counterparts at Diamond-Star did not receive their colorful names.

—from "Global Alliances and Joint Ventures . . . Or, How to Avoid a Dangerous Liaison," by Joseph E. Cappy, Vice President, International Operations, Chrysler Corporation

To quote Frederick Douglass: "Men may not get all they pay for in this world, but they certainly pay for all that they get." In many instances, the payment must be a commitment of time.

—from "Securing the African-American Future: A Challenge for Today and Tomorrow," by Virgis Colbert, Vice President, Operations, Miller Brewing Company

Gary David Goldberg, one of TV's more creative forces, summed it up last month when he described the networks as a group that would televise live executions if they could, except for Fox, which would televise naked executions . . . One final Don't: Don't deal with bureaucrats who come to you with special event opportunities. They simply do not understand the realities of life. Another true story: In Boston, there's a cemetery called the Granury Burial Ground, where patriots like John Hancock are buried. A few years back, the city was having trouble coming up with funds to maintain the cemetery, so some bureaucrat called us and asked for $100,000. I said "We're happy to help the homeless, but not the dead. Call us if there's something we can do for people who are alive." But, being good bureaucrats, they didn't give up. They decided it was better to sweeten the deal, and they offered to let us have John Hancock's body if we made the contribution.

They finally gave up when we told them we wouldn't settle for anything less than Hancock plus a patriot to be named later.

—from "Event Marketing: The Good, the Bad, and the Ugly," by David F. D'Alessandro, Senior Executive Vice President, John Hancock Financial Services

Little boys were running around peddling Soviet Army hats and medals, but I didn't see anybody selling missiles in Red Square!

I *did* buy a hat. I'm going to put it on when things aren't going well in a meeting and announce that I'm making a command decision!

—from "Flash: The Sky is Not Falling! A Call for Balance," by Earnst W. Deavenport, Jr., President, Eastman Chemical Company

I think rock star Elton John put aging in clear perspective for many aging baby boomers. When asked what growing older meant to him, he replied, "I still want to play music, but I don't want to look like Donald Duck while I'm doing it." Bill Cosby put it another way. He said, "Experts agree that the elderly are usually not losing it, they are just not 'using it' as often." And Andy Rooney observes, "I don't notice too many bad things about getting older except that it hurts more to go barefoot."

—from "The Media and the Mature Marketplace," by Horace B. Deets, Executive Director, American Association of Retired Persons

In the world of international diplomacy, there is an old saying: "When *goods* cannot cross borders, *armies will.*"

—from "Passports—Not Provincialism: Marketers and Communicators Need New International Skills," by Jean L. Farinelli, Chairman and Chief Executive Officer, Creamer Dickson Basford and Eurocom Corporate & PR (U.S.)

Good news is seldom considered newsworthy. Walter Cronkite once observed that "a cat in the alley is not news, but a cat in a tree is." Or, as the late Warren Brookes of the *Detroit News* put it, "we cover crashes, we don't cover landings."

—from "Energy, the Environment, and the New World Economy: Reformulating the Regulatory Process," by H. L. Fuller, Chairman of the Board, Amoco Corporation

To paraphrase a famous Johnson (from another century), "The prospect of a hanging in a fortnight concentrates the mind wonderfully well."

—from "The Challenge of Change: Building a New Competitive Spirit for the 21st Century," by Ralph S. Larsen, Chairman and Chief Executive Officer, Johnson & Johnson

The great nineteenth-century French historian and political philosopher Alexis de Tocqueville observed in his famous book *Democracy in America* that the futures of the United States and Russia are bound tightly together by history. He spoke of "two great nations in the world which . . . have suddenly taken their place among the leading nations, making the world take note of their birth and of their greatness almost at the same instant." But, he added, "Their point of departure is different and their paths diverse; nevertheless, each seems called by some secret design of Providence one day to hold in its hands the destinies of half the world." . . . Winston Churchill once described Russia as "a riddle wrapped in a mystery inside an enigma."

—from "Economic Assistance and Business Opportunities in the Independent States of the Former Soviet Union," by Lawrence M. Lesser, Adjunct Professor of Business and Management, University of Maryland

President Harry Truman once observed that . . . "The only thing new is the history you don't know." In that context . . . I will look backward to see forward.

—from "Design for the Environment: The Challenge for Year 2000 and Beyond," by Dr. Joseph T. Ling, Vice President, Environmental Engineering and Pollution Control (retired), 3M

Carl Ally, founder of an advertising agency, once said that "the creative person wants to be a know-it-all. He wants to know about all kinds of things: ancient history, nineteenth-century mathematics, current manufacturing techniques, flower arranging, and hog futures. Because he never knows when these ideas might come together to form a new idea. It may happen six minutes later or six months or six years down the road. But he has faith that it will happen." . . . Like Henry Ford, who stated his vision very explicitly: "I will build a motor car for the great multitude . . . so low in price that no [one] will be unable to own one—and enjoy with his family the blessing of pleasure in God's great open spaces." . . . I think Isaac Asimov said it best: "Science can amuse and fascinate us all—but it is engineering that changes the world."

You have an opportunity to change the world. I urge you to make the most of it.

—from "Progress through Innovation: You Can't Have One without the Other," by Robert G. McVicker, Senior Vice President, Technology, Quality Assurance, and Scientific Relations, Kraft General Foods

Sam Rayburn had it right when he said, "Any jackass can kick down a barn, but it takes a real carpenter to build one."

—from "Reforming the Civil Justice System," by Stephen B. Middlebrook, Senior Vice President and Executive Counsel, Aetna Life & Casualty

In a way, I feel like the story that Kentucky Democratic Congressman Bill Natcher tells on himself: During one of his many reelection campaigns, Congressman Natcher stopped a man in the street, told him he was a candidate for reelection, and held out his hand to shake. The man asked Natcher what party he belonged to, and when Natcher said he was a Democrat, the man frowned. He held out his hand very reluctantly and said, "Well, all right, but just press it light."

I am afraid that many in our society are equally unwilling constituents of American agriculture.

—from "Agenda for Tomorrow's Agriculture," by Dale A. Miller, Chairman-elect, National Future Farmers of America Sponsors Board, and President & CEO, Sandoz Agro Inc.

They are left with little but Yogi Berra's line about hard choices: "When you're at a fork in the road, take it."

—from "Sticking to Your Knitting: The Increasing Trend toward Outsourcing," by Joe Neubauer, Chairman and CEO, ARA Services, Inc.

Apparently, the voters still haven't gotten mad enough to start throwing the politicians out of office in large enough numbers to make a difference. And so far, there's no sign the politicians have gotten the message. But then, I happen to believe that most politicians have the ability to screw up the working parts of a brick. If they don't start getting the message soon, then I am going to support term limits. Perhaps two terms: one in office . . . and one in jail.

—from "Is the Business of America Still Business?" by James R. Paul, President and CEO, The Coastal Corporation

Unfortunately, there can be no quick fix. This is the wisdom of an ancient Confucian proverb, which says: "If you think in terms of a year, plant seed; if in terms of ten years, plant trees; and if in terms of a hundred years, *teach the people.*" For our impatient society, perhaps the biggest difficulty is to set our minds to a task whose payoff is measured in decades, not in days or weeks.

—from "Learning to Compete: Developing Canada's Human Resources," by C. E. Ritchie, Chairman, and Chief Executive Officer, The Bank of Nova Scotia

I say this with a caveat uttered by the physicist Niels Bohr more than three decades ago: "Prediction is very difficult," he said. "Especially about the future." . . . The third component of success is technology—not technology of itself, but how efficiently that technology is used. The story of the traveler and the Arkansas chicken is a good illustration of this point. According to the story, a motorist was clipping along at about 65 mph through the Arkansas back country when he was passed by a three-legged chicken running along the shoulder of the road.

The amazed driver followed the chicken as it turned onto a dirt road that led up to a run-down poultry farm. As the chicken ran behind the barn, the man pulled up and asked a farmer standing nearby if he had seen the amazing sight.

"Yup," the farmer said. "Those are three-legged chickens I breed. My wife and boy and I all like drumsticks, and we grew three-leggers so we can all have a drumstick from one chicken."

"That's amazing," the traveler said. "How do they taste?"

"I do not know," the farmer replied. "I haven't caught one yet."

—from "Components of Success: Quality Control, Investment in Human Resources, and Applied Technology," by Richard M. Rosenberg, Chairman and Chief Executive Officer, BankAmerica Corporation

Democracy is not a smooth sauce.

Democracy is a chili of different currents, changes, and contradictions.

Democracy is the lone dish in constant need of seasoning, stirring, and tasting.

Democracy is never, never done.

—from "An Uneven Playing Field in America," by Bernard Shaw, Principal Washington Anchor, CNN

And, as the saying goes: "The nearest thing to immortality in this world is a government bureaucracy."

—from "Global Competitiveness: Five Steps to Failure," by Richard J. Stegemeier, Chairman, President and Chief Executive Officer, Unocal Corporation

Before I begin, I'd like to answer the question I know you're too polite to ask: "How long is this going to take?"

Let me answer this way: Lincoln's Gettysburg Address used 266 words, the Ten Commandments used 297 words, and the Bill of Rights used 463. I hear that the latest Federal directive to regulate the price of cabbage in American contains 26,911 words.

My comments will fall somewhere in between.

—from "Closing the Impact Gap through Leadership," by Barry Sullivan, Electronic Data Services Corporation

I'm also flattered to be invited to speak about business to your business school, but I can't help feeling a bit like the man whose proudest accomplishment was being one of the few survivors of the great Jamestown flood. This man loved bending the ear of any listener with his story. After he died and entered heaven, St. Peter asked if he had any special requests. The man said, "Yes. I'd like to speak before a large audience about surviving that big flood in Pennsylvania in 1889."

St. Peter arranged a meeting and told the man he was scheduled to speak that afternoon on Cloud Nine. "But just one thing," said St. Peter. "I want to warn you that one person in the audience will be a guy named *Noah*."

I know there are many Noahs in the audience today, but I hope I can enhance *your* business expertise by sharing some personal experiences from nearly fifty years in business. . . . There's a story about a professor, a college student, and a dean riding in a small plane. The engine stalled, and their pilot announced they'd have to bail out. But he had only three parachutes for the four of them.

The pilot said he had a wife and children, grabbed a parachute, and jumped. The professor said he was one of the smartest men in the world, and his knowledge was too valuable to lose. So he jumped. The dean told the college student, "I've had a full life and yours is still ahead. Take the last parachute." The college student said, "That won't be necessary. We have two parachutes left. The smartest man in the world just jumped with my backpack." . . . They say a person who speaks three languages is trilingual, one who speaks two languages is bilingual, and someone who speaks just one language is an American. . . . That's illustrated by the story of the man in the former Soviet Union who finally earned enough to buy a car, but because of slow production methods he was told he'd have to wait several years for delivery. When he pressed the dealer further, he was given an exact delivery date of June 30, 2002.

"Will that be delivered in the morning or the afternoon?" the man asked the dealer. The dealer replied, "What's the difference?" And the man said, "I have a leaky faucet, and my plumber is scheduled to come that morning."

—from "Beyond the Horizon: The Pursuit of Goals," by Jay Van Andel, Co-founder and Chairman, Amway Corporation

As Jack Kennedy once remarked, "The Ship of State is the only one that leaks from the top."

—from "Clintonomics: The Information Revolution and the New Global Market Economy," by Walter B. Wriston, Citicorp

You know about the heavyweights of invention. I've mentioned some already— Edison, Bell, McCoy, and the Wright brothers. But did you know about Abe Lincoln? He was granted a patent in 1849 for a device for buoying vessels over shoals. Mark Twain, who is better known for creating great literature, found time to get *three* patents, including one he called, "An Improvement in Adjustable and Detachable Straps for Garments." (You would think that Twain would be the appropriate source for "a device for buoying vessels over shoals," but Lincoln beat him to it!) . . . How do you capture the importance of five million patents, stretching across more than two hundred years?

Well, the U.S. Patent and Trademark Office put it *this* way in one of their pamphlets: "Under the patent system, a small, struggling nation has grown into the greatest industrial power on earth." Now, if that sounds like the patent office was tooting its own horn, try this next quote, which was made by a *Japanese* official in the year 1900: "We have looked about us," he said, "to see what nations are the greatest, so that we can be like them. We said, 'What is it that makes the United States such a great nation?' and we investigated and found that it was patents, and we will have patents."

—from Remarks by Jerome B. York, Executive Vice President and Chief Financial Officer, Chrysler Corporation

CHOICE CLOSINGS

This is our domain—to hold or to lose. What say ye?

—from "Publishing for the Individual: Alternatives to Traditional Textbooks," by Joseph L. Dionne, Chairman and Chief Executive Officer, McGraw-Hill, Inc.

As marketers and communicators, we have a proud role to play. We are the people who can help promote international understanding through international trade and competition. Together, we could do more good than all the debates in the United Nations General Assembly.

And I ask you: What could be better than making a profit while promoting prosperity all over the world?

—from "Passports—Not Provincialism: Marketers and Communicators Need New International Skills," by Jean L. Farinelli, Chairman and Chief Executive Officer, Creamer Dickson Basford and Eurocom Corporate & PR (U.S.)

In closing, I am reminded of the words of our old friend Pogo: "We is confronted by insurmountable opportunities." It often seems that way, I'll admit. But higher education has overcome even greater challenges in the past and will continue to do so in the future.

—from "Facing the Facts: Reshaping the Academic Enterprise," by John T. Hartley, Chairman, Harris Financial Corporation

All of these forces profoundly affect the way the new administration has to go about its business, because they affect the very foundation of modern society and international relations. The president said the "urgent question of our age is whether we can make change our friend and not our enemy." Americans handle change better than most of the world's people. We know that new circumstances will require new solutions, but diplomats and politicians, like old soldiers, often concentrate on fighting the last war, not the new one. Whatever the new policies, the screens will light up all over the world and judgments will be instantly reflected in the cross rate of our currency. There no longer is any place to hide.

—from "Clintonomics: The Information Revolution and the New Global Market Economy," by Walter B. Wriston, Citicorp

Index